China

PHRASEBOOK & DICTIONARY

Acknowledgments
Editors Francesca Coles, Laura Crawford, Branislava Vladisavljevic, Tracy Whitmey
Production Support Chris Love
Cartographer Wayne Murphy
Illustrations Yukiyoshi Kamimura
Cover Researcher Naomi Parker

Thanks
James Hardy, Angela Tinson

Published by Lonely Planet Publications Pty Ltd
ABN 36 005 607 983

2nd Edition – September 2015
ISBN 978 1 74321 434 3

Cover Image Diners at Yikeyin Lao Fangzi restaurant, Kūnmíng, Yunnan, China/Katie Garrod, AWL
Printed in Singapore 10 9 8 7 6 5 4 3 2 1

Contact lonelyplanet.com/contact

acknowledgments

This book was based on existing editions of Lonely Planet's *Cantonese, Mandarin* and *Tibetan* phrasebooks and developed with the help of the following people:

- PAEN Language Services for the Dongbei Hua, Hakka, Sichuanese, Uighur, Xi'an and Yunnan Hua chapters
- David Holm for the Hunanese, Zhuang & Chaozhou chapters
- Lance Eccles for the Shanghainese chapter
- Emyr RE Pugh for the Mongolian chapter
- Tughluk Abdurazak for the Uighur chapter

Thanks also to Will Gourlay for the language introductions for Dongbei Hua, Hakka, Hunanese, Shanghainese, Sichuanese, Uighur, Xi'an and Yunnan Hua; Jodie Martire for the Culture chapter; and Dora Chai and Shahara Ahmed for additional language expertise.

contents

	Man	Can	Cha	Don	Hak	Hun	Sha	Sic	Xi'a	Yun	Zhu	Mon	Tib	Uig
tones	10	36	62	86	110	134	158	182	206	230	254	–	–	–
alphabet	–	–	–	–	–	–	–	–	–	–	–	278	310	336
introduction	11	37	63	87	111	135	159	183	207	231	255	279	311	337
pronunciation	12	38	64	88	112	136	160	184	208	232	256	280	312	338
language difficulties	13	39	65	89	113	137	161	185	209	233	257	281	313	339
time & dates	14	40	66	90	114	138	161	186	201	234	258	282	314	340
border crossing	15	40	–	–	–	–	–	–	–	–	–	–	–	–
tickets & luggage	15	41	–	–	–	–	–	–	–	–	–	–	–	–
transport	16	42	67	91	115	139	163	187	211	235	259	283	315	342
directions	18	43	67	91	115	139	163	187	211	235	259	283	315	342
accommodation	19	44	68	92	116	140	164	188	212	236	260	285	317	343
banking & communications	20	45	69	93	117	141	165	189	213	237	261	286	318	344
sightseeing	21	47	70	94	117	142	166	190	214	238	262	286	319	344
shopping	22	48	70	95	118	142	166	190	215	239	262	288	320	345

	Man	Can	Cha	Don	Hak	Hun	Sha	Sic	Xi'a	Yun	Zhu	Mon	Tib	Uig
meeting people	–	–	71	96	119	143	167	191	215	240	263	289	321	346
photography	24	50	–	–	–	–	–	–	–	–	–	–	–	–
making conversation	24	50	72	96	120	144	168	192	216	241	264	290	322	347
feelings & opinions	–	–	75	99	123	147	171	194	219	243	267	294	325	350
farewells	–	–	75	100	123	147	171	195	219	244	268	295	326	351
eating out	26	52	76	101	124	148	172	196	220	245	268	296	327	352
special diets & allergies	27	54	79	104	127	151	175	199	223	248	272	300	329	355
emergencies	28	54	80	104	128	152	175	200	224	248	272	303	329	356
health	29	55	80	104	128	152	175	200	224	248	272	303	329	356
dictionary	31	57	81	105	129	153	177	201	225	249	273	305	331	357

culture section 361
history timeline 362
food 366
festivals 370

index 374

China

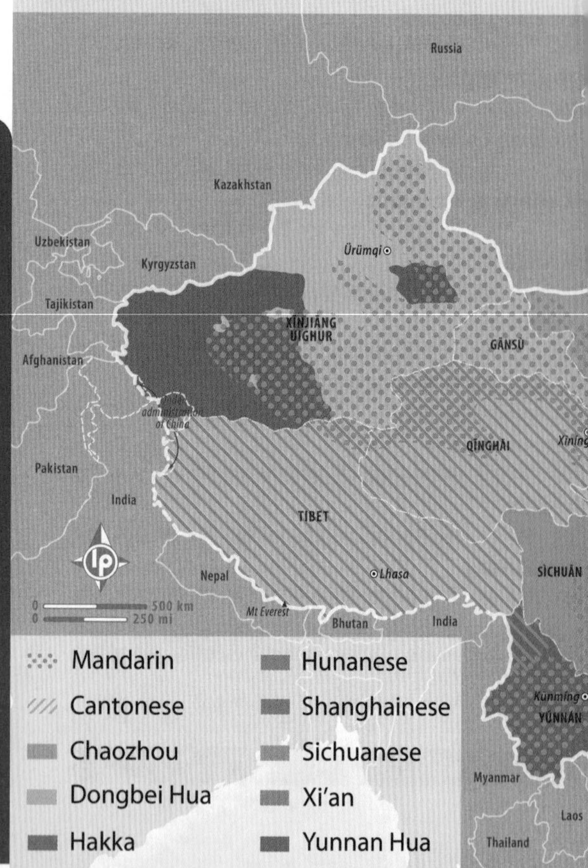

LANGUAGE MAP

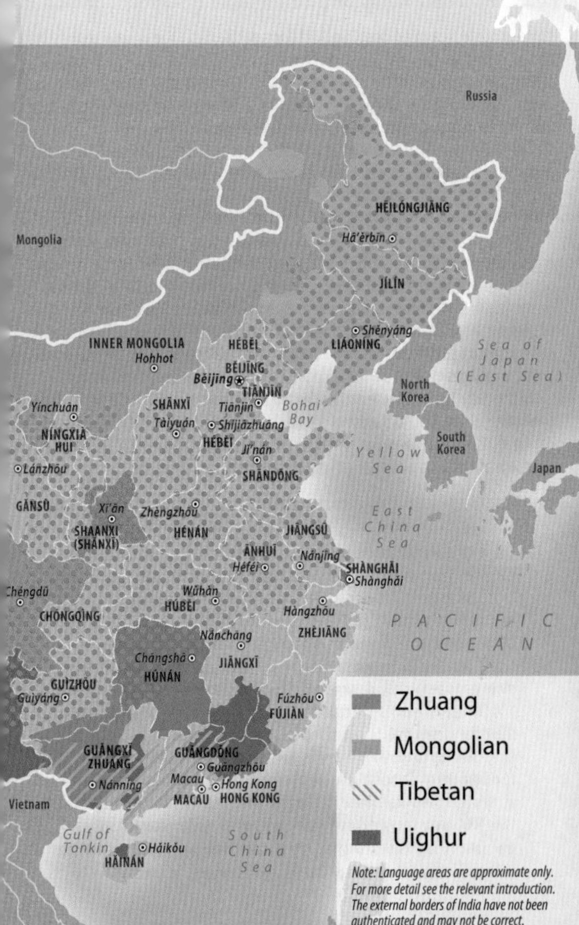

Russia
Mongolia
HĒILÓNGJIĀNG
Hā'ěrbīn
JÍLÍN
Shěnyáng
LIÁONÍNG
INNER MONGOLIA
Hohhot
HÉBĚI
BĚIJĪNG
Běijīng
TIĀNJĪN
Tiānjīn
Bohai Bay
Sea of Japan (East Sea)
North Korea
South Korea
Japan
Yínchuān
NÍNGXIÀ HUÍ
SHĀNXĪ
Tàiyuán
Shíjiāzhuāng
HÉBĚI
Jǐ'nán
SHĀNDŌNG
Yellow Sea
Lánzhōu
GĀNSÙ
Xī'ān
SHAANXI (SHĀNXĪ)
Zhèngzhōu
HÉNÁN
JIĀNGSŪ
East China Sea
ĀNHUĪ
Nánjīng
Héféi
SHÀNGHĂI
Shànghǎi
Chéngdū
CHÓNGQÌNG
Wǔhàn
HÚBĚI
Hángzhōu
ZHÈJIĀNG
PACIFIC OCEAN
Nánchāng
Chángshā
HÚNÁN
JIĀNGXĪ
GUÌZHŌU
Guìyáng
Fúzhōu
FÚJIÀN
GUĂNGXĪ ZHUÀNG
GUĂNGDŌNG
Guǎngzhōu
Macau
Hong Kong
Nánníng
MACAU
HONG KONG
Vietnam
Gulf of Tonkin
Hǎikǒu
HǍINÁN
South China Sea
Zhuang
Mongolian
Tibetan
Uighur
Note: Language areas are approximate only. For more detail see the relevant introduction. The external borders of India have not been authenticated and may not be correct.

china – at a glance

China is home to a mind-boggling 1.3 billion people, who live in such contrasting environments as the fast-paced modern cities of Shànghǎi and Hong Kong, the mountains and forests of the southwest, and the rolling steppes of Inner Mongolia. So it's little wonder that China is also home to a cacophony of languages – more than 200, and counting – and to countless dialects and subdialects.

China's languages are traditionally classified into seven main groups: Gan, spoken in Jiāngxī and adjoining areas; Hakka, spoken across a number of areas but particularly in the south and southeast; Mandarin, spoken in the north, central and western provinces, but with speakers right across the country; Min, which has speakers in Fújiàn and Taiwan; Wu, spoken on the east coast; Xiang (also called Hunanese), mainly spoken in Húnán province; and Yue (also known as Cantonese), a language of the Guǎngdōng area. These are all Sinitic languages within the Sino-Tibetan language family and each one has numerous regional dialects. More than two-thirds of Chinese speakers, for example, speak various dialects of Mandarin. The linguistic variety doesn't stop there, however. Outside these major groups are the many non-Sinitic languages of China's ethnic minorities, including Mongolian and Uighur.

In the early 1900s Chinese authorities sought to reinforce national unity with the promotion of the Běijīng dialect of Mandarin as 'Modern Standard Chinese', mandating its use in education and for official purposes. This is now the official national language of China, as well as one of the official languages of the UN.

did you know?

- The writing system common to China's main Sinitic languages (Mandarin and Cantonese) contains more than 50,000 different characters, and this number continues to grow. However, a mere 3000 or so are all you need to read a local newspaper or to make it past senior high school in China.
- Of the more than 80 languages and dialects 'discovered' around the world in recent decades, 30 are native to China. Linguists agree that there are many more yet to be formally documented. Meanwhile, Unesco has listed more than 100 Chinese languages and dialects as in danger of becoming extinct; some of these have fewer than 50 remaining speakers.
- In the lead-up to the 2008 Olympics, Běijīng officials established a committee to rid the city of 'Chinglish', the often perplexing and amusing results of locals' attempts to translate Chinese into English. The committee had replaced more than 4000 occurrences of the offending prose on signs with accepted 'standard' translations. Authorities could only do so much, though, and you can still find fine examples of Chinglish in private businesses throughout the city.

Mandarin

TONES	10
ABOUT MANDARIN	11
PRONUNCIATION	12
LANGUAGE DIFFICULTIES	13
TIME & DATES	14
BORDER CROSSING	15
TICKETS & LUGGAGE	15
TRANSPORT	16
DIRECTIONS	18
ACCOMMODATION	19
BANKING & COMMUNICATIONS	20
SIGHTSEEING	21
SHOPPING	22
PHOTOGRAPHY	24
MAKING CONVERSATION	24
EATING OUT	26
SPECIAL DIETS & ALLERGIES	27
EMERGENCIES	28
HEALTH	29
ENGLISH–MANDARIN DICTIONARY	31

tones

Mandarin is a tonal language ('tonal quality' refers to the raising and lowering of pitch or certain syllables). Mandarin is commonly described as having four tones, as well as a fifth one, the neutral tone. Apart from the unmarked neutral tone, Pinyin (the official system of writing Chinese using the Roman alphabet) uses symbols above the vowels to indicate each tone, as shown in the table below for the vowel 'a'. Bear in mind that the tones are relative to the natural vocal range of the speaker, eg the high tone is pronounced at the top of one's vocal range. Note also that some tones slide up or down in pitch.

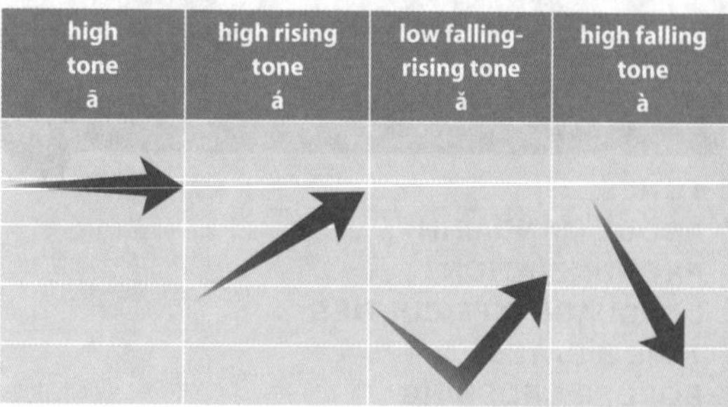

The tonal quality plays a crucial role in distinguishing the meaning of words in Mandarin. For instance, the table below shows how the same combination of sounds, ma, can have five different meanings depending on the tone.

Tone	Example	Meaning
1st – high	mā	mother
2nd – high rising	má	hemp
3rd – low falling-rising	mǎ	horse
4th – high falling	mà	scold
neutral	ma	question marker

about Mandarin

It may surprise you to learn that the term 'Mandarin' is not really the name of a language. It actually refers to the largest of the various Chinese dialect groups, all members of the Sino-Tibetan language family. The language of this chapter is more accurately described as Modern Standard Chinese and is based on the Běijīng dialect. Whatever you choose to call it, Mandarin (pǔtōnghuà 普通话) has been a powerful force for linguistic and political unity in a country with countless dialects. It's the main language used in official contexts and, aside from its use in mainland China, Mandarin has official status in Taiwan (where it's called *Guóyǔ*) and Singapore (where it's known as *Huáyǔ*). The total number of its speakers worldwide is over 800 million, making Mandarin the most widely spoken 'language' in the world. However, there are two versions of the written language. Simplified Chinese is used in mainland China and has been adopted by Singapore, Malaysia and other Southeast Asian countries. Traditional Chinese is used in Taiwan, Hong Kong and Macau. In this chapter, we've used simplified Chinese characters, along with Pinyin (the official system of writing Chinese using the Roman alphabet) in the pronunciation guides.

mandarin

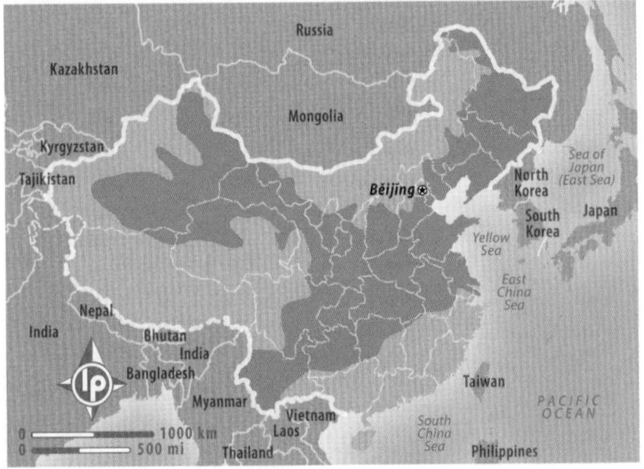

pronunciation

Vowels		Consonants	
Pinyin	**English sound**	**Pinyin**	**English sound**
a (an/ang)	father (fun, sung)	b	bed
ai	aisle	c	hats
ao	now	ch	cheat
e (en/eng)	her (broken, Deng)	d	dog
ei	pay	f	fat
i (in/ing)	peel (pin, ping)	g	go
i (after c/s/z)	girl	h	hat
i (after ch/sh/zh/r)	like the 'r' in Grrr!	j	joke
ia	yard	k	kit
ian	yen	l	lot
iang	young	m	man
iao	yowl	n	not
ie	yes	ng	ring
iong	Jung	p	pet
iu	yolk	q	cheat
o (ong)	more (Jung)	r	red
ou	low	s	sun
u (un)	tool (tune)	sh	shot
ua	wah!	t	top
uai	why	w	win
uan	won	x	shot
uan (after j/q/x/y)	went	y	yes
uang	swung	z	sounds
ue	you wet	zh	gem
ui	way		
uo	war		
ü (and u or un after j/q/x/y)	'new' pronounced with rounded lips		

In this chapter, the Pinyin is given in blue after each phrase.

For pronunciation of tones, see p10.

essentials		
Yes./No.	是。/不是。	Shì./Bùshì.
Please ...	请……	Qǐng ...
Hello./Goodbye.	你好。/再见。	Nǐhǎo./Zàijiàn.
Thank you.	谢谢你。	Xièxie nǐ.
Excuse me. (to get past)	借光。	Jièguāng.
Sorry.	对不起。	Duìbùqǐ.

language difficulties

Do you speak English?
你会说英文吗？ — Nǐ huìshuō Yīngwén ma?

Do you understand?
你明白吗？ — Nǐ míngbai ma?

I (don't) understand.
我(不)明白。 — Wǒ (bù) míngbai.

Could you please ...?	请你……?	Qǐng nǐ ...?
repeat that	再说一遍	zài shuō yībiàn
speak more slowly	慢一点说	màn yīdiǎn shuō

numbers					
0	零	líng	20	二十	èrshí
1	一	yī	30	三十	sānshí
2	二/两	èr/liǎng	40	四十	sìshí
3	三	sān	50	五十	wǔshí
4	四	sì	60	六十	liùshí
5	五	wǔ	70	七十	qīshí
6	六	liù	80	八十	bāshí
7	七	qī	90	九十	jiǔshí
8	八	bā	100	一百	yībǎi
9	九	jiǔ	1000	一千	yīqiān
10	十	shí	1,000,000	一百万	yībǎiwàn

time & dates

What time is it?
现在几点钟？ Xiànzài jǐdiǎn zhōng?

It's (10) o'clock.
（十）点钟。 (Shí)diǎn zhōng.

Quarter past (10).
（十）点十五分。 (Shí)diǎn shíwǔfēn.

Half past (10).
（十）点三十分。 (Shí)diǎn sānshífēn.

Quarter to (11). (literally: Forty-five minutes past (10).)
（十）点四十五分。 (Shí)diǎn sìshíwǔfēn.

At what time (does it start)?
什么时候（开始）？ Shénme shíhòu (kāishǐ)?

(it starts) At 10.
十点钟（开始）。 Shídiǎn zhōng (kāishǐ).

It's (18 October).
（十月十八号）。 (Shíyuè shíbā hào).

yesterday	昨天	zuótiān
today	今天	jīntiān
tomorrow	明天	míngtiān
Monday	星期一	xīngqī yī
Tuesday	星期二	xīngqī èr
Wednesday	星期三	xīngqī sān
Thursday	星期四	xīngqī sì
Friday	星期五	xīngqī wǔ
Saturday	星期六	xīngqī liù
Sunday	星期天	xīngqī tiān

border crossing

I'm …	我是……来的。	Wǒ shì … láide.
in transit	过境	guòjìng
on business	出差	chūchāi
on holiday	度假	dùjià
I'm here for …	我要住……	Wǒ yào zhù …
(three) days	(三)天	(sān) tiān
(three) months	(三)个月	(sān)ge yuè
(three) weeks	(三)个星期	(sān)ge xīngqī

I'm going to (Běijīng).
我到(北京)去。 — Wǒ dào (Běijīng) qù.

I'm staying at (the Pujiang Hotel).
我住(浦江宾馆)。 — Wǒ zhù (Pǔjiāng Bīnguǎn).

I have nothing to declare.
我没有东西申报。 — Wǒ méiyǒu dōngxi shēnbào.

I have something to declare.
我有东西申报。 — Wǒ yǒu dōngxi shēnbào.

That's (not) mine.
那(不)是我的。 — Nà (bù)shì wǒde.

tickets & luggage

Where do I buy a ticket?
哪里买票? — Nǎli mǎi piào?

Do I need to book?
要先订票吗? — Yào xiān dìngpiào ma?

A … ticket to (Dàlián).	一张到(大连)的……票。	Yīzhāng dào (Dàlián) de … piào.
one-way	单程	dānchéng
return	双程	shuāngchéng

I'd like to … my ticket.	我想……票。	Wǒ xiǎng … piào.
cancel	退	tuì
change	改	gǎi
confirm	确定	quèdìng

I'd like a (non)smoking seat.
我想要(不)吸烟的座位。 Wǒ xiǎngyào (bù) xīyān de zuòwèi.

Is there a toilet/air-conditioning?
有厕所/空调吗? Yǒu cèsuǒ/kōngtiáo ma?

How long does the trip take?
几个小时到站? Jīge xiǎoshí dàozhàn?

Is it a direct route?
是直达的吗? Shì zhídáde ma?

My luggage has been …	我的行李被……了。	Wǒde xíngli bèi … le.
damaged	摔坏	shuāihuài
lost	丢	diū
stolen	偷走	tōuzǒu

transport

Where does flight (BJ8) arrive/depart?
(BJ8) 飞机在哪里抵达/起飞? (bee jay bā) fēijī zài nǎli dǐdá/qǐfēi?

Is this the … to (Hángzhōu)?	这个……到(杭州)去吗?	Zhège … dào (Hángzhōu) qù ma?
boat	船	chuán
bus	车	chē
plane	飞机	fēijī
train	火车	huǒchē

When's the ... (bus)?	……(车)几点走?	... (chē) jǐdiǎn zǒu?
first	首趟	Shǒutàng
last	末趟	Mòtàng
next	下一趟	Xià yītàng

How long will it be delayed?
推迟多久? — Tuīchí duōjiǔ?

Can you tell me when we get to (Hángzhōu)?
到了(杭州)请叫我,好吗? — Dàole (Hángzhōu) qǐng jiào wǒ, hǎoma?

That's my seat.
那是我的座。 — Nà shì wǒde zùo.

I'd like a taxi ...	我要订一辆出租车,……	Wǒ yào dìng yīliàng chūzū chē, ...
to depart at (9am)	(早上9点钟)出发	(zǎoshàng jiǔ diǎn zhōng) chūfā
now	现在	xiànzài

How much is it to (the Great Wall)?
到(长城)多少钱? — Dào (Chángchéng) duōshǎo qián?

Please put the meter on.
请打表。 — Qǐng dǎbiǎo.

Please take me to (this address).
请带我到(这个地址)。 — Qǐng dàiwǒ dào (zhège dìzhǐ).

Please stop/wait here.
请在这儿停/等 — Qǐng zài zhèr tíng/děng.

I'd like to hire a self-drive car.
我想租一辆轿车。 — Wǒ xiǎng zū yīliàng jiàochē.

I'd like to hire a car with a driver.
我想包一辆车。 — Wǒ xiǎng bāo yīliàng chē.

How much is it per day/week?
一天/星期多少钱? — Yī tiān/xīngqī duōshǎo qián?

directions

Where's a/the …?	……在哪儿?	… zài nǎr?
bank	银行	Yínháng
place to change foreign money	换外币的地方	Huàn wàibì de dìfang
post office	邮局	yóujú

Can you show me where it is on the map?
请帮我找它在地图上的位置。 Qǐng bāngwǒ zhǎo tā zài dìtú shàng de wèizhi.

What's the address?	什么地址?	Shénme dìzhǐ?
How far is it?	有多远?	Yǒu duō yuǎn?
How do I get there?	怎么走?	Zěnme zǒu?
Turn left/right.	往左/右拐。	Wǎng zuǒ/yòu guǎi.
It's straight ahead.	一直往前。	Yīzhí wǎngqián.

It's …	在……	Zài …
behind …	……的后面	… de hòumian
in front of …	……的前面	… de qiánmian
near …	……附近	… fùjìn
on the corner	拐角	guǎijiǎo
opposite …	……的对面	… de duìmiàn
there	那里	nàli

signs

入口/出口	rù kǒu/chū kǒu	**Entry/Exit**
派出所	pàichūsuǒ	**Police Station**
浴室	yù shì	**Bathroom**
男/女	nán/nǚ	**Male/Female**
不许吸烟	bùxǔ xīyān	**No Smoking**
不许吐痰	bùxǔ tǔtán	**No Spitting**

accommodation

Where's a guest house/hotel?
哪里有宾馆/酒店？ Nǎli yǒu bīnguǎn/jiǔdiàn?

Can you recommend somewhere cheap/good?
你能推荐一个便宜/好的地方住吗？ Nǐ néng tuījiàn yīge piányi/hǎo de dìfang zhù ma?

I'd like to book a room.
我想订房间。 Wǒ xiǎng dìng fángjiān.

I have a reservation.
我有预订。 Wǒ yǒu yùdìng.

Do you have a … room?	有没有……房？	Yǒuméiyǒu … fáng?
double (suite)	套	tào
single	单人	dānrén
twin	双人	shuāngrén

How much is it per night/person?
每天/人多少钱？ Měi tiān/rén duōshǎo qián?

For (three) nights.
住(三)天。 Zhù (sān) tiān.

What time is checkout?
几点钟退房？ Jǐdiǎnzhōng tuìfáng?

Could I have my key, please?
能不能给我房间钥匙？ Néngbùnéng gěi wǒ fángjiān yàoshi?

Can I get an extra (blanket)?
我能多拿一条(毛毯)吗？ Wǒ néng duōná yītiáo (máotǎn) ma?

The (air conditioning) doesn't work.
(空调)有毛病。 (Kōngtiáo) yǒu máobìng.

Do you have a/an …?	有没有……？	Yǒuméiyǒu …?
elevator	电梯	diàntī
safe	保险箱	bǎoxiǎn xiāng

Could I have my …, please?	我想拿回我的……	Wǒ xiǎng náhuí wǒde …
deposit	押金	yājīn
passport	护照	hùzhào
valuables	贵重物品	guìzhòng wùpǐn

banking & communications

Where's a/an …?	……在哪儿？	… zài nǎr?
ATM	自动取款机	Zìdòng qǔkuǎnjī
public phone	公用电话	Gōngyòng diànhuà

I'd like to …	我要……	Wǒ yào …
change a travellers cheque	换旅行支票	huàn lǚxíng zhīpiào
change money	换钱	huànqián
withdraw money	取现金	qǔ xiànjīn

What's the …?	……是多少？	… shì duōshǎo?
charge for that	手续费	Shǒuxùfèi
exchange rate	兑换率	Duìhuànlǜ

Where's the local internet cafe?
附近有网吧吗？ Fùjìn yǒu wǎngbā ma?

How much is it per hour?
每小时多少钱？ Měi xiǎoshí duōshǎo qián?

I'd like to …	我想……	Wǒ xiǎng …
get internet access	上网	shàngwǎng
use a printer/scanner	打印/扫描	dǎyìn/sǎomiáo

I'd like a …	我想买一……	Wǒ xiáng mǎi yī …
mobile/cell phone	个手机	ge shǒujī
SIM card	张SIM卡	zhāng SIM kǎ

What are the rates?
电话费怎么算？ Diànhuàfèi zěnme suàn?

What's your phone number?
您的电话号码是多少？ Nín de diànhuà hàomǎ shì duōshǎo?

The number is ...
号码是…… Hàomǎ shì ...

I want to ...	我想……	Wǒ xiǎng ...
buy a phonecard	买一张电话卡	mǎi yīzhāng diànhuà kǎ
call collect	打对方付款的电话	dǎ duìfāng fùkuǎn de diànhuà
call (Singapore)	打电话到(新加坡)	dǎ diànhuà dào (Xīnjiāpō)

I want to buy a/an ...	我想买一……	Wǒ xiǎng mǎi yī ...
envelope	个信封	ge xìnfēng
stamp	张邮票	zhāng yóupiào

I want to send a fax.
我想发个传真。 Wǒ xiǎng fā ge chuánzhēn.

I want to send a parcel.
我想寄一个包裹。 Wǒ xiǎng jì yī gè bāoguǒ.

Please send it by airmail/surface mail to (Australia).
请寄航空信/平信到(澳大利亚)。 Qǐng jì hángkōng xìn/píngxìn dào (Àodàlìyà).

sightseeing

What time does it open/close?
几点开门/关门？ Jǐdiǎn kāimén/guānmén?

What's the admission charge?
门票多少钱？ Ménpiào duōshǎo qián?

Is there a discount for students/children?
给学生/儿童打折扣吗？ Gěi xuésheng/értóng dǎzhékòu ma?

I'd like a ...	我想买一……	Wǒ xiǎng mǎi yī ...
catalogue	本画册	běn huàcè
guide	本指南书	běn zhǐnán shū
(local) map	张(本地)地图	zhāng (běndì) dìtú

I'd like to see ...	我想看……	Wǒ xiǎng kàn ...
What's that?	那是什么？	Nà shì shénme?
Can I take a photo?	我能拍吗？	Wǒ néng pāima?

When's the next tour?
下一个向导游是什么时候？ — Xiàyīge xiàngdǎoyóu shì shénme shíhòu?

How long is the tour?
向导游要多长时间？ — Xiàngdǎoyóu yào duōcháng shíjiān?

Is (the) ... included?	包括……吗？	Bāokuò ... ma?
accommodation	住宿	zhùsù
admission	门票钱	ménpiàoqián
food	饮食	yǐnshí
transport	交通	jiāotōng

sightseeing		
Army of Terracotta Warriors	西安兵马俑	Xī'ān Bīngmǎyǒng
Forbidden City	故宫	Gùgōng
Great Wall	长城	Chángchéng
Guìlín	桂林	Guìlín
Píngyáo (ancient walled city)	平遥	Píngyáo
Tài Shān	泰山	Tàishān
West Lake of Hángzhōu	杭州西湖	Hángzhōu Xīhú

shopping

Where's a ...?	……在哪儿？	... zài nǎr?
camera shop	照相店	Zhàoxiàng diàn
market	市场	Shìchǎng
souvenir shop	纪念品店	Jìniànpǐn diàn

I'd like to buy ...
我想买…… — Wǒ xiǎng mǎi ...

Can I look at it?
我能看看吗？ — Wǒ néng kànkan ma?

Can I have it sent overseas?
你能寄到国外吗？ — Nǐ néng jìdào guówài ma?

Can I have my (camera) repaired here?
你能修我的（照相机）吗？ — Nǐ néngxiū wǒde (zhàoxiàngjī) ma?

It's faulty.
有毛病。 — Yǒu máobìng.

How much is it?
多少钱？ — Duōshǎo qián?

Please write down the price.
请把价钱写下来。 — Qǐng bǎ jiàqián xiěxià lái.

That's too expensive.
太贵了。 — Tàiguì le.

I'll give you (five kuai).
给你（五块）钱。 — Gěinǐ (wǔkuài) qián.

There's a mistake in the bill.
帐单上有问题。 — Zhàngdān shàng yǒu wèntí.

Do you accept ...?	你们收……吗？	Nǐmen shōu ... ma?
credit cards	信用卡	xìnyòng kǎ
debit cards	借记卡	jièjìkǎ
travellers cheques	旅行支票	lǚxíng zhīpiào
I'd like ..., please.	可以……吗？	Kěyǐ ... ma?
a bag	一个袋子	yīge dàizi
a receipt	发票	fāpiāo
a refund	退钱	tuì qián
my change	找零钱	zhǎo língqián
less	少	shǎo
enough	足够	zúgòu
more	多	duō

photography

Can you burn a CD from my memory card?
能不能帮我从内存卡刻录到CD光盘? — Néng bù néng bāng wǒ cóng nèi cún kǎ ke lu dào CD guāng pán?

Can you develop this film?
能洗这个胶卷吗? — Néng xǐ zhège jiāojuǎn ma?

I need a memory card for this camera.
我需要一张用于这部相机的内存卡。 — Wǒ xūyào yī zhāng yòng yú zhè bù xiāng jī de nèi cún kǎ.

I want to buy a film for this camera.
我想买这个机子的胶卷。 — Wǒ xiǎng mǎi zhège jīzi de jiāojuǎn.

When will it be ready?
什么时候来取? — Shénme shíhòu lái qǔ?

making conversation

Hello. (general)	你好。	Nǐhǎo.
Hello. (Běijīng)	您好。	Nínhǎo.
Goodbye.	再见。	Zàijiàn.
Good night.	晚安。	Wǎn'ān.
Mr	先生	xiānsheng
Mrs	女士	nǚshì
Ms/Miss	小姐	xiǎojiě
How are you? (general)	你好吗?	Nǐhǎo ma?
How are you? (Běijīng)	您好吗?	Nínhǎo ma?
Fine.	好。	Hǎo.
And you?	你呢?	Nǐ ne?
What's your name?	你叫什么名字?	Nǐ jiào shénme míngzi?
My name is …	我叫……	Wǒ jiào …
I'm pleased to meet you.	幸会。	Xìnghuì.

This is my …	这是我的……	Zhè shì wǒde …
brother	兄弟	xiōngdì
daughter	女儿	nǚ'ér
father	父亲	fùqīn
friend	朋友	péngyou
husband	丈夫	zhàngfu
mother	母亲	mǔqīn
partner (intimate)	对象	duìxiàng
sister	姐妹	jiěmèi
son	儿子	érzi
wife	太太	tàitai

Here's my (address).
给你我的(地址)。 Gěi nǐ wǒde (dìzhǐ).

What's your (email)?
你的(网址)是什么? Nǐde (wǎngzhǐ) shìshénme?

Where are you from?
你从哪儿来? Nǐ cóngnǎr lái?

I'm from …	我从……来。	Wǒ cóng … lái.
Australia	澳大利亚	Àodàlìyà
Canada	加拿大	Jiānádà
England	英国	Yīngguó
New Zealand	新西兰	Xīnxīlán
the USA	美国	Měiguó

What's your occupation?	你做什么工作?	Nǐ zuò shénme gōngzuò?

I'm a/an …	我当……	Wǒ dāng …
businessperson	商人	shāngrén
office worker	白领	báilǐng
tradesperson	工匠	gōngjiàng

Do you like …?	你喜欢……吗？	Nǐ xǐhuān … ma?
I (don't) like …	我(不)喜欢……	Wǒ (bù) xǐhuān …
art	艺术	yìshù
films	看电影	kàn diànyǐng
music	听音乐	tīngyīnyuè
reading	看书	kànshū
sport	体育	tǐyù

eating out

Can you recommend a …?	你可以推荐一个……吗？	Nǐ kěyǐ tuījiàn yīge … ma?
bar	酒吧	jiǔbā
dish	盘	pán
restaurant	饭馆	fànguǎn
I'd like a/the …	我要……	Wǒ yào …
bill	帐单	zhàngdān
drink list	酒水单	jiǔshuǐ dān
local speciality	一个地方特色菜	yīge dìfāng tèsè cài
menu	菜单	càidān
(non)smoking table	(不)吸烟的桌子	(bù)xīyān de zhuōzi
table for (five)	一张(五个人的)桌子	yīzhāng (wǔge rén de) zhuōzi
I'll have that.	来一个吧。	Lái yīge ba.
breakfast	早饭	zǎofàn
lunch	午饭	wǔfàn
dinner	晚饭	wǎnfàn
drink (alcoholic)	酒	jiǔ
drink (nonalcoholic)	饮料	yǐnliào
(cup of) coffee …	(一杯)咖啡……	(yībēi) kāfēi …
(cup of) tea …	(一杯)茶……	(yībēi) chá …
with (milk)	加(牛奶)	jiā (niúnǎi)
without (sugar)	不加(糖)	bù jiā (táng)

(orange) juice	(橙)汁	(chéng) zhī
soft drink	汽水	qìshuǐ

I'll have boiled/still mineral water.
我来一个开/矿泉水。 Wǒ lái yīge kāi/kuàngquán shuǐ.

What are you drinking?
喝什么？ Hē shénme?

I'll buy you one.
我请客。 Wǒ qǐng kè.

What would you like to drink?
你想喝什么？ Nǐ xiǎng hē shénme?

a … of beer	一……啤酒	yī … píjiǔ
glass	杯	bēi
large bottle	大瓶	dàpíng
small bottle	小瓶	xiǎopíng
a shot of (whisky)	一樽(威士忌)	yīzūn (wēishìjì)
a bottle/glass of … wine	一瓶/一杯……葡萄酒	yīpíng/yībēi … pútáo jiǔ
red	红	hóng
white	白	bái

special diets & allergies

Do you have … food?	有没有……食品？	Yǒuméiyǒu … shípín?
halal	清真	qīngzhēn
kosher	犹太	yóutài
vegetarian	素食	sùshí

Could you prepare a meal without …?
能不能做一个不放……的菜？ Néngbùnéng zuòyīge bùfàng … de cài?

I'm allergic to ...	我对……过敏。	Wǒ duì ... guòmǐn.
dairy produce	奶制品	nǎizhìpǐn
eggs	鸡蛋	jīdàn
meat	肉	ròu
nuts	果仁	guǒrén
seafood	海鲜	hǎixiān

emergencies

Help!	救命！	Jiùmìng!
Stop!	站住！	Zhànzhù!
Go away!	走开！	Zǒukāi!
Thief!	小偷！	Xiǎotōu!
Fire!	着火啦！	Zháohuǒ la!
Watch out!	小心！	Xiǎoxīn!

Call a doctor!
请叫医生来！ Qǐng jiào yīshēng lái!

Call an ambulance!
请叫一辆 Qǐng jiào yīliàng
急救车！ jíjiù chē!

Could you please help?
你能帮我吗？ Nǐ néng bāngwǒ ma?

Can I use your phone?
我能借用 Wǒ néng jièyòng
你的电话吗？ nǐde diànhuà ma?

I'm lost.
我迷路了。 Wǒ mílù le.

Where are the toilets?
厕所在哪儿？ Cèsuǒ zài nǎr?

Where's the police station?

派出所在哪里?	Pàichūsuǒ zài nǎli?

I want to contact my embassy/consulate.

我要联系我的大使馆/领事馆。	Wǒ yào liánxì wǒde dàshǐguǎn/lǐngshìguǎn.

I've been ...	我被……了。	Wǒ bèi ... le.
assaulted	侵犯	qīnfàn
raped	强奸	qiángjiān
robbed	抢劫	qiǎngjié

I've lost my ...	我的……丢了。	Wǒde ... diū le.
My ... was/were stolen.	我的……被偷了。	Wǒde ... bèitōu le.
bags	行李	xíngli
credit card	信用卡	xìnyòng kǎ
money	钱	qián
passport	护照	hùzhào
travellers cheques	旅行支票	lǚxíng zhīpiào

health

Where's the nearest ...?	最近的……在哪儿?	Zuìjìnde ... zài nǎr?
dentist	牙医	yáyī
doctor	医生	yīshēng
hospital	医院	yīyuàn
pharmacist	药房	yàofáng

I need a doctor (who speaks English).

我要看(会说英文的)医生。	Wǒ yào kàn (huìshuō Yīngwénde) yīshēng.

Could I see a female doctor?

最好要看一位女医生。	Zuìhǎo yàokàn yīwèi nǚyīshēng.

I've run out of my medication.

我用完了我的处方药。	Wǒ yòngwánle wǒde chǔfāngyào.

It hurts here.	这里痛。	Zhèlǐ tòng.
I have (a) …	我有……	Wǒ yǒu …
asthma	哮喘	xiàochuǎn
constipation	便秘	biànmì
diarrhoea	拉稀	lāxī
fever	发烧	fāshāo
heart condition	心脏病	xīnzàngbìng
nausea	反胃	fǎnwèi
I'm allergic to …	我对……过敏。	Wǒ duì … guòmǐn.
antibiotics	抗菌素	kàngjūnsù
anti-inflammatories	抗炎药	kàngyányào
aspirin	阿斯匹林	āsīpǐlín
bees	蜜蜂	mìfēng
codeine	可待因	kědàiyīn

english–mandarin dictionary

In this dictionary, words are marked as n (noun), a (adjective), adv (adverb), v (verb), sg (singular), pl (plural), inf (informal) and pol (polite) where necessary.

A

accident 事故 shìgù
accommodation 住宿 zhùsù
adaptor 双边插座 shuāngbiān chāzuò
address n 地址 dìzhǐ
after 以后 yǐhòu
air-conditioned 有空调的 yǒu kōngtiáo de
airplane 飞机 fēijī
airport 飞机场 fēijī chǎng
alcohol 酒精 jiǔjīng
all 所有的 suǒyǒu de
allergic 过敏 guòmǐn
ambulance 急救车 jíjiù chē
and 和 hé
ankle 脚踝 jiǎohuái
antibiotics 抗菌素 kàngjūnsù
arm 胳膊 gēbo
ATM 自动取款机 zìdòng qǔkuǎnjī

B

baby n 小娃娃 xiǎo wáwa
back (body) 背 bèi
backpack 背包 bèibāo
bad 坏 huài
bag 包 bāo
baggage claim 行李领取处 xíngli lǐngqǔ chù
bank (money) 银行 yínháng
bar 酒吧 jiǔbā
bathroom 浴室 yù shì
battery 电池 diànchí
beautiful 美丽 měilì
bed 床 chuáng
beer 啤酒 píjiǔ
before 以前 yǐqián
behind 背面 bèimiàn
bicycle n 自行车 zìxíngchē
big 大 dà
bill (restaurant etc) n 帐单 zhàngdān
blanket 毛毯 máotǎn
blood group 血型 xuèxíng
boat 船 chuán
book (make a booking) v 定 dìng
bottle 瓶子 píngzi
boy 男孩子 nán háizi
brakes 车闸 chēzhá
breakfast 早饭 zǎofàn
broken 坏了 huài le
bus (city) 大巴 dàbā
bus (intercity) 长途车 chángtú chē
business n 生意 shēngyì
buy v 买 mǎi

C

camera 照相机 zhàoxiàngjī
cancel 取消 qǔxiāo
car 轿车 jiàochē
cash n 现金 xiànjīn
cash (a cheque) v 兑现 duìxiàn
cell phone 手机 shǒujī
centre 中心 zhōngxīn
change (money) v 换钱 huànqián
cheap 实惠 shíhuì
check (bill) n 账单 zhàngdān
check-in (desk) 登记台 dēngjì tái
chest (body) 胸 xiōng
child 孩子 háizi
cigarette 香烟 xiāngyān
city 城市 chéngshì
clean a 干净 gānjìng
closed 关门 guānmén
cold a 冷 lěng
collect call 对方付款电话 duìfāng fùkuǎndiànhuà
come 来 lái
computer 电脑 diànnǎo
condom 避孕套 bìyùntào
contact lenses 隐形眼镜 yǐnxíng yǎnjìng
cook v 炒菜 chǎocài
cost (price) n 价格 jiàgé
credit card 信用卡 xìnyòng kǎ
currency exchange 货币兑换 huòbì duìhuàn
customs (immigration) 海关 hǎiguān

D

dangerous 危险 wēxiǎn
date (day) n 日期 rìqī

day 白天 báitiān
delay 往后退 wǎnghòutuì
dentist 牙医 yáyī
depart (leave) 离开 líkāi
diaper 尿裤 niàokù
dinner 晚饭 wǎnfàn
direct 直接 zhíjiē
dirty 脏 zāng
disabled 残疾 cánjí
discount 折扣 zhékòu
doctor 医生 yīshēng
double bed 双人床 shuāngrén chuáng
double room 双人间 shuāngrén jiān
drink (alcoholic) n 酒 jiǔ
drink (nonalcoholic) n 饮料 yǐnliào
drive v 开车 kāichē
driving licence 驾照 jiàzhào
drug (illicit) 毒品 dúpǐn

E

ear 耳朵 ěrduo
east 东方 dōngfāng
eat 吃饭 chīfàn
economy class 经济舱 jīngjì cāng
electricity 电 diàn
elevator 电梯 diàntī
email n 电子邮件 diànzǐ yóujiàn
embassy 大使馆 dàshǐguǎn
emergency 出事 chūshì
English 英文 Yīngwén
evening 晚上 wǎnshàng
exit n 出口 chūkǒu
expensive 贵 guì
eye(s) 眼睛 yǎnjīng

F

far 远 yuǎn
fast 快 kuài
father 父亲 fùqīn
film (for camera) 胶卷 jiāojuǎn
finger 指头 zhǐtou
first-aid kit 急救装备 jíjiù zhuāngbèi
first class 头等 tóuděng
fish n 鱼 yú
food n 食品 shípǐn
foot 脚 jiǎo
free (no charge) 免费 miǎnfèi
friend 朋友 péngyou
fruit 水果 shuǐguǒ
full 满 mǎn

G

gift 礼物 lǐwù
girl 女孩子 nǚháizi
glass (drinking) 玻璃杯 bōli bēi
glasses (spectacles) 眼镜 yǎnjìng
go 去 qù
good 好 hǎo
guide (person) 导游 dǎoyóu

H

half 半个 bànge
hand 手 shǒu
happy 快乐 kuàilè
have 有 yǒu
he 他 tā
head 头 tóu
heart 心脏 xīnzàng
heavy 重 zhòng
help 帮助 bāngzhù
here 这里 zhèlǐ
high 高 gāo
highway 高速公路 gāosù gōnglù
hike v 步行 bùxíng
holiday 度假 dùjià
homosexual 同性恋 tóngxìng liàn
hospital 医院 yīyuàn
hot 热 rè
hotel 酒店 jiǔdiàn
hungry (to be) 饿 è
husband 丈夫 zhàngfu

I

I 我 wǒ
identification card (ID) 身份证 shēnfèn zhèng
ill 有病 yǒubìng
important 重要 zhòngyào
injury 伤害 shānghài
insurance 保险 bǎoxiǎn
internet 因特网 yīntèwǎng
interpreter 翻译 fānyì

J

jewellery 首饰 shǒushì
job 工作 gōngzuò

K

key 钥匙 yàoshi
kilogram 公斤 gōngjīn
kitchen 厨房 chúfáng
knife 刀 dāo

L

laundry (place) 洗衣店 xǐyīdiàn
lawyer 律师 lǜshī
left (direction) 左边 zuǒbian
leg 腿 tuǐ
lesbian 女同性恋 nǚ tóngxìng liàn
less 少 shǎo
letter (mail) 信 xìn
light 光 guāng
like adv 同……一样 tóng … yīyàng
lock n 锁 suǒ
lock v 锁上 suǒshàng
long a 长 cháng
lost (one's way) 迷路 mílù
love v 爱 ài
luggage 行李 xíngli
lunch 午饭 wǔfàn

M

mail n 来信 láixìn
man 男人 nánrén
map 地图 dìtú
market 市场 shìchǎng
matches (for lighting) 火柴 huǒchái
meat 肉 ròu
medicine (medication) 医药 yīyào
message 信息 xìnxī
milk 牛奶 niúnǎi
minute 分钟 fēnzhōng
mobile phone 手机 shǒujī
money 钱 qián
month 月 yuè
morning (after breakfast) 早上 zǎoshàng
morning (before lunch) 上午 shàngwǔ
mother 母亲 mǔqin
motorcycle 摩托车 mótuō chē
mouth 口 kǒu

N

name n 名字 míngzi
near 近 jìn
new 新 xīn
newspaper 报纸 bàozhǐ
night 晚上 wǎnshàng
no 不对 bùduì
nonsmoking 不吸烟 bù xīyān
north 北边 běibiān
nose 鼻子 bízi
now 现在 xiànzài
number 号码 hàomǎ

O

old 老 lǎo
one-way (ticket) 单程（票）dānchéng (piào)
open a 开放 kāifàng
outside 外面 wàimian

P

passport 护照 hùzhào
pay v 付 fù
pharmacy 西药房 xīyào fáng
phone card 电话卡 diànhuà kǎ
photo 照片 zhàopiàn/zhàopiānr
police 警察局 jǐngchájú
postcard 明信片 míngxìnpiàn
price 价格 jiàgé

Q

quiet 安静 ānjìng

R

rain n 下雨 xiàyǔ
razor 剃刀 tìdāo
receipt 发票 fāpiào
refund n 退钱 tuì qián
registered (mail) 挂号 guàhào
rent 租赁 zūlìn
repair 修理 xiūlǐ
reservation (booking) 预定 yùdìng
restaurant 饭馆 fànguǎn
return (come back) 回来 huílái
return (ticket) 双程（票）shuāngchéng (piào)
right (direction) 右边 yòubiān
road 道路 dàolù
room 房间 fángjiān

S

safe 安全 ānquán
sanitary napkin 卫生巾 wèishēngjīn
seat (hard; on train) 硬座 yìngzuò
seat (place) 座位 zuòwèi

seat (soft; on train) 软座 ruǎnzuò
send 寄送 jìsòng
sex 男女事 nánnǚ shì
shampoo 洗发膏 xǐfàgāo
share 公用 gōngyòng
she 她 tā
sheet (bed) 床单 chuángdān
shirt 衬衫 chènshān
shoes 鞋子 xiézi
shop n 店 diàn
short (height) 矮 ǎi
short (length) 短 duǎn
shower 浴室 yùshì
single room 单人间 dānrén jiān
skin 皮肤 pífū
skirt 裙子 qúnzi
sleep 睡觉 shuìjiào
slowly 慢慢地 mànmande
small 小 xiǎo
soap 肥皂 féizào
some 一些 yīxiē
soon 快 kuài
south 南 nán
souvenir shop 纪念品店 jìniànpǐn diàn
stamp 邮票 yóupiào
stand-by ticket 站台票 zhàntái piào
station 车站 chēzhàn
stomach 肚子 dùzi
stop (bus, tram) n 停 tíng
stop v 停止 tíngzhǐ
street 街头 jiētóu
student 学生 xuéshēng
sun 太阳 tàiyáng
sunblock 防晒油 fángshài yóu
swim 游泳 yóuyǒng

T

tampon 棉条 miántiáo
teeth 牙齿 yáchǐ
telephone n 电话 diànhuà
temperature (weather) 温度 wēndù
that (one) 那个 nàge
they 他们 tāmen
thirsty (to be) 渴 kě
this (one) 这个 zhège
throat 脖子 bózi
ticket 票 piào
time 时间 shíjiān
tired 累 lèi
tissues 纸巾 zhǐjīn
toilet 厕所 cèsuǒ
tomorrow 明天 míngtiān
tonight 今天晚上 jīntiān wǎnshàng
toothbrush 牙刷 yáshuā
toothpaste 牙膏 yágāo
torch (flashlight) 手电筒 shǒudiàntǒng
tour 向导游 xiàngdǎo yóu
tourist office 旅行店 lǚxíng diàn
towel 毛巾 máojīn
train 火车 huǒchē
translate 翻译 fānyì
travel agency 旅行社 lǚxíng shè
travellers cheque(s) 旅行支票 lǚxíng zhīpiào
trousers 休闲裤 xiūxián kù
twin room 双人房 shuāngrén fáng

U

underwear 内衣 nèiyī
urgent 要紧 yàojǐn

V

vacant 有空 yǒukòng
vegetable 蔬菜 shūcài
vegetarian 吃素的 chīsù de
visa 签证 qiānzhèng

W

walk 走路 zǒulù
wallet 钱包 qiánbāo
wash 洗 xǐ
watch n 手表 shǒubiǎo
water 水 shuǐ
we 我们 wǒmen
weekend 周末 zhōumò
west 西 xī
wheelchair 轮椅 lúnyǐ
when 什么时候 shénme shíhòu
where 哪里 nǎli
who 谁 shéi
why 为什么 wèi shénme
wife 老婆 lǎopo
with 跟 gēn
without 以外 yǐwài
woman 女人 nǚrén

Y

yes 是 shì
yesterday 昨天 zuótiān
you sg inf 你 nǐ
you sg pol 您 nín
you pl 你们 nǐmen

Cantonese

TONES 36
ABOUT CANTONESE 37
PRONUNCIATION 38
LANGUAGE DIFFICULTIES 39
TIME & DATES 40
BORDER CROSSING 40
TICKETS & LUGGAGE 41
TRANSPORT 42
DIRECTIONS 43
ACCOMMODATION 44
BANKING & COMMUNICATIONS 45
SIGHTSEEING 47
SHOPPING 48
PHOTOGRAPHY 49
MAKING CONVERSATION 50
EATING OUT 52
SPECIAL DIETS & ALLERGIES 54
EMERGENCIES 54
HEALTH 55
ENGLISH–CANTONESE DICTIONARY 57

tones

Cantonese is a tonal language ('tonal quality' refers to the raising and lowering of pitch on certain syllables). Tones in Cantonese fall on vowels and on n. The same combination of sounds pronounced with different tones can have a very different meaning, eg gwa̱t 掘 means 'dig up' and gwàt 骨 means 'bones'.

Cantonese has between six and 10 tones, depending on which definition you use. In our pronunciation guide they've been simplified to five tones, indicated with accents or underscores on the symbol letters (as shown in the tables below for the vowel 'a'), in addition to a sixth, level tone. Higher tones involve tightening the vocal cords to get a higher sounding pitch, while lower tones are made by relaxing the vocal cords to get a lower pitch. Bear in mind that the tones are relative to the natural vocal range of the speaker, eg the high tone is pronounced at the top of one's vocal range. Note also that some tones slide up or down in pitch.

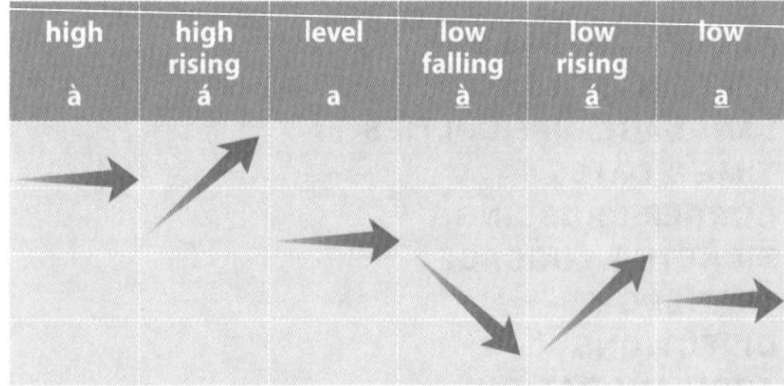

Symbol	Tone	Example	
à	high	睇	tái
á	high rising	嬲	nàu
a	level	角	gawk
à̱	low falling	人	yà̱n
á̱	low rising	被	pá̱y
a̱	low	問	ma̱n

about Cantonese

Cantonese is the official language of Hong Kong and Macau, and in mainland China it's the local language of the southeast, including most of the province of Guǎngdōng. Standard Cantonese is based on the language spoken in the city of Guǎngzhōu (Canton), and it's colloquially known as gwáwng·dùng·wáa 廣東話 (Guǎngdōng speech), while its more formal name is yue yu 粤语 (Yue language). Cantonese has over 70 million speakers, as it's also spoken among minority groups in Southeast Asia, most notably in Singapore, and by emigrant communities worldwide. For over 50 years, official Chinese policy has encouraged the use of Mandarin as the national language of China. However, Cantonese speakers have persisted in using their native language, a key part of their pride and cultural identity. Today's Cantonese can trace its history back over 2000 years to the Qin Dynasty (221–206 BC). Both Cantonese and Mandarin belong to the Sino-Tibetan language family and have developed from the same tongue, but Cantonese has preserved certain intricate elements of Middle Chinese (AD 581–907), which Mandarin has lost. Various systems have been developed to show Cantonese sounds in Roman script. In this chapter, we've used a slightly simplified version of the widely accepted Yale system.

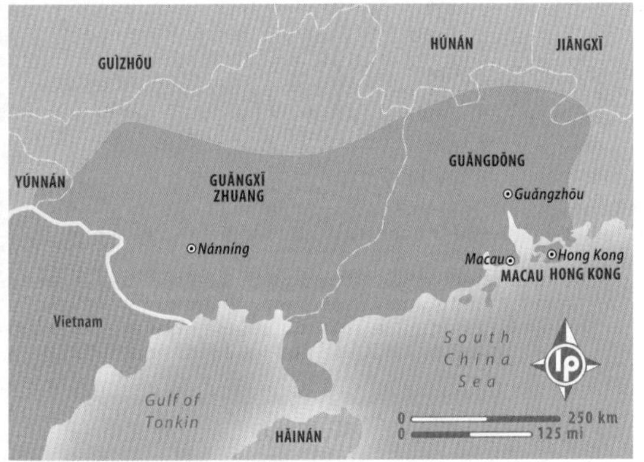

pronunciation

Vowels		Consonants	
Symbol	**English sound**	**Symbol**	**English sound**
a	run	b	bed
aa	father	ch	cheat
aai	aisle (long)	d	dog
aau	now (long)	f	fat
ai	aisle (short)	g	go
au	now (short)	h	hat
aw	law	j	joke
ay	say	k	kit
e	bet	l	lot
eu	nurse	m	man
eui	eu followed by i	n	not
ew	i pronounced with rounded lips	ng	ring
i	see	p	pet
iu	youth	s	sun
o	note	t	top
oy	toy	w	win
u	put	y	yes
ui	with		

In this chapter, the Cantonese pronunciation is given in turquoise after each phrase.

The sound ng (found in English at the end or in the middle of words, eg 'ringing') can appear at the start of words in Cantonese or as a word on its own. Note that words ending with the sounds p, t and k must be clipped, eg in English the p sound is much shorter in 'tip' than in 'pit'. For pronunciation of tones, see p36.

Syllables within a word are separated by a dot, for example:
多謝。 dàw·je

essentials

Yes./No.	係。/唔係。	hai/ǹg·hai
Please ...	唔該……	ǹg·gòy ...
Hello./Goodbye.	哈佬。/再見。	hàa·ló/joy·gin
Thank you (very much).	多謝(你)。	dàw·je (láy)
You're welcome.	唔駛客氣。	ǹg·sái haak·hay
Excuse me. (to get past)	唔該借借。	ǹg·gòy je·je
Sorry.	對唔住。	deui·ǹg·jew

language difficulties

Do you speak English?
你識唔識講
英文啊？ — láy sìk·ǹg·sìk gáwng yìng·mán aa

Do you understand?
你明唔明啊？ — láy mìng·ǹg·mìng aa

I (don't) understand.
我 (唔)明白。 — ngáw (ǹg) mìng·baak

Could you please ...?	唔該你……?	ǹg·gòy láy ...
repeat that	再講一次	joy gáwng yàt chi
speak more slowly	講慢啲	gáwng maan dì

numbers

0	零	lìng	**20**	二十	yi·sap
1	一	yàt	**30**	三十	sàam·sap
2	二	yi	**40**	四十	say·sap
3	三	sàam	**50**	五十	ńg·sap
4	四	say	**60**	六十	luk·sap
5	五	ńg	**70**	七十	chàt·sap
6	六	luk	**80**	八十	baat·sap
7	七	chàt	**90**	九十	gáu·sap
8	八	baat	**100**	一百	yàt·baak
9	九	gáu	**1000**	一千	yàt·chìn
10	十	sap	**1,000,000**	一百萬	yàt·baak·maan

time & dates

What time is it?	而家幾點鐘？	yi·gàa gáy·dím·jùng
It's (10) o'clock.	(十)點鐘。	(sap)·dím·jùng
Quarter past (10).	(十)點三。	(sap)·dím sàam
Half past (10).	(十)點半。	(sap)·dím bun
Quarter to (11). (literally: Forty-five minutes past (10).)	(十)點九。	(sap)·dím gáu
At what time?	幾時開始?	gáy·si hòy·chí
At …	夜晚……	ye·máan …
It's (18 October).	(十月十八)號。	(sap·yewt sap·baat) ho
yesterday	寢日	kàm·yat
today	今日	gàm·yat
tomorrow	听日	tìng·yat
Monday	星期一	sìng·kày·yàt
Tuesday	星期二	sìng·kày·yi
Wednesday	星期三	sìng·kày·sàam
Thursday	星期四	sìng·kày·say
Friday	星期五	sìng·kày·ńg
Saturday	星期六	sìng·kày·luk
Sunday	星期日	sìng·kày·yat

border crossing

I'm …	我係……	ngáw hai …
in transit	過境	gaw·gíng
on business	出差嚟嘅	chèut·chàai lái ge
on holiday	嚟度假嘅	lái do·gaa ge
I'm here for …	我要住……	ngáw yiu jew …
(two) days	(二)天	(yi) yat
(four) weeks	(四) 個星期	(say) gaw sìng·kày
(three) months	(三) 個月	(sàam) gaw yewt

I'm going to (Shēnzhèn).
我要去(深圳)。 — ngáw yiu heui (sàm·jan)

I'm staying at (the China Hotel).
我住(中國大酒店)。 — ngáw jew (jùng·gawk daai jáu·dim)

I have nothing to declare.
我冇嘢報。 — ngáw mó yé bo

I have something to declare.
我有嘢報。 — ngáw yáu yé bo

That's (not) mine.
(唔)係我嘅。 — (ǹg) hai ngáw ge

tickets & luggage

Where do I buy a ticket?
去邊度買飛？ — heui bìn·do máai fày

Do I need to book?
駛唔駛定飛先呀？ — sái·ǹg·sái deng·fày sìn a

A … ticket to (Panyu).	一張去(番禺)嘅……飛。	yàt jèung heui (pùn·yèw) ge … fày
one-way	單程	dàan·chìng
return	雙程	sèung·chìng

I'd like to … my ticket, please.	唔該，我想……飛。	ǹg·gòy ngáw séung … fày
cancel	退	teui
change	改	góy
confirm	確定張	kawk·ding jèung

I'd like a smoking/nonsmoking seat.
有冇吸煙/不吸煙位？ — yáu·mó kàp·yìn/bàt·kàp·yìn wái

Is there a toilet/air conditioning?
有冇廁所/空調呀？ — yáu·mó chi·sáw/hùng·tìu aa

How long does the trip take?
幾多個鐘頭到？ — gáy·dàw gaw jùng·tàu do

Is it a direct route?
係唔係直達嘅？ — hai·ǹg·hai jik·daat ge

My luggage has been …	我嘅行李……	ngáw ge hàng·láy …
damaged	爛咗	laan·jáw
lost	唔見咗	ǹg·gin·jáw
stolen	俾人偷咗	báy·yàn tàu·jáw

transport

Where does flight (12) arrive/depart?
(十二)號飛機喺邊度起飛／降落？ — (sap·yi) ho fày·gày hái bìn·do háy·fày/gawng·lawk

Is this the … to (Guǎngzhōu)?	呢班……係唔係去(廣州)㗎？	lày bàan … hai·ǹg·hai heui (gwáwng·jàu) gaa
boat	船	sèwn
bus	巴士	bàa·sí
plane	飛機	fày·gày
train	火車	fáw·chè

When's the … (bus)?	……(巴士)幾點開？	… (bàa·sí) gáy dím hòy
first	頭班	tàu·bàan
last	尾班	máy·bàan
next	下一班	haa·yàt·bàan

How long will it be delayed?
推遲幾耐？ — tèui·chì gáy·loy

Please tell me when we get to (Guǎngzhōu).
到(廣州)嘅時候，唔該叫聲我。 — do (gwáwng·jàu) ge si·hau ǹg·gòy giu sèng ngáw

That's my seat.
呢個係我個位。 — lày·gaw hai ngáw gaw wái

I'd like a taxi at (9am).
我想(9點鐘)坐的士。 — ngáw séung (gáu dím·jùng) cháw dìk·sí

I'd like a taxi now.
我想坐的士而家。 — ngáw séung cháw dìk·sí yì·gàa

How much is it to ...?
去……幾多錢？ heui ... gáy·dàw chín

Please put the meter on.
唔該打咪表。 ǹg·gòy dáa mài·biù

Please take me to (this address).
唔該帶我去 (呢個地址)。 ǹg·gòy daai ngáw heui (lày gaw day·jí)

Please stop/wait here.
唔該喺呢度/等。 ǹg·gòy hái lày·do tìng/dáng

I'd like to hire a 4WD/car (with a driver).
我想租架4WD/車(有司機)。 ngáw séung jò gaa fàw·wiù·jàai·fù/chè (yáu sì·gày)

How much for ... hire?	租……幾多錢？	jò ... gáy·dàw chín
daily	一日	yàt yat
weekly	一個禮拜	yàt gaw lái·baai

directions

Where's a/the ...?	……喺邊度？	... hái·bìn·do
bank	銀行	ngàn·hàwng
foreign exchange office	換外幣嘅地方	wun ngoy·bai ge day·fàwng
post office	郵局	yàu·gúk

Can you show me (on the map)?
你可唔可以(喺地圖度)指俾我睇我喺邊度？ láy háw·ǹg·háw·yí (hái day·to do) jí báy ngáw tái ngáw hái bìn·do

What's the address?	地址係？	day·jí hai
How far is it?	有幾遠？	yáu gáy yéwn
How do I get there?	點樣去？	dím·yéung heui
Turn left/right.	向左/右轉。	heung jáw/yau jewn

It's …	喺……	hái …
behind …	……嘅後面	… ge hau·min
in front of …	……嘅前面	… ge chìn·min
near …	……附近	… fu·gan
on the corner	十字路口	sap·ji·lo·háu
opposite …	……嘅對面	… ge deui·min
straight ahead	前面	chìn·min
there	嗰度	gáw·do

signs		
入口/出口	yap·háu/chèut·háu	**Entry/Exit**
有房	yáu fáwng	**Vacancy**
冇房	mó fáwng	**No Vacancy**
派出所	paai·chèut·sáw	**Police Station**
廁所	chi·sáw	**Bathroom**
男	laam	**Male**
女	léui	**Female**

accommodation

Where's a guest house/hotel?
邊度有賓館/酒店? bìn·do yáu bàn·gún/jáu·dim

Can you recommend somewhere …?	你可唔可以推薦個……嘅地方住呀？	láy háw·ǹg·háw·yí tèui·jin gaw … ge day·fàwng jew a
cheap	平	peng
good	好	hó

I'd like to book a room, please.
我想定房。 ngáw séung deng fàwng

I have a reservation.
我預定咗。 ngáw yew·deng jáw

Do you have a … room?	有冇……房？	yáu·mó … fáwng
double	雙人	sèung·yàn
single	單人	dàan·yàn
twin	雙人	sèung·yàn

How much is it per ...?	一……幾多錢？	yàt ... gáy·dàw chín
night	晚	máan
person	個人	gaw yàn

For (three) nights.
住(三)日。 jew (sàam) yat

Could I have my key, please?
可唔可以俾條門匙我？ háw·ǹg·háw·yí báy tiù mùn sì ngáw

Can I get an extra (blanket)?
我可唔可以攞多張(氈)呀？ ngáw háw·ǹg·háw·yí láw dàw jèung (jìn) aa

The (air-conditioning) doesn't work.
(空調)壞咗。 (hùng·tiu) waai·jáw

Do you have an elevator/a safe?
有冇電梯/甲萬？ yáu mó din·tài/gàap·maan

What time is checkout?
幾點鐘退房？ gáy dím·jùng teui·fáwng

Could I have my ..., please?	唔該，我嘅攞……	ǹg·gòy ngáw lày láw ...
deposit	押金	ngaat·gàm
passport	護照	wu·jiu
valuables	貴重物品	gwai·jung mat·bán

banking & communications

Where's a/an ...?	……喺邊度？	... hái bìn·do
ATM	自動提款機	ji·dung tài·fún·gày
public phone	公眾電話	gùng·jung din·wáa

I'd like to ...	我要……	ngáw yiu ...
change a travellers cheque	換旅行支票	wun léui·hàng jì·piu
change money	換錢	wun chín
withdraw money	攞現金	láw yin·gàm

What's the …?	……係乜嘢？	… hai gáy·dàw
charge for that	手續費	sáu·juk·fai
exchange rate	兌換率	deui·wun·léut

Where's the nearest public phone?
呢度附近有冇公眾電話呀？
lày·do fu·gan yáu·mó gùng·jung din·wáa aa

Where's the local internet cafe?
附近有冇網吧？
fu·gan yáu·mó máwng·bàa

How much is it per hour?
每個鐘幾多錢？
muí gaw jùng gáy·dàw chín

I'd like to …	我想……	ngáw séung …
get internet access	上網	séung·máwng
use a printer/scanner	打印/掃描	dáa·yan/so·miù

I'd like a …	我想買個……	ngáw séung máai gaw …
mobile/cell phone for hire	出租手機	chèut·jò sáu·gày
SIM card for your network	你地網絡用嘅SIM卡	láy·day máwng·làwk yung ge sím·kàat

What are the rates?
電話費點計？
din·wáa·fai dím gai

What's your phone number?
你嘅電話號碼係幾多號？
láy ge din·wáa ho·máa hai gáy·dàw ho

The number is …
號碼係……
ho·máa hai …

I want to …	我想……	ngáw séung …
buy a phonecard	買張電話卡	máai jèung din·wáa·kàat
call collect	打對方付款嘅電話	dáa deui·fàwng fu·fún ge din·wáa
call (Singapore)	打電話去（新加坡）	dáa din·wáa heui (sàn·gaa·bàw)

I want to send a …	我想……	ngáw séung …
fax	發傳真	faat chèwn·jàn
parcel	寄包裹	gay bàau·gwáw

I want to buy a/an …	我想買……	ngáw séung máai …
envelope	個信封	gaw seun·fùng
stamp	張郵票	jèung yàu·piu

Please send it by airmail to (Australia).
唔該寄航空
去(澳大利亞)。
ǹg·gòy gay hàwng·hùng
heui (ngo·daai·lay·a)

sightseeing

What time does it open/close?
幾點開/關門？
gáy dím hòy/gwàan·mùn

What's the admission charge?
入場券幾多錢？
yap·chèung·gewn gáy·dàw chín

Is there a discount for children/students?
有冇小童/學生折扣呀？
yáu·mó siú·tùng/hawk·sàang ji·kau aa

I'd like a …	我想買……	ngáw séung máai …
catalogue	目錄	muk·luk
guide	指南	jí·làam
(local) map	(本地)地圖	(bún·day) day·tò

I'd like to see …
我想睇下……
ngáw séung tái háa …

What's that?
嗰啲係乜嘢？
gáw dì hai màt·yé

Can I take a photo?
我可唔可以影
嘅像呀？
ngáw háw·ǹg·háw·yí yíng
ge séung aa

When's the next tour?
下個旅遊團係幾時？
haa·gaw léui·yàu·tèwn hai gáy·sì

How long is the tour?
呢團要幾長時間？
lày tèwn yiu gáy chèung sì·gaan

Is (the) … included?	包唔包……呀？	bàau·ng·bàau … aa
accommodation	住宿	jew·sùk
admission	票價	piu·gaa
food	飲食	yúm·sik
transport	交通	gàau·tùng

sightseeing		
garden	花園	fàa·yéwn
Great Wall	長城	chèung·sìng
palace	宮殿	gùng·din
ruins	廢墟	ai·hèu
square (town)	廣場	gwáwng·chèung
temple (shrine)	廟	miú

shopping

Where's a …?	……喺邊度？	… hái·bìn·do
camera shop	相機鋪	séung·gày·pó
market	街市	gàai·sí
souvenir shop	紀念品店	gay·lim·bán·dim

Where can I buy locally produced goods/souvenirs?
邊度可以買倒本地製品/紀念品？
bìn·do háw·yí máai·dó bún·day jai·bán/gáy·lim·bán

What's this made from?
係乜嘢做㗎？
hai màt·yé jo gaa

I'd like to buy …
我想買……
ngáw séung máai …

Can I look at it?
我可唔可以睇下？
ngáw háw·ng·háw·yí tái haa

Can I have it sent abroad?
可唔可以寄出國外啊？
háw·ng·háw·yí gay chèut gawk·ngoy aa

Can I have my (camera) repaired here?
你可唔可以修好我個（相機）呀？
láy háw·ng·háw·yí sàu·hó ngáw gaw (séung·gày) aa

It's faulty.
壞咗。
waai·jáw

How much is it?
幾多錢？ — gáy·dàw chín

Can you write down the price?
唔該寫低個价錢。 — ǹg·gòy sé dài gaw gaa·chìn

That's too expensive.
太貴啦。 — taai gwai laa

I'll give you (five RMB).
俾(五百蚊人民幣)你。 — báy (ńg baak màn yàn·màn·bai) láy

There's a mistake in the bill.
帳單錯咗。 — jeung·dàan chaw jáw

Do you accept ...?	你地收唔收……呀？	láy·day sàu·ǹg·sàu ... aa
credit cards	信用卡	seun·yung·kàat
debit cards	提款卡	tài·fún·kàat
travellers cheques	旅行支票	léui·hàng jì·piu

I'd like ..., please.	唔該，我要……	ǹg·gòy ngáw yiu ...
a bag	個袋	gaw dóy
a receipt	張單	jèung dàan
a refund	退錢	teui·chín
my change	找錢	jáau·chín

less/enough/more	少/夠/多	siú/gau/dàw

photography

Can you ...?	可唔可以……呀？	háw·ǹg·háw·yí ... aa
develop this film	沖晒呢筒菲林	chùng·saai lày tung fày·lám
transfer photos from my camera to CD	幫我將相機啲相轉落CD	bàwng ngáw jèung séung·gày dì séung jewn lawk sì·dì

Do you have … for this camera?	你有冇啱呢部相機嘅……？	láy yáu·mó ngàam làybo séung·gày ge …
batteries	電池	din·chi
memory cards	儲存卡	chéw·chèwn·kàat

I need film for this camera.
我想買呢架相機嘅 — ngáw séung máai lày gaa séung·gày ge

When will it be ready?
幾時嚟攞？ — gáy·si lày láw

making conversation

In Cantonese, titles are attached to the end of the surname.

Hello.	哈佬。	hàa·ló
Goodbye.	再見。	joy·gin
Good night.	晚安。	máan·ngàwn
Mr/Sir	先生	·sìn·sàang
Ms	小姐	·siú·jé
Mrs	太太	·taai·táai
Madam	女士	·léui·si

How are you?
你幾好啊嗎？ — láy gáy hó à maa

Fine. And you?
幾好。你呢？ — gáy hó láy lè

What's your name?
你叫乜嘢名？ — láy giu màt·yé méng aa

My name is …
我叫…… — ngáw giu …

I'm pleased to meet you.
幸會！ — hang·wui

This is my …	呢個係我嘅⋯⋯	lày gaw hai ngáw ge …
brother (older)	哥哥	gàw·gàw
brother (younger)	細佬	sai·ló
daughter	女	léui
father	爸爸	baa·bàa
friend	朋友	pàng·yáu
husband	老公	ló·gùng
mother	媽媽	màa·màa
partner (intimate)	伴	pún
sister (older)	家姐	gàa·jè
sister (younger)	妹妹	mui·muí
son	仔	jái
wife	老婆	ló·pò

Here's my (address).
呢個係我嘅(地址)。 — lày·gaw hai ngáw ge (day·jí)

What's your (email)?
你嘅(電子郵箱)呢？ — láy ge (din·jí yàu·sèung) lè

Where are you from?
你係邊度人？ — láy hai bìn·do yàn

I'm from …	我係喺⋯⋯嚟嘅。	ngáw hai hái … lài ge
Australia	澳大利亞	ngò·daai·lay·aa
Canada	加拿大	gàa·làa·daai
England	英國	yìng·gawk
New Zealand	新西蘭	sàn·sài·làan
the USA	美國	máy·gawk

What's your occupation?	你做邊行㗎?	láy jo bìn hàwng gaa

I'm a/an …	我係⋯⋯	ngáw hai …
businessperson	生意人	sàang·yi·yàn
office worker	白領	baak·líng
tradesperson	技工	gay·gùng

Do you like …?	你鍾唔鍾意……啊？	láy jùng·ǹg·jùng·yi … aa
I (don't) like …	我(唔)鍾意……	ngáw (ǹg·)jùng·yi …
art	藝術	ngai·seut
films	睇戲	tái·hay
music	聽音樂	tèng yàm·ngawk
reading	睇書	tái·sèw
sport	體育	tái·yuk

I'd like to learn some of your local dialects.
我想學啲你地嘅本地話。
ngáw séung hawk dì láy·day ge bún·day wáa

Would you like me to teach you some English?
你想不想我教你學啲英文？
láy séung·ǹg·séung ngáw gaau láy hawk dì yìng·mán

Is this a local or national custom?
呢啲係唔係本地嘅或者係全國嘅風俗？
lày·dì hai·ǹg·hai bún·day ge waak·jé hai chèwn·gwawk ge fùng·juk

eating out

Can you recommend a …?	有乜好……介紹？	yáu màt hó … gaai·xiu
bar	酒吧	jáu·bàa
dish	碟	díp
restaurant	茶樓	chàa·làu
I'd like a/the…, please.	唔該我要……	ǹg·gòy ngáw yiu …
bill	埋單	màai·dàan
drink list	酒料單	jáu·liú·dàan
menu	菜單	choy·dàan
(non)smoking table	(不)吸煙嘅檯	(bàt)·kàp·yìn ge tóy
table for (five)	(五位)嘅檯	(ńg wái) ge tóy

I'd like …	我想食……	ngáw séung sik …
a local speciality	地方風味菜	day·fàwng fùng·may choy
that dish	嗰個菜	gáw gaw choy
breakfast	早餐	jó·chàan
lunch	午餐	ńg·chàan
dinner	晚飯	máan·faan
drinks	飲料	yám·liu
(cup of) coffee …	(一杯)咖啡……	(yàt buì) gaa·fè …
(cup of) tea …	(一杯)茶……	(yàt buì) chàa …
with (milk)	加(牛奶)	gàa (ngàu·láai)
without (sugar)	唔加(糖)	ǹg gàa (tàwng)
orange juice	橙汁	cháang·jàp
soft drink	汽水	hay·séui
… water	……水	…·séui
boiled	滾	gún
cold	凍滾	dung·gún
sparkling mineral	礦泉氣	kawng·chèwn·hay
still mineral	礦泉	kawng·chèwn

I'll buy you a drink.
飲乜嘢我請。 yám màt·yé ngáw chéng

What would you like?
你想飲乜嘢？ láy séung yám màt·yé

a … of beer	一……啤酒	yàt … bè·jáu
glass	杯	buì
small bottle	細樽	sai jèun
large bottle	樽	jèun
a shot of (whisky)	一杯(威士忌)	yàt buì (wài·si·gáy)
a bottle/glass of … wine	一樽/杯……葡萄酒	yàt jèun/buì … pò·tò·jáu
red	紅	hung
white	白	baak

special diets & allergies

Do you have … food?	有冇……食品？	yáu·mó … sik·bán
halal	清真	chìng·jàn
kosher	猶太	yàu·tàai
vegetarian	齋	jàai
Could you prepare a meal without …?	可唔可以煮味餸唔落……㗎？	háw·ǹg·háw·yí jéw may sung ǹg lawk … gaa
I'm allergic to …	我對……	ngáw deui …
dairy produce	奶製品	láai·jai·bán
eggs	雞蛋	gài·dáan
meat	肉	yuk
nuts	果仁	gwáw·yàn
seafood	海鮮	hóy·sìn

emergencies

Help!	救命！	gau·meng
Stop!	企喺度！	káy hái·do
Go away!	走開！	jáu·hòy
Thief!	有賊啊！	yáu cháat aa
Fire!	火燭啊！	fó·jùk aa
Watch out!	小心！	siú·sàm
Call …!	快啲叫……！	faai·dì giu …
a doctor	醫生	yì·sàng
an ambulance	救傷車	gau·sèung·chè

the police	警察	gíng·chaat

Could you please help?
唔該幫幫忙。 ǹg·gòy bàwng bàwng màwng

Can I use your phone?
唔該借個電話用下。 ǹg·gòy je gaw din·wáa yung háa

I'm lost.
我蕩失路。 ngáw dawng·sàk·lo

Where are the toilets?
廁所喺邊度？ chi·sáw hái bìn·do

Where's the police station?
警察局喺邊度？ gíng·chaat·gúk hái·bìn·do

I want to contact my embassy.
我要聯繫我嘅大使館。 ngáw yiu lèwn·hai ngáw ge daai·si·gún

I've been …	有人……我。	yáu·yàn … ngáw
assaulted	打	dáa
raped	強奸	kèung·gàan
robbed	打劫	dáa·gip

I've lost my …	我……唔見咗。	ngáw … ǹg·gin·jáw
My … was/were stolen.	我……俾人偷咗。	ngáw … báy·yàn tàu·jáw
bags	啲行李	dì hang·láy
credit card	張信用卡	jèung seun·yung·kàat
money	啲錢	dì chín
passport	個護照	gaw wu·jiu
travellers cheques	啲旅行支票	dì léui·hang jì·piu

health

Where's the nearest …?	最近嘅……喺邊度？	jeui kán ge … hái bìn·do
dentist	牙醫	ngàa·yì
doctor	醫生	yì·sàng

hospital	醫院	yì·yéwn
pharmacist	藥房	yeuk·fàwng

I need a doctor (who speaks English).
我要睇（識講英文嘅）醫生。
ngáw yiu tái (sìk gáwng yìng·mán ge) yì·sàng

Could I see a female doctor?
最好睇個女醫生。
jèui·hó tái gaw léui yì·sàng

I've run out of my medication.
我啲藥用完啦。
ngáw dì yeuk yung yèwn laa

It hurts here.
呢度痛。
lày·do tung

I have (a) …	我有……	ngáw yáu …
asthma	哮喘	hàau·chéwn
constipation	便秘	bin·bay
diarrhoea	肚痾	tó·ngàw
fever	發燒	faat·siù
heart condition	心臟病	sàm·jawng·beng
nausea	作嘔	jawk·ngáu

I'm allergic to …	我對……過敏。	ngáw deui … gaw·mán
antibiotics	抗菌素	kawng·kún·so
anti-inflammatories	消炎藥	siù·yim yeuk
aspirin	阿斯匹林	àa·sì·pàt·làm
bees	蜜蜂	mat·fùng
codeine	可待因	háw·doy·yàn

english–cantonese dictionary

is dictionary, words are marked as n (noun), a (adjective), v (verb), sg (singular) and pl (plural) where necessary.

A

accident 意外 yi·ngoy
accommodation 住宿 jew·sùk
adaptor 轉換插頭 jéwn·wun chaap·tàu
address 地址 day·jí
after 以後 yí·hau
air-conditioned 有冷氣嘅 yáu láang·hay ge
airplane 飛機 fày·gày
airport 飛機場 fày·gày·chèung
alcohol 酒精 jáu·jìng
all 所有嘅 sáw·yáu·ge
allergic 過敏 gaw·mán
ambulance 急傷車 gau·sèung·chè
and 同埋 tùng·mài
ankle 腳踭 geui·jàang
antibiotics 抗菌素 kawng·kún·so
arm 胳膊 sáu·bay
ATM 自動提款機 ji·dung tài·fún·gày

B

baby BB仔 bì·bì·jái
back (body) 背脊 bui·jek
backpack 背囊 bui·làwng
bad 壞 waai
bag 包 bàau
baggage claim 行李認領處 hàng·láy ying·líng·chew
bank n 銀行 ngàn·hàwng
bar 酒吧 jáu·bàa
bathroom 廁所 chi·sáw
battery 電池 din·chì
beautiful 美麗 máy·lai
bed 床 chàwng
beer 啤酒 bè·jáu
before 以前 yí·chìn
behind 後面 hau·min
bicycle 單車 dàan·chè
big 大 daai
bill (restaurant etc) 單 dàan
blanket 氈 jìn
blood group 血型 hewt·ying
boat 船 sèwn
book v 訂 deng
bottle 樽 jèun
boy 男仔 làam·jái
brakes 逼力 bik·lìk
breakfast 早餐 jó·chàan
broken 壞咗 waai·jáw
bus (intercity) 長途汽車 chèung·tò hay·chè
bus (local) 公共汽車 gùng·gung hay·chè
business 生意 sàang·yi
buy 買 màai

C

camera 相機 séung·gày
cancel 取消 chéui·siù
car 車 chè
cash n 現金 yin·gàm
cash (a cheque) v 兌現 deui·yin
cell phone 手機 sáu·gày
change (money) v 換錢 wun chín
cheap 平 pèng
check (bill) 單 dàan
check-in (desk) 登記（台）dàng·gay·(tóy)
chest (body) 胸 hùng
child 細路仔 sai·lo·jái
cigarette 香煙 hèung·yìn
city 城市 sìng·sí
clean a 乾淨 gàwn·jeng
closed 關門 gwàan·mùn
cold a 凍 dung
collect call 對方付款 deui·fàwng fu·fún
come 嚟 lài
computer 電腦 din·ló
condom 避孕套 bay·yan·to
contact lens 隱形眼鏡 yán·yìng ngáan·géng
cook v 煮飯 jéw·faan
cost (price) n 價錢 gaa·chìn
credit card 信用卡 seun·yung·kàat
currency exchange 外幣兌換 ngoy·bai deui·wun
customs (immigration) 海關 hóy·gwàan

D

dangerous 危險 ngài·hím
date (calendar) n 日期 yat·kày
day 日頭 yat·táu
delay n 推遲 tui·chì

dentist 牙科 ngàa·fò
depart 離開 lày·hoy
diaper 尿片 liu·pín
dinner 晚飯 máan·faan
direct 直接 jik·jip
dirty 污糟 wù·jò
disabled 傷殘 sèung·chàan
discount 折扣 jit·kau
doctor 醫生 yì·sàng
double bed 雙人床 sèung·yàn·chàwng
double room 雙人房 sèung·yàn·fáwng
drink n 飲料 yám·liu
drive v 開車 hòy·chè
driving licence 駕駛執照 gaa·sái jàp·jiu
drug(s) 毒品 duk·bán

E

ear 耳仔 yí·jái
east 東方 dùng·fàwng
eat 食 sik
economy class 經濟艙 gìng·jai·chàwng
electricity 電 din
elevator 電梯 din·tài
email n 電子郵件 din·jí yàu·gín
embassy 大使館 daai·si·gún
emergency 緊急意外 gán·gàp yi·ngoy
English 英文 yìng·man
evening 夜晚 ye·máan
exit n 出口 chèut·háu
expensive 貴 gwai
eye 眼睛 ngáan·jing

F

far 遠 yéwn
fast a 快 faai
father 爸爸 baa·bàa
film (for camera) 菲林 fày·lám
finger 手指 sáu·jí
first-aid kit 救傷用品 gau·sèung yung·bán
first class 頭等艙 tàu·dáng·chàwng
fish n 魚 yéw
food 食物 sik·mat
foot 腳 geui
free (no charge) a 免費 mín·fai
friend 朋友 pàng·yáu
fruit 水果 séui·gwáw
full 滿 mún

G

gift 禮物 lái·mat
girl 女仔 léui·jái
glass (drinking) 杯 buì
glasses (spectacles) 眼鏡 ngáan·géng
go 去 heui
good 好 hó
guide (person) n 導游 do·yàu

H

half 半 bun
hand n 手 sáu
happy 快樂 faai·lawk
have 有 yáu
he 佢 kéui
head 頭 tàu
heart 心臟 sàm·jawng
heavy 重 chúng
help n 幫助 bàwng·jaw
here 呢度 lày·do
high 高 gò
highway 高速公路 gò·chùk gùng·lo
hike 遠足 yéwn·jùk
holiday(s) 假期 gaa·kày
homosexual 同性戀 tung·sing·léwn
hospital 醫院 yì·yéwn
hot 熱 yit
hotel 酒店 jáu·dim
hungry 餓 ngaw
husband 老公 ló·gùng

I

I 我 ngáw
identification card (ID) 身份證 sàn·fán·jing
ill 有病 yáu·beng
important 重要 jung·yiu
injury 傷 séung
insurance 保險 bó·hím
internet 互聯網 wu·lèwn·máwng
interpreter 翻譯 fàan·yik

J

jewellery 首飾 sáu·sik
job 工作 gùng·jawk

K

key 鑰匙 sáw·si
kilogram 公斤 gùng·gàn
kitchen 廚房 chèw·fáwng
knife 刀 dò

L

laundry (place) 洗衣店 sái·yì·dim
lawyer 律師 leut·sì
left (direction) 左邊 jáw·bìn
leg 腿 téui
lesbian n 女同性戀 léui tung·sing·léwn
less 少 siú
letter (mail) 信 seun
light n 光 gwàwng
like v 同……一樣 tung … yàt·yeung
lock n 鎖 sáw
long 長 chèung
lost (one's way) 蕩失路 dawng·sàt·lo
love v 愛 ngoy
luggage 行李 hàng·láy
lunch 午餐 ńg·chàan

M

mail n 信 seun
man (male person) 男人 làam·yán
map 地圖 day·tò
market 街市/市場 gàai·sí/ sí·chèung HK/China
matches (for lighting) 火柴 fó·chàai
meat 肉 yuk
medicine (medication) 醫藥 yì·yeuk
message 口信 háu·seun
milk 牛奶 ngàu·láai
minute 分鐘 fàn·jùng
mobile phone 手機 sáu·gày
money 錢 chín
month 月 yewt
morning 朝早 jiù·jó
mother 媽媽 màa·màa
motorcycle 電單車 din·dàan·chè
mouth 口 háu

N

name 名 méng
near 近 kán
new 新 sàn
newspaper 報紙 bo·jí
night 夜晚 ye·maan
no 唔得 ǹg·dàk
noisy 嘈 cho
nonsmoking 不吸煙 bàt·kàp·yìn
north 北邊 bàk·bin
nose 鼻 bay
now 而家 yì·gàa
number 號碼 ho·máa

O

old 老 ló
one-way (ticket) 單程(飛) dàan·chìng (fày)
open a 開放 hòy·fawng
outside 外面 ngoy·min

P

passport 護照 wu·jiu
pay v 俾錢 báy·chín
pharmacy 藥房 yeuk·fàwng
phonecard 電話卡 din·wáa·kàat
photo 相 séung
police (officer) 警察 gíng·chaat
postcard 明信片 mìng·seun·pín
post office 郵局 yàu·gúk
pregnant 懷孕 wàai·yan
price 價錢 gaa·chìn

Q

quiet 安靜 ngàwn·jing

R

rain n 落雨 lawk·yéw
razor 剃刀 tai·dò
receipt 收據 sàu·geui
refund n 退錢 teui·chín
(by) registered mail 掛號 gwaa·ho
rent v 租 jò
repair v 修理 sàu·láy
reservation (booking) 預定 yew·deng
restaurant 酒樓 jáu·làu
return (come back) v 返嚟 fàan·lày
return (ticket) 雙程(飛) sèung·chìng (fày)
right (direction) 右邊 yau·bìn
road 路 lo
room 房 fáwng

S

safe a 安全 ngàwn·chèwn
sanitary napkin 衛生巾 wai·sàng·gàn
seat (hard; on train) 硬座 ngaang·jaw
seat (place) 座位 jawk·wái
seat (soft; on train) 軟座 yéwn·jaw
send 寄 gay
sex 性 sing

shampoo n 洗頭水 sái·tàu·séui
share v 公用 gùng·yung
she 佢 kéui
sheet (bed) 床單 chàwng·dàan
shirt 恤衫 sèut·sàam
shoe(s) 鞋 hàai
shop n 店 dim
short (height) 矮 ngái
shower 沖涼室 chùng·lèung·fáwng
single room 單人房 dàan·yàn·fáwng
skin 皮膚 pày·fù
skirt 裙 kùn
sleep v 瞓覺 fan·gaau
slowly 慢慢 maan·máan
small 細 sai
soap 肥皂 fày·jo
some 一啲 yàt·dì
soon 快 faai
south 南 làam
souvenir shop 紀念品店 gay·lim·bán·dim
stamp n 郵票 yàu·piu
stand-by ticket 月台票 yewt·tòy·piu
station 車站 chè·jaam
stomach 肚 tó
stop (bus, tram etc) 停 ting
stop (cease) 停止 ting·jí
street 街 gàai
student 學生 hawk·sàang
sun 太陽 taai·yèung
sunblock 防曬油 fàwng·saai·yàu
swim v 游水 yàu·séui

T

tampon 棉塞 min·sàk
teeth 牙齒 ngàa·chí
telephone n 電話 din·wáa
temperature (weather) 溫度 wàn·do
that (one) 嗰個 gáw·gaw
they 佢地 kéui·day
thirsty (to be) 頸渴 géng·hawt
this (one) 呢個 lày·gaw
throat 喉嚨 hàu·lùng
ticket 票 piu
time n 時間 sì·gaan
tired 攰 gui
tissues 紙巾 jí·gàn
today 今日 gàm·yat
toilet 廁所 chi·sáw
tomorrow 听日 tìng·yat
tonight 今晚 gàm·máan
toothbrush 牙刷 ngàa·cháat
toothpaste 牙膏 ngàa·gò
torch (flashlight) 電筒 din·túng
tour n 旅游團 léui·yáu·tèwn
tourist office 旅行社 léui·hàng·sé
towel 毛巾 mò·gàn
train n 火車 fó·chè
translate 翻譯 fàan·yik
travel agency 旅行社 léui·hàng·sé
travellers cheque 旅行支票 léui·hàng jì·piu
trousers 褲 fu
twin room 雙人房 sèung·yàn·fáwng

U

underwear 底衫褲 dái·sàam·fu
urgent 緊要 gán·yiu

V

vacant 有空闕 yáu hùng·kewt
vegetable n 蔬菜 sàw·choy
vegetarian a 食齋嘅 sik·jàai ge
visa 簽證 chìm·jing

W

walk v 行路 hàang·lo
wallet 個銀包 gaw ngàn·bàau
wash 洗 sái
watch n 手錶 sáu·biù
water 水 séui
we 我地 ngáw·day
weekend 週末 jàu·mut
west 西 sài
wheelchair 輪椅 lèun·yí
when 幾時 gáy·sì
where 邊度 bìn·do
who 邊個 bìn·gaw
why 點解 dím·gáai
wife 老婆 ló·pò
window 窗 chèung
with 同埋 tùng·màai
without 之外 jì·ngoy
woman 女人 léui·yán
write 寫 sé

Y

yes 係 hai
yesterday 尋日 kàm·yat
you sg 你 láy
you pl 你地 láy·day

Chaozhou

TONES 62
ABOUT CHAOZHOU 63
PRONUNCIATION 64
LANGUAGE DIFFICULTIES 65
TIME & DATES 66
TRANSPORT & DIRECTIONS 67
ACCOMMODATION 68
BANKING & COMMUNICATIONS 69
SIGHTSEEING 70
SHOPPING 70
MEETING PEOPLE 71
MAKING CONVERSATION 72
FEELINGS & OPINIONS 75
FAREWELLS 75
EATING OUT 76
SPECIAL DIETS & ALLERGIES 79
EMERGENCIES & HEALTH 80
ENGLISH–CHAOZHOU DICTIONARY 81

tones

Chaozhou is a tonal language ('tonal quality' refers to the raising and lowering of pitch on certain syllables). Tones in Chaozhou fall on vowels, on n and on m when it appears as a word on its own. The same combination of sounds pronounced with different tones can have a very different meaning.

Chaozhou has eight tones. In our pronunciation guide they've been simplified to seven tones, indicated with accents or underscores on the letters, as shown in the table below for the vowel 'a'. Note that we haven't indicated the tone on m when it appears as a word on its own – in all these instances it carries a low falling tone.

Higher tones involve tightening the vocal cords to get a higher sounding pitch, while lower tones are made by relaxing the vocal cords to get a lower pitch. Bear in mind that the tones are relative to the natural vocal range of the speaker, eg high tones are pronounced at the top of one's vocal range. Note also that some tones slide up or down in pitch.

high flat & short high flat	high falling	high rising	mid flat	low falling	low falling-rising	low flat & short low fla
ā	â	á	a	à	ǎ	a̲

about Chaozhou

Chaozhou (tio tsiu ue 潮州話) is a southern dialect of Chinese and is also known as Teochiu. It's spoken in the eastern part of Guǎngdōng province, centring on the old cultural capital Cháozhōu and the port city of Shàntóu, but also in many overseas Chinese communities, including in Thailand, Hong Kong, Singapore, Malaysia, Cambodia, Indonesia, Vietnam and the Philippines. The total number of speakers within the Cháozhōu-Shàntóu region is about 12 million, with an almost equal number of speakers internationally. Linguistically, the dialect is closely related to those of southern Fújiàn. There was once a distinctive literary language based on Chaozhou speech. This fell into disuse in the 20th century but there have been local efforts to revive it. In recent decades the language has been enriched by new vocabulary reflecting scientific and technical advances. Chaozhou dialect varies from place to place but local varieties are mutually intelligible. The dialect on which this chapter is based is that of Jiēyáng, a county halfway between Cháozhōu and Shàntóu.

chaozhou

pronunciation

Vowels	
Symbol	**English sound**
a	father
e	bet
ew	as the 'oo' in 'soon' with the lips spread widely
i	bit (in syllables ending in -k, -m, -ng, -p); machine (in syllables ending in a vowel)
o	ought
u	rule

In this chapter, the Chaozhou pronunciation is given in green after each phrase.

In Chaozhou vowels can appear in combinations of two (diphthongs) or three (triphthongs). All vowels in combinations are always pronounced – they are simply pronounced in series.

Some vowels in Chaozhou are nasalised (pronounced with air escaping through the nose). In our pronunciation guides the nasalised vowels are indicated with ng after the vowel.

For pronunciation of tones, see p62.

Consonants	
Symbol	**English sound**
b	**b**ed
g	**g**ood
h	**h**at
k	ti**ck**le; like English g but unvoiced
k'	**k**it
l	**l**ot
m	**m**an
n	**n**ot
ng	ri**ng** (both at the start and at the end of words)
p	ni**pp**le; like English b but unvoiced
p'	**p**et
q	glottal stop (the sound heard between 'uh-oh')
s	**s**un
t	li**tt**le; like English d but unvoiced
t'	**t**op
ts	ca**ts**
ts'	like ts, but with a strong puff of air following
z	**z**ero

essentials

Yes.	是 。	sí
No.	不是 。	m sí
Please …	请 …	ts'iăng …
Hello.	你好 。	lêw chô
Goodbye.	再见 。	tsâi kiăng
Thank you.	谢谢你 。	tsoi sia léw
Excuse me. (to get past)	借光 。	tuî m tsú
Excuse me. (asking for directions/assistance)	请问 。	ts'iáng mung
Sorry.	对不起 。	tuî m tsú

language difficulties

Do you speak (English)?	你会说(英文)吗?	lêw òi tâng (eng būng) bòi
Do you understand?	你明白吗?	lêw òi ts'eng ts'ô bòi
I (don't) understand.	我(不)明白 。	uâ (m) meng pēk
I (don't) speak Chaozhou.	我(不)会潮州話 。	uâ (bòi) tâng tio tsiu ue

Could you please …?	请你 …?	ts'iáng léw …
repeat that	再说一遍	tsâi tâng ke kuê
speak more slowly	慢一点说	tâng mang tiq kiăng

numbers

0	零	lēng	20	二十	zí tsāp
1	一	tsēk	30	三十	sang tsāp
2	二/两	nó	40	四十	sí tsāp
3	三	sang	50	五十	ngóung tsāp
4	四	sĭ	60	六十	lak tsāp
5	五	ngóung	70	七十	ts'eq tsāp
6	六	lāk	80	八十	poiq tsāp
7	七	ts'eq	90	九十	káu tsāp
8	八	poiq	100	一百	tsek peq
9	九	kâu	1000	一千	tsek ts'aing
10	十	tsāp	1,000,000	一百万	tsek peq buang

time & dates

What time is it?	现在几点钟?	hèng tsái kúi tiâm
It's (10) o'clock.	(十)点钟 。	(tsap) tiâm
Quarter past (10).	(十)点十五分 。	(tsap) tiâm tsap ngòung hung
Half past (10).	(十)点三十分 。	(tsap) tiâm puǎng
Quarter to (11). **(literally: Forty-five minutes past (10).)**	(十)点四十五分 。	(tsap) tiâm sî tsap ngòung hung

At what time (does it start)?
什么时候(开始)? — ti tiang si (k'ai sî)

(It starts) At 10.
十点钟(开始) 。 — tsap tiâm (k'ai sî)

It's (18 October).
(十月十八号) 。 — (tsap gueq tsap poiq ho)

yesterday	昨天	tsau zēk
today	今天	kim zēk
now	现在	hēng tsái
tonight	今晚	kim mē
tomorrow	明天	mâ zēk
sunrise	日出	zēk ts'uq
morning (after breakfast)	早上	tsá sēng
morning (before lunch)	上午	tsìong ngôung
afternoon	下午	è kuǎ
sunset	日落	zēk lōq
spring	春天	ts'ung ting
summer	夏天	he ting
autumn	秋天	ts'iu ting
winter	冬天	tang ting
Monday	星期一	ts'eng k'i ek
Tuesday	星期二	ts'eng k'i zí
Wednesday	星期三	ts'eng k'i sang
Thursday	星期四	ts'eng k'i sǐ
Friday	星期五	ts'eng k'i ngóung
Saturday	星期六	ts'eng k'i lāk
Sunday	星期天	ts'eng k'i zēk

January	一月	ek gue
February	二月	zí gue
March	三月	sang gue
April	四月	sǐ gue
May	五月	ngóung gue
June	六月	lāk gue
July	七月	ts'eq gue
August	八月	poiq gue
September	九月	kāu gue
October	十月	tsāp gue
November	十一月	tsap ek gue
December	十二月	tsap zí gue

transport & directions

Is this the … to (Zhōngshān Park)?	这个 … 是不是去 (中山公园)?	tsí tsiaq … sì m sì kêw (tong suang kong hn̄g)
boat	船	tsūng
bus	公共汽车	kong kang k'ǐ ts'ia
train	火车	hué ts'ia

Where's a/the …?	… 在哪儿?	… tò ti·kǒ
bank	银行	ngeng hang
place to change foreign money	换外币的地方	uang guà pí kai ti hng
post office	邮局	iu kēq

Is this the road to (Haibin Park)?
这条路是不是去 (海边公园)? — tsí tiau lou sì m sì k'êw (hai piang kong hn̄g)

Can you show me where it is on the map?
请帮我找它在地图上的位置 。 — lau lêw kai uá tò ti tōu sìong ts'ue i kai ui tǐ

What's the address?	什么地址?	ti tsî sì meq kāi
How far is it?	有多远 ?	ù zioq hńg
How do I get there?	怎么走?	tsô ni kiāng
Turn left/right.	往左/右拐 。	hiâng tsô/íu
It's straight ahead.	一直往前 。	tsek tēk hiâng tsaing kiāng
Can I get there on foot?	可以走路过去吗?	kiang lou òi kǎu bòi

It's …	在 …	tó …
behind …	… 的后面	… ka̲i àu pāing
in front of …	… 的前面	… ka̲i tsa̲ing me̲ng
near …	… 附近	… ka̲i hû kéng
on the corner	拐角	tsuáng uang ka̲i kaq lōk
opposite …	… 的对面	… ka̲i tuî me̲ng
there	那里	hió kŏ

accommodation

Where's a guest house?
哪里有宾馆? — ti̲ kô ù piang kuâng

Where's a hotel?
哪里有酒店? — ti̲ kô ù tsíu tiăm

Can you recommend somewhere cheap?
你能推荐一个便宜的地方住吗? — lēw k'ó m k'ó í ka̲i uá kâi siàu ka̲i p'ing ka̲i li̲ tiăm k'iá

Can you recommend somewhere good?
你能推荐一个好的地方住吗? — lēw k'ó m k'ó í ka̲i uá kâi siàu ka̲i hô ka̲i li̲ tiăm k'iá

I'd like to stay at a locally run hotel.
我想住在本地人开的旅馆 。 — uâ sìong k'ià tse̲k kaing púng ti̲ nāng k'ui ka̲i lí kuâng

I'd like to book a room.
我想订房间 。 — uâ âing tia̲ng pa̲ng kaing

I have a reservation.
我有预订 。 — uá ú éw tia̲ng

Do you have a … room?	有没有 … 房?	ù … pāng bo̲
double (suite)	套	t'ău
single	单人	tuang nāng
twin	双人	sang nāng

How much is it per night/person?
每天/人多少钱? — tsek nāng/zēk zio̲q tso̲i tsīng

I'd like to stay for (three) nights.
住(三)天 。 — uâ âing k'ià (sang) zēk

Could I have my key, please?
能不能给我房间钥匙? hó mó k'eq uá pang kaing kai só sī

Can I get an extra (blanket)?
我能多拿一条(毛毯吗)? uâ hó mó k'ioq ke tiao (mo t'âng)

The (air conditioning) doesn't work.
(空调)有毛病 。 (k'ong t'iāu) ù mung toī

What time is checkout?
几点钟退房? kuí tiám tseng t'ô pāng

Could I have my ..., please?	我想拿回我的 ⋯	uâ hó mó k'ioq tńg uá kai ...
deposit	押金	âng kim
passport	护照	hù tsiŏ

banking & communications

Where's a/an ...?	⋯ 在哪儿?	... tò ti kô
ATM	自动取款机	tsew tóng ts'uq k'uáng ki
public phone	公用电话	kong eng tiàng ue

Where's the local internet cafe?
附近有网吧吗? hû kéng ù màng pa bo

I'd like to ...	我想 ⋯	uâ âing ...
get internet access	上网	tsìo máng
use a printer	打印	eng hoq êng ki
use a scanner	扫描	sâu miau ki

What's your phone number?
您的电话号码是多少? lêw kai tiàng ue ho bê sì zioq tsoi

The number is ...
号码是 ⋯ tiàng ue ho mê sì ...

sightseeing

I'd like to see some local sights.
我想看一些有特色的景点 。 — uâ âing t'óing tńg tí kai tsek seng kéng tiâm

I'd like to see ...
我想看 … — uâ siò âing t'óing ...

What's that?
那是什么? — hiá kāi sì meq kāi

Can I take a photo?
我能拍吗? — uâ hó p'ak sîong p'iǎng me

I'd like to go somewhere off the beaten track.
我想看一些旅客较少的地方 。 — uâ siò lái k'êw t'óing lang kai iu k'eq tsío kěw kai ti hńg

How long is the tour?
向导游要多长时间? — kiang tiāng tioq zioq tsoi si kang

sights		
Haimen Lotus Blossom Hill	海门莲花峰	hái mēng nai hue hong
Lin Baixin International Convention Centre	林百欣国际会议中心	lim peq heng koq tsǐ huè i tong sim
Seaview Promenade	观海长廊	kuang hâi ts'iang lāng
Shàntóu University	汕头大学	suang t'au tài hāq
Temple of Matsu	老妈宫	làu ma keng
Zhōngshān Park	中山公园	tong suang kong hn̄g
Zhōngxìn Tourist Resort	中信度假村	tong sêng tou kiáng ts'ng

shopping

Where's a ...?	… 在哪儿?	... tò ti kǒ
camera shop	照相店	tsiô sióng tiǎm
market	市场	ts'ì tiōng
souvenir shop	纪念品店	kî niàm p'éng tiǎm

Where can I buy locally produced goods?
哪里可以买当地生产的产品? tò ti kô hó pói tiõq t'óu teq suâng

Where can I buy locally produced souvenirs?
哪里可以买当地生产的纪念品? tò ti kô hó pói tiõq kî niàm p'êng

What's this made from?
这是用什么材料做的? tsiá kāi sì meq kai tsŏ kai

I'd like to buy ...
我想买 ... uâ âing bói ...

Can I look at it?
我能看看吗? uâ hó mó t'ói t'ôi tse

How much is it?
多少钱? zioq tsoi tsīng

That's too expensive.
太贵了 。 k'aq kuĭ

Please write down the price.
请把价钱写下来 。 ts'iang tsiang kê tsīng siâ lok lai

I'll give you (five kuai).
给你(五块)钱 。 k'eq lew (ngòu kai) ngēng

Do you accept credit cards?
你们收信用卡吗? nêng ù siu sêng êng k'â bò

There's a mistake in the bill.
帐单上有问题 。 tiô tuang ù ts'uq zīp

less	少	tsiô
enough	足够	ngam ngam
more	多	tsoi
bigger	更大	tsoi
smaller	更小	sŏi

meeting people

Hello.	你好 。	lêw hô
Goodbye.	再见 。	tsâi kiăng
Goodbye. (to person leaving)	再见 。	k'uang kiāng

Mr	先生	seng seng
Mrs	女士	ńg séw
Ms/Miss	小姐	siáu tsê
How are you?	你好吗?	lêw tsuê kéng tsa̲i seng
Fine. And you?	好 。你呢?	hô hô, lêw ne̲
What's your name?	你叫什么名字?	lêw kîo meq miāng
My name is ...	我叫 …	uâ kîo ...
This is my ...	这是我的 …	tsî ka̲i/u̲i sì uá ka̲i ... **inf/pol**
brother	兄弟	hiang tí
child	孩子	nou kiâng
daughter	女儿	tsáu kiâng
father	父亲	pèq ts'eng
friend	朋友	p'e̲ng îu
husband	老公	ang/tsiàng hu **inf/pol**
mother	母亲	bó ts'eng
partner (intimate)	对象	tuî siáng
sister (older/younger)	姐/妹	tsé/mue̲
son	儿子	kiâ
wife	太太	lâu p'uā/t'āi t'āi **inf/pol**

making conversation

Do you live here?	你住这里吗?	lêw sì m sì k'ià to̲ tsío kǒ
Where are you going?	上哪儿去?	lêw âing k'êw ti̲ kǒ
Do you like it here?	喜欢这里吗?	lêw oì hí huang tsío kǒ bòi
I love it here.	我很喜欢这里 。	uâ hoq hí huang tsío kǒ
Have you eaten?	吃饭了吗?	tsia̲k pu̲ng bue̲
Are you here on holiday?	你来这里旅游吗?	lêw sì m sì la̲i lí īu
I'm here ...	我来这里 …	uâ la̲i tsío kǒ ...
for a holiday	旅游	lí īu
on business	出差	ts'uq ts'e
to study	留学	li̲u hāq

How long are you here for?
你在这里住多久? lêw âing la̲i tsío kǒ k'ià ziōq kû

I'm here for (four) weeks.
我住(四)个星期 。 uâ k'ià (sî) ka̲i ts'eng k'ī

潮州話 – making conversation

Can I take a photo (of you)?
我可以拍(你的)相片吗? — uâ k'ó íng p'aq (léw) kai sîong p'iăng mè

Do you speak (Chaozhou)?
你会说(潮州话)吗? — lêw òi tâng (tio tsiu ue) bòi

What language do you speak at home?
你家里讲什么话? — lêw tò lái tâng meq ue

What do you call this in (Chaozhou)?
这个东西(潮州话)叫什么? — tsiá kāi (tio tsiu ue) tsô ni tăng

What's this called?
这个叫什么? — tsiá kāi kiô meq kāi

I'd like to learn some (Chaozhou).
我想学点(潮州话)。 — uâ siòng âing oq kuí kû (tio tsiu ue)

Would you like me to teach you some English?
你想让我教你一点英语吗? — lêw âing uá kâ léw kuí kû eng būng mè

Is this a local custom?
这是地方风俗吗? — tsiá kāi sì m sì ti hng kai hong sōq

local talk

Great! (food/things)	真棒!	k'iâng/hó sî
Hey!	劳驾!	uê
It's OK.	还行。	hang k'ó îng
Just a minute.	等一下。	tâng tsek e
Maybe.	有可能。	ù k'ó nēng
No problem.	没事。	bo sew
No way!	不可能!	mô
Sure, whatever.	行,行,行。	hô hô hô
That's enough!	够了,够了!	kău lău kău lău
Just joking.	开玩笑。	tâng sńg ts'îo

Where are you from?	你从哪儿来?	lêw ti kô nāng
I'm from …	我从 … 来 。	uâ kāi … nāng
Australia	澳大利亚	ô tài lì a
Canada	加拿大	kia ná tái
England	英国	eng koq
New Zealand	新西兰	seng sai lāng
the USA	美国	múi koq
What's your occupation?	你做什么工作?	lêw kāi tsoq meq kai kang tsaq kai
I'm a/an …	我当 …	uâ kāi …
businessperson	商人	siang zēng
office worker	白领	paing kong sek nang uāng
tradesperson	工匠	kang tsiáng
How old …?	… 多大了?	… tsioq tsoi huě
are you	你	lêw
is your daughter	你的女儿	lêw kai tsáu kiâng sì
is your son	你的儿子	lêw kai kiâng sì
I'm … years old.	我 … 岁 。	uâ … huě
He/She is … years old.	他/她 … 岁 。	i … huě
Too old!	太老了！	k'aq láu
I'm younger than I look.	我还小了 。	uâ t'ôing k'í lai hang sǒi
Are you married?	你结婚了吗?	lêw kaq hung bue
Do you have a family?	你成家了吗？	lêw ts'eng ke bue
I live with someone.	我有伴儿 。	uâ ù kai tuî siáng lǎu
I'm …	我 …	uâ …
married	结婚了	kaq hung lǎu
single	单身	tuang seng
Do you like …?	你喜欢 … 吗?	lêw òi hí huang … bòi
I (don't) like …	我(不)喜欢 …	uâ (m) hí huang …
art	艺术	goi sūk
film	看电影	t'óing tiàng iâng
music	听音乐	t'iang im gāuq
reading	看书	t'óing tsew
sport	体育	t'í īoq

feelings & opinions

I'm …	我 …	uâ …
I'm not …	我不 …	uâ bòi …
Are you …?	你 … 吗?	lêw òi bòi …
cold	冷	ngāng
hot	热	zuāq
hungry	饿	tôu k'ûng
thirsty	渴	āu ta
tired	累	hēq

I feel …	我感到 …	uâ kaq teq …
I don't feel …	我不感到 …	uâ m kaq teq …
Do you feel …?	你感到 … 吗?	lêw òi bòi kaq teq …
happy	高兴	kau hĕng
sad	不高兴	m kau hĕng
worried	着急	kéng tsiang

What do you think of it?	你觉得怎么样?	lêw kaq teq tsài seng iong

awful (quality)	很差劲	âu sî
awful (taste)	不好吃	mó tsiâk
beautiful	美丽	ngiá sî
boring	很无聊	bo î sĕw
great	很棒	hui siong hô
interesting	很有意思	hoq ù î sĕw
OK	还行	hang k'ó îng
strange	奇怪	k'i kuăi

farewells

Tomorrow I'm leaving.
明天我要走了 。 — mâ zēk uâ tsù tsáu liǎu

If you come to (Scotland), you can stay with me.
有机会来(苏格兰),
可以来找我 。 — ù ki hué lai (sou keq lāng)
tioq lai ts'ue uá

Keep in touch!
保持联系! — po t'i liang hī

It's been great meeting you.		
认识你实在很高兴 。		zeng seq léw uâ hui siong kau hĕng
Here's my (address).		
给你我的(地址) 。		tsîo kāi uá kai (ti tsî)
What's your (email)?		
你的(网址)是什么?		lêw kai (màng tsî) sì meq kāi

well-wishing

Bon voyage!	一路平安!	tsek lou p'eng ang
Congratulations!	恭喜,恭喜!	kiong hî kiong hî
Good luck!	祝你好运!	tsok léw hó ung
Happy birthday!	生日快乐!	seng zēk k'uâi lāk
Happy New Year!	新年好!	seng nī hô

eating out

Where would you go for (a) ...?	… 该到哪里去?	... tioq k'êw ti kŏ
banquet	办宴席	paing toq
celebration	举行庆祝会	kéw kiang k'êng tsôk hué
cheap meal	吃得便宜一点的	tsiāk hiá ping tiq kiáng kai
local specialities	地方小吃	ti hng siáu tsiāk
yum cha	饮茶	tsiāk tē

Can you recommend a ...?	你可以推荐一个 … 吗?	lêw k'ó íng kâi siàu kai ... me
bar	酒吧	tsíu pa
cafe	咖啡屋	kia hui kuâng
dish (food item)	菜	ts'ăi
noodle house	面馆	mi tiăm
restaurant	饭馆	pung tiăm
snack shop	小吃店	siáu tsiak tiăm
(wonton) stall	(馄饨)摊	(hung t'ung) tiăm
street vendor	街头小吃	koi t'āu siáu tsiāk
teahouse	茶馆	tē kuâng

I'd like a/the …	我要 …	uâ âing …
table for (five)	一张(五个人的)桌子	tsek tio (ngòung nāng) kai ts'n̄g
bill	帐单	pói tuang
drink list	酒水单	tsíu tsuí tuang
local speciality	一个地方特色菜	ti hng teq seq ts'ăi
menu	菜单	tsâi tuang
(non)smoking table	(不)吸烟的桌子	(bo) tsiak hung kai ts'n̄g

Are you still serving food?
你们还营业吗？ nêng kueng mūng bue

What would you recommend?
有什么菜可以推荐的? ù meq ts'ăi hó kâi siáu

What do you normally eat for breakfast?
早饭一般吃什么? tsaq ts'ang tsek puang tsiak meq kāi

What's in that dish?
这道菜用什么东西做的? tsí kai ts'ăi eng meq kai liau tsŏ kai

What's that called?
那个叫什么? hiá kāi kîo meq kāi

I'll have that.
来一个吧 。 lāi tsek kai

I'd like it with …	多放一点 …	pâng ke kô …
I'd like it without …	不要放 …	mâi pâng …
chilli	辣椒	lak tsio
garlic	大蒜	sn̄g t'āu
MSG	味精	bi tseng
nuts	果仁	kué zēng
oil	油	īu

I'd like …, please.	请给我 …	ts'iáng k'eq uá …
one slice	一块	tsēk kŏ
a piece	一份	tsek hung
a sandwich	一个三明治	tsek kai sang bung ti
that one	那一个	hêw tsek kai
two	两个	nò kāi

This dish is …	这个菜 … 了 。	tsí kai ts'ăi …
(too) spicy	(太)辣	(k'aq) hiam
superb	好极	hó tsiăk sî

I love this dish.
这道菜真香 。 — uâ hoq hí huang tsí kai ts'ǎi

That was delicious!
真好吃！ — hó tsiāk sî

I'm full.
吃饱了 。 — tsiak pâ lǎu

breakfast	早饭	tsaq ts'ang
lunch	午饭	tong ngóu pung
dinner	晚饭	múng pung
drink (alcoholic)	酒	tsîu
drink (nonalcoholic)	饮料	ím liau
… water	… 水	… tsuî
boiled	开	kûng
cold	凉开	gang kúng
sparkling mineral	矿泉汽	k'uâng tsuang k'ĭ
still mineral	矿泉	k'uâng tsuang
(cup of) coffee …	(一杯)咖啡 …	(tsek pue) kia hui …
(cup of) tea …	(一杯)茶 …	(tsek pue) tē …
with (milk)	加(牛奶)	kia (gu ní)
without (sugar)	不加(糖)	mâi pâng (t'n̄g)
black tea	红茶	ang tē
chrysanthemum tea	菊花茶	keq hue tē
green tea	绿茶	lek tē
jasmine tea	花茶	hue tē
oolong tea	乌龙茶	ou leng tē
fresh drinking yoghurt	酸奶	sng ní
(orange) juice	(橙)汁	(ts'eng) tsap
lychee juice	荔枝汁	nài kuâing tsap
soft drink	汽水	k'ĭ tsûi
sour plum drink	酸梅汤	sng bue tng

What are you drinking?	喝什么?	âing tsiak meq kāi
I'll pay.	我请客 。	uâ ts'iáng k'eq
What would you like?	我来买饮料， 你喜欢喝什么?	uâ âing bói kai ím liau lêw âing tsiak meq kāi
Cheers!	干杯!	kang pue
I'm feeling drunk.	我有点醉 。	uâ ù tiq kiáng tsuî tsuǐ

a … of beer	一 … 啤酒	tsek … pi tsîu
glass	杯	pue
large bottle	大瓶	tua tsung
small bottle	小瓶	sòi tsung
a shot of (whisky)	一樽(威士忌)	tsek pue (ui sèw kí)
a bottle/glass of … wine	一瓶/一杯 … 葡萄酒	tsek p'eng/tsek pue … p'u to tsîu
red	红	āng
white	白	pēq

street eats

Chaozhou steamed dumplings	潮洲粉果	tio tsiu húng kuê
corn on the cob	玉米棒	îung muí zēng
dumpling (boiled)	饺子	kiâu
dumpling (fried)	锅贴	tsiang kiâu
dumpling (steamed)	包子	pau
oyster omelette	蚝煎	o luaq
radish cake	萝卜糕	ts'âi t'au ko
sticky rice in bamboo leaves	粽子	tsâng kīu
wonton soup	馄饨	hung t'ung

special diets & allergies

Do you have vegetarian food?
有没有素食食品？ ù bo tse ts'ǎi

Could you prepare a meal without …?
能不能做一个不放 … 的菜? hó mó tsô tsek kai mâi pâng … kai ts'ǎi

I'm allergic to …	我对 … 过敏 。	uâ tuî … kuê miâng
dairy produce	奶制品	nî tsî p'êng
eggs	鸡蛋	koi ńg
meat	肉	nēk
nuts	果仁	kué zēng
seafood	海鲜	hái ts'ing

emergencies & health

Help!	救命！	kîu miang
Go away!	走开！	lêw tsáu k'ui
Fire!	着火啦！	tioq huê lău a
Watch out!	小心！	siáu sim

Where's the nearest …?	最近的 … 在哪儿?	li tsío tsuê kéng kai … tò ti kŏ
dentist	牙科医生	ge ui
doctor	医生	ui seng
hospital	医院	ui ngi
pharmacist	药房	ioq pāng

Could you please help?
你能帮我吗？ — lêw hó mó pang tsó uă

Can I use your phone?
我能借用你的电话吗? — uâ hó mó tsioq léw kai tiàng ue eng e

I'm lost.
我迷路了 。 — uâ m pak lou

Where are the toilets?
厕所在哪儿？ — ts'eq sô tò ti kŏ

Where's the police station?
派出所在哪里? — p'âi ts'uq sô tò ti kŏ

english–chaozhou dictionary

s dictionary, words are marked as n (noun), a (adjective), v (verb), sg (singular), pl (plural), inf (informal) and polite) where necessary.

A

accident (mishap) 灾祸 ìng gua̱
accommodation 食宿 tsù sua̱q
adaptor 插头转接器 piâng iâp k'ĭ
address n 地址 ti̱ tsî
after 之后 ĭng áu
air conditioning 空调 k'ong t'iāu
airplane 飞机 pue ki
airport 机场 ki tiōng
alcohol 酒 tsiú
all 所有的 ts'ua̱ng póu
allergy 过敏 kuê miâng
ambulance 救护车 kîu hù ts'ia
and 和 ka̱q
ankle 踝 k'a māk
antibiotics 抗生素 k'âng seng sŭ
arm 手臂 ts'íu kôu
ATM 自动取款机 tse̱w tóng ts'úq k'uáng ki

B

baby 婴儿 eng zĭ
back (of body) 背 ka tsia̱q
backpack 背包 puê pau
bad (behaviour) 坏的 huái
bag 包 pau
baggage 行李 he̱ng lî
bank 银行 nge̱ng ha̱ng
bar 酒吧 tsíu pa
bathroom 浴室 e̱k se̱k/e̱k pāng
battery 电池 tiáng tī/tiáng t'ōu
beautiful 美丽的 múi lí/ngiâ pol/inf
bed 床 me̱ng ts'ng
beer 啤酒 pi̱ tsîu
before 之前 íng tsāing
behind 后面 áu pāing
bicycle 自行车 k'a ta̱q ts'ia
big 大的 tuă
bill 帐单 tiông tuang
blanket 毛毯 mō t'âng
blood group 血型 huēq hēng
boat 船 tsūng
book (make a reservation) v 预订 tia̱ng
bottle 瓶 tsung
boy 男孩 ta pou kiâng
brakes (car) 车煞 ts'ia tsâp
breakfast 早饭 tsaq ts'ang
broken (out of order) 坏掉的 seq tia̱u
bus 共公汽车 kong ka̱ng k'î ts'ia
business 生意 seng lî
buy v 买 pôi

C

camera 照相机 tsîo sîong ki
cancel 取消 ts'ŭ siau
car 汽车 k'î ts'ia
cash n 兑现 hua̱ng
cash (a cheque) v 把 … 兑现
tsiang . . . hua̱ng he̱ng kim
cell phone 手机 ts'íu ki
centre n 中心 tong sim
cheap 便宜的 p'ing
check (bill) 帐单 tiông tuang
check-in n 登记 tsú pāng teng kì
chest (body) 胸膛 heng
children 孩子 no̱u kiâng
cigarette 香烟 hung
city 城市 sia̱ng ts'í
clean a 干净的 kang tséng
closed 关闭的 kueng
cold a 冷的 ngáng
collect call 对方付费电话
tûi huang hû huĭ tiàng ue̱
come 来 lāi
computer 电脑 tiàng nâu
condom 避孕套 pi̱ uèng t'ău
contact lenses 隐形眼镜 êng hēng ma̱k kiăng
cook v 做饭 lî lo̱k tsiāk
cost n 价钱 kê ke̱q
credit card 信用卡 sêng êng k'â
currency exchange 货币兑换 guà hué tuî ua̱ng
customs (immigration) 海关 hái kuang

D

dangerous 危险的 ngui̱ng hiâm
date (time) 日期 ho̱
day 天 zēk
delay v 延迟 tam go̱u
dentist 牙科医生 ge̱ ui

A

english–chaozhou

depart 离开 li k'ui
diaper 尿布 zio pǒu
dinner 晚饭 múng pung
direct a 直接的 tek tsiq
dirty 脏的 ts'i gī
disabled 残废的 ts'ang huī
discount v 打折 kiám kě
doctor 医生 ui seng
double bed 双人床 sang nang ts'ng
double room 双人房 sang nang pāng
drink n 饮料 ím liau
drive v 开车 k'ui ts'ia
driving licence 驾照 tsip tsǐo
drug (illicit) 毒品 tak p'êng

E

ear 耳朵 híng
east 东 tang
eat 吃 tsiāk
economy class 经济舱 keng tsì ts'ng
electricity 电 tiáng
elevator 电梯 tiàng t'ui
email 电子邮件 tiàng tséw iu kiáng
embassy 大使馆 tài sâi kuâng
emergency 紧急状况 kéng kip ts'eng k'uǎng
English (language) 英语 eng būng/eng gêw
evening 傍晚 mé âm
exit n 出口 ts'uq k'âu
expensive 贵的 kuī
eye 眼睛 māk

F

far 远的 hńg
fast 快的 mê
father 父亲 pèq ts'eng
film (camera) 胶卷 ka kng
finger 手指 síu tsâing
first-aid kit 急救箱 kip kîu siong
first class 头等舱 t'au téng ts'ng
fish n 鱼 hēw
food 食物 tsiak muēk
foot 脚 k'a
free (of charge) 免费的 miáng huī
friend 朋友 p'eng îu
fruit 水果 tsuí kuê
full 满 muâng

G

gift 礼物 lí muēk
girl 女孩 tsew nio kiāng
glass (drinking) 杯子 po li pue
glasses 眼镜 mak kiāng
go 去 k'ěw
good 好的 hô
guide n 向导 tàu īu

H

half n 一半 puǎng
hand 手 ts'īu
happy 高兴的 kau hěng
he 他 i
head n 头 t'āu
heart 心 sim
heavy 重的 táng
help 帮助 pang tsó
here 这里 tsió kǒ
high 高的 kau/kuīng pol/inf
highway 高速公路 kau soq gong lou
hike v 徒步旅行 iáng tsok
holiday 假期 kiáng k'ī
homosexual 同性恋 tang sêng luǎng
hospital 医院 ui ing
hot (food) 热的 sio
hot (weather) 热的 zuāq
hotel 旅馆 lí tiǎm
(be) hungry 饿的 tôu k'ûng
husband 老公 tsiàng hu

I

I 我 uâ
identification (card) 身份证 seng hung tsěng
ill 生病的 seng peng
important 重要的 tông iǎu
injury (harm) 伤害 siong hai
injury (wound) 伤口 siong k'âu
insurance 保险 pó hiâm
internet 英特网 eng tek máng
interpreter 翻译 huang ēk

J

jewellery 珠宝 tsu pô
job 工作 kang tsaq

K

key 钥匙 só sī
kilogram 公斤 kong keng
kitchen 厨房 tou pāng
knife 刀 to

L

laundry (place) 洗衣店 sói i pang
lawyer 律师 luk sew
left (direction) 左 tsô
leg (body) 腿 k'a
lesbian 女同性恋 ńg tang sêng luǎng
less 少 tsiô
letter (mail) 信 sěng
light n 光 teng
like v 喜欢 hí huang
lock n 锁 só t'āu
long 长的 tng
lost 失去的 m kiǎng
love v 爱 ǎing
luggage 行李 heng lî
lunch 午饭 tong ngóu pung

M

mail n 邮件 iu kiáng
man 男人 nam zēng/ta pou pol/inf
map 地图 ti tôu
market 市场 ts'i tīong
matches 火柴 hué ts'ā
meat 肉 nēk
medicine 药 iōq
message 信息 k'áu sěng
milk 牛奶 gu ní
minute 分钟 hung tseng
mobile phone 手机 ts'íu ki
money 钱 tsīng
month 月 guēq
morning 早上 tsá sēng
mother 妈妈 bó ts'eng
motorcycle 摩托车 mo toq ts'ia
mouth 嘴 ts'uǐ

N

name 名字 miāng
near 近的 kéng
neck n 脖子 ám
new 新的 seng
newspaper 报纸 pô tsuâ
night 晚上 me hng
no (not this) 不是 m sí
noisy 喧闹的 ts'âu tsāk
nonsmoking 禁止吸烟 bo eng k'u
north 北 paq
nose 鼻子 p'ing
now 现在 heng tsǎi
number (room/telephone) 号码 ho bê

O

old (people) 老 láu
old (things) 旧 ku
one-way ticket 单程票 tuang t'iang p'iǒ
open a 开的 k'ui
outside 外面的 gua pāing

P

passport 护照 hù tsiǒ
pay v 付钱 hû tsīng
pharmacy 药房 ioq pāng
phonecard 电话卡 tiàng ue k'â
photo 照片 siô p'iāng
police 警察 kèng ts'ak
postcard 明信片 meng sêng p'iǎng
post office 邮局 iu kēq
pregnant 怀孕的 huai uéng
price n 价格 kê tsīng

Q

quiet a 安静的 tséng

R

rain n 雨 hóu
razor 剃刀 t'î ts'iu to
receipt n 收据 huaq p'iǒ
refund n 退款 t'ô tsīng
registered (mail) 挂号信 kuâ ho sěng
rent v 租 tsou
repair v 修理 siu lî
reserve v 预订 èr tiang
restaurant 饭馆 pung tiǎm
return (give back) 还 hāing
return (go back) 回来 tńg kêw
return ticket 返程票 lai hue p'iǒ
right (direction) 右 íu
road 路 lou
room n 房间 pang kaing

S

safe a 安全的 uang ts'uāng
sanitary napkin 卫生棉 gueq keng tuǎ
seat n 座位 tsò ui
send 发送 sǎng
sex (intercourse) 性 sêng kau
sex (gender) 性别 sêng piāq

english–chaozhou

shampoo 洗发精 sói huaq tseng
share (a dorm) 分租 haq k'iá
she 她 i
sheet (bed) 床单 ts'ng tuang
shirt 衬衫 soq sang
shoes 鞋 ōi
shop n 商店 siang tiăm
short 短的 tô
shower n 淋浴 sói ēk
single room 单人间 tuang nang pāng
skin n 皮肤 p'uē hu
skirt n 裙子 kūng
sleep v 睡 íng
slow 慢的 mang
small 小的 sōi
soap 肥皂 piáng iōq
some 一些 tsek seng
soon 马上 tsek e
south 南 nām
souvenir 纪念品 kî niàm p'êng
stamp 邮票 iu p'iŏ
stand-by ticket 候车票 hau ts'ia p'iŏ
station (train) 火车站 hué ts'ia tsám
stomach 胃 ui
stop v 停止 t'ēng
stop (bus) n 站台 tsám
street 街 koi
student 学生 hak seng
sun 太阳 t'âi iāng
sunscreen 防晒油 huang sâi sng
swim v 游泳 iu iōng

T

tampon 月经棉塞 gueq keng mi sak
telephone n 电话 tiàng ue
temperature (weather) 温度 k'î ung
that 那个 héw kai
they 他们 i nang
(be) thirsty 口渴的 āu ta
this 这个 tsí kai
throat 喉咙 āu
ticket 票 p'iŏ
time 时间 si kang
tired 累的 hēq
tissues 纸巾 poq tsuá keng
today 今天 kim zēk
toilet 厕所 ts'eq sô
tomorrow 明天 mâ zēk
tonight 今晚 kim mē
tooth 牙齿 ge k'î
toothbrush 牙刷 ge sueq
toothpaste 牙膏 ge ko
torch (flashlight) 手电筒 ts'íu tiàng tāng
tour n 旅行 lî iu t'uāng
tourist office 游客信息中心 iu k'eq sêng sêng tong sim
towel 毛巾 tua ek keng
train n 火车 hué ts'ia
translate 翻译 huang ēk
travel agency 旅行社 lí kiang siá
travellers cheque 旅行支票 lí iu tsing piŏ
trousers 裤子 k'ŏu
twin-bed room 双床房 sang ts'ng pāng

U

underwear 内衣裤 lài sang k'ŏu
urgent 紧急的 kéng kip

V

vacancy 空房 ù k'ong pāng
vegetable n 蔬菜 ts'ăi
vegetarian a 吃素的 tsiak tse
visa 签证 ts'iam tsěng

W

walk v 步行 kiāng
wallet 钱包 tsi to
wash (something) 洗 sôi
watch n 手表 ts'íu pio
water n 水 tsuî
we 我们 nāng
weekend 周末 tsiu muăk
west 西 sai
wheelchair 轮椅 lung îng
when 当 … 时 kai si hau
where 在哪里 tò ti kǒ
who 谁 ti tiāng
why 为什么 ui sìm moq
wife 妻子 ts'i tsêw/làu p'uā pol/inf
window 窗户 t'eng
with 和 kaq
without 没有 bō
woman 妇女 hû ng/tsew niō pol/inf
write 写 siâ

Y

yes 是 tuī
yesterday 昨天 tsau zēk
you 你/你们 lêw/nêng sg/pl

Dongbei Hua

TONES 86
ABOUT DONGBEI HUA 87
PRONUNCIATION 88
LANGUAGE DIFFICULTIES 89
TIME & DATES 90
TRANSPORT & DIRECTIONS 91
ACCOMMODATION 92
BANKING & COMMUNICATIONS 93
SIGHTSEEING 94
SHOPPING 95
MEETING PEOPLE 96
MAKING CONVERSATION 96
FEELINGS & OPINIONS 99
FAREWELLS 100
EATING OUT 100
SPECIAL DIETS & ALLERGIES 103
EMERGENCIES & HEALTH 104
ENGLISH–DONGBEI HUA DICTIONARY 105

tones

Dongbei Hua is a tonal language ('tonal quality' refers to the raising and lowering of pitch on certain syllables). In this chapter Dongbei Hua is represented with four tones, as well as a fifth one, the neutral tone. Apart from the unmarked neutral tone, we have used symbols above the vowels to indicate each tone, as shown in the table below for the vowel 'a'. Bear in mind that the tones are relative to the natural vocal range of the speaker, eg the high tone is pronounced at the top of one's vocal range. Note also that some tones slide up or down in pitch.

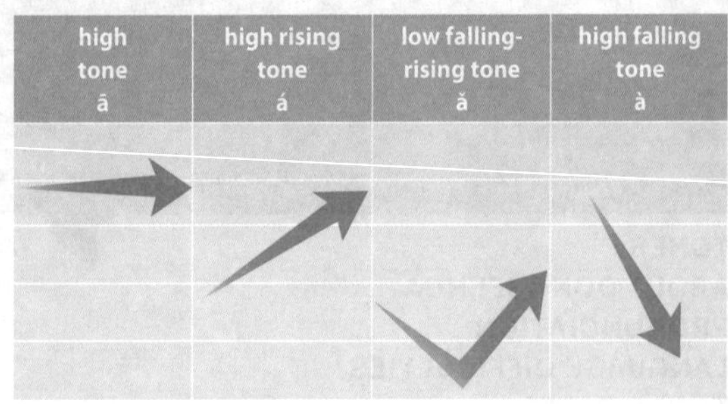

DONGBEI HUA
东北话

about Dongbei Hua

Tucked up in the northeastern provinces of Liáoníng, Jílín and Hēilóngjiāng you'll encounter speakers of Dongbei Hua (dōong bǎy hwà 东北话), the northeastern dialect of Mandarin. It's spoken by around 100 million people and is very similar to the Běijīng dialect, which is the basis of Modern Standard Chinese. Dongbei Hua developed with the arrival of Han immigrants from the southern provinces who came to this corner abutting Russia and Korea in the early years of the 20th century. The dialect took on elements from Siberian and Manchurian languages as well as Korean. In the bustling industrial cities of the northeast, Dongbei Hua also has city-specific sub-dialects, so if you want to impress locals with your street-smart banter in Hā'ěrbīn, Shěnyáng and Chángchūn you'll have to be on your toes. Dongbei Hua is recognisable to Mandarin speakers for its distinctive accent and its lively and informal character, and if you're an aficionado of the Chinese comedy circuit you'll often hear it used by Chinese stand-up comedians.

dongbei hua

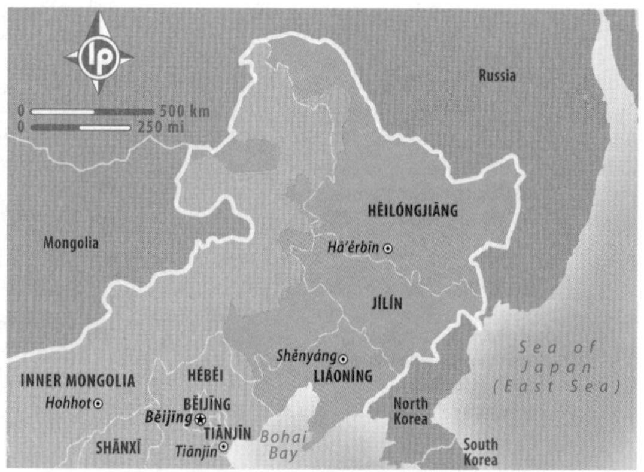

pronunciation

Vowels		Consonants	
Symbol	English sound	Symbol	English sound
a	father	b	bed
ai	aisle	ch	cheat
air	hair	d	dog
ao	Mao	f	fun
ay	pay	g	go
e	bet	h	hat
ee	see	j	jump
er	her without the 'r'	k	kid
ew	similar to new, pronounced with rounded lips	l	lot
i	hit	m	man
ir	girl with strong 'r'	n	not
o	low	ng	ring
oo	tool	p	pet
or	more	r	run
u	cut	s	sun
		sh	shot
		t	top
		ts	cats
		w	win
		y	yes
		z	lads

In this chapter, the Dongbei Hua pronunciation is given in green after each phrase.

For pronunciation of tones, see p86.

Some syllables are separated by a dot, and should be pronounced run together.
For example: 点儿 dyěn·er

essentials

Yes.	是。	shìr
No.	不是。	bóo shìr
Please …	请 …	chǐng …
Hello.	你好。	née hǎo
Goodbye.	拜拜。	bái bái
Thank you.	谢谢。	shyàir shyair
Excuse me. (to get past)	借光儿。	jyàir gwūng·er
Excuse me. (asking for directions or assistance)	帮个忙儿。	bāng gèr máng·er
Sorry.	不好意思。	bòo hǎo yèe sir

language difficulties

Do you speak English?
你说英语不? — něe shwōr yīng yěw boo

Do you understand?
明白不? — míng bài boo

I understand.
我明白。 — wǒr míng bai

I don't understand.
我不明白。 — wǒr bòo míng bai

I (don't) speak Dongbei Hua.
我(不)会说东北话。 — wǒr (bòo) hwày shwōr dōong bǎy hwà

Could you please …?	请你 …?	chǐng něe …
repeat that	再说一遍	zài shwōr yée byèn
speak more slowly	说慢点儿	shwōr mùn dyěn·er

numbers					
0	零	líng	20	二十	èr shír
1	一	yēe	30	三十	sūn shír
2	二/两	èr/lyǎ	40	四十	sìr shír
3	三	sūn	50	五十	wǒo shír
4	四	sìr	60	六十	lyò shír
5	五	wǒo	70	七十	chēe shír
6	六	lyò	80	八十	bā shír
7	七	chēe	90	九十	jyǒ shír
8	八	bā	100	一百	yèe bǎi
9	九	jyǒ	1000	一千	yèe chyēn
10	十	shír	1,000,000	一百万	yèe bǎi wùn

time & dates

What time is it?	现在几点了？	shyèn zài jeé dyěn ler
It's (10) o'clock.	(十)点。	(shír) dyěn
Quarter past (10).	(十)点十五分。	(shír) dyěn shír wǒo fērn
Half past (10).	(十)点半。	(shír) dyěn bùn
Quarter to (11). **(literally: Forty-five minutes past (10).)**	(十)点四十五。	(shír) dyěn sìr shír wǒo

At what time (does it start)?
啥时候(开始)？ shá shír ho (kāi shǐ)

(It starts) At 10.
十点(开始)。 shír dyěn (kāi shǐ)

It's (18 October).
(十月十八号)。 (shír ywàir shír bā hào)

this …	这个 …	zày gè …
morning (after breakfast)	早上	zǎo sùng
morning (before lunch)	头午	tó wǒo
afternoon	下午	shyà wǒo

sunrise	日出	rìr chōo
sunset	日落	rìr lwòr

yesterday	昨天	zwór tyēn
today	今天	jīn tyēn
now	现在	syèn zài
tonight	今儿晚	jīn·er wŭn
tomorrow	明天	míng tyēn
spring	春天	chōon tyen
summer	夏天	shyà tyen
autumn	秋天	chyō tyen
winter	冬天	dōong tyen
Monday	礼拜一	lĕe bài yēe
Tuesday	礼拜二	lĕe bài èr
Wednesday	礼拜三	lĕe bài sūn
Thursday	礼拜四	lĕe bài sìr
Friday	礼拜五	lĕe bài wŏo
Saturday	礼拜六	lĕe bài lyò
Sunday	礼拜天	lĕe bài tyēn
January	一月	yēe ywàir
February	二月	èr ywàir
March	三月	sūn ywàir
April	四月	sìr ywàir
May	五月	wŏo ywàir
June	六月	lyò ywàir
July	七月	chēe ywàir
August	八月	bā ywàir
September	九月	jyŏ ywàir
October	十月	shír ywàir
November	十一月	shír yīr ywàir
December	十二月	shír èr ywàir

transport & directions

Is this the … to (Hā'ĕrbīn)?	这 … 到 (哈尔滨) 那疙瘩去吗？	zày … dào (hā ĕr bīn) nà gā der chèw ma
boat	船	tswún
bus	公交车	gōong jyāo tsēr
train	火车	hwŏr tsēr

Where's a/the ...?	… 在哪儿疙瘩啊?	... zài nǎ·er gā der a
bank	银行	yín húng
place to change foreign money	换外币那疙瘩	hwùn wài bì nà gā der
post office	邮局	yó jéw

Is this the road to (Jílín)?
这是去(吉林)那疙瘩的路吗? — zày shìr chèw (jée lín) nà gā der der lòo mā

Can you show me where it is on the map?
请帮我指下它在地图上哪儿行不? — chǐng būng wǒr zǐr syà tā zài dèe tú sùng nǎ·er shíng boo

Is it walking distance?
走路能到吗? — zǒ lòo nérng dào ma

What's the address?	啥地址啊?	shá dèe zǐr a
How far is it?	多儿老远啊?	dwór·er lǎo ywǔn a
How do I get there?	咋走啊?	zǎ zǒ a
Turn left/right.	往左/右拐。	wǔng zwǒr/yò gwǎi
It's straight ahead.	一直往前走。	yèe zír wǔng chyén zǒ

It's ...	在 …	zài ...
behind ...	… 的后头儿	... der hò to·er
in front of ...	… 的前头儿	... der chyén to·er
near ...	… 附近	fòo jìn
on the corner	拐角	gwǎi jyǎo
opposite ...	… 的对面儿	... de dwày myèn·er
there	那疙瘩	nà gā der

accommodation

Where's a hotel?
哪儿疙瘩有酒店啊? — nǎ·er gā der yǒ jyǒ dyèn a

Can you recommend somewhere cheap?
你能推荐个便宜的地方住吗? — nǐ nérng twāy jyèn gèr pyén yèe der dèe fūng zòo ma

Can you recommend somewhere good?
你能推荐个好的地方住吗? — nǐ nérng twāy jyèn gèr hǎo der dèe fūng zòo ma

I'd like to book a room.
我想订间房儿。 wǒr shyǔng dìng jyēn fúng·er

I have a reservation.
我有预订。 wǒr yǒ yèw dìng

Do you have a … room?	有没有 … 房间啊?	yǒ máy yǒ … fúng jyēn a
double (suite)	套房	tào fúng
single	单人间	dūn rérn jyēn
twin	双人房儿	shwūng rérn fúng·er

How much is it per night?
每晚多少钱? mǎy wǔn dwór sǎo chyén

How much is it per person?
每人多少钱? mǎy rérn dwór sǎo chyén

I'd like to stay for (three) nights.
我想呆(三)天。 wǒr shyǔng dāi (sūn) tyēn

Could I have my key, please?
能不能把钥匙给我啊? nérng bòo nérng bǎ yào sìr gǎy wǒr a

Can I get an extra (blanket)?
我能多拿条(毛毯)吗? wǒr nérng dwōr ná tyáo (máo tǔn) ma

The (air conditioning) doesn't work.
(空调)坏了。 (kōong tyáo) hwài ler

What time is checkout?
啥时候退房啊? shá shír ho twày fúng a

Could I have my …, please?	我想拿回我的 …	wǒr shyǔng ná hwáy wǒr der …
deposit	押金	yā jīn
passport	护照	hòo zào

banking & communications

Where's a/an …?	… 在哪儿疙?	… zài nǎ·er gā
ATM	自动取款机	zìr dòong chêw kwǔn jēe
public phone	公用电话	gōong yòong dyèn hwà

Where's the local internet cafe?
跟前儿有网吧儿吗? gērn chyěn·er yǒ wǔng bā·er ma

I'd like to ...	我想 …	wŏr shyŭng ...
get internet access	上网	sùng wŭng
use a printer	用打印机	yòong dă yìn jēe
use a scanner	用扫描仪	yòong săo myáo yée

What's your phone number?
你的电话号码是多少啊? — nĕe der dyèn hwà hào mă sìr dwór sao a

The number is ...
号码是 … — hào mă sìr ...

sightseeing

I'd like to see ...	我想看 …	wŏr shyŭng kùn ...
What's that?	那是啥啊?	nà sìr shá a
Can I take a photo?	我能拍照吗?	wŏr nérng pāi zào ma

I'd like to see some local sights.
我想去当地这疙瘩景点转转。 — wŏr shyŭng chèw dūng dèe zày gā der jĭng dyĕn zwèn zwèn

I'd like to go somewhere off the beaten track.
我想去人不多的地方转转。 — wŏr shyŭng chèw rérn bòo dwōr der dèe fūng zwèn zwèn

How long is the tour?
这旅游一次多长时间啊? — zày lĕw yó yée chìr dwór tsáng shír jyēn a

sightseeing		
Chángbái Shān	吉林长白山	jée lín tsúng bái sūn
Dàlián	辽宁大连	lyáo níng dà lyén
Mòhé in Hēilóngjiāng	黑龙江漠河北极村风景区	hāy lóong jyūng mòr hér băy jée chōon fērng jĭng chēw
Shĕnyáng Imperial Palace	沈阳故宫	shĕrn yúng gòo gōong
Sun Island Park in Hā'ĕrbīn	哈尔滨太阳岛	hā ĕr bīn tài yúng dăo
Zhālóng Nature Reserve in Qíqíhā'ĕr	齐齐哈尔扎龙自然保护区	chée chée hā ĕr jā lóong zìr rún băo hòo chēw

shopping

Where's a ...?	… 在哪儿疙?	... zài nǎ·er gā
camera shop	照相馆	zào shyùng gwǔn
market	市场	shìr tsǔng
souvenir shop	纪念品店儿	jèe nyèn pǐn dyèn·er
supermarket	超市儿	tsāo sìr·er

Where can I buy locally produced souvenirs?
哪儿能买到纪念品? nǎ·er nérng mǎi dào jèe nyèn pǐn

I'd like to buy ...	我想买 …	wǒr shyǔng mǎi ...
Can I look at it?	我能看看不?	wǒr nérng kùn kùn boo
How much is it?	多儿少钱?	dwór·er sǎo chyén
That's too expensive.	忒贵了。	tāy gwày ler

What's this made from?
这是啥做的? zày shìr shá zwòr der

Please write down the price.
请把价钱写下来。 chǐng bǎ jyà chyén syǎir syà lái

I'll give you (five kuai).
给你(五块)钱。 gǎy něe (wǒo kwài) chyén

Do you accept credit cards?
你们收信用卡不? něe mern sō shìn yòong kǎ boo

There's a mistake in the bill.
帐单儿上有问题。 zùng dūn·er sùng yǒ wèrn tée

less	更少	gèrng sǎo
enough	够了	gò ler
more	更多	gèrng dwōr
bigger	大点儿	dà dyěn·er
smaller	小点儿	syǎo dyěn·er

meeting people

Hello.	你好。	née hăo
Good morning.	早上好。	zăo shung hăo
Good evening.	晚上好。	wŭn shùng hăo
Goodbye.	再见。	zài jyèn
Good night.	晚安。	wŭn ūn
Mr	先生	shyēn sherng
Mrs	女士	nĕwn sìr
Ms/Miss	小姐	shyăo jyăir
How are you?	你咋样啊？	nĕe ză yùng a
Fine. And you?	挺好。你呢？	tĭng hăo, nĕe ner
What's your name?	你叫啥？	nĭr jyào sá
My name is ...	我叫 …	wŏr jyào ...
I'm pleased to meet you.	幸儿会。	shìng·er hwày
This is my ...	这是我的 …	zày sìr wŏr der ...
brother	兄弟	shyōong dee
child	孩子	hái zir
daughter	闺女	gwāy newn
father	爹	dyaīr
friend	朋友	pérng yŏ
husband	丈夫	zùng foo
mother	妈	mā
partner (intimate)	对象	dwày shyàng
sister	姐妹儿	jĭe mày·er
son	儿子	ér zir
wife	媳妇儿	shée fern·er

making conversation

Do you live here?	你住这儿？	nĕe jòo jèr·er
Where are you going?	上哪儿去？	shùng nă·er chew
Do you like it here?	得意这儿吗？	dér yee jèr·er ma
I love it here.	我得意这儿。	wŏr dér yee jèr·er

Have you eaten?
吃了吗? — chīr ler ma

Are you here on holidays?
你在这儿旅游吗? — née zăi jèr·er lĕw yó ma

I'm here ...	我在这儿 …	wór zăi jèr·er ...
for a holiday	旅游	lĕw yó
on business	出差	chōo chāi
to study	留学	léw shwáir

How long are you here for?
你在这儿呆多久? — née zăi jèr·er dāi dwór jyŏ

I'm here for (four) weeks.
我在这儿(四)个星期。 — wór zăi jèr·er (sir) gèr sīng chēe

Can I take a photo (of you)?
可以给(你)拍照吗? — kér yĕe gáy (nĕe) pāi jào ma

Do you speak (Dongbei Hua)?
你说(东北话)吗? — nĕe shwōr (dōong bǎy hwà) ma

What language do you speak at home?
你在家说啥话? — nĕe zài jyā shwōr shá hwà

What do you call this in (Dongbei Hua)?
这个用(东北话)怎么说? — zày gèr yòong (dōong bǎy hwà) zĕrn mor shwōr

What's this called?
这个叫啥? — zày gèr jyào shá

I'd like to learn some (Dongbei Hua).
我想学一些(东北话)。 — wór syŭng shwáir yèe syāir (dōong bǎy hwà)

Would you like me to teach you some English?
你介意我教你些英文吗? — nĕe jyàir yèe wŏr jyāo nĕe syāir yīng wérn ma

Is this a local custom?
这是地方风俗吗? — zày shìr dèe fūng fērng shóo ma

local talk		
Great!	好！	hǎo
Hey!	最近咋样？	zwày jìn zǎ yùng
It's OK.	挺好的。	tíng hǎo der
Just a minute.	等一会儿。	děrng yèe hwǎy·er
Just joking.	闹着玩儿。	nào jer wún·er
Maybe.	差不多。	chà bòo dwōr
No problem.	没问题。	máy wèrn tée
No way!	不可能！	bòo kěr nérng
Sure, whatever.	行，行，行。	síng, síng, síng
That's enough!	够了，够了！	gò ler, gò ler

Where are you from?	你从哪儿来？	něe tsóong nǎ·er lái
I'm from …	我从 … 来。	wǒr tsóong … lái
Australia	澳大利亚	ào dà lèe yà
Canada	加拿大	jyā ná dà
England	英国	yīng gwór
New Zealand	新西兰	sīn sēe lún
the USA	美国	mǎy gwór
What's your occupation?	你干啥的啊？	něe gùn shá der a
I'm a/an …	我是 …	wǒr shìr …
businessperson	商人	shūng rérn
office worker	白领	bái lǐng
tradesperson	工匠	gōong jyùng
How old …?	… 多大了？	… dwōr dà ler
are you	你	něe
is your daughter	你闺女	něe gwāy newn
is your son	你儿子	něe ér zir
I'm … years old.	我 … 岁。	wǒr … shwày
He/She is … years old.	他/她 … 岁。	tā/tā … shwày
Too old!	太老了！	tài lǎo ler

I'm younger than I look.
我看上去年轻。 wǒr kùn shùng chèw nyún chīng

Are you married?
你结婚了吗？ něe jyaír hōon ler ma

东北话 – making conversation

I live with someone.		
我和别人一起住。		wŏr hér byaír rérn yèe chĕe jòo
I'm ...	我 …	wŏr ...
married	结婚了	jyaír hōon ler
single	单身	dūn shērn
Do you like ...?	你得意 … 吗？	nĕe dér yèe ... ma
I (don't) like ...	我(不)得意 …	wŏr (bòo) dér yèe ...
art	艺术	yèe shòo
film	电影	dyèn yĭng
music	音乐	yīn ywàir
reading	看书	kùn shōo
sport	运动	yòon dòong

feelings & opinions

I'm (not) ...	我(不) …	wŏr (bòo) ...
Are you ...?	你 … 吗？	nĕe ... ma
cold	冷	lĕrng
hot	热	rèr
hungry	饿	èr
thirsty	渴	kĕr
tired	累	lày
I (don't) feel ...	我(不)觉得 …	wŏr (bòo) jwáir der ...
Do you feel ...?	你觉得 … 吗？	nĕe jwáir der ... ma
happy	高兴	gāo shìng
sad	不高兴	bòo gāo shìng
worried	着急	jáo jée
What do you think of it?	你觉得怎么样？	nĕe jwáir der jĕrn mor yùng
It's ...	它 …	tā ...
awful	差劲	chà jìn
beautiful	漂亮	pyào lyùng
boring	很没劲	hĕrn máy jìn
great	好	hăo
interesting	很有意思	hĕrn yŏ yèe sir
OK	还行	hái síng
strange	奇怪	chée gwài

farewells

Tomorrow I'm leaving.
明天我就走了。 míng tyēn wǒr jyò zǒ ler

If you come to (Scotland) you can stay with me.
有机会来(苏格兰)，可以来找我。 yǒ jēe hwày lái (sōo gér lún) kér yěe lái jǎo wǒr

Keep in touch!
保持联系！ báo chír lyén see

Here's my (address).
这是我的(地址)。 zày shìr wǒr der (dèe zǐr)

What's your (email)?
你的(电子邮件儿)是啥? něe der (dyàn zǐr yó jyèn er) shìr shá

well-wishing

Bon voyage!	一路平安！	yée lòo píng ūn
Congratulations!	恭喜！	gōong shěe
Good luck!	祝你好运！	jòo něe hǎo yòon
Happy birthday!	生日快乐！	shērng rìr kwài lèr
Happy New Year!	拜年了！	bài nyén ler

eating out

Where would you go for (a) ...?	… 该到哪里去?	... gāi dào nǎ lěe chèw
banquet	吃喜酒	chīr sěe jyǒ
celebration	庆贺	chìng hèr
cheap meal	吃得便宜一点的	chīr der pyén yee yèe dyěn der
local specialities	地方小吃	dèe fūng syǎo chīr
yum cha	喝茶	hēr chá

Can you recommend a …?	你能介绍一个 … 吗？	něe némg jyàir shào yée gèr … ma
bar	酒吧	jyǒ bā
cafe	咖啡厅	kā fāy tīng
dish	盘子	pán zir
noodle house	面馆儿	myèn gwǔn·er
restaurant	饭店	fùn dyèn
snack shop	小吃部	shyǎo chīr bòo
(wonton) stall	(馄饨)摊儿	(hóon dòon) tūn·er
street vendor	街头小吃	jyāir tóu syǎo chīr
teahouse	茶馆儿	chá gwǔn·er

I'd like (a/the) …	我要 …	wǒr yào …
table for (five)	一张(五个人的)桌子	yèe zhūng (wǒo gèr rérn der) jwōr zir
bill	帐单儿	zùng dūn·er
drink list	酒水单儿	jyó shwǎy dūn·er
local speciality	一个地方特色菜	yée gèr dèe fūng tèr sèr tsài
menu	菜单	tsài dūn
(non)smoking table	(不)抽烟的桌子	(bòo) chō yūn der jwōr zir

Are you still serving food?
你们还营业吗？ něe mérn hái yíng yèr ma

What would you recommend?
有啥菜可以推荐的? yǒ shá tsài kér yěe twāy jyèn der

What's in that dish?
这道菜用啥做的? zày dào tsài yòong shá jwòr der

What do you normally eat for (breakfast)?
(早饭)一般吃啥？ (zǎo fùn) yèe būn chīr shá

What's that called?	那个叫啥？	nà gèr jyào shá
I'll have that.	来一个吧。	lái yée gèr ba

I'd like it with …	多放一点 …	dwōr fùng yèe dyěn …
I'd like it without …	别放 …	bái fùng …
chilli	辣椒	là jyāo
garlic	大蒜	dà swùn
MSG	味精	wày jīng
nuts	果仁	gwǒr rérn
oil	油	yó

I'd like ..., please.	请给我 …	chǐng gáy wǒr ...
one slice	一块	yée kwài
a piece	一份	yée fèrn
a sandwich	一个三明治	yée gèr sūn míng zìr
that one	那一个	nà yée gèr
two	两个	lyǔng gèr
This dish is ...	这个菜 …	zày gèr tsài ...
(too) spicy	(太)辣	(tài) là
superb	相当好	syūng dūng hǎo
I love the local cuisine.	这个地方的菜相当不错。	zày gèr dèe fūng der tsài syūng dūng bóo tswòr
That was delicious!	真好吃!	jērn hǎo chīr
I'm full.	吃饱了。	chīr bǎo ler
breakfast	早饭	zǎo fùn
lunch	午饭	wǒo fùn
dinner	晚饭	wǔn fùn
drink (alcoholic)	酒	jyǒ
drink (nonalcoholic)	饮料	yǐn lyào
... water	… 水	... shwǎy
boiled	凉开水	lyúng kāi shwǎy
cold	凉	lyúng
still mineral	矿泉水	koo·ùng chwún shwǎy
(cup of) coffee ...	(一杯)咖啡 …	(yèe bāy) kā fāy ...
(cup of) tea ...	(一杯)茶 …	(yèe bāy) chá ...
with (milk)	加(牛奶)	jyā (nyó nǎi)
without (sugar)	不带(糖)	bòo dài (túng)
black tea	红茶	hóong chá
chrysanthemum tea	菊花茶	jéw hwā chá
green tea	绿茶	lèw chá
jasmine tea	花茶	hwā chá
oolong tea	乌龙茶	wōo lúng chá
fresh drinking yoghurt	酸奶	shwān nǎi
(orange) juice	(橙)汁	(chérng) jīr
soft drink	汽水	chèe shwǎy
sour plum drink	酸梅汤	shwān máy tūng

a … of beer	一 … 啤酒	yèe … pée jyǒ
glass	杯	bāy
large bottle	大瓶儿	dà píng·er
small bottle	小瓶儿	syǎo píng·er
a shot of (whisky)	一瓶儿(威士忌)	yèe píng·er (wāy shìr jèe)
a bottle/glass of … wine	一瓶/杯 … 葡萄酒	yèe píng/bāy … póo táo jyǒ
red	红	hóong
white	白	bái
I'll buy you a drink.	我请客。	wǒr chǐng kèr
What would you like?	你要点啥？	nǐ yào dyěn shá
Cheers!	干！	gūn
I'm feeling drunk.	我有点醉了。	wǒr yǒ dyěn jwày ler

street eats

cold clear bean-flour noodles	凉粉儿	lyúng fěrn·er
corn on the cob	苞米	bāo měe
dumpling (fried)	煎饺子	jyēn jyǎo zir
dumpling (steamed)	蒸饺儿	jērng jyǎo·er
pork pie (small)	馅儿饼	syèn·er bǐng
steamed bread stuffed with meat	包子	bǎo zir
sticky rice in bamboo leaves	粽子	zòong zir

special diets & allergies

Do you have vegetarian food?
有没有素食？ — yǒ mày yǒ sòo shír

Could you prepare a meal without …?
能不能做一个不放 … 的菜？ — nérng bòo nérng zwòr yée gèr bóo fùng … der tsài

I'm allergic to ...	我对 … 过敏。	wŏr dwày ... gwòr mĭn
dairy produce	奶制品	năi jìr pĭn
eggs	鸡蛋	jēe dùn
meat	肉	rò
nuts	果仁儿	gwŏr rérn·er
seafood	海鲜	hăi syēn

emergencies & health

Help!	救命！	jyò mìng
Go away!	走开！	zŏ kāi
Fire!	着火啦！	jáo hwŏr la
Watch out!	加点儿小心！	jyā dyĕn·er syăo sīn

Could you please help?
你能帮儿帮儿忙儿吗？ — nĕe nérng būng·er būng·er múng·er ma

Can I use your phone?
我能借用你的电话用用吗？ — wŏr nérng jyàir nĕe der dyèn hwà yòong yòong ma

Where's the police station?
派出所在哪儿？ — pài chōo swŏr zài nă·er

I'm lost.
我迷路了。 — wŏr mée lù ler

Where are the toilets?
厕所在哪儿？ — tsèr swŏr zài nă·er

Where's the nearest ...?	最近的 … 在哪儿？	zwày jìn der ... zài nă·er
dentist	牙医	yá yēe
doctor	医生	yēe shērng
hospital	医院	yēe ywùn
pharmacist	药店	yào dyèn

东北话 – emergencies & health

english–dongbei hua dictionary

dictionary, words are marked as n (noun), a (adjective), v (verb), sg (singular), pl (plural), inf (informal) and
olite) where necessary.

A

accident (mishap) 意外 yèe wài
accident (traffic) 事故 shìr gòo
accommodation 住宿 zòo sòo
adaptor 适配器 sìr pày chèe
address n 地址 dèe zǐr
after … 之后 … zīr hò
air conditioning 空调 kōong tyáo
airplane 飞机 fāy jēe
airport 机场 jēe tsǔng
alcohol 酒 jyǒ
all 所有的 swǒr yǒ der
allergy 过敏 gwòr mǐn
ambulance 救护车 jyò hòo tsēr
and 和 hér
ankle 脚踝 jyǎo hwaí
antibiotics 抗生素 kùng sērng sòo
arm 手臂 sǒ bèe
ATM 自动取款机 zìr dòong chěw kwǔn jēe

B

baby 婴儿 yīng·ér
back (of body) 后背 hò bày
backpack 背包儿 bāy bāo·er
bad 坏的 hwài der
bag 袋儿 dài·er
baggage 行李 shíng lee
bank 银行 yín húng
bar 酒吧 jyǒ bā
bathroom 浴室 yèw sìr
battery 电池 dyàn tsír
beautiful 漂亮的 pyào lyùng der
bed 床 tswúng
beer 啤酒 pée jyǒ
before … 前头 … chyén to
behind … 后头 … hò to
bicycle 自行车 zìr síng tsēr
big 大的 dà der
bill 帐单儿 zùng dūn·er
blanket 毛毯 máo tǔn
blood group 血型 swàir síng
boat 船 tswún
book (make a reservation) v 预订 yèw dìng
bottle 瓶儿 píng·er
boy 小男孩儿 shyǎo nún hái·er
breakfast 早饭 zǎo fùn
broken (out of order) 坏掉了 hwài dyào ler
bus 公交车 gōong jyāo tsēr
business 买卖 mǎi mai
buy v 买 mǎi

C

camera 照相机 zào syùng jēe
cancel 取消 chěw syāo
car 汽车 chèe tsēr
cash n 现金 shyèn jīn
cell phone 手机 sǒ jēe
centre n 中心 zōong sīn
change (money) v 零钱儿 líng chyén·er
cheap 便宜的 pyén yèe der
check (bill) n 帐单儿 zùng dūn·er
check-in n 登记 dērng jèe
chest (body) 胸 syōong
children 孩子 hái zir
cigarette 烟 yūn
city 城市 tsérng shìr
clean a 干净的 gūn jìng der
closed 关门了 gwūn mérn ler
cold a 凉的 lyúng der
collect call 对方付费电话 dwày fūng fòo fày dyèn hwà
come 来 lái
computer 电脑 dyèn nǎo
condom 避孕套儿 bèe yòon tào·er
contact lenses 隐形眼镜 yǐn shíng yǔn jìng
cook v 烹饪 pērng yìn
cost n 花费 hwā fày
credit card 信用卡 shìn yòong kǎ
currency exchange 货币汇兑 hwòr bèe dwày hwùn
customs (immigration) 海关 hǎi gwūn

D

dangerous 危险的 wāy shyěn der
date (time) 日期 rìr chēe
day 天 tyēn
delay v 延迟 yún chír

A

english–dongbei hua

dentist 牙科医生 yá kèr yēe shērng
depart 出发 tsōo fā
diaper 尿布 nyào bòo
dinner 晚饭 wǔn fùn
dirty 埋汰 mái tai
disabled 残疾的 tsún jée der
discount v 打折儿 dǎ zér
doctor 大夫 dài foo
double bed 双人床 swūng yín tswúng
double room 双人房儿 swūng yín fúng-er
drink n 饮料 yǐn lyào
drive v 开车 kāi tsēr
drivers licence 驾照 jyà zào
drug (illicit) 毒品 dóo pǐn

E

ear 耳朵 ěr dwor
east 东 dōong
eat 吃 chīr
economy class 经济舱 jīng jèe tsūng
electricity 电 dyèn
email 电子邮件儿 dyèn zǐ yó jyèn-er
embassy 大使馆 dà sǐr gwǔn
emergency 紧急状况 jǐn jée chúng kwùng
English (language) 英语 yīng yěw
evening 傍晚 bùng wǔn
exit n 出口 tsōo kǒ
expensive 贵 gwày
eye 眼睛 yǔn jing

F

far 远的 ywǔn der
fast 快的 kwài der
father 爸 bà
film (camera) 胶卷 jyāo jwǔn
finger 手指 sǒ zǐr
first-aid kit 急救箱 jée jyò syūng
first class 头等舱 tó děrng tsūng
fish n 鱼 yéw
food 食物 sír wòo
foot 脚 jyǎo
free (of charge) 免费的 myěn fày der
friend 朋友 pérng yǒ
fruit 水果 sǎy gwǒr
full 饱的 bǎo der

G

gift 礼物 lěe wòo
girl 女孩儿 něw hái-er
glass (drinking) 杯子 bāy zir
glasses 眼镜 yǔn jìng
go 去 chèw
good 好的 hǎo der
guide n 导游 dǎo yó

H

half n 一半 yée bùn
hand 手 shǒ
happy 高兴的 gāo shìng der
he 他 tā
head n 头 tó
heart 心 shīn
heavy 重的 zòong der
help 帮助 būng zòo
here 这旮瘩 zày gā da
high 高 gāo
highway 高速公路 gāo sòo gōong lòo
hike v 徒步旅行 tóo bòo lěw shíng
holiday 假期 jyà chēe
homosexual 同性恋 tóong shìng lyèn
hospital 医院 yēe ywùn
hot 热乎 yàir hoo
hotel 酒店 jyǒ dyèn
(be) hungry 饿了 nèr ler
husband 丈夫 zùng fōo

I

I 我 wǒr
identification (card) 身份证 sērn fèrn zèrng
ill 生病 sērng bìng
important 重要的 zòong yào der
injury (harm) 侮辱 wǒo rǒo
injury (wound) 伤口 sūng kǒ
insurance 保险 bǎo shyěn
internet 因特儿网 yīn tè-er wǔng
interpreter 翻译 fūn yèe

J

jewellery 珠宝 zōo bǎo
job 工作 gōong zwòr

K

key 钥匙 yào sìr
kilogram 公斤 gōong jīn
kitchen 厨房 tsóo fúng
knife 小刀 syǎo dāo

L

laundry (place) 洗衣店 shěe yēe dyèn
lawyer 律师 lèw shīr
left (direction) 左 zwŏr
leg (body) 腿 twăy
lesbian 女同 nĕw tóong
less 更少 gèrng săo
letter (mail) 信 shìn
light n 光 gwūng
like v 中意 zōong yèe
lock n 锁 swŏr
long 长的 chúng der
lost 遗失的 yée sīr der
love v 爱 ài
luggage 行李 síng lee
lunch 午饭 wŏo fùn

M

mail n 信 shìn
man 男人 nún yín
map 地图儿 dèe tú·er
market 市场 shìr tsŭng
matches 比赛 bĕe sài
meat 肉 rò
medicine 药 yào
message 消息 shyāo shee
milk 牛奶 nyó năi
minute 分钟 fērn zōong
mobile phone 手机 sŏ jēe
money 钱 chyén
month 月份 ywàir fern
morning 早上 zăo sùng
mother 妈 mā
motorcycle 摩托车 mór twōr tsēr
mouth 嘴 zwăy

N

name 名字 míng zìr
near 近 jìn
neck n 脖子 bór zir
new 新的 shīn der
newspaper 报纸 bào zhĭr
night 晚上 wŭn shùng
no (not at all) 不用 bóo yòong
no (not this) 不是 bóo shìr
noisy 嘈嘈 tsāo tsāo
nonsmoking 无烟区 wóo yūn chēw
north 北 băy
nose 鼻子 bée zir
now 现在 syèn zài
number 数 shòo

O

old (people) 老 lăo
old (things) 旧 jyò
one-way ticket 单程票 dūn chérng pyào
open a 开着的 kāi jēr der
outside 外头 wài to

P

passport 护照 hòo zhào
pay v 付钱 fòo chyén
pharmacy 药店 yào dyèn
phonecard 电话卡 dyèn hwà kă
photo 照片 zhào pyēn
police 警察 jĭng chá
postcard 明信片 míng sìn pyèn
post office 邮局 yó jéw
pregnant 怀孕了 hwái yèwn ler
price n 价格 jyà gér

Q

quiet a 安静的 ūn jìng der

R

rain n 雨 yĕw
razor 剃须刀 tèe shēw dāo
receipt n 收据 shō jèw
refund n 赔钱 páy chyén
registered (mail) 注册 zhòo tsèr
rent v 出租 chōo zōo
repair v 维修 wáy shyō
reserve v 预订 yèw dìng
restaurant 餐馆 tsūn gwŭn
return (give back) 还 hwún
return (go back) 回去 hwáy chèw
return ticket 返程票 fŭn chérng pyào
right (direction) 右 yò
road 马路 mă lòo
room n 房间 fúng jyēn

S

safe a 安全的 ūn chwún der
sanitary napkin 卫生巾 wày shērng jīn
seat n 座位 zwòr wày
send 发送 fā sòong
sex (intercourse) 做爱 zwòr ài

sex (gender) 性别 sìng byáir
shampoo 洗发水 sěe fà shwǎy
share (a dorm) 分享 fērn syǔng
she 她 tā
sheet (bed) 床单 chwúng dūn
shirt 衬衫 chèrn shūn
shoes 鞋 syáir
shop n 商店 shūng dyèn
short 短的 dwǔn der
shower n 冲凉 chōong lyúng
single room 单人间 dūn rérn jyēn
skin n 皮肤 pée fōo
skirt n 裙子 chóon zir
sleep v 睡觉 shwài jyào
slow 慢 mùn
small 小 syǎo
soap 香皂 syūng zào
some 一些 yèe syāir
soon 马上 mǎ shùng
south 南 nún
souvenir 纪念品 jèe nyèn pǐn
stamp 邮票 yó pyào
stand-by ticket 站票 zhùn pyào
station (train) 车站 chēr zùn
stomach 胃 wày
stop v 停止 tíng zǐr
stop (bus) n 公车站 gōong chēr zùn
street 街 jyāir
student 学生 swáir shērng
sun 太阳 tài yúng
sunscreen 防晒霜 fúng shài shwūn
swim v 游泳 yó yǒong

T

tampon 棉球 myén chyó
telephone n 电话 dyèn hwà
temperature (weather) 气温 chèe wērn
that 那个 này gèr
they 他们 tā mern
(be) thirsty 渴了 kěr ler
this 这个 zày ger
throat 嗓子 sǔng zir
ticket 车票 chēr pyào
time 时间 shír jyēn
tired 累挺 lày ting
tissues 纸巾 jǐr jīn
today 今天 jīn tyēn
toilet 茅房 máo fúng
tomorrow 明天 míng tyēn
tonight 今儿晚 jīn-er wǔn
tooth 牙齿 yá chǐr
toothbrush 牙刷 yá shwā
toothpaste 牙膏 yá gāo
torch (flashlight) 电棒儿 dyèn bùng-er
tour n 旅游 lěw yó
tourist office 旅游局 lěw yó jéw
towel 毛巾 máo jīn
train n 火车 hwǒr tsēr
translate 翻译 fūn yèe
travel agency 旅行社 lěw síng shèr
travellers cheque 旅游支票 lěw yó jīr pyào
trousers 裤子 kòo zir
twin-bed room 双人房 shwūng rérn fúng

U

underwear 内衣 này yēe
urgent 紧急 jǐn jée

V

vacancy 空缺 kòong chwāir
vegetable n 蔬菜 shōo tsài
vegetarian n 素食者 sòo shír jěr
visa 签证 chyēn jèrng

W

walk v 走道儿 zǒ dào-er
wallet 钱包儿 chyén bāo-er
wash (something) 洗 sěe
watch n 手表 shǒ byǎo
water n 水 shwǎy
we 我们 wǒr mérn
weekend 周末 zhō mòr
west 西 sēe
wheelchair 轮椅 lóon yěe
when 啥时候 shá shír ho
where 哪 nǎ
who 谁 shwáy
why 为啥 wày shá
wife 媳妇儿 shée fern-er
window 窗户 chwūng hoo
with 带 dài
without 不带 bóo dài
woman 女人 něwn rérn
write 写 syǎir

Y

yes 是 shìr
yesterday 昨天 zwór tyēn
you sg inf 你 něe
you sg pol 您 nín
you pl 你们 něe mern

Hakka

TONES 110
ABOUT HAKKA 111
PRONUNCIATION 112
LANGUAGE DIFFICULTIES 113
TIME & DATES 114
TRANSPORT & DIRECTIONS 115
ACCOMMODATION 116
BANKING & COMMUNICATIONS 117
SIGHTSEEING 117
SHOPPING 118
MEETING PEOPLE 119
MAKING CONVERSATION 120
FEELINGS & OPINIONS 122
FAREWELLS 123
EATING OUT 124
SPECIAL DIETS & ALLERGIES 127
EMERGENCIES & HEALTH 127
ENGLISH–HAKKA DICTIONARY 129

tones

Hakka is a tonal language ('tonal quality' refers to the raising and lowering of pi on certain syllables). In this chapter Hakka is represented with four tones, as well a fifth one, the neutral tone. Apart from the unmarked neutral tone, we have us symbols above the vowels to indicate each tone, as shown in the table below for t vowel 'a'. Bear in mind that the tones are relative to the natural vocal range of t speaker, eg the high tone is pronounced at the top of one's vocal range. Note al that some tones slide up or down in pitch.

high tone ā	high rising tone á	low falling-rising tone ǎ	high falling tone à

about Hakka

There are 34 million speakers of Hakka (kā gā wā 客家话) spread across southern China, with populations also in Malaysia, Indonesia, Singapore and Thailand. Originally from Hénán and Shānxī provinces, through the course of Chinese history the Hakka moved south, encountering Cantonese speakers. Their language has proved resolute, remaining similar to the languages of the Tang and Song dynasties of the 10th century. However, spoken in scattered regions and across difficult terrain, Hakka is believed to have absorbed elements of other languages, including the non-Sinitic She language, evolving into an estimated 30 dialects across south and southeast China and Taiwan. Most speakers are found in the Guǎngdōng, Fújiàn and Jiāngxī region, with Méixiàn, in northeast Guǎngdōng, considered the centre of 'standard' Hakka (represented in this chapter). It's a Sino-Tibetan language but isn't mutually intelligible with Mandarin or Cantonese. Enterprising, adventurous and occasionally revolutionary, Hakka speakers, such as the late Deng Xiaoping, have played an important role in broader Chinese and Southeast Asian history, rising to become military, business and political leaders.

hakka

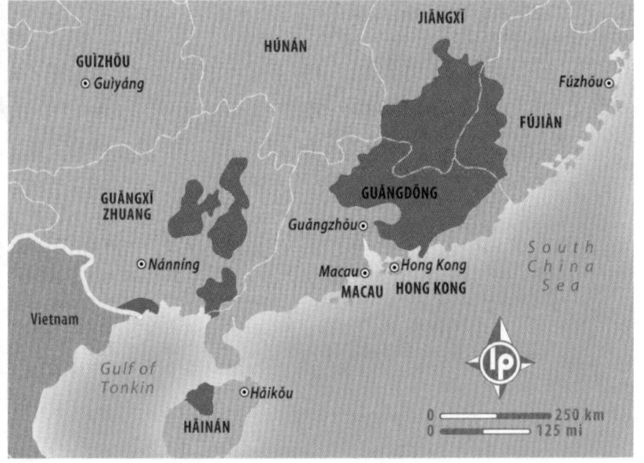

about – HAKKA

pronunciation

Vowels		Consonants	
Symbol	**English sound**	**Symbol**	**English sound**
a	father	b	bed
ai	aisle	ch	cheat
air	lair	d	dog
ao	Mao	f	fun
ay	say	g	go
e	bet	h	hot
ee	see	j	jump
i	hit	k	kit
o	go	l	lot
oo	tool	m	man
or	more	n	not
oy	toy	ng	ring
u	cut	p	pet
		r	run
		s	sun
		sh	shot
		t	top
		ts	cats
		w	win
		y	yes
		z	lads

In this chapter, the Hakka pronunciation is given in purple after each phrase.

In Hakka, the sound ng (found in English at the end or in the middle of words, eg 'ringing') can appear at the start of words, or represent an entire word.

For pronunciation of tones, see p110.

Some syllables are separated by a dot, and should be pronounced run together.
For example: 月 ngi·āir

essentials		
Yes./No.	是。/吾是。	hè/ng hè
Please …	请 …	chyǔng …
Hello.	你好。	ngée hao
Goodbye.	再见。	zwài jyèn
Thank you.	谢谢你。	chyă chyă ngée
Excuse me. (to get past)	借光。	jyà kwò
Excuse me. (asking for directions/assistance)	请问。	chyǔng mwèn
Sorry.	对吾助。	dwày ng chŏo

language difficulties

Do you speak English?	你讲不讲英语?	ngée gwǔng ng gwǔng yīng ngēe
Do you understand?	你明白吗?	ngée míng pā mā
I (don't) understand.	涯(不)明白。	yái (ng) míng pā
I (don't) speak Hakka.	涯(不)讲客家话。	yái (ng) gwǔng kā gā wā
Could you please …?	请你 …?	chyǔng ngée …
repeat that	再说一遍	zwài gwǔng yēe pyèn
speak more slowly	慢一点讲	mūn yēe dēe gwǔng

numbers					
0	零	lyúng	20	二十	ngèe shēe
1	一	yēe	30	三十	sūng shēe
2	二/两	ngèe/lyǔng	40	四十	sèe shēe
3	三	sūng	50	五十	ng shēe
4	四	sèe	60	六十	lyŏ shēe
5	五	ng	70	七十	chĕe shēe
6	六	lyŏ	80	八十	bāi shēe
7	七	chĕe	90	九十	jyŏ shēe
8	八	bāi	100	一百	yēe bā
9	九	jyŏ	1000	一千	yēe chyēn
10	十	shēe	1,000,000	一百万	yēe bā wùn

time & dates

What time is it?	今来几点钟?	jīn lái jěe dō dyǔng
It's (10) o'clock.	(十)点钟。	(shēe) dyǔng
Quarter past (10).	(十)点十五分。	(shēe) dyǔng shēe ng fēn
Half past (10).	(十)点三十分。	(shēe) dyǔng sūng shēe fēn
Quarter to (11). (literally: Forty-five minutes past (10).)	(十)点四十五分。	(shēe) dyǔng sèe shēe ng fēn
(It starts) At 10.	十点(开始)。	shēe dyǔng (kwāi shǐ)
It's (18 October).	(十月十八号)。	(shēe ngi·āir shēe bāi hǎo)

yesterday	昨不日	tsyō pōo ngēe
today	今日	jīn ngēe
now	今来	jīn lái
tonight	今日昂布	jīn ngēe àm pōo
tomorrow	天光日	tyēn kwōong ngēe

this …	这个 …	é kè …
morning (after breakfast)	早晨头	tsāo sén twǒo
morning (before lunch)	上布	shǔng tsòo
afternoon	下午	hā tsòo

sunrise	日出	ngēe tsōo
sunset	日落	ngēe lòo

spring	春天	tsūn tyēn
summer	夏天	hā tyēn
autumn	秋天	tsyō tyēn
winter	冬天	dōong tyēn

Monday	星期一	sīn kée yēe
Tuesday	星期二	sīn kée ngì
Wednesday	星期三	sīn kée sūng
Thursday	星期四	sīn kée sèe
Friday	星期五	sīn kée ng
Saturday	星期六	sīn kée lyǒ
Sunday	星期天	sīn kée tyēn

January	一月	yēe ngi·āir
February	二月	ngèe ngi·āir
March	三月	sūng ngi·āir
April	四月	sèe ngi·āir
May	五月	ng ngi·āir
June	六月	lyǒ ngi·āir
July	七月	chěe ngi·āir
August	八月	bāi ngi·āir
September	九月	jyǒ ngi·āir
October	十月	shēe ngi·āir
November	十一月	shēe yēe ngi·āir
December	十二月	shēe ngèe ngi·āir

transport & directions

Is this the … to (Méixiàn)?	这个 … 到 (梅县) 去吗?	é kè … dào (móy yèn) hèe mā
boat	船	shwún
bus	车	chā
train	火车	hwǒr chā
Where's a/the …?	… 在哪儿?	… tsōr lái lēe
bank	银行	ngyún hóong
place to change foreign money	换外币的地方	wùn ǒy bèe kè těe fōong
post office	邮局	yó kyō

Is this the road to (Méixiàn)?
列系去 (梅县) 的路吗? — é hè dào (móy yèn) gè lòo mā

Can you show me where it is on the map?
请帮涯寻它在地图上的位置。 — chyǔng bōong yái chín jée tsōr těe tóo shùng kè wìr zěe

Is it walking distance?
系不系布行的其离? — hè ng hè pǒo húng gè kēe lée

What's the address?	什么地址?	syēn mō těe jěe
How far is it?	有多远?	yō jěe ywūn
How do I get there?	怎呢行?	nyǔng nē húng
Turn left/right.	尚左/右。	shùng zǒr/yǒ

It's straight ahead.	一直尚前。	yēe chēe shùng chyén
It's …	错 …	tsōr …
behind …	… 后面	… hǒ myèn
in front of …	… 前面	… chyén myèn
near …	… 附近	… fòo kwīm
on the corner	转角	zwǔn wūn
opposite …	… 对面	… dwày myèn
there	那里	kái lēe

accommodation

Can you recommend somewhere cheap?		
你能推荐一个便宜的地方住吗?		ngée nyén twāy jyùng yēe kè pyén yēe kè tǐ fōong chǒo mā
Can you recommend somewhere good?		
你能推荐一个好的地方住吗?		ngée nyén twāy jyùng yēe kè hǎo kè tǐ fōong chǒo mā
Where's a guest house?	来里有宾馆?	lái lēe yō bēen gwǔn
Where's a hotel?	来里酒店?	lái lēe jyǒ dyùng
I'd like to book a room.	涯想订房间。	yái syǔng dùng fóong gūn
I have a reservation.	涯有预订。	yái yō yèe dùng
Do you have a … room?	有毛有 … 房?	yō máo yō … fóong
double (suite)	套	tào
single	单人	dūn ryén
twin	标准	pyāo zwǔng
How much is it per night/person?		
每天/人多少钱?		mēe tyēn/ryén jǐ dwōr chyén
I'd like to stay for (three) nights.		
涯想住(三)天。		yái syǔng chǒo (sūng) tyēn
Could I have my key, please?		
能不能给涯房间钥匙?		nyén ng nyén bwēn yái fóong gūn swǒr shée
Can I get an extra (blanket)?		
涯能多拿一条(毛毯)吗?		yái nyén dwōr nā yēe tyáo (māo tūn) mā

The (air conditioning) doesn't work.
(空调)有毛病。 (kōong tyáo) yō māo pyùng

What time is checkout?
几点钟退房? jĭ dyŭng jōong twày fóong

Could I have my …, please?	涯想拿回 涯的 …	yái syŭng nā jwŭn yái kè …
deposit	押金	yā jīn
passport	护照	fòo jào

banking & communications

Where's the local internet cafe?
附近有网吧吗? fòo kwīm yō mwūng bā mā

Where's a/an …?	… 在哪儿?	… tsōr lái lēe
ATM	自动取款机	zēe tòong chĕe kwŭn jēe
public phone	公用电话	gōong yŏong tyèn wā

I'd like to …	涯想 …	yái syŭng …
get internet access	上网	shūng mwūng
use a printer/scanner	打印/扫描	dă yìn/săo myáo

What's your phone number?
您的电话号码是多少? ngée kè tyèn wā hăo mā hè jĕe dwōr

The number is …
号码是 … hăo mā hè …

sightseeing

I'd like to see some local sights.
涯想看一些当体景色。 yái syŭng kwùn yēe dēe dūng tēe jĭm sèe

I'd like to see …	涯想看 …	yái syŭng kwùn …
What's that?	那是麻个?	kái hè má kè
Can I take a photo?	涯能拍照吗?	yái nyén pā jyào mā

banking & communications – HAKKA

sightseeing		
Hua Cheng	华城	fá shōon
Ling-Guang Temple	灵光寺	líng kwūn sèe
Mei Zhou	梅洲	móy jō
Thousand-Buddha Pagoda	千佛塔	chyēn fō tă
Wu Hua	五华	ng fá
Zi Jin	紫金	tsēe jīn

I'd like to go somewhere off the beaten track.
涯想去看人少的景点。 — yái syŭng hèe kwùn nyén shăo gè jĭm sèe

How long is the tour?
向导游要多长时间? — shùng dăo yó òy jĕe chóong shée jyūng

shopping

Where's a ...?	... 在哪儿?	... tsōr lái lēe
camera shop	照相店	jào syùng dyùng
market	市场	shèe chúng
souvenir shop	纪念品店	jèe nyùn pĭm dyùng
supermarket	超市	chāo shèe

Where can I buy locally produced souvenirs?
涯可以在来里买地方纪念品? — yái kwŏr yēe tswōr lái lēe māi tĕe fōong jèe nyùn pĭm

What's this made from?
这个是用麻个做的? — é kè hè yòong má kè zwòr gé

I'd like to buy ...	涯想买 ...	yái syŭng māi ...
Can I look at it?	涯能看看吗?	yái nyén kwùn kwùn mā
How much is it?	多少钱?	jĕe dwōr chyén
That's too expensive.	太贵。	tài kwày

Please write down the price.
请把价钱写下来。 — chyŭng bă gà chyén syă hā lái

I'll give you (five kuai).
给你(五块)钱。 — bwēn ngée (ng kwày) chyén

Do you accept credit cards?
你们收信用卡吗? ngée mwēn shwāy sìn yòong ká mā

There's a mistake in the bill.
帐单上有问题。 jùng dūn yō mwèn tée

less	少	shǎo
enough	够	gò
more	多	dwōr
bigger	大一点	tà yēe dēe
smaller	小一点	syè yēe dēe

meeting people

Hello.	你好。	ngée hǎo
Good morning.	早上好。	tsāo shàng hǎo
Good afternoon.	下午好。	hā ng hǎo
Good evening.	晚上好。	mān shàng hǎo
Goodbye.	再见。	zwài jyèn
Good night.	晚安。	wǔn ūn
Mr	先生	syēn sūng
Mrs	女士	ngěe sèe
Ms/Miss	小姐	syǎo jyǎ
How are you?	你好吗?	ngée hǎo mā
Fine. And you?	好。你呢?	hǎo, ngée nē

What's your name?
你很措麻个名? ngée hēn tswōr má kè myúng

My name is ...
涯很措 ··· yái hēn tswōr ...

I'm pleased to meet you.
幸会。 hèn hwāy

This is my …	这是涯的 …	é hè yái kè …
brother	兄弟	shyōong tĕe
child	小孩子	syè ryén nēe
daughter	妹子	mòy tsĕe
father	爷俄	yá é
friend	朋友	pyén yō
husband	老公	lăo gōong
mother	母亲	ōy jè
partner (intimate)	对象	dwày shyùng
sister	姐妹	jyă mòy
son	莱子	lài tsĕe
wife	老婆	lăo pó

making conversation

Do you live here?	你住列里吗?	ngée chŏo lyáir lēe mā
Where are you going?	上来里?	shùng lái lēe
Do you like it here?	中意列里吗?	jòong yèe lyáir lēe mā
I love it here.	涯很中意这里。	yái hĕn jòong yèe lyáir lēe
Have you eaten?	吃过饭吗?	shēe gò fŭn mā
Are you here on holiday?	你来来里旅游吗?	ngée lái lyáir lēe lēe jó mā

I'm here …	涯来来里 …	yái lái lyáir lēe …
for a holiday	旅游	lēe jó
on business	出差	chōo tsāi
to study	留货	lyó hō

How long are you here for?
你在这里住几久? — ngée tsai lyáir lēe chŏo jĕe jŏ

I'm here for (four) weeks.
涯住(四)个星期。 — yái chŏo (sèe) kè sīn kée

Can I take a photo (of you)?
涯可不可以拍(你)吗? — yái kwŏr bù kwŏr yēe pā (ngée) mā

local talk		
Great!	真好！	zēn hăo
Hey!	劳驾！	láo gà
It's OK.	毛问题。	máo mwèn tī
Just a minute.	等下。	dĕn hà
Just joking.	开玩笑。	kwāi yún syào
Maybe.	有可能。	yō kwŏr nyén
No problem.	没事。	máo sèe
No way!	不可能！	máo kwŏr nyén
Sure, whatever.	得, 得, 得。	dyāir dyāir dyāir
That's enough!	够啦！	gìr·ò lā

Do you speak (Hakka)?
你讲(客家话)吗? — ngée gwŭng (kā gā wā) mā

What language do you speak at home?
你在屋喀讲麻个话? — ngée tswōr kā gwŭng má gè wā

What do you call this in (Hakka)?
这个用(客家话)酿般讲? — é kè yōong (kā gā wā) nyĕn būn gwŭng

What's this called?
这个很措麻个名? — é kè hēn tswōr má kè myúng

I'd like to learn some (Hakka).
我想学一些(客家话)。 — yái syŭng hō yēe dēe (kā gā wā)

Would you like me to teach you some English?
你想涯教你一些英语吗? — ngée syŭng yái jyāo ngée yēe dēe yīng ngēe mā

Is this a local custom?
这是地方风俗吗? — é hè tĕe fōong fōon sōo mā

Where are you from?	你从哪儿来?	ngée chyóong lái lēe lái
I'm from ...	涯从 … 来。	yái chyóong ... lái
Australia	澳大利亚	ào tài lèe à
Canada	加拿大	gā ná tài
England	英国	yīng gē
New Zealand	新西兰	sīn sī lán
the USA	美国	mī gē

What's your occupation?	你做麻个工作?	ngée zwòr má gè gōong zwōr
I'm a/an …	涯系 …	yái hè …
businessperson	商人	shūng nyén
office worker	白领	pā lyēn
tradesperson	贸易商	myào yēe shūng
How old …?	… 几大?	… jěe tāi
are you	你	ngée
is your daughter	你的女儿	ngée gè mòy tsěe
is your son	你的儿子	ngée gè lài tsěe
I'm … years old.	涯 … 岁。	yái … swòy
He/She is … years old.	他/她 … 岁。	jée … swòy
I'm younger than I look.	涯还细。	yái hún sèe
Are you married?	你结婚了吗?	ngée gě hōon lē mā
I live with someone.	涯有阵。	yái yō chèn
Do you have a family of your own?	你成家了吗?	ngée shyén gā lē mā
I'm …	涯 …	yái …
married	结了婚	gě dēe hōon
single	单身	dūn shyēn
Do you like …?	你中意 … 吗?	ngée jòong yèe … mā
I (don't) like …	涯(吾)中意 …	yái (ng) jòong yèe …
art	艺术	ngèe sōo
film	看电影	kwùn tyēn yǔng
music	听音乐	tùng yīng lwōr
reading	看书	kwùn shōo
sport	体育	tǐ yōo

feelings & opinions

I'm (not) …	涯(吾) …	yái (ng) …
Are you …?	你 … 吗?	ngée … mā
cold	冷	lūm
hot	热	ngè
hungry	饿	ngò
thirsty	渴	hwǒr
tired	累	kwǎy

I (don't) feel …	涯(不)觉得 …	yái (ng) kwór dē …
Do you feel …?	你觉得 … 吗?	ngée kwór dē … mā
happy	欢喜	hwūn shēe
sad	不欢喜	ng hwūn shēe
worried	担心	dūng sīng

What do you think of it?	你觉得酿办?	ngée kwór dē nyěn būn

It's …	它 …	jée …
awful	好差劲	hǎo tsā jìn
beautiful	好美	hǎo mī
boring	好无聊	hǎo wú lyáo
great	真好	zēn hǎo
interesting	好有意思	hǎo yō yèe sēe
OK	还可以	hái kwǒr yēe
strange	奇怪	kí gwày

farewells

Tomorrow I'm leaving.
天光布涯要走。 — yái tyēn kwōong ngēe òy zwǒr

If you come to (Scotland) you can stay with me.
有机会来(苏格兰),
可以来找涯。 — yō jī hwày lái (sū gē lán)
kwǒr yēe lái chyín yái

Keep in touch!	保持联络!	bǎo chée lyén lwōr
Here's my (address).	给你涯的(地址)。	bwūn ngée yái gè (těe jěe)
What's your (email)?	你的(电邮)是麻个?	ngée gè (tyěn yó) hè má gè

well-wishing

Bon voyage!	一路平安!	yēe lù pín ūn
Congratulations!	恭喜, 恭喜!	gōong shěe, gōong shěe
Good luck!	祝你好运!	jòo ngée hǎo yòon
Happy birthday!	生日快乐!	shūn ngèe kwày lwò
Happy New Year!	新年好!	sīn nyén hǎo

eating out

Where would you go for (a) ...?	应该到. . . 去?	yīng gwāy dào ... hèe
banquet	办宴会	pùn yùn hwày
celebration	举行庆祝会	jěe húng chìng jōo hwày
cheap meal	吃便宜一点	shēe pyén yēe yēe dēe
local specialities	地方小吃	tèe fōong syǎo shēe
yum cha	饮茶	yǐm tsá
Can you recommend a ...?	你可以推荐一个 … 吗?	ngée kwǒr yēe twāy jyùng yēe kè ... mā
bar	酒吧	jyǒ bā
cafe	咖啡厅	kā fī tyūng
dish	盘	pún
noodle house	面馆	myèn kwǔn
restaurant	饭店	fǔn dyùng
snack shop	小吃店	syǎo shēe dyùng
(wonton) stall	(馄饨)摊	(wóon tōon) tūn
street vendor	街头小吃	gwāy tyó syǎo shēe
teahouse	茶馆	tsá gwǔn
I'd like (a/the) ...	涯要 …	yái òy ...
table for (five)	一个(五位)台	yēe kè (ng wì) tái
bill	帐单	jùng dūn
drink list	酒水单	jyǒ shwǎy dūn
local speciality	一个地方特色菜	yēe kè tèe fōong tì sèe chòy
menu	菜单	chòy dūn
(non)smoking table	(毛)吃烟的台	(máo) shēe yōon kè tái

Are you still serving food?
你们还营业吗? — ngée mwén hái yúng nyā mā

What would you recommend?
有麻个菜可以推荐的? — yō má gè chòy kwǒr yēe twāy jyùng gé

What's in that dish?
这个菜用麻个做的? — é kè chòy yòong má gè zwòr gé

What's that called?
那个很错麻个？ é kè hēn tswōr má gè

I'll have that.
来一个。 lái yēe kè

I'd like it with …	多放一点 …	dwōr fòon yēe dēe …
I'd like it without …	不要放 …	ng òy fòon …
chilli	辣椒	lāi jyāo
garlic	大蒜	tài swùn
MSG	味精	mī jīm
nuts	果仁	gwǒ ním
oil	油	yó

I'd like …, please.	请给涯 …	chyǔng bwēn yái …
one slice	一块	yēe kwày
a piece	一份	yēe fwùn
that one	那一个	yái yēe kè
two	两个	lyǔng kè

This dish is …	这个菜 …	é kè chòy …
(too) spicy	(太)辣	(tài) lāi
superb	好吃	hǎo shēe

That was delicious!
真好吃！ zēn hǎo shēe

I'm full.
吃饱啦。 shēe bǎo lā

breakfast	早饭	zǎo fūn
lunch	午饭	ng fūn
dinner	晚饭	mwūn fūn
drink (alcoholic)	酒	jyǒ
drink (nonalcoholic)	饮料	yǐm lyào

... water	··· 水	... shwǎy
boiled	必	bì
cold	凉开	lyǔng
sparkling mineral	矿泉汽	kwòon chwún chèe
still mineral	矿泉	kwòon chwún
(cup of) coffee ...	(一杯)咖啡 ···	(yēe bwāy) kā fī ...
(cup of) tea ...	(一杯)茶 ···	(yēe bwāy) tsá ...
with (milk)	加(牛念)	gā (nyó nyèn)
without (sugar)	不加(糖)	ng gā (tóon)
black tea	红茶	hwóon tsá
chrysanthemum tea	菊花茶	chyó fā tsá
green tea	绿茶	lyō tsá
jasmine tea	花茶	fā tsá
fresh drinking yoghurt	酸奶	swūn nāi
lychee juice	荔枝汁	lài chēe zēe
(orange) juice	(橙)汁	(chúng) zēe
soft drink	汽水	chèe shwǎy
sour plum drink	酸梅汁	swūn móy zēe
a ... of beer	一 ··· 啤酒	yēe ... pée jyǒ
glass	杯	bwāy
large bottle	大瓶	tài pyén
small bottle	小瓶	sèe pyén
a shot of (whisky)	一樽(威士忌)	yēe zōon (wī sēe jēe)
a bottle/glass of	一瓶/杯 ···	yēe pyén/bwāy ...
... wine	葡萄酒	pú tāo jyǒ
red	红	fóon
white	白	pā

I'll buy you a drink.
涯请客。 yái chyǔng kè

What would you like?
你想要麻个? ngée syǔng òy má gè

Cheers!
干杯! gwūn bī

I'm feeling drunk.
涯有点醉。 yái yō dēe zwày

客家话 – eating out

street eats		
bun (steamed)	包子	bāo lēe
cold clear bean-flour noodles	凉粉	lyúng fwùn
corn on the cob	包苏	bāo syǒo
dumpling (boiled)	饺子	jyáo lēe
flat bread with sesame seeds	烧饼	shāo byūn
pork pie	肉饼	nyǒ byūn
sticky rice in bamboo leaves	粽子	zòong lēe
wonton soup	馄饨	wóon tōon

special diets & allergies

Do you have vegetarian food?
有毛有素食食品？ — yō máo yō sòo shée shée pǐm

Could you prepare a meal without ...?
能不能做一个不放 … 的菜? — nyén ng nyén zwòr yēe kè ng fòon ... gè chòy

I'm allergic to ...	涯对 … 过敏。	yái dwày ... gwòr myěn
dairy produce	奶制品	nǎi zèe pǐm
eggs	鸡蛋	gāi chōong
meat	肉	nyǒ
nuts	果仁	gwǒ ním
seafood	海鲜	hǎi syēn

emergencies & health

Help!	救命！	jyò myèn
Go away!	走开！	zwǒr kwāy
Fire!	着火啦！	chōr hǒ lā

Watch out!	小心！	syǎo sīm

Could you please help?
你能帮涯吗？ — ngée nyén bōong yái mā

Can I use your phone?
涯能借用你的电话吗? — yái nyén jyà yòong ngée gè tyèn wǎ mā

I'm lost.
涯迷了路。 — yái mí lyǎo lòo

Where are the toilets?
厕所在哪儿? — tsèe swǒr tswōr lái lēe

Where's the police station?
派出所在哪里? — pài chōo swǒr tswōr lái lēe

Where's the nearest ...?	最近的 … 在哪儿?	zwày kǐm gè ... tswōr lái lēe
dentist	牙医	ngá yēe
doctor	医生	yēe sūm
hospital	医院	yēe ywùn
pharmacist	药房	yōr fóon

english–hakka dictionary

dictionary, words are marked as n (noun), a (adjective), v (verb), sg (singular), pl (plural), inf (informal) and
olite) where necessary.

A

accident (mishap) 厄运 ò yōon
accident (traffic) 意外 yèe òy
accommodation 食宿 shēe sōo
adaptor 插座 tsā tswǒr
address n 地址 tēe jěe
after 之后 jēe hǒ
air conditioning 空调 kōong tyáo
airplane 飞机 fēe jēe
airport 飞机场 fēe jēe chúng
alcohol 酒 jyǒ
all 所有 swǒr yō
allergy 过敏 gwòr myěn
ambulance 救护车 jyò hòo chā
and 和 hó
ankle 脚曾 tjyǒ zūng
antibiotics 抗生素 kwòong sūm sòo
arm 穷 kyóong
ATM 自动取款机 zēe tòong chěe kwǔn jēe

B

baby 哦亚里 ō ngá lēe
back (of body) 背囊 bòy nóong
backpack 背包 bòy bāo
bad 坏 fāi
bag 包 bāo
baggage 行李 húng lēe
bank 银行 ngyún hóong
bar 酒吧 jyǒ bā
bathroom 洗手间 sěr shǒ gūn
battery 电池 tyěn chée
beautiful 靓 lyùng
bed 床 chóong
beer 啤酒 pée jyǒ
before 前面 chyén myèn
behind 后面 hǒ myèn
bicycle 单车 dūn chā
big 大 tài
bill 帐单 jùng dūn
blanket 毛毯 māo tūn
blood group 血型 shyǎir shíng
boat 船 shwún
book (make a reservation) v 预定 yèe dùng
bottle 瓶 pyén
boy 攘子 núng tsǎi
brakes (car) 刹车 tsāi chā
breakfast 早饭 zǎo fūn
broken (out of order) 坏 fāi
bus 车 chā
business 商务 shūng wòo
buy v 买 māi

C

camera 照相机 jào syùng jēe
cancel 取消 chěe syāo
car 车 chā
cash n 现金 syǔm jēen
cash (a cheque) v 兑现 dwày syǔm
cell phone 手机 syǒ jēe
centre n 中心 jōong sīm
change (money) v 兑换 dwày wùn
cheap 便宜 pyén yēe
check (bill) 帐单 jùng dūn
check-in n 登记 dēn jēe
chest (body) 胸脯 shyōong póo
children 小孩子 syè ryén nēe
cigarette 烟 yōon
city 城市 shúng shèe
clean a 干净 gwūn chyùng
closed 关 gūn
cold a 冷 lūm
collect call 向受话者收费的电话 shùng syò wà jǎ syō fēe gè tyěn wā
come 来 lái
computer 电脑 tyěn nǎo
condom 皮孕套 pèe ywùn tào
contact lenses 隐形眼镜 yǐm shím ūn jyèm
cook v 煮 chǒo
cost n 值 chēe
credit card 信用卡 sìn yòong ká
currency exchange 外币兑换 ōy bèe dwày wùn
customs (immigration) 海关 hwǎy gwūn

D

dangerous 危险 wée shǔng
date (time) 日期 ngèe kēe

day 天 tyēn
delay v 推迟 twāy chée
dentist 牙医 ngá yēe
depart 出发 chōo fāi
diaper 尿布 ngyào bòo
dinner 晚饭 mwūn fūn
direct a 直接 chēe jyā
dirty 奈 nài
disabled 残废 chún fèe
discount v 打折 dǎ jě
doctor 医生 yēe sūm
double bed 双人床 sōong ryén chóong
double room 双人房 sōong ryén fóong
drink n 饮料 yǐm lyào
drive v 开 kwāy
driving licence 驾照 gà jyào
drug (illicit) 毒品 tōo pǐm

E

ear 拟多 ngěe dwōr
east 东 dōon
eat 吃 shēe
economy class 经济舱 jīm jèe tsūng
electricity 电 tyěn
elevator 电梯 tyěn twōy
email 电邮 tyěn yó
embassy 大使馆 tǎi sěe gwǔn
emergency 急症 jī zyǔn
English (language) 英语 yīng ngēe
evening 晚上 mān shàng
exit n 出口 chōo kwǒr
expensive 贵 kwày
eye 眼金 ngwǔn jīm

F

far 远 ywūn
fast 几乎 jēe hōo
father 爷俄 yá é
film (camera) 录像 lōo syùng
finger 手指 sǒr jěe
first-aid kit 急救箱 jī jyò syūng
first class 头等舱 tóo děm tsūng
fish n 吾 ng
food 食物 shēe wōo
foot 脚 kjyǎo
free (of charge) 免费 myūn fi
friend 朋友 pyén yō
fruit 水果 shwāy gwǒ
full 饱 bǎo

G

gift 礼物 lī mwōo
girl 妹子人 mòy tsěe ryén
glass (drinking) 杯 bwāy
glasses 眼剑 ngwǔn jyùm
go 去 hèe
good 好 hǎo
guide n 导游 dǎo yó

H

half n 一半 yēe bùn
hand 手 shwǒr
happy 欢喜 hwūn shēe
he 几 jée
head n 头 twór
heart 心 sīm
heavy 重 chōong
help 帮助 bōong chòo
here 列里 lyáir lēe
high 高 gāo
highway 高速公路 gāo sōo gōong lòo
hike v 布行 pòo húng
holiday 节日 jyē ngēe
homosexual 同性恋 tóong sìm lyèn
hospital 医院 yēe ywùn
hot 热 ngè
hotel 酒店 jyǒ dyùng
(be) hungry 饿 ngò
husband 老公 lǎo gōong

I

I 涯 yái
identification (card) 身份 shēm fwùn
ill 病 pyǔng
important 重要 chǒong yào
injury (harm) 伤害 shūng hài
injury (wound) 伤口 shūng kwǒo
insurance 保险 bǎo shǔng
internet 网 mwūng
interpreter 口译 kwǒo yī

J

jewellery 宝贝 bǎo bì
job 工作 gōong zwōr

K

key 琐石 swǒr shée
kilogram 公斤 gōong jīm

chen 厨房 chóo fóon
fe 刀 dāo

L

ndry (place) 洗衣房 sī yēe fóon
wyer 律师 lwāy sī
t (direction) 左 zǒr
g (body) 腿 twǎy
sbian 女同性恋 ngǐr tóong sìm lyèn
s 少 shǎo
tter (mail) 信 sìm
ht n 灯 dēm
e v 中意 jòong yèe
ck n 锁 swǒr
ng 长 chóong
st 丢失 dwāy shēe
ve v 爱 òy
ggage 行李 húng lī
nch 午饭 ng fūn

M

ail n 信 sìm
an 人 ryén
ap 地图 těe tóo
arket 市场 shèe chúng
atches 配对 pwày dwày
eat 肉 nyǒ
edicine 药 yōr
essage 信息 sìm sī
ilk 牛念 nyó nyèn
inute 分钟 fwūn jōong
obile phone 手机 syǒ jēe
oney 钱 chyén
onth 月 ngi·āir
orning 早晨头 tsāo sén twǒo
other 母亲 ōy jè
otorcycle 电动车 tyèn dòong chā
outh 嘴 jwòy

N

ame 名 myúng
ear 附近 fòo kwīm
eck n 江津 jyǔng jīm
ew 新的 sīm gè
ewspaper 新闻 sīm wún
ight 昂布晨 àm pōo sén
o (not at all) 吾 ng
o (not this) 吾是 ng hè
oisy 吵 tsáo
onsmoking 毛吃烟的 máo shēe yōon kè
orth 北 bě
nose 啤工 pǐ gōong
now 今来 jīn lái
number 号码 hǎo mā

O

old (people) 老 lǎo
old (things) 旧 chyǒ
one-way ticket 单程票 dūn tsún pyào
open a 开 kwāy
outside 外面 ngǒy myùn

P

passport 护照 fòo jào
pay v 付钱 fòo chyén
pharmacy 药房 yōr fóon
phonecard 电话卡 tyèn wā kā
photo 照片 jào pyēn
police 警察 jīm tsāi
postcard 明信片 míng sìm pyēn
post office 邮局 yó kyō
pregnant 有养 yō yōong
price n 价钱 gà chyén

Q

quiet a 安静 ūn chìm

R

rain n 雨 yǐ
razor 剃刀 tèe dāo
receipt n 收据 sōr jì
refund n 本还 būn wún
registered (mail) 注册的 jòo tsā gè
rent v 租 tsōo
repair v 修 syō
reserve v 预订 yèe dùng
restaurant 饭店 fūn dyùng
return (give back) 给回 būn fée
return (go back) 回来 fí lóy
return ticket 来回票 lóy fée pyào
right (direction) 右 yǒ
road 路 lòo
room n 房间 fóong gūn

S

safe a 安全 ūn chyén
sanitary napkin 卫生巾 wěe sūm jīm
seat n 座位 tswǒr wěe
send 寄 jèe

sex (intercourse) 性交 sìm jyāo
sex (gender) 性别 sìm pyé
shampoo 洗发水 sěe fā shwǎy
share (a dorm) 共用 gwōon yòong
she 她 jée
sheet (bed) 床单 chóong dūn
shirt 衬衫 chùn sūng
shoes 鞋 hái
shop n 商店 shùng dyùng
short 短 dwǔn
shower n 冲凉 tsōon lyúng
single room 单人房 dūn ryén fóong
skin n 皮肤 pí fōo
skirt n 裙 kwóon
sleep v 睡目 shwǎy mòo
slow 慢 mǔn
small 细 sèe
soap 翻甘 fūn gǔn
some 一些 yēe syā
soon 马上 mā shùng
south 南 nún
souvenir 纪念品 jèe nyùn pǐm
stamp 邮票 yó pyào
stand-by ticket 补票 bǒo pyào
station (train) 车站 chā chùng
stomach 胃 wèe
stop v 停 tíng
stop (bus) n 汽车站 chèe chā chùng
street 街道 gāi tào
student 学生 hō sām
sun 日头 ngēe tóo
sunscreen 防晒油 fóong sài yó
swim v 游泳 yó yǒong

T

tampon 棉塞 myén sāi
telephone n 电话 tyèn wā
temperature (weather) 温度 wūn tòo
that 来个 lyáir kè
they 几豆 jée dwōo
(be) thirsty 渴 hwǒr
this 这个 é kè
throat 喉咙 hó lōong
ticket 票 pyào
time 时间 shée jyūng
tired 累 kwǎy
tissues 事 sée
today 今日 jīn ngēe
toilet 厕所 tsèe swǒr
tomorrow 天光日 tyēn kwōong ngēe
tonight 今日昂布 jīn ngēe àm pōo
tooth 牙齿 ngá chēe
toothbrush 牙刷 ngá swōr
toothpaste 牙膏 ngá gāo
torch (flashlight) 手电筒 shǒ tyèn tǒong
tour n 向导游 shùng dǎo yó
tourist office 旅行局 lī húng kyō
towel 毛巾 máo jīm
train n 火车 hwǒr chā
translate 翻译 fūn yī
travel agency 旅行社 lī húng shā
travellers cheque 旅行支票 lī húng jēe pyào
trousers 裤 fòo
twin-bed room 标准房 pyāo zwǔng fóong

U

underwear 内衣 nǒy yēe
urgent 紧急 jīm jī

V

vacancy 空闲 kòong hún
vegetable n 蔬菜 swōr tsài
vegetarian a 素食 sòo shée
visa 签证 chyūng zèm

W

walk v 行 húng
wallet 钱包 chyén bāo
wash (something) 洗 sě
watch n 手表 shǒ byāo
water n 水 shwǎy
we 我们 ō mwūn
weekend 周末 jō māi
west 西 sī
wheelchair 轮椅 lóon yěe
when 几时 jěe shée
where 来里 lái lēe
who 莱萨 lǎi sá
why 为何 wèe hé
wife 老婆 lǎo pó
window 窗 tswūn
with 捞 lāo
without 毛 máo
woman 女人 ngěe ryén
write 写 syǎ

Y

yes 是 hè
yesterday 昨不日 tsyō pōo ngēe
you sg inf/pol 你/您 ngée/ngéen
you pl 你们 ngée mwén

Hunanese

TONES 134
ABOUT HUNANESE 135
PRONUNCIATION 136
LANGUAGE DIFFICULTIES 137
TIME & DATES 138
TRANSPORT & DIRECTIONS 139
ACCOMMODATION 140
BANKING & COMMUNICATIONS 141
SIGHTSEEING 142
SHOPPING 142
MEETING PEOPLE 143
MAKING CONVERSATION 144
FEELINGS & OPINIONS 147
FAREWELLS 147
EATING OUT 148
SPECIAL DIETS & ALLERGIES 151
EMERGENCIES & HEALTH 152
ENGLISH–HUNANESE DICTIONARY 153

tones

Hunanese is a tonal language ('tonal quality' refers to the raising and lowering of pitch on certain syllables). Tones in Hunanese fall on vowels and on z. The same combination of sounds pronounced with different tones can have a very different meaning.

Hunanese has six tones, including a neutral tone. In our pronunciation guide the six tones are indicated with accents or underscores on the letters, as shown in the table below for the vowel 'a'. Syllables with neutral tone are unmarked, and are usually pronounced in the middle of your natural pitch range.

Higher tones involve tightening the vocal cords to get a higher sounding pitch, while lower tones are made by relaxing the vocal cords to get a lower pitch. Bear in mind that the tones are relative to the natural vocal range of the speaker, eg high tones are pronounced towards the top of one's vocal range. Note also that some tones slide up or down in pitch.

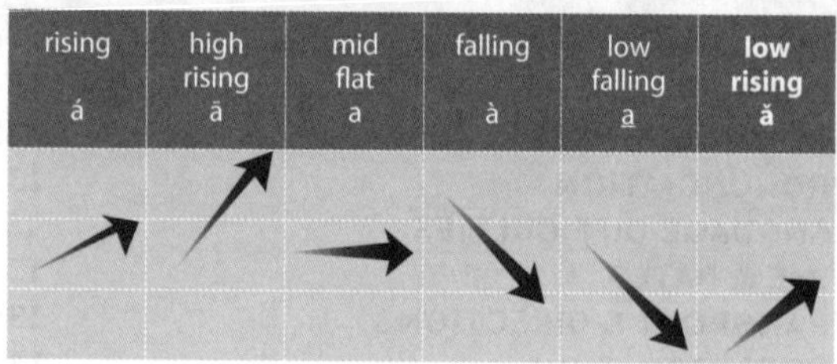

rising á
high rising ā
mid flat a
falling à
low falling a̲
low rising ă

HUNANESE
湖南话

about Hunanese

A Sino-Tibetan language, also known as Xiang, Hunanese (fŭ lăn fa̲ 湖南话) is spoken by around 35 million people in central and southwestern Húnán and parts of the nearby Sìchuān, Guǎngdōng and Guǎngxī provinces. Hunanese speakers are surrounded by speakers of several different languages – Mandarin, Gan, Tujia and Hmong – and their language has been influenced by these linguistic neighbours, and by Mandarin in particular. Hunanese is usually classified into two varieties: Old Xiang, which has absorbed fewer elements of Mandarin; and New Xiang, which is intelligible to speakers of the Southwestern Mandarin dialect. There are also local variations of these dialects. Hunanese speakers are noted for their skill as craftspeople, creating silk scarves and jade carvings that are sold internationally, and Húnán has a well-developed television and entertainment industry (the Chinese version of *Pop Idol* was filmed here). Try using a few of the phrases that follow and you'll be in some interesting historical company – Mao Zedong, who was born in Sháoshān, was perhaps the most well-known Hunanese speaker.

hunanese

pronunciation

Vowels		Consonants	
Symbol	**English sound**	**Symbol**	**English sound**
a	father	b	nipple; like English b but unvoiced
aw	loud	ch	cheat
e	bet	d	little; like English d but unvoiced
eu	as the 'oo' in 'soon' with the lips spread widely	f	fat
i	machine	g	tickle; like English g but unvoiced
o	vote	h	hat
u	rule	j	joke
uh	but	k	kit
uhw	uh followed by u	l	lot
y	i with the lips rounded	m	man
		n	not
		ng	ring (both at the start and at the end of words)
		p	pet
		s	sun
		sh	shut
		t	top
		ts	like tz, but with a strong puff of breath following
		tz	as in 'it's'
		y	yes
		w	win
		z	zero

In this chapter, the Hunanese pronunciation is given in pink after each phrase.

In Hunanese, vowels can appear in combinations of two (diphthongs). The vowels in combinations are always pronounced – they are simply pronounced in series.

Some vowels in Hunanese are nasalised (pronounced with air escaping through the nose). In our pronunciation guides the nasalised vowels are indicated with ng after the vowel.

For pronunciation of tones, see p134.

essentials

Yes./No.	是。/不是。	sz/bú sz
Please …	请…	chìn …
Hello.	你好。	lì hàw
Goodbye.	再见。	tzāi jyēng
Thank you.	谢谢你。	siē siē lì
Excuse me. (asking for directions or assistance)	不好意思。	bú hàw ī sz
Sorry. (general apology)	对不起啊。	tēi bú chì a

language difficulties

Do you speak (English)?
你晓得讲(英文)不? — lì siàw duh gàng (in wǔhn) bú

I (don't) speak Hunanese.
我(不)晓得讲湖南话。 — ngò (bú) siàw duh gàng fǔ lǎn fa

Do you understand?	你懂不啦?	lì dùhn bú la
I (don't) understand.	我(不)懂。	ngò (bú) dùhn
Could you please …?	累你…?	liá lì …
repeat that	再讲一遍	tzāi gàn í biēng
speak more slowly	讲慢点	gàng man dièng

numbers

0	零	lǐn	20	二十	eu sź
1	一	í	30	三十	san sź
2	二/两	eu	40	四十	sz sź
3	三	san	50	五十	ù sź
4	四	sz	60	六十	lúhw sź
5	五	ù	70	七十	chí sź
6	六	lúhw	80	八十	bá sź
7	七	chí	90	九十	jiùhw sź
8	八	bá	100	一百	í béu
9	九	jiùhw	1000	一千	í chieng
10	十	sź	1,000,000	一百万	í béu wan

time & dates

What time is it?	现在几点嗒?	sieng tzai jì dièng ta
It's (10) o'clock.	(十)点嗒。	(sź) dièng ta
Quarter past (10).	(十)点十五分。	(sź) dièng sź ù fuhn
Half past (10).	(十)点三十分。	(sź) dièng san sź fuhn
Quarter to (11). (literally: Forty-five minutes past (10).)	(十)点四十五分。	(sź) dièng sź sz ù fuhn

At what time (does it start)?
么子时候(开始)? — mò tz sž huhw (kai sz)

(It starts) At 10.
十点钟(开始)。 — sź dièng tzuhn (kai sz)

It's (18 October).
(十月十八号)。 — (sź yé sź bá haw)

now	现在	sieng tzai
today	今天	jin tieng
tonight	今天晚上	jin tieng wàn san
yesterday	昨天	tzǒ tieng
tomorrow	明天	mǐn tieng
afternoon	下午	sia ù
morning (after breakfast)	早上	tzàw san
morning (before lunch)	上午	san ù
sunrise	日出	zź chý
sunset	日落	zź ló
spring	春天	chyn tieng
summer	夏天	sia tieng
autumn	秋天	chiuhw tieng
winter	冬天	duhn tieng
Monday	星期一	shin chi í
Tuesday	星期二	shin chi eu
Wednesday	星期三	shin chi san
Thursday	星期四	shin chi sź
Friday	星期五	shin chi ù
Saturday	星期六	shin chi lúhw
Sunday	星期天	shin chi tieng

January	一月	í yé
February	二月	e̲u yé
March	三月	san yé
April	四月	sz yé
May	五月	ù yé
June	六月	lúhw yé
July	七月	chí yé
August	八月	bá yé
September	九月	jiuhw yé
October	十月	sź yé
November	十一月	sź í yé
December	十二月	sź e̲u yé

transport & directions

Is this the ... to (Chángshā)?	这个…去(长沙)吧?	gó gō ... keū (tza̲n sa) ba
boat	船	jye̲ng
bus	公共汽车	guhn gūhn chī cheu
train	火车	hò tseu
Where's a/the ...?	…在哪里?	... tza̲i là li
bank	银行	ĭn hăng
place to change foreign money	换外币的地方	tiàw wa̲i bēi di di̲ fang
post office	邮局	iŭhw jý

Is this the road to (the Yuèlù Academy)?
这是去(岳麓书院)的路吧? — gó sz̲ keū (ió lúhw shy yēng) di lúhw ba

Can you show me where it is on the map?
累你帮我找下它在地图上的位置好吧? — liá lì bang ngò tsàw ha ta tza̲i dī du̲hw sa̲ng di we̲i tz hàw ba

Can I get there on foot?
我可以走起去吧? — ngò kò ì tzùhw chì keū ba

What's the address?	地址是么子啦?	di tz sz mò tz la
How far is it?	好远咧?	hàw yèng lie
How do I get there?	何什走咧?	ǒ sz tzùhw lie
Turn left/right.	往左/右拐。	wáng tzò/iuhw gwài
It's straight ahead.	一直往前走。	í tź wan chiěng tzùhw

It's …	在…	tzai …
behind …	…的后头	… di huhw tuhw
in front of …	…的前头	… di chiěng tuhw
near …	…旁边	… bàng bieng
on the corner	拐弯的地方	gwài wan di di fang
opposite …	…的对过	… di dēi gō
there	那里	lā li

accommodation

Where's a guest house?
哪里有宾馆啊? — là li iùhw bin gòng a

Where's a hotel?
哪里有酒店啊? — là li iùhw jiùhw diēng a

Can you recommend somewhere cheap?
你可以推荐一个便宜的地方住不? — lì kò ì tei jiēng í go biěng i di di fang jy bú

Can you recommend somewhere good?
你可以推荐一个好的地方住不? — lì kò ì tei jiēng í go hàw di di fang jy bú

I'd like to stay at a locally run hotel.
我想住当地的酒店。 — ngò shiàng jy dang di jiùhw diēng

I'd like to book a room.
我想订间房。 — ngò siàng din gan fǎng

I have a reservation.
我预订嗒。 — ngò ȳ din da

Do you have a … room?	有…房吧?	iùhw … fǎng ba
double (suite)	套房	tāw fǎng
single	单人间	dan zǔhn gan
twin	双人间	shyang zǔhn gan

How much is it ...?	…好多钱啦?	... hàw do chiěng la
per night	一天	í tieng
per person	个人	í gō zǔhn

I'd like to stay for (three) nights.
我要住(三)天。 — ngò iāw jy (san) tieng

Could I have my key, please?
可以把房间钥匙把我不? — kò ì bà fǎng gan ió sž bà ngò bú

Can I get an extra (blanket)?
我可以多拿一条(毛毯)不? — ngò kò ì do lǎ í diǎw (mǎw tàn) bú

The (air conditioning) doesn't work.
(空调)有问题。 — (kuhn diǎw) iùhw wūhn dǐ

What time is checkout?
几点钟退房? — jì dièng tzuhn tei fǎng

Could I have my ..., please?	我想拿回我的…	ngò siàng lǎ fěi ngò di ...
deposit	押金	iá jin
passport	护照	fū tzāw

banking & communications

Where's a/an ...?	…在哪里?	... tzai là li
ATM	自动取款机	tz dūhn chỳ kuàn ji
public phone	公用电话	guhn in diēng fa
Where's the local internet cafe?	旁边有网吧不?	báng bieng iùhw uàng ba bú
I'd like to ...	我想…	ngò siàng ...
get internet access	上网	sang uàng
use a printer	打印	dà īn
use a scanner	扫描	sàw miǎw

What's your phone number?
您的电话号码是好多啦？ lì di diēng fa haw mà sz hàw do la

The number is ...
号码是··· haw mà sz ...

sightseeing

I'd like to see ...	我想看···	ngò siàng kān ...
What's that?	那是么子啦？	lā sz mò tz la
Can I take a photo?	我可以拍照吧？	ngò kò ì péu tzāw ba

I'd like to see some local sights.
我想去这里的景点看下子。 ngò siàng gēu go li di jìn dièng kān ha tz

I'd like to go somewhere off the beaten track.
我想去常规路线以外的地方玩。 ngò siàng kēu tzăw gwei luhw siēng ì uai di di fang uăn

How long is the tour?
这个行程要好久啊？ gó go hăng tzuhn iāw hàw jiùhw a

sightseeing		
Nányuè	南岳	lăn ió
Sháoshān Mountain	韶山	săw san
Yuèlù Academy	岳麓书院	ió lúhw shy yēng
Yuèlù Mountain	岳麓山	ió lúhw san
Yuèyáng Temple	岳阳楼	ió iăng lŭhw
Zhāngjiājiè	张家界	tzang jia gāi

shopping

Where's a ...?	···在哪里？	... tzai là li
camera shop	照相器材店	tzăw siāng chī tzăi diēng
market	市场	sz tzăn
souvenir shop	纪念品店	ji niēng pìn diēng
supermarket	超市	tsāw sz

I'd like to buy …	我想买…	ngō siàng mài …
Can I look at it?	我可以看下子吧?	ngō kò ì kān ha tz ba
What's this made from?	这用么子做的啦?	gó sz mò tz tzūhw di la
How much is it?	好多钱啦?	hàw do jiěng la
That's too expensive.	太贵嗒。	tāi gwēi da

Please write down the price.
累你把价钱写下来。 niá lì bà jiā jiěng shiè ha lǎi

I'll give you (five kuai).
把你(五块)钱。 bà lì (ù kwài) chiěng

Do you accept credit cards?
可以用信用卡吧? kò ì in shīn in kà ba

There's a mistake in the bill.
帐单上有点问题。 tzāng dan sang iùhw tièng uen tǐ

less	少	sào
enough	足够	tzúhw gūhw
more	多	do
bigger	大得多	dai déu do
smaller	细得多	shī déu do

meeting people

Hello.	你好。	lì hàw
Good morning.	早上好。	tzàw tzǎng hàw
Good afternoon.	下午好。	shia ù hàw
Good evening.	晚上好。	uàn sang hàw
Goodbye.	再见。	tzai jiēng
Good night.	晚安。	uàn an
Mr	先生	shieng suhn
Mrs	女士	nỳ sz̄
Ms/Miss	小姐/妹子	siàw jiè/mei tz

How are you?	你好吧?	lì hàw ba
Fine. And you?	还可以啊。 你咧?	hǎi kò ìa, lì lie
What's your name?	你叫么子名字啊?	lì jiāw mò tz mǐ tz a
My name is …	我叫…	ngò jiāw …
I'm pleased to meet you.	幸会。	shīn fei

This is my …	这是我的…	gó sz ngò di …
brother (older)	哥哥	go go
brother (younger)	弟弟	dī di
child	细伢子	shì ngǎ tz
daughter	妹子	mei tz
father	爷	iǎ
friend	朋友	bǔhn iùhw
husband	老公	làw guhn
mother	娘	niǎng
partner (intimate)	男朋友 m	lǎn bǔhn iùhw
	女朋友 f	nỳ bǔhn iùhw
son	崽	tzài
sister (older)	姐姐	jiè jie
sister (younger)	妹妹	méi mei
wife	堂客	dǎng kéu

making conversation

Do you live here?	你住这里吧?	lì jy gó li ba
Where are you going?	去哪里啦?	kēu là li la
Do you like it here?	喜欢这里吧?	shì hong gó li ba
I love it here.	我時喜欢这里。	ngò téu shì hong gó li
Have you eaten?	呷饭哒冒?	chiá fan da maw
Are you here on holiday?	你是来这里旅游的吧?	lì sz lǎi gó li lỳ iǔhw di ba

I'm here …	我来这里…	lì ngò lǎi gó li …
for a holiday	旅游	lỳ iǔhw
on business	出差	chý tsai
to study	留学	liǔhw sió

How long are you here for?
你要在这里住好久? lì iāw tzai gó li jý hàw jiùhw

I'm here for (four) weeks.
我住（四）个礼拜。 — ngò jy (sz̄) go lì bāi

Can I take a photo (of you)?
我可以照（你）吧？ — ngò kò ì tzāw (lì) ba

Do you speak (Hunanese dialect)?
你晓得讲（湖南话）吧？ — lì siàw déu gàng (fŭ lăn fa) ba

What language do you speak at home?
你老家讲么子话啊？ — lì làw jia gàng mò tz hua a

What do you call this in (Hunanese dialect)?
这用（湖南话）何什讲啦？ — kó in (fŭ lăn fa) ŏ sz gàng la

What's this called?
这喊么子啦？ — gó hàn mò tz la

I'd like to learn some (Hunanese).
我想学点（湖南话）。 — ngò shiàng shió dieng (fŭ lăn fa)

Would you like me to teach you some English?
你要我教你英文吧？ — lì iāw ngò gāw lì in wŭhn ba

Is this a local custom?
这是地方风俗吧？ — gó sz di fang hun súhw ba

local talk

Great!	蛮好！	măn hàw
It's OK.	还可以。	hăi kò ì
Just a minute.	等下子。	dùhn ha tz
Just joking.	我是斗把的。	ngò sz dūhw bā di
Maybe.	有可能。	iùhw kò lŭhn
No problem.	冒事。	maw sz
No way!	不可能！	bŭ kò lŭhn
Sure, whatever.	可以。	kò ì
That's enough!	够哒。	gūhw da

Where are you from?	你是哪里来的咧?	lì sz là li lǎi di lie
I'm from ...	我从…来。	ngò tzǔhn ... lǎi
Australia	澳大利亚	ngāw dā lī iā
Canada	加拿大	jia lǎ dā
England	英国	in gó
New Zealand	新西兰	shin shi lǎn
the USA	美国	mèi gó
What's your occupation?	你做么子的啊?	lì tzūhw mò tz di a
I'm a/an ...	我是…	ngò sz ...
businessperson	做生意的	tzūhw suhn ī di
office worker	白领	béu lìn
tradesperson	工匠	guhn jiang
How old ... ?	…好多岁嗒?	... hàw do suēi da
are you	你	lì
is your daughter	你妹子	lì mei tz
is your son	你崽	lì tzài
I'm ... years old.	我…岁。	ngò ... suēi
He/She is ... years old.	他/她…岁。	ta ... suēi
Too old!	太老嗒!	tāi làu da
I'm younger than I look.	我还小咧。	ngò hǎi siàw lie
Are you married?	你结婚了嗒冒?	lì jié fuhn da maw
Do you have a family?	你成家嗒吧?	lì tzǔhn jia da ba
I live with someone.	我有伴嗒。	ngò iùhw bong da
I'm ...	我…	ngò ...
single	单身	dan suhn
married	结婚嗒	jié fuhn da
Do you like ...?	你喜欢…吧?	lì shì hong ... ba
I (don't) like ...	我(不)喜欢…	ngò (bú) shì hong ...
art	艺术	nyī shý
film	看电影	kān diēng ìn
music	听歌	tīn go
reading	看书	kān shy
sport	运动	yū dūhn

feelings & opinions

I'm (not) …	我(不)…	ngò (bú) …
Are you … ?	你…吧?	lì … ba?
cold	冷	lùhn
hot	热	lé
hungry	饿	ngo
thirsty	口干	kùhw gan
tired	累	liá
I (don't) feel …	我(不)觉得…	ngò (bú) chió déu …
Do you feel …?	你觉得…吧?	lì chió déu … ba
happy	高兴	gaw shīn
sad	不高兴	bǔ gaw shīn
worried	急	jí
What do you think of it?	你觉得怎么样?	lì chió déu tzùhn mo ian
It's …	它…	ta …
awful	连不好	liěng bú hàw
beautiful	好漂亮的	hàw piāw liang di
boring	无聊	ǔ liǎw
great	几好的	jì hàw di
interesting	好有味的	hàw iùhw uei di
OK	还可以	hǎi kò ì
strange	奇怪	jǐ guāi

farewells

Tomorrow I'm leaving.
明天我要走嗒。 mǐn tieng ngò iāw tzuhw da

If you come to (Scotland) you can stay with me.
有机会来(苏格兰),可以来找我。 iùhw jì fēi lǎi (suhw géu lǎn) kò ì lǎi tzàw ngò

Keep in touch!	保持联系!	bàw tsź liěng shī
Here's my (address).	这是我的(地址)。	gó sz ngò di (di dz)
What's your (email)?	你的(邮箱)是么子?	lì di (iǔhw siang) sz mò tz

well-wishing

Bon voyage!	一路平安！	í luhw bǐn ngan
Congratulations!	恭喜，恭喜！	guhn shì, guhn shì
Good luck!	祝你好运！	tzúhw lì hàw yn
Happy birthday!	生日快乐！	suhn zź kuāi ló
Happy New Year!	新年好！	shin niēng hàw

eating out

Where would you go for (a) ...?	…去哪里咧？	... kēu là li lie
banquet	办酒席	ban jiùhw shí
celebration	举行庆祝会	jỳ shǐn chīn tzúhw fei
cheap meal	呷便宜点的	chí biēng i dièng di
local specialities	地方小吃	di fang siàw chiá
yum cha	喝茶	hó tzǎ

Can you recommend a ...?	你可以推荐一个…吧？	lì kò ì tei jiēng í go ... ba
bar	酒吧	jiùhw ba
cafe	咖啡屋	ka fei ú
noodle house	面馆	mieng gòng
dish	盘	bǒng
restaurant	饭馆	fān gòng
(wonton) stall	（馄饨）摊子	(fǔhn tuhn) tan tz
street vendor	路边摊	luhw bieng tan
teahouse	茶馆	tzǎ gòng

I'd like (a/the) ...	我要…	ngò iāw ...
table for (five)	一张（五个人的）桌子	í tzan (ù go zǔhn di) tzó tz
bill	帐单	tzān dan
drink list	酒水单	jiùhw shyèi dan
local speciality	地方特色菜	di fang teú séu tsāi
menu	菜单	tsāi dan
(non)smoking table	（不）呷烟的桌子	(bú) chiá ieng di tzó tz

Are you still serving food?
还有呷的吧? hǎi iùhw chiá di ba

What would you recommend?
有么子推荐菜吧? iùhw mò tz tei jiēng tsāi ba

What do you normally eat for (breakfast)?
(早饭)一般呷么子? (tzàw fa̲n) í ban chiá mò tz

What's in that dish?
这只菜是么子家伙做的啦? gó tzá tsāi sz̲ mò tz jia ho tzūhw di la

What's that called?
那个喊么子啰? lá go ha̲n mò tz lo

I'll have that.
来一个啰。 lǎi í go lo

I'd like it with ...	多放点···	do fāng dièng ...
I'd like it without ...	不要放···	bú iāw fāng ...
chilli	辣椒	lá jiaw
garlic	大蒜	da̲i sōng
MSG	味精	wēi jin
nuts	果仁	gò zǔhn
oil	油	iǔhw

I'd like ..., please.	我要···	ngò iāw ...
one slice	一块	í kwài
a piece	一份	í fuhn
a sandwich	一个三明治	í go san mǐn tz
that one	那个	lā go
two	两个	liǎng go

This dish is ...	这只菜···嗒。	gó tzá tsāi ... da
(too) spicy	(太)辣	(tāi) lá
superb	几好的	jì hàw di

That was delicious!	几好呷!	jì hàw chiá
I'm full.	呷饱嗒。	chiá bàw da

breakfast	早饭	tzàw fan
lunch	中饭	tzuhn fan
dinner	夜饭	ia fan
drink (alcoholic)	酒	jiùhw
drink (nonalcoholic)	饮料	ìn liaw

… water	…水	… shyèi
boiled	开	kai
cold	冷开	lùhn kai
sparkling mineral	矿泉汽	kuāng chyěng chī
still mineral	矿泉	kuāng chyěng

(cup of) coffee …	(一杯)咖啡…	(í bei) ka fei …
(cup of) tea …	(一杯)茶…	(í bei) tzǎ …
with (milk)	加(牛奶)	jia (liǔhw lài)
without (sugar)	不加(糖)	bú jia (dǎng)

fresh drinking yoghurt	酸奶	song lài
lychee juice	荔枝	lī tz
orange juice	橙汁	tzúhn tź
soft drink	汽水	chī shyèi
sour plum drink	酸梅汤	song měi tang

black tea	红茶	hǔhn tzǎ
chrysanthemum tea	菊花茶	jý hua tzǎ
green tea	绿茶	lúhw tzǎ
jasmine tea	花茶	fa tzǎ
oolong tea	乌龙茶	u lěn tzǎ

What are you drinking?
喝么子? — hǒ mò tz

I'll buy you a drink.
我请客。 — ngò chìn kéu

What would you like?
你要点么子? — lì iāw dièng mò tz

Cheers!
干杯! — gan bei

I'm feeling drunk.
我有点醉嗒。 — ngò iùhw dièng tzèi da

a … of beer	一…啤酒	í … bǐ jiùhw
glass	杯	bei
large bottle	大瓶	da̲i bǐn
small bottle	细瓶	shī bǐn
a shot of (whisky)	一樽(威士忌)	í tzun (uei sz̄ jī)
a bottle/glass of … wine	一瓶/杯…葡萄酒	í bǐn/bei … bǔ dǎw jiùhw
red	红	hǔhn
white	白	béu

street eats

cold clear bean-flour noodles	凉粉	liǎng fùhn
dumpling (boiled)	饺子	jiàw tz
dumpling (fried)	锅贴	go tié
dumpling (steamed)	包子	bau tz
pork pie (large)	肉饼	zúhw bìn
pork pie (small)	馅饼	shiēng bìn
sticky rice in bamboo leaves	粽子	zūhn tz
stinky bean curd	臭豆腐	tsūhw du̲hw fu
wonton soup	馄饨	fǔhn tuhn

special diets & allergies

Do you have vegetarian food?
有素食食品吧？ iùhw sūhw sź ba

Could you prepare a meal without …?
可以做一个不放…的菜吧？ kó í tzūhw í go bú fāng … di tsāi ba

I'm allergic to …	我对…过敏。	ngò dēi … gō mìn
dairy produce	奶制品	lài tz pìn
eggs	鸡蛋	jī dan
meat	肉	zúhw
nuts	果仁	gò zŭhn
seafood	海鲜	hài shieng

emergencies & health

Help!	救命啊！	jiūhw min a
Go away!	走开！	tzùhw kai
Fire!	起火嗒！	chì hò da
Watch out!	小心！	shiàw shin

Could you please help?
你可以帮下我吧？ — lì kò ì bang ha ngò ba

Can I use your phone?
我可以用下你的电话吧？ — ngò kò ì i ha lì di diēng fa ba

I'm lost.
我迷路嗒。 — ngò mĭ luhw da

Where are the toilets?
厕所在哪里啊？ — tséu sò tzai là li a

Where's the police station?
公安局在哪里？ — guhn ngan jý tzai là li

Where's the nearest …?	最近的…在哪里？	tzēi jin di … tzai là li
dentist	牙医	iă i
doctor	医生	i suhn
hospital	医院	i yēng
pharmacist	药房	ió fāng

english–hunanese dictionary

dictionary, words are marked as n (noun), a (adjective), v (verb), sg (singular), pl (plural), inf (informal) and olite) where necessary.

A

accident (mishap) 灾祸 tzai hō
accident (traffic) 交通事故 jiaw tuhn sz gū
accommodation 食宿 sź súhw
address n 地址 di tz
after 之后 tz huhw
air conditioning 空调 kuhn diǎw
airplane 飞机 fei ji
airport 机场 ji tzǎn
alcohol 酒 jiùhw
all 所有的 sò iùhw di
allergy 过敏 gò mìn
ambulance 救护车 jiūhw fū tseu
and 和 hǒ
ankle 踝 guài
antibiotics 抗生素 kāng suhn sō
arm 手杆子 sùhw gàn tz
ATM 自动取款机 tz dūhn chỳ kuàn ji

B

baby 毛毛 mǎw māw
back (of body) 背 bēi
backpack 背包 bei baw
bad 坏 fai
bag 包 baw
baggage 行李 shǐn lì
bank 银行 ǐn hǎng
bar 吧 ba
bathroom 浴室 zúhw sź
battery 电池 diēng tź
beautiful 好看 hàw kān
bed 床 jyǎng
beer 啤酒 bǐ jiùhw
before 之前 tz jiěng
behind 之后 tz huhw
bicycle 单车 dan tseu
big 大 dai
bill 帐单 tzān dan
blanket 毯子 tàw tz
blood group 血型 shyé shǐn
boat 船 jyěng
book (make a reservation) v 预订 ȳ din
bottle 瓶子 bǐn tz
boy 伢子 ngǎ tz
brakes (car) 煞车 sá tseu
breakfast 早饭 tzàw fan
broken (out of order) 坏咖嗒 fai gà da
bus 公共汽车 guhn gūhn chī cheu
business 生意 suhn ī
buy v 买 mài

C

camera 相机 shiāng ji
cancel 取消 chỳ shiaw
car 汽车 chī tseu
cash n 现金 shieng jin
cell phone 手机 sùhw ji
centre n 中心 tsuhn shin
change (money) n 零钱 ling jiěng
cheap 便宜 biěng ǐ
check (bill) 帐单 tzān dan
check-in n 登记 duhn jī
chest (body) 胸口 shin kùhw
children 细伢子 shī ngǎ tz
cigarette 香烟 shiang ieng
city 城市 tzǔhn sz
clean a 干净 gan jin
closed 关闭 guan bēi
cold a 冷 lùhn
collect call 对方付费电话
dēi fang fū fēi diēng fa
come 来 lai
computer 电脑 diēng làw
condom 避孕套 bēi ȳn tāw
contact lenses 隐形眼镜 ìn shǐn ngàn jīn
cook v 烹饪 puhn zūhn
cost n 花费 fa fēi
credit card 信用卡 shīn in kà
currency exchange 货币汇兑 hō bēi fēi dēi
customs (immigration) 海关 hài guan

D

dangerous 危险 uěi shièng
date (time) 日期 zź chi
day 天 tieng
delay v 延迟 ieng tź
dentist 牙科医生 iǎ ko i suhn

depart 出发 chý fá
diaper 尿布 liaw bū
dinner 夜饭 ia fan
direct a 直接 tź jié
dirty 邋遢 lá tá
disabled 残废 tzăn fēi
discount v 打折 dà tzéu
doctor 医生 i suhn
double bed 双人床 shyang zŭhn chyăng
double room 套房 tāw făn
drink n 饮料 ìn liaw
drive v 开车 kai tseu
driving licence 驾照 jiā tzāw
drug (illicit) 毒品 dúhw pìn

E

ear 耳朵 èu do
east 东 duhn
eat 吃 chiá
economy class 经济舱 jin jī tsang
electricity 电 diēng
elevator 电梯 diēng ti
email 电子邮件 diēng tz iŭhw jieng
embassy 大使馆 dai sz gòng
emergency 紧急状况 jìn jí jīn kuāng
English (language) 英文 in wŭhn
evening 晚上 uàn san
exit n 出口 chý kùhw
expensive 贵 guēi
eye 眼睛 ngàn jin

F

far 远 yèng
fast 快 kuāi
father 爷 iă
film (camera) 胶卷 jiaw jyèng
finger 手指 sùhw tz
first-aid kit 急救箱 jí jiūhw shiang
first class 头等舱 dŭhw dùhn tsang
fish n 鱼 ỳ
food 食物 sź ú
foot 脚 jió
free (of charge) 免费 mièng fēi
friend 朋友 bŭhn iùhw
fruit 水果 shyèi gò
full 饱 bàw

G

gift 礼物 lì ú
girl 妹子 mei tz
glass (drinking) 杯子 bei tz
glasses 眼镜 ngàn jīn
go 去 kēu
good 好 hàw
guide n 向导 shiāng dàw

H

half n 一半 í bōng
hand 手 sùhw
happy 高兴 gaw shīn
he 他 ta
head n 头 dŭhw
heart 心 shin
heavy 重 tzuhn
help 帮助 ban tsūhw
here 这里 gó li
high 高 gaw
highway 高速公路 gaw súhw guhn luhw
hike v 徒步旅行 dŭhw bu lỳ shĭn
holiday 假期 jià chi
homosexual 同性恋 dŭhn shīn liēng
hospital 医院 i yēng
hot 热 yé
hotel 旅馆 lỳ gòng
(be) hungry 饿 ngo
husband 老公 làw guhn

I

I 我 ngò
identification (card) 身份证 suhn fūhn tzūhn
ill 生病 suhn bin
important 重要 tzūhn iāw
injury (harm) 侮辱 ù zúhw
injury (wound) 伤口 sang kùhw
insurance 保险 bàw shièng
internet 英特网 in téu uàng
interpreter 翻译 fan í

J

jewellery 珠宝 jy bàu
job 工作 guhn tzó

K

key 钥匙 ió sz
kilogram 公斤 guhn jin
kitchen 厨房 jỳ făng
knife 刀子 daw tz

undry (place) 洗衣店 shì i diēng
wyer 律师 lý sz
ft (direction) 左 tzò
g (body) 腿 tèi
sbian 女同性恋 lỳ dǔhn shīn liēng
ss 少 sàw
tter (mail) 信 shīn
ht n 光 guang
e v 喜欢 shì hong
ck n 锁 sò
ng 长 tzǎng
st 失咖嗒 séu gà da
ve v 爱 ngāi
ggage 行李 shǐn lì
nch 中饭 tzuhn fan

M

ail n 信 shin
an 男人 lǎn zǔhn
ap 地图 dī dǔhw
arket 市场 sz tzǎng
atches 火柴 hò tzǎi
eat 肉 zúhw
edicine 药 ió
essage 信息 shīn shí
ilk 牛奶 niǔhw lài
inute 分钟 fuhn tzuhn
obile phone 手机 sùhw ji
oney 钱 jiěng
onth 月 yé
orning 早上 tzàw san
other 娘 niǎng
otorcycle 摩托车 mó tó tseu
outh 嘴巴 tzèi ba

N

ame 名字 mǐn tz
ear 近 jin
eck n 颈根 jìn guhn
ew 新 shin
ewspaper 报纸 bāw tz
ight 晚上 wàn san
o (not at all) 一点也不 í diēng iè bú
oisy 吵死哒 tsàw sz da
onsmoking 禁止吸烟 jīn tz shí ieng
orth 北 béu
ose 鼻子 bǐ tz
ow 现在 shieng tzai
umber 数字 sūhw tz

O

old (people) 老 làw
old (things) 旧 jiuhw
one-way ticket 单程票 dan tzǔhn piāw
open a 开的 kai di
outside 外面 wai mieng

P

passport 护照 fū tzāw
pay v 付钱 fū jiě
pharmacy 药房 ió fǎng
phonecard 电话卡 diēng fa kà
photo 像片 shiáng piēng
police 警察 jìn tsá
postcard 明信片 mǐn shīn piēng
post office 邮局 iǔhw jý
pregnant 怀孕 fāi ȳn
price n 价格 jiā géu

Q

quiet a 安静 ngan jin

R

rain n 雨 ỳ
razor 刮胡刀 guá fū daw
receipt n 收据 tzuhw jȳ
refund n 退款 tēi kòng
registered (mail) 挂号 guā haw
rent v 出租 chý tzuhw
repair v 修理 shiuhw lì
reserve v 预订 ȳ din
restaurant 饭馆 fan gòng
return (give back) 还 fǎn
return (go back) 回来 fěi lai
return ticket 返程票 fàn tzǔhn piāw
right (direction) 右 iuhw
road 路 iuhw
room n 房间 fǎng gan

S

safe a 安全 ngan jyeng
sanitary napkin 卫生巾 uēi suhn jin
seat n 座位 tzo uei
send 寄 jī
sex (intercourse) 性 shīn
sex (gender) 性别 shīn bíe
shampoo 洗发精 shì fá jin

L

english–hunanese

share (a dorm) 分享 fuhn shiàng
she 她 ta
sheet (bed) 床单 jyǎng dan
shirt T恤衫 ti shyé san
shoes 鞋 hǎi
shop n 商店 sang diēng
short 短 dòng
shower n 淋浴 lǐn tzúhw
single room 单人间 dan zǔhn gan
skin n 皮肤 bǐ fu
skirt n 裙子 juě tz
sleep v 困觉 kuūhn gāw
slow 慢 man
small 细 shī
soap 肥皂 fěi tzāw
some 一些 í shie
soon 马上 mà san
south 南 lǎn
souvenir 纪念品 jī niēng pìn
stamp 邮票 iǔhw piāw
stand-by ticket 站台票 tzan tǎi piāw
station (train) 火车站 hò tseu tzan
stomach 胃 uēi
stop v 停止 dǐn tz
stop (bus) n 站台 tzān dǎi
street 街 gai
student 学生 shió suhn
sun 太阳 tāi iǎng
sunscreen 防晒油 fǎng sāi iǔhw
swim v 游泳 iǔhw ìn

T

tampon 止血棉球 tz shié miěng jiǔhw
telephone n 电话 diēng fa
temperature (weather) 温度 wuhn dūhn
that 那个 lā go
they 他们 ta muhn
(be) thirsty 口干 kò gan
this 这个 gó go
throat 喉咙 hǔhw lǔhn
ticket 票 piāw
time 时间 sž gan
tired 累 liá
tissues 卫生纸 uēi suhn tz
today 今天 jin tieng
toilet 厕所 tséu sò
tomorrow 明天 mǐn tieng
tonight 今天晚上 jin tieng wàn san
tooth 牙齿 ngǎ tz
toothbrush 牙刷 iǎ shyá
toothpaste 牙膏 iǎ gaw
torch (flashlight) 手电筒 sùhw diēng dǔhn
tour n 旅行 lỳ shǐn
tourist office 旅行社 lỳ shǐn séu
towel 毛巾 mǎw jin
train n 火车 hò tseu
translate 翻译 fan í
travel agency 旅行社 lỳ shǐn sūh
travellers cheque 旅行支票 lỳ shǐn tz piāw
trousers 裤子 kù tz
twin-bed room 双人间 shyang zǔhn gan

U

undershirt 内衣 lēi i
underpants 内裤 lēi kù
urgent 紧急 jìn jí

V

vacancy 空缺 kūhn chyé
vegetable n 蔬菜 suhw tsāi
vegetarian a 素食者 sūhw sź tzèu
visa 签证 chieng tzūhn

W

walk v 步行 bu shǐng
wallet 钱包 jiěng baw
wash (something) 洗 shì
watch n 看 kān
water n 水 shyèi
we 我们 ngò muhn
weekend 周末 tzuhw mó
west 西 shi
wheelchair 轮椅 lǔhn ì
when 当…时 dan … sž
where 在哪里 tzai là li
who 哪个 la gō
why 何解 ǒ gài
wife 堂客 dǎng kéu
window 窗户 chyang fu
with 和 hǒ
without 冒得 maw déu
woman 堂客 dǎng kéu
write 写 shiè

Y

yes 是 sz
yesterday 昨天 tzǒ tieng
you sg inf 你 lì
you sg pol 你郎家 lì lang ga
you pl 你们 lì muhn

Shanghainese

TONES 158
ABOUT SHANGHAINESE 159
PRONUNCIATION 160
LANGUAGE DIFFICULTIES 161
TIME & DATES 161
TRANSPORT & DIRECTIONS 163
ACCOMMODATION 164
BANKING & COMMUNICATIONS 165
SIGHTSEEING 166
SHOPPING 166
MEETING PEOPLE 167
MAKING CONVERSATION 168
FEELINGS & OPINIONS 171
FAREWELLS 171
EATING OUT 172
SPECIAL DIETS & ALLERGIES 175
EMERGENCIES & HEALTH 175
ENGLISH–SHANGHAINESE DICTIONARY 177

tones

Shanghainese is a tonal language ('tonal quality' refers to the raising and lowering of pitch on certain syllables). Tones in Shanghainese fall on vowels and on z and n. In this chapter Shanghainese is represented with four tones, as well as a fifth one, the neutral tone. Apart from the unmarked neutral tone, we have used symbols above the vowels to indicate each tone, as shown in the table below for the vowel 'a'. Bear in mind that the tones are relative to the natural vocal range of the speaker, eg the high tone is pronounced at the top of one's vocal range. Note also that some tones slide up or down in pitch.

high tone ā	high rising tone á	low falling-rising tone ǎ	high falling tone à

about Shanghainese

In dynamic Shànghǎi nothing sits still for long. Even Shanghainese (zǔng hay ǎy woo 上海话) is evolving as the city attracts immigrants and entrepreneurs, opportunists and global citizens. The most important dialect of Wu Chinese, Shanghainese has around 14 million speakers and is similar to the dialects of Níngbō, Sūzhōu and Kūnshān. Like the city itself, the dialect might appear brash and uppity: it's not mutually intelligible with other Wu dialects nor is it with Standard Mandarin. Nonetheless, those who come seeking opportunity in Shànghǎi are infusing the dialect with elements of Mandarin, so that Shanghainese is effectively experiencing a generation gap of its own as it moves from the historic Bund to the futuristic skyline of Pǔdōng. The younger generation of Shànghǎi residents casually flip Mandarin idioms and expressions into their banter and, with government campaigns to encourage the use of Mandarin only, some fear for the future of the dialect. But, while Shanghainese is rarely heard in schools or in the media, it remains a source of pride and identity for many Shànghǎi natives.

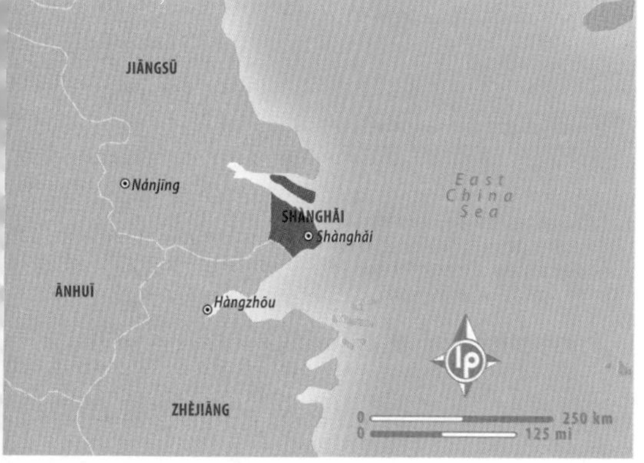

pronunciation

Vowels		Consonants	
Symbol	**English sound**	**Symbol**	**English sound**
a	father	b	bed
aw	saw	ch	cheat
ay	say	d	dog
ee	see	ds	lads
er	mother (without the 'r')	f	fun
ew	few	g	go
i	bit (very short)	h	hot
o	mock (very short)	j	jump
oe	as the 'e' in 'send', with rounded lips	k	kid
oo	took	l	lot
uh	uh-huh	m	man
ung	rung	n	not
urr	purr (strongly pronounced 'rr')	ng	ring
		p	pet
		r	run
		s	sun
		sh	shot
		t	top
		ts	cats
		v	very
		w	win
		y	yes
		z	zero
		zh	pleasure

In this chapter, the Shanghainese pronunciation is given in red after each phrase.

In Shanghainese, some consonants and consonant combinations (dz, ng, m, sz and z) can appear at the start of words, or represent an entire word.

For pronunciation of tones, see p158.

essentials

Yes./No.	是。/勿是。	ź/vŭh z
Please …	请 …	ching …
Hello.	侬好。	nóong haw
Goodbye.	再会。	dsāy way
Thank you.	谢谢侬。	zhă zhā noong
Excuse me. (to get past)	让一让。	nyŭng yī nyung
Excuse me. (asking for direction/assistance)	勿好意思。	vŭh haw yēe sz
Sorry.	对勿起。	day vūh chee

language difficulties

Do you speak (English)?
侬会讲(英语)伐? — noong wǎy duh gung (yīng new) va

Do you understand?
侬懂伐? — noong doong vā

I (don't) understand.
吾(勿)懂。 — ngoo (vŭh) doong

I (don't) speak Shanghainese.
吾(勿)会讲上海闲话。 — ngoo (vŭh) way duh gung zŭng hay ǎy woo

Could you please …?	请侬 …?	ching nōong …
repeat that	再讲一遍	dsāy gung yi bee
speak more slowly	慢点讲	mǎy dēe gung

time & dates

What time is it?	现在几点钟?	yěe zay jee dēe dsoong
It's (10) o'clock.	(十)点钟。	(zŭh) dee dsoong
Quarter past (10).	(十)点一刻。	(zŭh) dee yi kūh
Half past (10).	(十)点半。	(zŭh) dee boe
Quarter to (11). (literally: Forty-five minutes past (10).)	(十)点四十五分。	(zŭh) dee sz sūh ňg ferng

numbers					
0	零	líng	20	二十	nyáy suh
1	一	yī	30	三十	sāy suh
2	二/两	nyée/lyúng	40	四十	sz sūh
3	三	sày	50	五十	ňg suh
4	四	sz	60	六十	lŏ suh
5	五	ňg	70	七十	chi sūh
6	六	ló	80	八十	buh sūh
7	七	chī	90	九十	jer sūh
8	八	būh	100	一百	yī buh
9	九	jer	1000	一千	yī chee
10	十	zúh	1,000,000	一百万	yī buh vay

At what time (does it start)?
萨辰光(开始)? sa zēng kwung (kāy sz)

(It starts) At 10.
十点钟(开始)。 zǔh dee dsoong (kāy sz)

It's (18 October).
(十月十八号)。 (zǔh ywi zǔh buh aw)

yesterday	昨日	zŏ nyi
today	今朝	jīng dsaw
now	现在	yěe zay
tonight	今晚夜里	jīng dsaw yă der
tomorrow	明朝	mǐng dsaw
sunrise	日出	zǔh tsuh
sunset	日落	zǔh lo
this ...	今朝 ...	jīng dsaw ...
afternoon	下半日	wŏo bōe nyi
morning (after breakfast)	早上	dsaw zūng
morning (before lunch)	上半日	zǔng bōe nyi
spring	春天	tsērng tee
summer	夏天	wŏo tee
autumn	秋天	cher tee
winter	冬天	dōong tee

Monday	礼拜一	lĕe ba yī
Tuesday	礼拜二	lĕe ba lyúng
Wednesday	礼拜三	lĕe ba sày
Thursday	礼拜四	lĕe ba sz
Friday	礼拜五	lĕe ba ňg
Saturday	礼拜六	lĕe ba ló
Sunday	礼拜天	lĕe ba tèe

January	一月份	yī ywi verng
February	二月份	lyŭng ywī verng
March	三月份	sāy ywi verng
April	四月份	sz ywī verng
May	五月份	ňg ywī verng
June	六月份	lŏ ywi verng
July	七月份	chi ywī verng
August	八月份	buh ywī verng
September	九月份	jer ywī verng
October	十月	zŭh ywi
November	十一月	zŭh yi ywi
December	十二月	zŭh nyee ywi

transport & directions

Is this the … to (Hàngzhōu)?	这只 … 到 (杭州) 去吗?	gŭh dsuh … daw (hŭng dser) chee vā
boat	船	zóe
bus	公车	gōong tswoo
train	火车	hoo tswōo

Where's a/the …?	… 在哪里?	… luh ă lēe duh
bank	银行	nyīng ung
place to change foreign money	换外币的地方	woe ngă bēe uh dĕe fung
post office	邮局	yĕr jwi

Is this the road to (the Bund)?
这条路是去(外滩)的吗? gŭh dyaw lóo z chee (ngă tay) uh vā

Can you show me where it is on the map?
请帮我寻寻看它在地图上头的位置。 ching būng ngoo zhĭng zhing koe yĕe luh dĕe dōo gaw der uh wăy dz

transport & directions – SHANGHAINESE

What's the address?	啥地址?	sa dĕe dz
How far is it?	多少远?	dōo saw yóe
Is it walking distance?	走过去远吗?	dser gōo chee yŏe vā
How do I get there?	哪能走?	na nĕrng dser
Turn left/right.	左/右转弯。	dser/yer dsoe wày
It's straight ahead.	一直往前。	yi zūh mung zhée
It's …	在 …	luh …
behind …	… 后头	… ĕr der
in front of …	… 前头	… zhĕe der
near …	… 附近	… vŏo jing
on the corner	转弯角落	dsoe wāy gō lo
opposite …	… 对过	… day gōo
there	那里	āy duh

accommodation

Can you recommend somewhere cheap?
依好推荐一只便宜点的地方蹲吗? — noong haw tāy jee yi dsūh bee nyēe ngāy uh dĕe fung dērng va

Can you recommend somewhere good?
依好推荐一只好点的地方蹲吗? — noong haw tāy jee yi dsūh haw ngāy uh dĕe fung dērng va

Where's a guest house?	哪里有宾馆?	ă lēe duh yer bīng gwoe
Where's a hotel?	哪里酒店?	ă lēe duh yer jer dēe
I'd like to book a room.	我想订房间。	ngoo shung ding vŭng gay
I have a reservation.	我有预订。	ngoo yer yĕw ding
What time is checkout?	几点钟退房?	jee dēe dsoong tay vúng
How much per night?	一天几钿?	yi tēe jee dēe
How much per person?	一个人几钿?	yi ūh nying jee dēe
Do you have a … room?	有 … 房间伐?	yer … vŭng gay va
double	大床	dŏo zung
single	单人	dāy nying
twin	双床	sūng zung

I'd like to stay for (three) nights.
我要蹲(三)个晚上。 ngoo yaw dèrng (sāy) uh yǎ der

Could I have my key, please?
房间钥匙给我好伐? vŭng gay yŭh z buh ngōo haw vā

Can I get an extra (blanket)?
我好多拿条(毛毯)吗? ngoo haw dōo này dyaw (mǎw tay) va

The (air conditioning) doesn't work.
(空调)有毛病。 (kōong dyaw) yer mǎw bing

Could I have my ..., please?	拿我的 … 给我好吗?	nāw ngoo ūh ... buh ngōo haw vā
deposit	押金	uh jīng
passport	护照	vŏo dsaw

banking & communications

Where's a/an ...?	… 在哪儿?	... luh ǎ lēe duh
ATM	自动取款机	z doong chew kwōe jee
public phone	公用电话	gōong yoong dĕe woo

Where's the local internet cafe?
附近有网吧吗? vŏo jing yer mŭng bā va

I'd like to ...	我想 …	ngóo shung ...
get internet access	上网	zúng múng
use a printer	打印	dung ying
use a scanner	扫描	saw myāw

What's your phone number?
侬电话号码是多少? noong dĕe woo hăw der dōo saw

The number is ...
号码是 … hăw der z ...

sightseeing

I'd like to see some local sights.
我想看一些当地的景点。 — ngóo shung koe yī shi dūng dee uh jing dēe

I'd like to see …
我想看 … — ngóo shung koe …

What's that?
那是啥? — gŭh uh z sa

Can I take a photo?
我能拍张照片吗? — ngóo haw pūh dsung dsaw pēe va

I'd like to go somewhere off the beaten track.
我想去常规路线以外的地方白相相。 — ngóo shung chee zŭng gway lŏo shee yi ngă uh dĕe fung bŭh shung shung

How long is the tour?
这趟旅行要用多少辰光? — gŭh tung lĕw ying yaw yŏong dōo saw zĕrng gwung

shopping

Where's a …?	… 在哪儿?	… luh ă lēe duh
camera shop	照相店	dsaw shūng dee
market	市场	ž zung
souvenir shop	纪念品商店	jee nyēe ping sūng dee
supermarket	超市	tsāw z

sightseeing

The Bund	外滩	ngă tay
Chóngmíng Island	崇明岛	zŏong mīng daw
Huangpu River	黄浦江	wŭng pōo gung
Jĭnjiāng Park	锦江乐园	jĭng gung ló yoe
Nánjīng Road	南京路	nŏe jīng loo
Oriental Pearl Tower	东方明珠电视塔	dōong fung mĭng dz dĕe z tuh
Shēshān	佘山	zwŏo say

What's this made from?	这什么做的?	gŭh uh sa ūh dsoo ūh
I'd like to buy …	我想买 …	ngóo shung má …
Can I look at it?	给我看看好吗?	buh ngōo koe kōe haw vā
How much is it?	多少钱?	jee dée
That's too expensive.	太贵了。	tuh jew luh

Where can I buy locally produced goods/souvenirs?
啥地方能买到本地特产? — sa dēe fung yer má berng dēe dŭh tsay

Please write down the price.
请把价钱写下来。 — ching này ga dēe sha wōo lay

I'll give you (five kuai).
给侬(五块)钱。 — buh nōong (ňg kway) ŭng dee

Do you accept credit cards?
侬们收信用卡吗? — ná sèr shing yōong ka va

There's a mistake in the bill.
帐单上有问题。 — dsung dāy gāw der yer vĕrng dee

less	少	saw
enough	足够	dso gēr
more	多	dòo
bigger	大一点	dōo yī ngay
smaller	小一点	shaw yī ngay

meeting people

Hello.	侬好。	nóong haw
Good morning.	早上好。	dsaw zūng haw
Good evening.	夜头好。	yă der haw
Goodbye.	再会。	dsāy way
Good night.	明朝会。	mĭng dsāw way

Mr	先生	shēe sung
Mrs	女士	nĕw z
Ms/Miss	小姐	shaw jā

How are you?	侬好吗?	noong haw
Fine. And you?	好的。侬呢?	haw ūh, nŏong nay
What's your name?	侬叫啥名字?	nŏong jaw sa mĭng dz
My name is ...	我叫 …	ngŏo jaw ...
I'm pleased to meet you.	幸会。	shīng way

This is my ...	这是我的 …	gŭh uh z ngŏo uh ...
brother (older)	阿哥	uh gōo
brother (younger)	阿弟	uh dēe
child	小人	shaw nyīng
daughter	女儿	nŏe
father	爹	yá
friend	朋友	bŭng yer
husband	老公	lăw goong
mother	娘	nyúng
partner (intimate)	对象	day yūng
sister (older)	阿姐	uh jyā
sister (younger)	阿妹	uh māy
son	儿子	nyĕe dz
wife	老婆	lăw boo

making conversation

Do you live here?	侬住在这里伐?	noong ž luh gŭh duh vā
Where are you going?	到哪里去?	daw ă lee chee
Do you like it here?	欢喜这里吗?	hwōe shee gŭh du vā
I love it here.	我老欢喜这里。	ngoo lăw hwōe shee gŭh duh
Have you eaten?	饭吃了吗?	văy chuh luh vā
Are you here on holidays?	侬来这里旅游吗?	noong lăy gŭh duh lĕw yer vā

I'm here ...	我来这里 …	ngoo lăy gŭh duh ...
for a holiday	旅游	lĕw yer
on business	出差	tsuh tsà
to study	留学	lyĕr o

How long are you here for?
依在这里住多久? | noong luh gŭh duh ž dōo jer

I'm here for (four) weeks.
我住(四)个星期。 | ngóo ž (sz) ūh lĕe ba

Can I take a photo (of you)?
我好拍(侬)伐? | ngóo haw puh (nōong) va

Do you speak (Shanghainese)?
侬讲(上海话)伐? | nóong gung (zŭng hay ăy woo) va

What language do you speak at home?
侬在家里讲啥话? | nóong luh o lēe gung sa ăy woo

What do you call this in (Shanghainese)?
这用(上海话)怎么讲? | gŭh uh yoong (zŭng hay ăy woo) nă nerng gung

What's this called?
这叫啥? | gŭh uh jaw sa

I'd like to learn some (Shanghainese).
我想学(上海话)。 | ngóo shung ō (zŭng hay ăy woo)

Would you like me to teach you some English?
侬要我教侬英语吗? | nóong yaw ngoo gaw nōong yīng new vā

Is this a local custom?
这是地方风俗吗? | gŭh uh z dĕe fung fŭng zo va

local talk

Great!	赞!	dsay
Hey!	诶!	ày
It's OK.	还可以。	ày koo yēe
Just a minute.	等一等。	derng yī derng
Just joking.	开玩笑。	kay wăy shaw
Maybe.	有可能。	yer khoo nērng
No problem.	没事情。	m muh z tee
No way!	不可能!	vŭh koo nerng
Sure, whatever.	好,好,好。	haw, haw, haw
That's enough!	够了,够了!	ger lūh, ger lūh

Where are you from?	侬从哪里来？	nóong zoong ǎ lee láy
I'm from …	我从 … 来。	ngóo zoong … láy
Australia	澳大利亚	aw dā lee ya
Canada	加拿大	gā na da
England	英国	yīng go
New Zealand	新西兰	shīng shee lay
the USA	美国	may gō
What's your occupation?	侬做啥工作？	nóong dsoo sa gōong dso
I'm a/an …	我做 …	ngóo dsoo …
businessperson	商人	sūng nying
office worker	白领	bǔh ling
tradesperson	工匠	gōong jung
How old …?	… 几岁了？	… jee sōe luh
are you (to child)	侬	nóong
is your daughter	侬的女儿	nóong uh nǒe ng
is your son	侬的儿子	nóong uh nyěe dz
How old are you? (to adult)	你多大年纪？	nóong dōo da nyěe jēe a
I'm … years old.	我 … 岁。	ngóo … soe
He/She is … years old.	他/她 … 岁。	yée … soe
Too old!	太老了！	tuh lǎw luh
I'm younger than I look.	我还小了。	ngóo ē shaw lūh
Are you married?	侬结婚了吗？	nóong ji hwērng luh va
I'm …	我 …	ngóo …
married	结婚了	ji hwērng luh
single	单身	dāy serng
I live with someone.	我有朋友了。	ngóo yér bǔng yēr luh
Do you have a family?	侬成家了吗？	nóong zérng gà luh va
Do you like …?	侬喜欢 … 吗？	nóong hwōe shee … va
I (don't) like …	我(不)喜欢 …	ngóo (vǔh) hwōe shee …
art	艺术	něe zōo
film	看电影	koe děe ying
music	听音乐	ting yīng ywi
reading	看书	koe sz
sport	体育	tee ywī

feelings & opinions

I'm (not) …	我(不) …	ngóo (vŭh) …
Are you …?	侬 … 吗?	nóong … va
cold	冷	lúng
hot	热	nyí
hungry	饿	ngóo
thirsty	干	gòe
tired	吃力	chuh lí
I (don't) feel …	我(不)感到 …	ngóo (vŭh) go zūh …
Do you feel …?	侬感到 … 吗?	nóong gaw zūh … va
happy	开心	kāy shing
sad	不开心	vŭh kāy shing
worried	急	jí
What do you think of it?	侬觉得哪能?	nóong gaw zūh nă nerng
It's …	这 …	gŭh uh …
awful	老差劲	law tāy bay
beautiful	老漂亮	law pyāw lyung
boring	老无聊	law vŏo lyaw
great	老灵	law líng
interesting	老有意思	law yĕr yēe sz
OK	还可以	ay kōo yee
strange	奇怪	jĕe gwa

farewells

Tomorrow I'm leaving.
明天我要走了。 mĭng dsaw ngóo yaw dser lūh

If you come to (Scotland) you can stay with me.
有机会来(苏格兰), 可以来寻我。 yĕr jēe way láy (sōo guh lay) koo yēe lay zhĭng ngoo

Keep in touch!	保持联系!	baw dz lēe shee
Here's my (address).	这是我的(地址)。	gŭh uh z ngŏo uh (dĕe dz)
What's your (email)?	侬的(网址)是啥?	nŏong uh (mŭng dz) z sa

well-wishing		
Bon voyage!	一路平安！	yi lōo bīng oe
Congratulations!	恭喜，恭喜！	gōong shee, gōong shee
Good luck!	祝侬好运！	dsuh nōong haw ywīng
Happy birthday!	生日快乐！	sērng nyi kwa lō
Happy New Year!	新年好！	shīng nyee haw

eating out

Where would you go for (a) …?	… 一应该到哪里去？	… yīng gay daw ǎ lēe duh chee
banquet	办酒水	bǎy jēr sz
celebration	庆祝	chīng zuh
cheap meal	吃得便宜一点	chuh lūh běe nyēe ngay
local specialities	地方小吃	děe fung shaw chūh
yum cha	吃茶	chūh zwóo

Can you recommend a …?	侬可以推荐一个 … 吗？	nóong koo yēe tāy jee yi dsūh … ù va
bar	酒吧	jer bā
cafe	咖啡屋	kā fee o
dish	盘	bérng
noodle house	面馆	měe gwoe
restaurant	饭店	vě dee
snack shop	小吃店	shaw chūh dee
(wonton) stall	（馄饨）摊	(wěrng derng) tāy der
street vendor	马路高头的小吃	mwǒo lōo gaw der uh shaw chūh
teahouse	茶馆	zwǒo gwoe

I'd like (a/the) …	我要 …	ngóo yaw …
table for (five)	一张（五个人的）桌子	yi dsūng (ňg nying) dāy dz
bill	帐单	dsūng day
drink list	酒水单	jer sz day
local speciality	特色菜	dǔh suh tsay
menu	菜单	tsāy day
(non)smoking table	（不）吸烟的桌子	(vūh) chuh shūng yee uh dāy dz

Are you still serving food?
依们还营业吗？ | ày yǐng yī va

What would you recommend?
有啥菜推荐的？ | yer sa tāy jee va

What do you normally eat for (breakfast)?
（早饭）一般吃什么？ | (dsaw vāy) yi bāy chūh sa

What's in that dish?	这道菜是啥做的？	gǔh uh tsay z sa ūh dsoo ūh
What's that called?	那个叫啥？	ày uh jaw sa
I'll have that.	拿一个。	này yi dsuh

I'd like it with ...	多放点 …	dòo fūng ngē ...
I'd like it without ...	不要放 …	vǔh yaw fung ...
chilli	辣椒	lǔh jaw
garlic	大蒜	dǎ soe
MSG	味精	věe jing
nuts	果仁	goo nyīng
oil	油	yér

I'd like ..., please.	请给我 …	ching buh ngōo ...
one slice	一块	yi kwāy
a piece	一份	yi vērng
a sandwich	一个三明治	yi dsūh sāy ming dz
that one	那一个	ày mee dsuh
two	两个	lyǔng dsuh

This dish is ...	这菜 … 了。	gǔh tsay ... luh
(too) spicy	（太）辣	(tuh) lúh
superb	好极	law haw

That was delicious!	真好吃！	dsērng haw chūh
I'm full.	吃饱了。	chuh bāw luh

breakfast	早饭	dsaw vāy
lunch	午饭	dsōong vay
dinner	晚饭	yǎ vay
drink (alcoholic)	酒	jer
drink (nonalcoholic)	饮料	ying lyāw

… water	… 水	… sz
boiled	开	kāy
cold	冷开	lǔng kāy
mineral	矿泉	kwung zhoe
(cup of) coffee …	(一杯)咖啡 …	(yi bāy) kā fee …
(cup of) tea …	(一杯)茶 …	(yi bāy) zwóo …
with (milk)	加(牛奶)	gà (nyěr na)
without (sugar)	不加(糖)	vǔh ga (dúng)
black tea	红茶	hǒong zwoo
chrysanthemum tea	菊花茶	jwi hwōo zwoo
green tea	绿茶	lǒ zwoo
jasmine tea	花茶	hwōo zwoo
oolong tea	乌龙茶	vōo loong zwoo
fresh drinking yoghurt	酸奶	sōe na
(orange) juice	(橙)汁	(dsěrng) dsūh
lychee juice	荔枝汁	lěe dz dsūh
soft drink	汽水	chēe sz
sour plum drink	酸梅汤	sōe may tung
I'll buy you a drink.	我请客。	ngóo ching kūh
What would you like?	侬要吃啥?	nóong yaw chūh sa
Cheers!	干杯!	gōe bay
I'm feeling drunk.	我有点醉。	ngóo yer ngǎy dsoe

a … of beer	一 … 啤酒	yi … běe jer
glass	杯子	bāy dsì
large bottle	大瓶	dǒo bīng
small bottle	小瓶	shaw bīng
a shot of (whisky)	一樽(威士忌)	yi dsērng (wāy sz jee)
a bottle/glass of	一瓶/杯	yi bīng/bāy
… wine	… 葡萄酒	… bǒo dāw jer
red	红	hóong
white	白	búh

street eats		
cold clear bean-flour noodles	凉粉	lyŭng ferng
corn on the cob	玉米棒	dsērng dz mee
dumpling (boiled)	饺子	jāw dz
dumpling (fried)	锅贴	gōo ti
dumpling (steamed)	包子	bāw dz
egg and spring onion pancake	煎饼	jēe bing
flat bread with sesame seeds	大饼	dă bing
pork pie (large)	肉饼	nyŏ bing
sticky rice in bamboo leaves	粽子	dsōong dz
wonton soup	馄饨汤	wĕrng dērng tung

special diets & allergies

Do you have vegetarian food?
有素食吗? yer sōo zuh va

Could you prepare a meal without …?
能做个不放 … 的菜吗? haw dsoo dsuh vŭh fung … uh tsay vā

I'm allergic to …	我对 … 过敏。	ngóo day … goo míng
dairy produce	奶制品	nă dz ping
eggs	鸡蛋	jēe day
meat	肉	nyó
nuts	果仁	goo nyīng
seafood	海鲜	hay shēe

emergencies & health

Help!	救命!	jer míng
Go away!	走开!	dser kāy
Fire!	着火啦!	zuh hŏo luh
Watch out!	小心!	dūng shing

Could you please help?
侬能帮我吗? nóong nérng būng ngoo va

Can I use your phone?
我能借侬电话用用吗? — ngóo haw ja nōong děe woo yǒong yōong va

I'm lost.
我迷路了。 — ngóo mee lǒo luh

Where are the toilets?
厕所在哪儿? — tsz sōo luh ǎ lēe duh

Where's the police station?
派出所在哪里? — pa tsūh soo luh ǎ lēe duh

Where's the nearest ...?	最近的 … 在哪儿?	dsoe jīng uh ... luh ǎ lēe duh
dentist	牙医	ngǎ yee
doctor	医生	yēe sung
hospital	医院	yēe yoe
pharmacist	药房	yǔh vung

english–shanghainese dictionary

dictionary, words are marked as n (noun), a (adjective), v (verb), sg (singular) and pl (plural) where necessary.

A

accident (mishap) 灾难 dsāy nay
accident (traffic) 交通事故 jāw toong sz gōo
accommodation 食宿 zŭh so
adaptor 编剧 bēe ji
address n 地址 dēe dz
after 之后 dz ér
air conditioning 空调 kōong dyaw
airplane 飞机 fēe jee
airport 机场 jēe zung
alcohol 酒 jer
all 所有的 soo yēr uh
allergy 过敏 goo míng
ambulance 救护车 jer ōo tswoo
and 跟 duh dz
ankle 踝关节 wă gwāy ji
antibiotics 抗生素 kung sērng soo
arm 手臂 ser bēe
ATM 自动取款机 z doong chew kwōe jee

B

baby 婴儿 yīng urr
back (of body) 背 bay
backpack 背包 bay bàw
bad 坏的 wă uh
bag 包 bàw
baggage 行李 hŭng lee
bank 银行 nyĭng ung
bar 酒吧 jer bā
bathroom 浴室 yŏ suh
battery 电池 dĕe z
beautiful 美丽的 haw kōe uh
bed 床 zúng
beer 啤酒 bĕe jēr
before 之前 dz zhée
behind 之后 dz ér
bicycle 脚踏车 juh dūh tswoo
big 大的 dŏo uh
bill 帐单 dsung dāy
blanket 毛毯 măw tay
blood group 血型 shwi yīng
boat 船 zóe
book (make a reservation) v 预订 yĕw ding
bottle 瓶 bīng
boy 男孩 nŏe shāw noe
brakes (car) 煞车 sūh tswoo
breakfast 早饭 dsaw vāy
broken (out of order) 坏掉的 wă dūh uh
bus 公车 gōong tswoo
business 生意 sūng yee
buy v 买 má

C

camera 照相机 dsaw shūng jee
cancel 取消 chew shāw
car 汽车 chee tswōo
cash n 现金 yĕe jing
cash (a cheque) v 把（支票）兑现
nàw (dz pyaw) dāy shee
cell phone 手机 ser jēe
centre n 中心 dsōong shìn
change (money) v 换钱 woe tsāw pyaw
cheap 便宜的 bĕe nyēe ù
check (bill) 帐单 dsung dāy
check-in n 登记 dērng jee
chest (body) 胸膛 shōong dung
children 小人 shaw nyĭng
cigarette 香烟 shūng yee
city 城市 zĕrng z
clean a 干净的 chĭng sung uh
closed 关闭的 gwāy tuh uh
cold a 冷的 lŭng uh
collect call 对方付费电话
day fūng foo fēe dĕe woo
come 来 láy
computer 电脑 dĕe naw
condom 避孕套 bĕe ywĭng taw
contact lenses 隐形眼镜 ying yĭng ngăy jing
cook v 烹饪 pērng zerng
cost n 花费 hwōo fee
credit card 信用卡 shing yōong ka
currency exchange 货币汇兑 hoo bēe wăy day
customs (immigration) 海关 hay gwāy

D

dangerous 危险的 wăy shēe uh
date (time) 日期 nyĭ jee

A

english–shanghainese

day 天 tèe
delay v 推迟 tāy z
dentist 牙医 ngă yee
depart 出发 tsuh fūh
diaper 尿布 sz boo
dinner 晚饭 yă vay
direct a 直接的 zŭh jī uh
dirty 龌龊的 o tsō uh
disabled 残疾的 zăy jēe uh
discount v 打折 dung dsūh
doctor 医生 yēe sung
double bed 双人床 sūng nying zung
double room 大床房 dŏo zūng vung
drink n 饮料 ying lyāw
drive v 开车 kāy tswòo
driving licence 驾照 ja dsāw
drug (illicit) 毒品 dŏo ping

E

ear 耳朵 nyĕe doo
east 东 dòong
eat 吃 chūh
economy class 经济舱 jīng jee tsung
electricity 电 dée
elevator 电梯 dĕe tee
email 电子邮件 dĕe dz yĕr jee
embassy 大使馆 dă sz gwoe
emergency 紧急状况 jing jī dsung kwūng
English (language) 英语 yīng nyew
evening 傍晚 yă der
exit n 出口 tsuh kēr
expensive 贵的 jew ūh
eye 眼睛 ngăy jing

F

far 远的 yŏe uh
fast 快的 kwa ūh
father 父亲 ŏo ching
film (camera) 影片 ying pēe
finger 手指 ser dz
first-aid kit 急救箱 ji jĕr shung
first class 头等舱 dĕr dērng tsung
fish n 鱼 ńg
food 食物 zŭh vuh
foot 脚 jūh
free (of charge) 免费的 mĕe fēe uh
friend 朋友 bŭng yer
fruit 水果 sz gōo
full 饱的 baw ūh

G

gift 礼物 lĕe vuh
girl 女孩 nĕw shāw noe
glass (drinking) 杯子 bāy dz
glasses 眼镜 ngăy jing
go 去 chee
good 好的 haw ūh
guide n 导游 dăw yer

H

half n 一半 yi bōe
hand 手 ser
happy 开心的 kāy shing uh
he 他 yēe
head n 头 dér
heart 心 shìng
heavy 重的 zŏong uh
help 帮忙 būng mung
here 这里 gŭh duh
high 高的 gāw uh
highway 高速公路 gāw so gōong loo
hike v 徒步旅行 dŏo boo lĕw ying
holiday 假期 ga jēe
homosexual 同性恋 dŏong shīng lee
hospital 医院 yēe yoe
hot 热 nyí
hotel 宾馆 bīng gwoe
(be) hungry 饿 ngóo
husband 老公 lăw goong

I

I 我 ngóo
identification (card) 身份证 sērng verng dserng
ill 生毛病的 sūng mŏr bīng uh
important 重要的 zŏong yāw uh
injury (harm) 伤害 sūng hay
injury (wound) 伤口 sūng ker
insurance 保险 baw shēe
internet 因特网 yīng tuh mung
interpreter 翻译 fāy yi

J

jewellery 珠宝 dz baw
job 工作 gōong dso

K

key 钥匙 yŭh z
kilogram 公斤 gōong jing

kitchen 厨房 ž vung
knife 小刀 shaw dăw

L

laundry (place) 洗衣店 shee yēe dee
lawyer 律师 lĭ sz
left (direction) 左 dsoo
leg (body) 腿 tay
lesbian 女同性恋 nyěw dōong shing lee
less 少 saw
letter (mail) 信 shing
light n 光 gwùng
like v 喜欢 hwōe shee
lock n 锁 soo
long 长的 zŭng uh
lost 失去的 suh chēe uh
love v 爱 ay
luggage 行李 hŭng lee
lunch 中饭 dsōong vay

M

mail n 邮件 yěr jee
man 人 nyíng
map 地图 děe doo
market 市场 ž zung
matches 自来火 zĭ lāy hoo
meat 肉 nyó
medicine 药 yúh
message 信息 shing shī
milk 牛奶 nyěr na
minute 分钟 fērng dsoong
mobile phone 手机 ser jēe
money 钞票 tsăw pyaw
month 月 yó
morning 早上 dsaw zūng
mother 母亲 mōo ching
motorcycle 摩托车 mōo tō tswoo
mouth 嘴巴 dz bwōo

N

name 名字 mĭng z
near 近的 jĭng uh
neck n 头颈 děr jing
new 新的 shīng uh
newspaper 报纸 baw dz
night 夜晚 yă der
no (none) 没有 m muh
no (not this) 不是 vú zī
noisy 吵的 tsaw ŭh
nonsmoking 不准吃香烟
vuh dsērn chuh shūng yee
north 北 bo
nose 鼻子 bĭ der
now 现在 yěe zay
number 数字 soo dz

O

old (people) 老 láw
old (things) 旧 jer
one-way ticket 单程票 dāy zerng pyaw
open a 开的 kāy uh
outside 外面的 ngă der

P

passport 护照 vŏo dsaw
pay v 付钞票 foo tsăw pyaw
pharmacy 药房 yŭh vung
phonecard 电话卡 děe wōo ka
photo 照片 dsaw pēe
police 警察 jīng tsuh
postcard 明信片 mĭng shĭng pee
post office 邮局 yěr jwi
pregnant 怀孕的 wă ywĭng uh
price n 价钱 ga dēe

Q

quiet a 安静的 ōe jing uh

R

rain n 雨 yéw
razor 刮胡子刀 gwŭh wŏo dz daw
receipt n 收据 sēr jwi
refund n 退款 tay kwōe
registered (mail) 已挂号的 gwoo āw uh
rent v 出租 tsŭh dz
repair v 修理 shēr lee
reserve v 预订 yěw ding
restaurant 饭店 văy dee
return (give back) 还 wáy
return (go back) 回来 wăy chee
return ticket 返程票 fay zērng pyaw
right (direction) 右 yer
road 路 lóo
room n 房间 vŭng gay

S

safe a 安全的 ōe zhoe uh
sanitary napkin 卫生棉 wăy sērng jing
seat n 座位 zŏo way

send 发送 fuh sōong
sex (intercourse) 性交 shīng jaw
sex (gender) 性别 shing bi
shampoo 洗发精 dǎ dēr gaw
share (a dorm) 分享 fērng shung
she 她 yēe
sheet (bed) 床单 zǔng day
shirt T恤 tēe shwi
shoes 鞋子 ǎ dz
shop n 商店 sūng dee
short 短的 doe ūh
shower n 淋浴 līng yo
single room 单人房 dāy nying vung
skin n 皮肤 běe foo
skirt n 裙子 jwǐng dz
sleep v 睡 kwerng
slow 慢的 mě uh
small 小的 shaw ūh
soap 肥皂 běe zaw
some 一些 yi ngáy
soon 马上 mwǒo zung
south 南 nóe
souvenir 纪念品 jee nyēe ping
stamp 邮票 yěr pyaw
stand-by ticket 站台票 zǎy dāy pyaw
station (train) 火车站 hoo tswōo zay
stomach 胃 wáy
stop v 停止 dīng dz
stop (bus) n 站台 tswōo zay
street 街 gà
student 学生 ǒ sung
sun 太阳 ta yūng
sunscreen 防晒油 fūng sā yer
swim v 游泳 yěr yoong

T

tampon 卫生巾 wǎy sērng jing
telephone n 电话 děe woo
temperature (weather) 温度 wērng doo
that 那个 āy uh
they 他们 yěe la
(be) thirsty 口渴的 dz bwōo gòe
this 这个 gǔh uh
throat 喉咙 ǒo loong
ticket 票 pyaw
time 时间 zěrng gwung
tired 累的 chuh lī uh
tissues 卫生纸 wǎy sērng dz
today 今朝 jīng dsaw
toilet 厕所 tsz sōo
tomorrow 明朝 mīng dsaw
tonight 今晚 jīng dsaw yǎ der
tooth 牙齿 ngǎ tsz
toothbrush 牙刷 ngǎ suh
toothpaste 牙膏 ngǎ gaw
torch (flashlight) 手电筒 ser dēe doong
tour n 旅行 lěw ying
tourist office 旅行社 lěw yīng zwoo
towel 毛巾 mǎw jing
train n 火车 hoo tswōo
translate 翻译 fāy yi
travel agency 旅行社 lěw yīng zwoo
travellers cheque 旅行支票 lěw ying dz pyaw
trousers 裤子 kòo dz
twin-bed room 双人间 sūng nying gay

U

underwear 内衣裤 nǎy yēe koo
urgent 紧急的 jing jī uh

V

vacancy 空缺 kōong chwi
vegetable n 蔬菜 sōo tsay
vegetarian a 吃素的 chuh sōo uh
visa 签证 chēe zerng

W

walk v 走 dser
wallet 皮夹子 běe gūh dz
wash (something) 洗 dá
watch n 手表 ser byaw
water n 水 sz
we 我们 uh lūh
weekend 周末 dsēr mo
west 西 shèe
wheelchair 轮椅 lěrng yee
when 当 dūng
where 在哪里 luh ǎ lēe duh
who 谁 sa nyīng
why 为啥 wǎy sa
wife 老婆 lǎw boo
window 窗户 tsūng merng
with 跟 duh dz
without 没 m muh
woman 女人 něw nying
write 写 sha

Y

yes 是 ź
yesterday 昨日 zǒ nyi
you sg 侬 nóong
you pl 你们 ná

Sichuanese

TONES 182
ABOUT SICHUANESE 183
PRONUNCIATION 184
LANGUAGE DIFFICULTIES 185
TIME & DATES 186
TRANSPORT & DIRECTIONS 187
ACCOMMODATION 188
BANKING & COMMUNICATIONS 189
SIGHTSEEING 190
SHOPPING 190
MEETING PEOPLE 191
MAKING CONVERSATION 192
FEELINGS & OPINIONS 194
FAREWELLS 195
EATING OUT 196
SPECIAL DIETS & ALLERGIES 199
EMERGENCIES & HEALTH 200
ENGLISH–SICHUANESE DICTIONARY 201

tones

Sichuanese is a tonal language ('tonal quality' refers to the raising and lowerinc pitch on certain syllables). In this chapter Sichuanese is represented with four tor as well as a fifth one, the neutral tone. Apart from the unmarked neutral tone, have used symbols above the vowels to indicate each tone, as shown in the ta below for the vowel 'a'. Bear in mind that the tones are relative to the natural vc range of the speaker, eg the high tone is pronounced at the top of one's vocal ran Note also that some tones slide up or down in pitch.

high tone ā	high rising tone á	low falling-rising tone ǎ	high falling tone à

SICHUANESE
四川话

about Sichuanese

It's classified as a southwestern dialect of Mandarin, but if it were viewed as a language in its own right Sichuanese (sěe tswūn hwǎ 四川话), with 120 million speakers, would be one of the most widely spoken languages in the world. The population of Sìchuān is 95% Han Chinese – with a small Tibetan minority, who also speak Sichuanese – and their dialect is regarded as one of the most uniform in China. The Sichuanese dialect is very similar to dialects spoken in the neighbouring provinces of Guìzhōu and Yúnnán, and if you wander across to Chóngqìng you'll hear the same dialect spoken. There are some variations – locals say, for example, that the Chóngqìng accent is different to the Chéngdū accent. If you have a grasp of Mandarin you should be able to chat with Sichuanese speakers, as the grammar and vocabulary are very similar. It's through its pronunciation that Sichuanese marks out its own linguistic territory. Perhaps it's the Szechuan cuisine – garnished with liberal sprinklings of Sìchuān peppercorns – that creates the nasal twang and clipped vowels that make Sichuanese distinctive.

pronunciation

Vowels		Consonants	
Symbol	English sound	Symbol	English sound
a	father	b	bed
ai	aisle	ch	cheat
air	lair	d	dog
ao	Mao	f	fun
au	haul	g	go
ay	pay	h	hot
e	bet	j	jump
ee	see	k	kit
er	her	l	lot
ew	new, with rounded lips	m	man
i	hit	n	not
o	home	ng	ring
oo	tool	p	pet
u	good	r	run
		s	sun
		sh	shot
		t	top
		ts	cats
		w	win
		y	yes
		z	lads
		zh	pleasure

In this chapter, the Sichuanese pronunciation is given in orange after each phrase.

Note that 'r' is always pronounced wherever it appears, including after a vowel (like in American English).

Some syllables are separated by a dot, and should be pronounced closely together.
For example: 月份 fěn·ěr

For pronunciation of tones, see p182.

essentials		
Yes./No.	是。/不是。	sèe/bóo sèe
Please …	请 …	chǐn …
Hello.	你好。	lèe hào
Goodbye.	再见。	zǎi jyèn
Thank you.	谢谢你。	syǎir syǎir lèe
Excuse me.	麻烦下子。	má fán hǎ zèe
Sorry.	不好意思。	bóo háo yée sēe

language difficulties

Do you speak (English)?
你说得来(英语)不? — lèe swáu dér lái (yīn yěw) bóo

I (don't) speak Sichuanese.
我说(不)来四川话。 — wàu swáu (bóo) lái sěe tswūn hwǎ

Do you understand?
你懂起没得? — lèe dòong chee máy dé

I understand.
我晓得啰。 — wǎu shyào dé lò

I don't understand.
我搞不伸展。 — wǎu gǎo bóo chēn zǎn

Could you please …?	麻烦你 …?	má fán lèe …
repeat that	再说一道	zǎi sáu yée dǎo
speak more slowly	慢滴点儿说	màn dēe dēr sáu

numbers					
0	零	lín	20	二十	ér sée
1	一	ée	30	三十	sān sée
2	二/两	ěr/lyùng	40	四十	sèe sée
3	三	sān	50	五十	wòo sée
4	四	sěe	60	六十	lyó sée
5	五	wòo	70	七十	ch sée
6	六	lyǒ	80	八十	bá sée
7	七	chi	90	九十	jyò sée
8	八	bá	100	一百	ée báy
9	九	jyò	1000	一千	ée chee yēn
10	十	sée	1,000,000	一百万	ée báy wǎn

time & dates

What time is it?	现在好多点喽?	shyěn zǎi hǎo dāu dyèn làu
It's (10) o'clock.	(十)点钟。	(sée) dyèn jyēn
Quarter past (10).	(十)点十五分。	(sée) dyèn sée wǒo fēn
Half past (10).	(十)点三十分。	(sée) dyèn sān sée fēn
Quarter to (11). (literally: Forty-five minutes past (10).)	(十)点四十五分。	(sée) dyèn sěe sée wǒo fēn
At what time (does it start)?	啥子时候 (开始)?	sà zěe sée hò (kāi sěe)
(It starts) At 10.	十点钟(开始)。	sée dyèn jyēn (kāi sèe)
It's (18 October).	(十月十八号)。	(sée ywáir sée bā hǎo)
yesterday	昨天	záu tyēn
today	今天	jīn tyēn
now	现在	shyěn zǎi
tonight	今晚上	jīn wǎn sàng
tomorrow	明天	mín tyēn
this …	这个 …	zǎy gǎu …
morning (after breakfast)	早上	zào sàng
morning (before lunch)	上午	sàng wǒo
afternoon	下午	syà wǒo
sunrise	日出	rée chú
sunset	日落	rée làu
spring	春天	chūn tyēn
summer	夏天	syà tyēn
autumn	秋天	chee·yā tyēn
winter	冬天	dōn tyēn
Monday	星期一	shīn chee ée
Tuesday	星期二	shīn chee ěr
Wednesday	星期三	shīn chee sān
Thursday	星期四	shīn chee sěe
Friday	星期五	shīn chee wǒo
Saturday	星期六	shīn chee lyǒ
Sunday	星期天	shīn chee tyēn

January	元月份	ywén ywáir fěn·ěr
February	二月份	ěr ywáir fěn·ěr
March	三月份	sān ywáir fěn·ěr
April	四月份	sěe ywáir fěn·ěr
May	五月份	wòo ywáir fěn·ěr
June	六月份	lyǒ ywáir fěn·ěr
July	七月份	chi ywáir fěn·ěr
August	八月份	bá ywáir fěn·ěr
September	九月份	jyò ywáir fěn·ěr
October	十月份	sée ywáir fěn·ěr
November	十一月份	sée yée ywáir fěn·ěr
December	十二月份	sée ěr ywáir fěn·ěr

transport & directions

Is this the ... to (Chéngdū)?	这个 … 是到 (成都) 的吗?	zǎi gǎu ... sěe dǎo (chen du) dé mā
boat	船	tswúng
bus	公共汽车	gōng gǒng chee chāy
train	火车	hàu chāy
Where's a/the ...?	… 在啥子地方?	... zài shà zěe dée fāng
bank	银行	yín háng
place to change foreign money	调外币的地方	tyǎo wǎi běe dé dée fāng
post office	邮局	yó jéw

Is this the road to (Tianfu Plaza)?

请问这条路是到 (天府广场) 的么?

chǐn wèn zǎy tyáo lù sée dào (tyēn fù gyùng chàng) dé māu

Can you show me where it is on the map?

请帮我指下子它在地图上的位置?

chǐn bāng wǎu jěe hà zěe tā zǎi děe tóo sàng dé wāy zhée

What's the address?	地址是那儿呢?	dée zèe sĕe lăr nē
How far is it?	有好远?	yéw hào ywèn
Is it walking distance?	走路要走好远啊?	jò lŭ yăo jò hào ywèn á
How do I get there?	咋个走?	já gău jò
Turn left/right.	往左/右拐。	wàn zău/yĕw gwài
It's straight ahead.	对直向前。	dwày jée sĭn chyèn
It's …	在 …	zăi …
behind …	… 的后头	… dé hò tó
in front of …	… 的前头	… dé chee·yén tó
near …	… 附近	… fŏo jĭn
on the corner	拐弯儿地方	gwài wàn·er dé dèe fāng
opposite …	… 的对面	… dē dwăy myĕn
there	那里	lă lĕe

accommodation

Where's a hotel?
哪个地方有旅馆? — là gàu dĕe fāng yò lèw gwèn

Can you recommend somewhere cheap?
你能介绍一个相因的地方住吗? — lèe lén jyĕn săo yée gău shyūng yīn dé dĕe fāng jŏo má

Can you recommend somewhere good?
你能介绍一个巴适的地方住吗? — lèe lén jyĕn săo yée gău bā sĕe dé dĕe fāng jŏo má

I'd like to book a room.
我想订一个房间。 — wău shyŭng dĭn yee gău fán jyēn

I have a reservation.
我订斗房间了。 — wău dĭn dŏ fáng jyēn ló

Do you have a … room?	有没的 … 房间得?	yò măy dé … fàng jyān dé
double	套间	tào jyēn
single	单人	dān rén
twin	标间	byāo jyēn

How much is it per night/person?
每天/人好多钱? — mày tyēn/rén hăo dāu chyén

I'd like to stay for (three) nights.
住(三)天。 jǒo (sān) tyēn

Could I have my key, please?
能不能给我房间钥匙? lén bóo lén gày wǎu fáng jyēn yǎo sěe

Can I get an extra (blanket)?
我能多拿一条(毛毯)吗? wǎu lén dāu ná yèe tyáo (máo tàn) má

The (air conditioning) doesn't work.
(空调)扯拐了。 (kōng tyén) chǎy gwǎi lò

What time is checkout?
好多点钟退房? hào dāu dyèn jōng twày fāng

Could I have my ..., please?	我想拿回我的 ··· ?	wǎu shyùng ná hwáy wǎu dé ...
deposit	押金	yā jīn
passport	护照	fù zào

banking & communications

Where's the local internet cafe?
周围有没的网吧得? jō wáy yǒ māy dé wàng bā dé

Where's a/an ...?	··· 在哪个地方?	... zài lǎ gàu dèe fāng
ATM	自动取款机	zěe dǒng chyèw kwèn jēe
public phone	公用电话	gōng yǒng dyěn hwǎ

I'd like to ...	我想 ···	wàu shyùng ...
get internet access	上网	sàng wàng
use a printer	打印	dà yìn
use a scanner	扫描	sào myáo

What's your phone number?
您的电话号码是好多? lín dé dyěn hwǎ hǎo mà sěe hǎo dāu

The number is ...
号码是 ··· hǎo mà sèe ...

sightseeing

I'd like to see some local sights.

我想看下子一些本地的景点。 — wàu shyùng kàn hà zĕe yèe syāir bèn dèe dé jìn dyèn

I'd like to go somewhere off the beaten track.

我想去一些人少的景点。 — wàu shyùng chyĕw ée syāir rén sào dē jìn dyèn

I'd like to see ...	我想看 …	wàu shyùng kàn ...
What's that?	那是啥子哦?	là sèe sà zèe ó
Can I take a photo?	我能拍不?	wàu lén pāy bóo
How long is the tour?	时间要好久啊?	sée jyēn yào hào jò ā

sightseeing		
Du Fu's Cottage	杜甫草堂	dŭ fù chào táng
Dūjiāngyàn irrigation project	都江堰	dū jyúng yán
Éméi Shān	峨眉山	áu máy sān
Jiŭzhàigōu Nature Reserve	九寨沟	jyŏ zài gō
Qīngchéng Shān	青城山	chīn chén sān
Qīngyáng Gōng	青羊宫	chīn yáng gōng
Wŭhóu Temple	武侯祠	wŏo hŏ ts

shopping

Where's a ...?	… 在哪儿?	... zăi nàr
camera shop	照相店	zăo shyŭng dyĕn
market	市场	sĕe chàng
souvenir shop	纪念品店	jĕe lyĕn pìn dyèn
supermarket	超市	chāo sèe

Where can I buy locally produced goods?

哪个地方我能买到本地的土产? — là gàu dèe fāng wàu lén gò mài dào bĕn dèe dé tòo tsàn

What's this made from?

这是啥子东西制成的? — zè sèe sà zée dōng sēe zwàu dé

I'd like to buy …	我想买 …	wǎu shyùng mài …
Can I look at it?	我能看下子么?	wàu nén kàn hō zěe māu
How much is it?	好多钱?	hǎo dāu chyén
That's too expensive.	太贵啰。	tǎi gwǎy lò

Please write down the price.
请把价钱写写下来。 — chǐn bà jyǎ chyén shyàir shyàir lǎi

I'll give you (five kuai).
给你(五块)钱。 — gāy lèe (wòo kwài) chyén

Do you accept credit cards?
你们收信用卡吗? — lèe mèn sō shìn yǒng kà mā

less	少	sào
enough	够了	gǒ lò
more	多	dāu
bigger	大	dǎ
smaller	小	shyào

meeting people

Hello.	你好。	lèe hào
Good morning.	早上好。	zào sàng hào
Good afternoon.	下午好。	syǎ wòo hào
Good evening.	晚上好。	wàn sǎng hào
Goodbye.	再见。	zài jyèn
Good night.	晚安。	wàn ān
Mr	先生	syā sēn
Mrs	女士	nèw sěe
Ms/Miss	小姐	shyào jyàir
How are you?	你好吗?	lèe hào mā
Fine. And you?	好。你呢?	hào, lèe nē
What's your name?	你叫啥子名字?	lèe jyǎo sǎ zèe mín zèe
My name is …	我叫 …	wàu jyǎo …
I'm pleased to meet you.	幸会。	shǐn hwǎy

This is my …	这是我的 …	zě sěe wàu dé …
brother	兄弟	syōong děe
child	娃儿	wár
daughter	女儿	léwr
father	老汉	lào hèr
friend	朋友	póng yò
husband	老公	lǎo gōng
mother	母亲	mòo chīn
partner (intimate)	对象	dwǎy shyǔng
sister	姐妹	jyàir mǎy
son	儿子	ér zěe
wife	老婆	lǎo pó

making conversation

Do you live here?	住在这里吗?	jǒo jǎi jě lèe mā
Where are you going?	上那里去?	sàng là lèe chyěw
Do you like it here?	喜欢这里撒?	shèe hwūn jè lèe sá
I love it here.	我很喜欢这里。	wàu hèn shèe hwūn zè lèe
Have you eaten?	吃过饭了吗?	chi gǎu fàn lyěn mā
Are you here on holidays?	你来这里旅游的吗?	lèe lái zè lèe lěw yó dé mā

I'm here …	我来这里 …	wǎu lái jě lèe …
for a holiday	旅游	lěw yó
on business	出差	chú chāi
to study	留学	lyó shwáir

How long are you here for?
你要在这里住好久? — lèe yào zǎi zé lǐ zǒo hào jyò

I'm here for (four) weeks.
我住(四)个星期。 — wǎu jǒo (sěe) gàu shīn chee

Can I take a photo (of you)?
我可以拍(你)吗? — wǎu kǎu yěe pāi (lèe) mā

Do you speak (Sichuanese)?
你会讲(四川话)不? — lèe hwày jyùng (sěe tswūn hwǎ) bòo

What language do you speak at home?
你在老家说得是啥子话? — lèe zǎi lào jyā sáu dé sěe sà zée hwǎ

local talk

Great!	安逸的很！	ān yèe dé hěn
Hey!	麻烦下子！	má fàn hà zěe
It's OK.	将就。	jyūng jyù
Just a minute.	等一下。	děn yée hà
Just joking.	扯把子。	tsè bà zèe
Maybe.	有可能。	yǒ kǎu nén
No problem.	没得啥子事。	máy dé sà zěe sèe
No way!	不可能！	bóo kǎu nén
Sure, whatever.	可以，可以，可以。	kàu yèe kàu yèe kàu yèe
That's enough!	够了，够了！	gò làu gò làu

What do you call this in (Sichuanese)?
你能告诉我这个东西（四川话）咋个讲？ — lèe lén gǎo sǒo wàu zé gǎu dōng sēe (sěe tswūn hwǎ) zá gàu jyǔng

What's this called?
这个叫啥子啊？ — zé gǎu jyǎo sà zěe á

I'd like to learn some (Sichuanese).
我想学点（四川话）。 — wàu syàng shōo·ǎu diàn (sěe tswūn hwǎ)

Would you like me to teach you some English?
你想不想我教你些英语？ — lèe shyùng bóo shyung wàu jyāo lèe syāir yīn yěw

Is this a local custom?
这是地方风俗么？ — zè sèe dèe fāng fōng sú māu

Where are you from?	你从哪儿来？	lèe sèe là·ér lái lē
I'm from ...	我从 … 来。	wàu tsóng ... lái
Australia	澳大利亚	ào dǎ lǐ yǎ
Canada	加拿大	jyā lá dǎ
England	英国	yīn gáu
New Zealand	新西兰	shīn shēe lán
the USA	美国	mày gáu
What's your occupation?	你是做啥子嘞？	lèe sèe zǔ sà zèe lé
I'm a/an ...	我当 …	wǎu dāng ...
businessperson	做生意的	jǔ sēn yée dé
office worker	白领	bày lǐn
tradesperson	工匠	gōng jyǔng

How old …?	…好大了?	… hào dǎ lò
are you	你	lèe
is your daughter	你的女儿	lèe dé lèwr
is your son	你的儿子	lèe dé·ér zèe

I'm … years old.	我 … 岁。	wàu … swày
He/She is … years old.	他/她 … 岁。	tā … swày
Too old!	老登了!	lǎo dēn lò
I'm younger than I look.	我还小了。	wàu shyǎo dé hèn
Are you married?	你结婚了没得?	lèe jyáir hōon lyǎo máy dé
I live with someone.	我有老婆了。	wàu yò lào pó lyào
Do you have a family?	你结婚了撒?	lèe jyáir hōon lē sá

I'm …	我 …	wàu …
married	结婚了	jyáir hōon lyào
single	单身	dān shēn

Do you like …?	你喜欢 … 不?	lèe shèe hwēn … bóo
I (don't) like …	我(不)喜欢 …	wàu (bóo) shèe hwēn …
art	艺术	èe sù
film	看电影	kàn dyèn yǐn
music	听音乐	tīn yīn ywàir
reading	看书	kàn sū
sport	体育	těe yèw

feelings & opinions

I'm (not) …	我(不) …	wàu (bóo) …
Are you …?	你 … 吗?	lèe … mā
cold	冷	lèn
hot	热	rè
hungry	饿	àu
thirsty	口干	kǒ gān
tired	累	lǎy

I (don't) feel …	我感(不)到 …	wàu gàn (bóo) dǎo …
Do you feel …?	你感到 … 吗?	lèe gàn dǎo … mā
happy	高兴	gāo shǐn
sad	不高兴	bóo gāo shǐn
worried	急得很	jyáir dé hèn
What do you think of it?	你觉得啷个样?	lèe jéw dé làng gǎu yàng
It's …	它 …	tā …
awful	歪的很	wǎi dé hěn
beautiful	漂亮的很	pyào lyùng dé hěn
boring	无聊的很	wóo lyáo dé hěn
great	巴适惨了	bā sèe tsǎn lò
interesting	有意思惨了	yǒ èe sēe tsǎn lò
OK	还将就	hái jyūng jèw
strange	怪的很	gwài dé hěn

farewells

Tomorrow I'm leaving.
明天我要走了。 mín tyēn wǎu yào jǒ làu

If you come to (Scotland), you can stay with me.
有机会来(苏格兰),可以来找我。 yǒ jēe hwày dào (sū gé lán) kǎu ěe lái zai wàu

Keep in touch!
保持联系! bǎo ts lyén sèe

Here's my (address).
给你我的(地址)。 gā lèe wàu dé (dèe zèe)

What's your (email)?
你的(网址)是啥子啊? lèe dé (wǎng zěe) sèe sà zěe ā

well-wishing

Bon voyage!	一路平安!	ée lǔ pín ān
Congratulations!	恭喜,恭喜!	gōng shée gōng shée
Good luck!	祝你好运!	zòo lèe hào yòon
Happy birthday!	生日快乐!	sēn rée kwài láu
Happy New Year!	新年好!	shīn lyén hào

eating out

Where would you go for (a) ...?	… 该到那儿去?	... gāi dào nǎ·ěr chyěw
banquet	办席	bàn sée
celebration	办庆祝会	bán chìn zóo hwǎy
cheap meal	吃的相因一点的	chi dē shyūng yīn ée dyén dé
local specialities	地方小吃	děe fāng shyǎo chi
yum cha	喝茶	hāu chá

Can you recommend a ...?	你可以介绍一个 … 吗?	lèe kàu èe jyěn sǎo ée gàu ... mā
bar	吧	bā
cafe	咖啡厅	kā fāy tīn
dish	盘	pán
noodle house	面馆	myěn gwèn
restaurant	餐厅	tsān tīn
snack shop	小吃店	shyǎo chi dyěn
(wonton) stall	(抄手)摊	(tsāo sǒ) tān
street vendor	街头小吃	gāi tó shyǎo chi
teahouse	茶馆	chá gwèn

I'd like (a/the) ...	我要 …	wàu yǎo ...
table for (five)	一张(五个人的)桌子	yée zāng (wòo gàu rén dé) zu·āu zěe
bill	账单	zàng dān
drink list	酒水单	jyǒ swǎy dān
local speciality	一个地方特色菜	ée gàu dèe fāng tè sè tsài
menu	菜单	tsài dān
(non)smoking table	(不)吸烟的桌子	(bóo) sée yān dé zu·áu zěe

Are you still serving food?
你们在还营业没得? — lèe mén zài hái yín yè máy dé

What would you recommend?
有啥子菜可以推荐没得? — yó sà zèe tsài kǎu ěe jyěn sǎo máy dé

What's in that dish?
这道菜是啥子东西做的? — zě dáo tsái sèe sà zěe dōng sēe zù dé

What do you normally eat for (breakfast)?
(早饭)一般吃啥子? — (zǎo fǎn) ée bān chi sà zěe

I'll have that.	来一个。	lái ée gàu
What's that called?	那个叫啥子?	là gàu jyào sá zěe
I'd like it with ...	多放一点 ···	dāu fàng ée dyèn ...
I'd like it without ...	不要放 ···	bóo yào fǎng ...
chilli	海椒	hǎi jyāo
garlic	大蒜	dà swèn
MSG	味精	wày jīn
nuts	果仁	gǎu rén
oil	油	yó

I'd like ..., please.	请给我 ···	chǐn gèi wàu ...
one slice	一块	ée kwài
a piece	一份	ée fèn
a sandwich	一个三明治	ée gàu sān mín zè
that one	那一个	là ée gàu
two	两个	lyǔng gàu
This dish is ...	这个菜 ··· 了。	zè gàu tsài ... làu
(too) spicy	(太)辣	(tài) là
superb	好极啦	hǎo jée là
That was delicious!	真好吃!	zhēn hào chi
I'm full.	吃饱啰。	chi bào ló
breakfast	早饭	zào fǎn
lunch	午饭	wòo fǎn
dinner	晚饭	wàn fǎn
drink (alcoholic)	酒	jyò
drink (nonalcoholic)	饮料	yìn lyǎo
... water	··· 水	... swày
boiled	开	kāi
cold	凉开	lyúng kāi
sparkling mineral	苏打饮料	sǒo dǎ yín lyào
still mineral	矿泉	kwùng chee·wèn

(cup of) coffee …	(一杯)咖啡 …	(ée báy) kā fāy …
(cup of) tea …	(一杯)茶 …	(ée báy) chà …
with (milk)	加(牛奶)	jyā (lyó lài)
without (sugar)	不加(糖)	bóo jyō (tàng)
black tea	红茶	hóng chà
chrysanthemum tea	菊花茶	jáu hwā chà
green tea	绿茶	lú chà
jasmine tea	花茶	hwā chà
oolong tea	乌龙茶	wū lóng chà
fresh drinking yoghurt	酸奶	swēn lài
(orange) juice	(橙)汁	(chén) zēe
lychee juice	荔枝汁	lěe zēe zēe
soft drink	汽水	chee swày
sour plum drink	酸梅汤	swēn máy tāng

What are you drinking?
喝啥子? — hāu sà zèe

I'll buy you a drink.
我帮你买一杯。 — wàu bǎn lèe mài yée bāy

What would you like?
你是不是想要? — lèe sèe bóo sèe syùng yǎo

Cheers!
干杯! — gān bāy

I'm feeling drunk.
我有点醉。 — wàu yò dyèn zwǎy

a … of beer	一 … 啤酒	ée … pée jyò
glass	杯	bāy
large bottle	大瓶	dǎ pín
small bottle	小瓶	shyào pín

a shot of (whisky)	一小杯(威士忌)	ée shyǎo bāy (wāy sée jèe)
a bottle/glass of	一瓶/杯 …	ée pín/bāy …
… wine	葡萄酒	póo táo jyò
red	红	hóng
white	白	báy

street eats

braised Dongpo pork hock with brown sauce	东坡肘子	dōng pō zò zèe
cold clear bean-flour noodles	凉粉	lyùng fèn
corn on the cob	苞谷棒	bǎo gǒo bàng
dumpling (boiled)	饺子	jyǎo zēe
pork lungs in chilli sauce	夫妻肺片	fū chee fày pyèn
pork pie (small)	锅魁	gāu kwāy
sticky rice in bamboo leaves	粽子	zǒng zěe
tofu with minced meat in a spicy sauce	麻婆豆腐	má pó dǒ fòo
twice-cooked pork	回锅肉	hwày gāu rò
wonton soup	抄手	tsāo sǒ
Yúxiāng shredded pork	鱼香肉丝	yéw syūng rǒ sèe

special diets & allergies

Do you have vegetarian food?
有没有素食食品? — yó māy dé sòo sèe sée pìn

Could you prepare a meal without …?
能不能做个不放 … 的菜? — len bu len zu gau bóo fang … dé tsai

I'm allergic to …	我对 … 过敏。	wàu dyèw … gǎu mìn
dairy produce	奶制品	lài zèe pìn
eggs	鸡蛋	jēe dǎn
meat	肉	rǒ
nuts	果仁	gàu rēn
seafood	海鲜	hǎi syèn

emergencies & health

Help!	救命！	jyǒ mín
Go away!	走开！	zò kāi
Fire!	起火喽！	chee hàu lò
Watch out!	当心！	dāng shīn
Where's the nearest ...?	最近的 … 在哪?	zùi jìn dé ... zài lár
dentist	牙医	yá ēe
doctor	医生	ēe sēn
hospital	医院	ēe ywèn
pharmacist	药店	yào dyèn

Could you please help?
你能帮我吗? — lèe lén bàng wàu mā

Can I use your phone?
我能借一下你的电话吗? — wàu lén jyǎir ée hà lèe dé dyèn hwà mā

I'm lost.
我迷路啰。 — wàu mée lù làu

Where are the toilets?
厕所在啥子地方? — chè sǎu zài sà zèe dèe fāng

Where's the police station?
派出所在啥子地方? — pài chú sàu zài sà zèe dèe fāng

english–sichuanese dictionary

dictionary, words are marked as n (noun), a (adjective), v (verb), sg (singular), pl (plural), inf (informal) and olite) where necessary.

A

accident (mishap) 灾祸 zāi hàu
accident (traffic) 交通事故 jyāo tōng sèe gǒo
accommodation 食宿 sée sǒo
adaptor 编剧 byēn jěw
address n 地址 děe zèe
after 之后 zēe hǒ
air conditioning 空调 kōng tyén
airplane 飞机 fāy jēe
airport 机场 jēe chàng
alcohol 酒 jyò
all 所有的 sò yǒ dé
allergy 过敏 gǎu mìn
ambulance 救护车 jèw fǒo chāy
and 和 hàu
ankle 踝 làu
antibiotics 抗生素 kàng sēn sǒo
arm 手臂 sò běe
ATM 自动取款机 zěe dǒng chyèw kwèn jēe

B

baby 婴儿 yīn ér
back (of body) 背 bāy
backpack 背包 bāy bāo
bad 坏的 hwài dē
bag 包 bāo
baggage 行李 shín lèe
bank 银行 yín háng
bar 吧 bā
bathroom 浴室 yèw sèe
battery 电池 dyèn chi
beautiful 漂亮的 pyào lyùng dé
bed 床 tswùng
beer 啤酒 pée jyò
before 之前 zēe chyèn
behind 之后 zēe hǒ
bicycle 自行车 zěe shín chāy
big 大的 dǎ dé
bill 帐单 zàng dān
blanket 毛毯 máo tàn
blood group 血型 shyáir shín
boat 船 tswúng
book (make a reservation) v 预订 yèw dìn
bottle 瓶 pín
boy 男孩 lán hái
brakes (car) 煞车 sá chēr
breakfast 早饭 zào fǎn
broken (out of order) 坏掉的 hwài dyào dé
bus 公共汽车 gōng gǒng chee chāy
business 生意 sēn èe
buy v 购买 gǒ mài

C

camera 相机 shyùng jēe
cancel 取消 chyěw shyāo
car 汽车 chee chāy
cash n 现金 shyèn jīn
cash (a cheque) v 付现金 fòo shyèn jīn
cell phone 手机 sò jēe
centre n 中心 zōng shīn
change (money) v 零钱 lìn chyèn
cheap 便宜的 shyūng yīn dé
check (bill) 帐单 zàng dān
check-in n 登记 dēn jěe
chest (body) 胸脯 shyōong pò
children 儿童 ér tóng
cigarette 香烟 shyūng yān
city 城市 chén sèe
clean a 干净的 gān jèe dè
closed 关闭的 gwēn bèe dé
cold (weather) a 冷的 lèn dé
collect call 对方付费电话 dwày fāng fòo fāy dyèn hwà
come 来 lái
computer 电脑 dyèn lào
condom 避孕套 bèe yòon tào
contact lenses 隐形眼镜 yìn shín yàn jìn
cook v 烹饪 pōng rěn
cost n 花费 hwā fāy
credit card 信用卡 shìn yǒng kà
currency exchange 货币汇兑 hàu bèe hwày dwày
customs (immigration) 海关 hài gwēn

D

dangerous 危险的 wāy shyèn dé
date (time) 日期 rée chee

day 天 tyēn
delay v 延迟 twāy chí
dentist 牙医 yá ēe
depart 出发 chū fā
diaper 尿布 lyào pòo
dinner 晚饭 wàn fàn
direct a 直接的 zée jyáir dé
dirty 脏的 fán dé
disabled 残废的 chán fāy dé
discount v 打折 dà zé
doctor 医生 ēe sēn
double bed 双人床 swūng rén tswúng
double room 套间房 tào jyēn fáng
drink n 饮料 yìn lyǎo
drive v 开车 kāi chēr
driving licence 驾照 jyà zào
drug (illicit) 毒品 dóo pìn

E

ear 耳朵 ér dǎu
east 东 dōng
eat 吃 chi
economy class 经济舱 jīn jēe tsāng
electricity 电 dyèn
elevator 电梯 dyèn tēe
email 电子邮件 dyèn zèe yó jyèn
embassy 大使馆 dà sèe gwèn
emergency 紧急状况 jìn jée chee-ín kwǖng
English (language) 英语 yīn yèw
evening 傍晚 bàng wàn
exit n 出口 chú kò
expensive 贵的 gwày dé
eye 眼睛 yàn jīn

F

far 远的 ywèn dé
fast 快的 kwài dé
father 老汉 lào hèr
film (camera) 影片 yìn pyěn
finger 手指 sò zèe
first-aid kit 急救箱 jwáir jěw shyūng
first class 头等舱 tó dèn tsāng
fish n 鱼 yéw
food 食物 sée wóo
foot 脚 jáu
free (of charge) 免费的 myèn fāy dé
friend 朋友 póng yò
fruit 水果 swày gàu
full 饱的 bào dé

G

gift 礼物 lèe wòo
girl 女孩 lěw hái
glass (drinking) 杯子 bāy zèe
glasses 眼镜 yàn jìn
go 去 chyèw
good 好的 hào dér
guide n 导游 dào yó

H

half n 一半 ée bǎn
hand 手 sò
happy 高兴的 gāo shǐn dé
he 他 tā
head n 头 tò
heart 心 shīn
heavy 重的 zǒng dé
help 帮助 bāng zóo
here 这里 zày lèe
high 高的 gāo dé
highway 高速公路 gāo sóo gōng lǒo
hike v 徒步旅行 tóo bǒo lěw shín
holiday 假期 jyà chee
homosexual 同性恋 tóng shìn lyèn
hospital 医院 ēe ywèn
hot 热的 ré dé
hotel 旅馆 lèw gwèn
(be) hungry 饿的 àu dé
husband 老公 lǎo gōng

I

I 我 wàu
identification (card) 身份证 sēn fěn zěn
ill 生病的 sēn bǐn dé
important 重要的 zòng yǎo dé
injury (harm) 侮辱 wōo ròo
injury (wound) 伤口 sāng kò
insurance 保险 bào shyèn
internet 因特网 yīn tèr wàng
interpreter 翻译 fān èe

J

jewellery 珠宝 zōo bǎo
job 工作 gōng zàu

K

key 钥匙 yáu sèe
kilogram 公斤 gōng jīn

tchen 厨房 chóo fáng
nife 小刀 shyǎo dāo

undry (place) 洗衣店 shì ēe dyèn
wyer 律师 lèw sēe
ft (direction) 左 zǎu
g (body) 腿 twày
sbian 女同性恋 lèw tóng shìn lyěn
ss 少 sào
tter (mail) 信 shìn
ght n 光 gwūng
ke v 喜欢 shèe hwēn
ck n 锁 sōo·àu
ng 长的 cháng dé
st (items) 过了的 go làu dé
ove v 爱 ài
uggage 行李 shín lèe
unch 午饭 wòo fǎn

M

mail n 信 shìn
man 男人 lán rén
map 地图 dēe tóo
market 市场 sèe chàng
matches 火柴 hàu tsái
meat 肉 rǒ
medicine 药 yào
message 信息 shìn shēe
milk 牛奶 lyó lài
minute 分钟 fēn zōng
mobile phone 手机 sò jēe
money 钱 chyìn
month 月 ywàir
morning 早上 zào sàng
mother 母亲 mòo chīn
motorcycle 摩托车 máu táu chāy
mouth 口 kò

N

name 名字 mín zèe
near 近的 jìn dé
neck n 脖子 bó zèe
new 新的 shīn dér
newspaper 报纸 bào zèe
night 夜晚 yèe wàn
no (not at all) 一点都不 yēe dyěn dō bòo
no (wrong) 不对头 bóo dwáy tó
noisy 闹哄哄的 lào hōng hōng dér
nonsmoking 禁止吸烟 jìn zěe shēe yān
north 北 báy

nose 鼻子 bée zèe
now 现在 shyěn zǎi
number 数字 sòo zèe

O

old (people) 老 lào
old (things) 旧 jěw
one-way ticket 单程票 dān chén pyǎo
open a 开的 kāi dé
outside 外头的 wài tó dé

P

passport 护照 fǔ zào
pay v 付钱 fǔ chyèn
pharmacy 药店 yào dyèn
phonecard 电话卡 dyèn hwà kà
photo 照片 zǎo pyěn
police 警察 jìn chà
postcard 明信片 mín shěe pyěn
post office 邮局 yó jéw
pregnant 怀孕的 hwái yòon dé
price n 价格 jyà gér

Q

quiet a 安静的 ān jìn dé

R

rain n 雨 yèw
razor 刮胡刀 gōo·wā hóo dāo
receipt n 收据 sō jèw
refund n 退款 twày kwèn
registered (mail) 已挂号的 èe gōo wà hào dé
rent v 出租 chǔ zōo
repair v 修理 shyō lèe
reserve v 预订 yèw dìn
restaurant 餐厅 tsān tīn
return (give back) 还 hwén
return (go back) 回来 hwáy lái
return ticket 返程票 fàn chēn pyào
right (direction) 右 yěw
road 路 lòo
room n 房间 fán jyēn

S

safe a 安全的 ān chwēn dé
sanitary napkin 卫生棉 wày sēn myén
seat n 座位 zōo·àu wày
send 发送 fá sòng

english–sichuanese

sex (intercourse) 性 shìn
sex (gender) 性别 shìn byáir
shampoo 洗发精 shì fà jīn
share (a dorm) 分享 fēn shyùng
she 她 tā
sheet (bed) 床单 chòn dān
shirt 衬衫 tsǒon sān
shoes 鞋 shyáir
shop n 商店 sāng dyěn
short 短的 dwèn dé
shower n 淋浴 lín yèw
single room 单人房 dān rén fāng
skin n 皮肤 pée fōo
skirt n 裙子 chee·óon zèe
sleep v 睡 swày
slow 慢的 màn dé
small 小的 shyào dé
soap 肥皂 fáy zào
some 一些 ée shyāir
soon 马上 mà sǎng
south 南 lán
souvenir 纪念品 jěe lyěn pìn
stamp 邮票 yó pyǎo
stand-by ticket 站台票 zàn tái pyào
station (train) 火车站 hàu chāy zǎn
stomach 胃 wày
stop v 停止 tín zěe
stop (bus) n 站台 zàn tái
street 街 gāi
student 学生 shōo·àu sēn
sun 太阳 tài yáng
sunscreen 防晒油 fáng sài yó
swim v 游泳 yó yòng

T

tampon 止血棉球 zèe shyàir myén chyó
telephone n 电话 dyèn hwà
temperature (weather) 温度 wēn dòo
that 那个 là gàu
they 他们 tā mèn
(be) thirsty 口干的 kò kàu
this 这个 zè gàu
throat 喉咙 hó lōng
ticket 票 pyǎo
time 时间 sée jyēn
tired 累的 lày dé
tissues 卫生纸 wǎy sēn zèe
today 今天 jīn tyēn
toilet 厕所 tsè sǎu
tomorrow 明天 mín tyēn
tonight 今晚上 jīn wàn sàng
tooth 牙齿 yá chi
toothbrush 牙刷 yá swā
toothpaste 牙膏 yá gāo
torch (flashlight) 手电筒 sò dyèn tòng
tour n 旅行 lèw shín
tourist office 旅行社 lèw shín sèr
towel 毛巾 máo jīn
train n 火车 hàu chāy
translate 翻译 fān èe
travel agency 旅行社 lèw shín sèr
travellers cheque 旅行支票 lèw shín zēe pyǒo
trousers 裤子 kòo zèe
twin-bed room 标间 byāo jyēn

U

underwear 内衣裤 lwày ēe kǒo
urgent 紧急的 jìn jée dé

V

vacancy 空缺 kòng chee·ēw
vegetable n 蔬菜 sōo chǎi
vegetarian a 吃素的 ts sòo dē
visa 签证 chyēn zěn

W

walk v 步行 bòo shìn
wallet 钱包 chyén bāo
wash (something) v 洗 shèe
watch n 观看 gwēn kěn
water n 水 swày
we 我们 wàu mèn
weekend 周末 zō màu
west 西 shēe
wheelchair 轮椅 lóon yèe
when 什么时候 sén máu sée hǒ
where 在哪里 zài là lèe
who 谁 swáy
why 为什么 wày sà zèe
wife 老婆 lǎo pó
window 窗户 tswūng fǒo
with 和 hāu
without 没有 māy yò
woman 女人 lèw rén
write 写 shyàir

Y

yes (right) 对头 dwáy tó
yesterday 昨天 záu tyēn
you sg inf 你 lèe
you sg pol 您 lín
you pl 你们 lèe mén

Xi'an

TONES 206
ABOUT XI'AN 207
PRONUNCIATION 208
LANGUAGE DIFFICULTIES 209
TIME & DATES 210
TRANSPORT & DIRECTIONS 211
ACCOMMODATION 212
BANKING & COMMUNICATIONS 213
SIGHTSEEING 214
SHOPPING 215
MEETING PEOPLE 215
MAKING CONVERSATION 216
FEELINGS & OPINIONS 219
FAREWELLS 219
EATING OUT 220
SPECIAL DIETS & ALLERGIES 223
EMERGENCIES & HEALTH 224
ENGLISH–XI'AN DICTIONARY 225

tones

Xi'an is a tonal language ('tonal quality' refers to the raising and lowering of pitch certain syllables). In this chapter Xi'an is represented with four tones, as well as a fi one, the neutral tone. Apart from the unmarked neutral tone, we have used symb above the vowels to indicate each tone, as shown in the table below for the vow 'a'. Bear in mind that the tones are relative to the natural vocal range of the speak eg the high tone is pronounced at the top of one's vocal range. Note also that son tones slide up or down in pitch.

high tone ā	high rising tone á	low falling-rising tone ǎ	high falling tone à

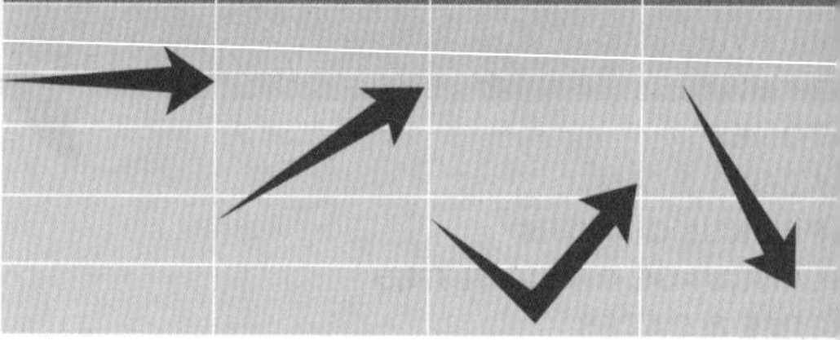

about Xī'an

Ancient Xī'ān, in the central northern province of Shaanxi, is one of the cradles of Chinese civilisation – legend has it that over four millennia ago a scribe from Shaanxi invented Chinese characters. During the Zhou dynasty (1100–221 BC) the city's dialect, a form of Old Chinese noted for its melodiousness and singsong intonation, was promoted as the standard language across the realm. During the same era, the stony-faced warriors of the Terracotta Army that has made Xī'ān so famous were created by speakers of this 'elegant dialect'. Situated at the eastern terminus of the fabled Silk Road, Xī'ān has absorbed speakers of countless languages over the years, yet always remained a bastion of the Mandarin language. These days, Xi'an dialect (shee·un hwā 西安话) is considered to be representative of the Shaanxi dialects of Mandarin spoken across the central plains and the reaches of the Yellow River. It doesn't share its ancient predecessor's reputation for melodiousness, but is characterised by its clever use of adjectives related to body parts and the 12 animals of the zodiac.

xi'an

pronunciation

Vowels		Consonants	
Symbol	**English sound**	**Symbol**	**English sound**
a	father	b	bed
ai	aisle	ch	cheat
ao	Mao	d	dog
ay	say	f	fun
e	bet	g	go
ee	see	h	hat
er	her	j	jump
ew	new with rounded lips	k	kid
ewe	ew followed by e	l	lot
i	hit	m	man
o	cold	n	not
oo	tool	ng	ring
or	more	p	pet
u	cut	r	run
		s	sun
		sh	shot
		t	top
		ts	cats
		w	win
		y	yes
		z	lads

In this chapter, the Xi'an pronunciation is given in brown after each phrase.

The nasal sound ng (found in English at the end or in the middle of words, eg 'ringing'), can represent an entire word in Xi'an.

Some syllables are separated by a dot, and should be pronounced closely together.
For example: 一点 dyen·er

For pronunciation of tones, see p206.

essentials		
Yes./No.	是。/不是。	sī/bŏo sī
Please …	请 …	chìng …
Hello.	你好。	nì hào
Goodbye.	再见。	zāi jyēn
Thank you.	谢谢你。	shyē shye ni
Excuse me. (to get past)	借光。	jyē gwung
Excuse me. (asking for directions/assistance)	麻烦一下。	má fún yěe ha
Sorry.	对不起。	dwāy boo chèe

language difficulties

Do you speak (English)?
你会说(英语)不? nèe hwāy shwor (yǐng yèw) boo

I (don't) speak Xi'an.
我(不)会说西安话。 ng (boo) hwāy shwor shee un hwā

Do you understand?	你明白吗?	nì míng bay boo
I (don't) understand.	我(不)明白。	ng (boo) míng bay
Could you please …?	请你 …?	chìng nì …
repeat that	再说一遍	zāi shwor yee byēn
speak more slowly	慢一点说	mūn dyen-er shwor

numbers					
0	零	líng	20	二十	ēr shí
1	一	yee	30	三十	sun shí
2	二/两	ēr/lyùng	40	四十	sēe shí
3	三	sun	50	五十	wòo shí
4	四	sī	60	六十	lyo shí
5	五	wòo	70	七十	chee shí
6	六	lyo	80	八十	ba shí
7	七	chee	90	九十	jyò shí
8	八	ba	100	一百	yée bay
9	九	jyò	1000	一千	yée chyen
10	十	shí	1,000,000	一百万	yée bay wūn

time & dates

What time is it?	现在几点钟?	chyēn zāi jee dyèn
It's (10) o'clock.	(十)点钟。	(shí) dyèn
Quarter past (10).	(十)点十五分。	(shí) dyèn shí wòo fern
Half past (10).	(十)点三十分。	(shí) dyèn sun shí fern
Quarter to (11). (literally: Forty-five minutes past (10).)	(十)点四十五分。	(shí) dyèn sī shí wòo fern
At what time (does it start)?	啥时候(开始)?	sā sí ho (kăi sì)
(It starts) At 10.	十点钟(开始)。	shí dyèn (kăi sì)
It's (18 October).	(十月十号)。	(shí ywē shír ba hāo)

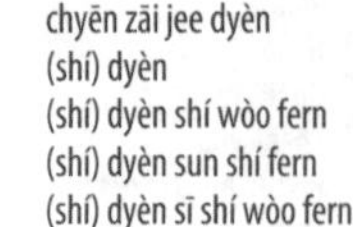
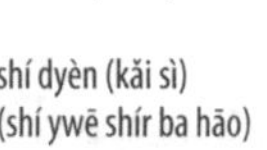

yesterday	昨天	zó tyen
today	今天	jin tyen
now	现在	shyēn zāi
tonight	今晚	jĭn wùn
tomorrow	明天	míng tyen
this …	这个 …	jày ger …
morning (after breakfast)	早上	zào shung
morning (before lunch)	上午	shŭng wòo
afternoon	下午	shyā wòo
sunrise	日出	rí choo
sunset	日落	rí lwor
spring	春天	choon tyen
summer	夏天	shyā tyen
autumn	秋天	chyŏ tyen
winter	冬天	dòong tyen

Monday	星期一	shǐng chée yee
Tuesday	星期二	shǐng chée ēr
Wednesday	星期三	shǐng chée sun
Thursday	星期四	shǐng chée sī
Friday	星期五	shǐng chée wòo
Saturday	星期六	shǐng chée lyo
Sunday	星期天	shǐng chée tyen

January	一月	yee ywe
February	二月	ēr ywe
March	三月	sun ywe
April	四月	sī ywe
May	五月	wòo ywe
June	六月	lyo ywe
July	七月	chee ywe
August	八月	ba ywe
September	九月	jyò ywe
October	十月	shí ywe
November	十一月	shí yee ywe
December	十二月	shí ēr ywe

transport & directions

Is this the … to Xī'ān?	这 … 到 (西安) 去不?	jèr … dāo (shee·un) chēe boo
boat	船	shwún
bus	车	cher
train	火车	hwòr cher

Where's a/the …?	… 在啥地方?	… zāi sā dēe fung
bank	银行	yín húng
place to change foreign money	换外币的地方	hwūn wāi bēe der dēe fung
post office	邮局	yó jóo

Is this the road to (the Bell Tower)?
走这条路能到 (钟楼) 不?
zò jèr tyáo lōo nérng dāo (jǒong ló) boo

Can you show me where it is on the map?
能帮我寻下它在地图上的位置不? — nérng bung ng shín ha tà zāi dēe tóo shung dee wāy jí boo

What's the address?	啥地方?	sā dēe fung
How far is it?	有多远?	yò dwor ywùn
Is it walking distance?	要走多远?	yāo zò dwŏr ywùn
How do I get there?	咋走?	zà zò
Turn left/right.	往左/右拐。	wūng zwòr/yō gwài
It's straight ahead.	一直往前。	yee jí wūng chyén

It's …	在 …	zāi …
behind …	… 后边	… hō byen
in front of …	… 前边	… chyén byen
near …	… 附近	… fōo jīn
on the corner	拐角	gwài jewe
opposite …	… 对过	… dwāy gwōr
there	无达	wóo da

accommodation

Where's a guest house?
啥地方有宾馆? — sā dēe fung yò bin gwùn

Where's a hotel?
啥地方有酒店? — sā dēe fung yò jyò dyēn

Can you recommend somewhere cheap?
你能推荐个便宜点的住处不? — nèe nérng tway jyen ger pyén yee dyen·er dee jōo chòo boo

Can you recommend somewhere good?
你能推荐个好点的住处不? — nèe nérng tway jyen ger hào dyen·er dee jōo chòo boo

I'd like to book a room.
我想订房。 — ng shyùng dīng fúng

I have a reservation.
我预订咧。 — ng yōo dīng lye

Do you have a … room?	有没有 … 间?	yò mer yò … jyen
double (suite)	套	tāo
single	单人	dun rérn
twin	双人	shwung rérn

How much is it per night?
每天多钱? — mày tyen dwor chyen

How much is it per person?
每人多钱? — mày rérn dwor chyen

I'd like to stay for (three) nights.
住(三)天。 — jōo (sun) tyen

Could I have my key, please?
能给把房间钥匙不? — nérng gày bà fúng jyen yewe si boo

Can I get an extra (blanket)?
我能多拿一条(毛毯)不? — ng nérng dwor ná ee tyáo (máo tùn) boo

The (air conditioning) doesn't work.
(空调)有问题。 — (kòng tyáo) yò wérn tée

What time is checkout?
几点退房? — jee dyèn twāy fúng

Could I have my …, please?	我想拿回我的 …	ng shyùng ná hwáy ng dee …
deposit	押金	ya jin
passport	护照	hōo jāo

banking & communications

Where's the local internet cafe?
附近有没有网吧? — fōo jīn yò mer yò wùng ba

Where's a/an …?	… 在啥地方?	… zāi sā dēe fung
ATM	自动取款机	zīr dōng chèw kwèn jee
public phone	公用电话	gong yōng dyēn hwā

I'd like to …	我想 …	ng shyùng …
get internet access	上网	shūng wùng
use a printer	打印	dà yīn
use a scanner	扫描	sào myáo

What's your phone number?
你电话号码是多少? nì dyēn hwā hāo mà si dwor shào

The number is …
号码是 … hāo mà si …

sightseeing

I'd like to see some local sights.
我想看看本地景点儿。 ng shyùng kūn kun bèrn dēe jìng dyèn·er

I'd like to go somewhere off the beaten track.
我想去人少的景点儿。 ng shyùng chēe rérn shào dee jìng dyèn·er

How long is the tour?
出行要多长时间? choo shíng yāo dwor chúng sí jyen

I'd like to see …
我想看 … ng shyùng kūn …

What's that?
握是啥? wòr si sā

Can I take a photo?
我能拍不? ng nérng pay boo

sightseeing		
Army of Terracotta Warriors	西安兵马俑	shee·un bǐng mà yòong
Big Goose Pagoda	大雁塔	dā yūn ta
Famen Temple	法门寺	fǎ mérn sī
Huà Shān	华山	hwā sun
Hukou Waterfall	壶口瀑布	hòo kò pōo bōo
Qian Tomb	乾陵	chyén líng
Tang Paradise Theme Park	大唐芙蓉园	dā túng fóo róong ywún

shopping

Where's a …?	… 在啥地方?	… zāi sā dēe fung
camera shop	照相馆	jāo shyūng gwùn
market	市场	sī chùng
souvenir shop	纪念品店	jēe nyēn pìn dyēn

Where can I buy locally produced souvenirs?
啥地方可买地方纪念品? — sā dēe fung kèr yee mài dēe fung jēe nyēn pìn

What's this made from?	这是用啥做的?	jer si yōng sā zō dee
I'd like to buy …	我想买 …	ng shyùng mài …
Can I look at it?	我能看下不?	ng nérng kūn ha boo
How much is it?	多钱?	dwor chyén
That's too expensive.	太贵咧。	tāi gwāy lye

Please write down the price.
请把价钱写下来。 — chìng ba jyā chyen shyè hā lai

I'll give you (five kuai).
给你(五块)钱。 — gày nì (woo kwài) chyen

Do you accept credit cards?
收信用卡不? — sho shīn yōng kà boo

less	少	shào
enough	足够	zóo gō
more	多	dwor
bigger	大一点	dā yee dyèn·er
smaller	小一点	swāy yee dyèn·er

meeting people

Hello.	你好。	nì hào
Good morning.	早上好。	zào shung hào
Good afternoon.	下午好。	shyā wòo hào
Good evening.	晚上好。	wùn shang hào
Goodbye.	再见。	zāi jyēn
Good night.	晚安。	wùn un

Mr	先生	shyen serng
Mrs	女士	nèw sī
Ms/Miss	小姐	shyao jye
How are you?	最近咋样?	zwāy jīn zà yūng
Fine. And you?	不错。你咋样?	bóo tswor nì zà yūng
What's your name?	你叫啥?	nì jyāo sā
My name is ...	我叫 …	ng jyāo ...
I'm pleased to meet you.	幸会。	shīng hwāy
This is my ...	这是我 …	jer sī ńg ...
brother	兄弟	shyoong dee
child	娃	wā
daughter	女子	nèw zi
father	爸	bā
friend	朋友	pérng yo
husband	丈夫	jūng foo
mother	妈	má
partner (intimate)	对象	dwāy shyūng
sister	姐妹	jyè may
son	儿子	ér zi
wife	媳妇	shee fer

making conversation

Do you live here?	你住这儿?	nì jōo jèr·er
Where are you going?	去阿达?	chēe á da
Do you like it here?	喜欢这儿不?	shèe hwun jèr·er boo
I love it here.	我很喜欢这儿。	ng hèrn shèe hwun jèr·er
Have you eaten?	吃咧么?	chee lye mer
Are you here on holiday?	你来这旅游不?	nì lái jèr lèw yó boo
I'm here ...	我来这 …	ng lái jer·er ...
for a holiday	旅游	lèw yó
on business	出差	chóo tsai
to study	留学	lyó shéwe

西安话 – making conversation

How long are you here for?
你在这儿住多久?　nì jāi jèr·er jōo dwǒr jyò

I'm here for (four) weeks.
我住(四)个星期。　ng joo (sī) ger shing chee

Can I take a photo (of you)?
我可以给(你)拍张照片不?　ng kè yee gày (nì) pay jung jāo pyēn boo

Do you speak (Xi'an)?
你会说(西安话)不?　nì hwāy shwor (shee·un hwā) boo

What language do you speak at home?
你在家说啥话?　nì zāi jya shwor sā hwā

What do you call this in (Xi'an)?
这个用(西安话)咋说?　jày ger yōong (shee·un hwā) za shwor

What's this called?
这叫啥?　jèr jyāo sā

I'd like to learn some (Xi'an).
我想学(西安话)。　ng shyùng shéwe (shee·un hwā)

Would you like me to teach you some English?
你愿意让我教你英文不?　nì ywūn yee rūng ng jyao nì yǐng wóon boo

Is this a local custom?
这是不是地方风俗?　jer sī boo sī dēe fung ferng sóo

local talk		
Great!	聊地很!	lyáo dee hèrn
Hey!	劳驾!	láo jyā
It's OK.	还行。	hái shíng
Just a minute.	稍微等一下。	sǎo wáy dèrng yee ha
Just joking.	开玩笑。	kǎi wún shyāo
Maybe.	有可能。	yò kèr nérng
No problem.	末麻达。	mǒr má da
No way!	没门!	mǒr mérn·er
Sure, whatever.	能成。	nérng chérng
That's enough!	够咧!	gō lye

Where are you from?	你从阿达来?	nì tsóong á da lai
I'm from …	我从 … 来。	ng tsóng … lai
Australia	澳大利亚	āo dā lēe yà
Canada	加拿大	jyǎ ná dā
England	英国	yìng gway
New Zealand	新西兰	shin shee lún
the USA	美国	mày gway
What's your occupation?	你做啥工作?	nì zō sā gong zwor
I'm a/an …	我是 …	ng sī …
businessperson	商人	shǔng rern
office worker	白领	báy lìng
tradesperson	工匠	gong jyung
How old …?	… 多大咧?	… dwǒr dā lye
are you	你	nì
is your daughter	你女子	nǐ nèw zi
is your son	你儿子	nǐ ér zi
I'm … years old.	我 … 岁。	ng … swāy
He/She is … years old.	他/她 … 岁。	tà … swāy
Too old!	太老咧!	tāi lào lye
I'm younger than I look.	我还小。	ng hái sway
Are you married?	你结婚咧吗?	nì jyé hoon lye mer
I live with someone.	我有伴儿。	ng yò bùn·er
Do you have a family?	你成家咧吗?	nì chérng jya lye mer
I'm …	我 …	ng …
married	结婚咧	jyé hoon lye
single	单身	dún shern
Do you like …?	你喜欢 … 不?	nì shèe hwun … boo
I (don't) like …	我(不)喜欢 …	ng (boo) shèe hwun …
art	艺术	yēe shōo
film	看电影	kūn dyēn yìng
music	听歌	tíng ger
reading	看书	kūn shoo
sport	体育	tèe yēw

feelings & opinions

I'm (not) …	我(不) …	ng (boo) …
Are you …?	你 … 不?	nì … boo
cold	冷	lèrng
hot	热	rer
hungry	饿	ng
thirsty	渴	ker
tired	累	lāy
I (don't) feel …	我(不)感到 …	ng (boo) gùn dāo …
Do you feel …?	你感到 … 不?	nì gùn dāo … boo
happy	高兴	gǎo shīng
sad	不高兴	boo gǎo shīng
worried	着急	jao jée
What do you think of it?	你觉得咋样?	nèe jewe dee za yūng
It's …	它 …	tà …
awful	差劲地很	tsǎ jīn dee hèrn
beautiful	漂亮地很	pyāo lyung dee hèrn
boring	无聊地很	wóo lyáo dee hèrn
great	增送地很	jěrng sóng dee hèrn
interesting	有意思地很	yò yēe si dee hèrn
OK	还行	hái shíng
strange	奇怪	chée gwāi

farewells

Tomorrow I'm leaving.

明天我要走。 míng tyen ng yāo zò

If you come to (Scotland), you can stay with me.

有机会来(苏格兰), yò jee hway lái (sǒo ger lún)
可以来寻我。 kèr yee lái shín ng

Keep in touch!	保持联系!	bào chée lyén shēe
Here's my (address).	这是我的(地址)。	jèr si ng dee (dēe zì)
What's your (email)?	你(邮箱)是啥?	nì (yó shyung) si sā

well-wishing		
Bon voyage!	一路平安！	yěe lōo píng un
Congratulations!	恭喜，恭喜！	gǒng shèe, gǒng shèe
Good luck!	祝你好运！	jōo nì hào yōon
Happy birthday!	生日快乐！	sěrng ri kwāi ler
Happy New Year!	新年好！	shǐn nyén hào

eating out

Where would you go for (a) ...?	··· 该到啥地方？	... gǎi dāo sā dēe fung
banquet	办宴席	būn yūn shée
celebration	举行庆祝会	jèw shíng chīng jōo hwāy
cheap meal	吃得便宜一点儿	chee dee pyén yee dyèn·er
local specialities	地方小吃	dēe fung shyào chi
yum cha	喝茶	hwǒr tsá

Can you recommend a ...?	能推荐个 ··· 不？	nérng twǎy jyēn ger ... boo
bar	酒吧	jyò ba
cafe	咖啡屋	ká fáy woo
dish	盘儿	pún·er
noodle house	面馆	myēn gwùn
restaurant	饭店	fūn dyen
snack shop	小吃店	shyào chee dyēn
(wonton) stall	(馄饨)摊	(hóon toon) tun·er
street vendor	大排档	dā pái dūng
teahouse	茶馆	tsá gwùn

I'd like (a/the) ...	我要 ···	ng yāo ...
table for (five)	一张(五个人的)桌子	yée jung (wòo ger rérn dee) jwor zi
bill	帐单	jūng dun
drink list	酒水单	jyò shwày dun
local speciality	一个地方特色菜	yěe gēr dēe fung táy say tsāi
menu	菜单	tsāi dun
(non)smoking table	(不)吸烟的桌子	(boo) shée yun dee jwor zi

Are you still serving food?
还营业不? hái yíng ye boo

What would you recommend?
有啥菜可以推荐? yò sà tsài kèr yee twǎy jyēn

What do you normally eat for (breakfast)?
(早饭)一般吃啥? (zào fūn) yée bun chee sā

What's in that dish?
这道菜用啥东西做的? jèr dāo tsāi yōng sā dong shee zō dee

What's that called?
为个叫啥? wày ger jyāo sā

I'll have that.
来一个。 lái yee ger

I'd like it with ...	多放点儿 ...	dwǒr fūng dyen·er ...
I'd like it without ...	不要放 ...	boo yāo fūng ...
chilli	辣子	là zi
garlic	大蒜	dā swēn
MSG	味精	wāy jing
nuts	果仁	gwòr rér
oil	油	yó
I'd like ..., please.	请给我 ...	chìng gày ng ...
one slice	一块	yěe kwài·er
a piece	一份	yěe fùn·er
a sandwich	一个三明治	yěe gē sǔn míng jēe
that one	为个	wày ge
two	两个	lyùng ge
This dish is ...	这道菜 ...	jèr dāo tsāi ...
(too) spicy	(太)辣	(tāi) la
superb	好地很	hào dee hèrn
That was delicious!	好吃地很!	hào chee dee hèrn
I'm full.	吃饱咧。	chěe bào lye

breakfast	早饭	zào fūn
lunch	午饭	wòo fūn
dinner	晚饭	wùn fūn
drink (alcoholic)	酒	jyò
drink (nonalcoholic)	饮料	yìn lyāo

... water	··· 水	... fày
boiled	开	kǎi
cold	凉开	lyúng kǎi
sparkling mineral	矿泉汽	kwūng chwún chēe
still mineral	矿泉	kwūng chwún

(cup of) coffee ...	（一杯）咖啡 ···	(yée bay) ká fay ...
(cup of) tea ...	（一杯）茶 ···	(yée bay) tsá ...
with (milk)	加（牛奶）	jyǎ (nyó nài)
without (sugar)	不加（糖）	bóo jya (túng)

black tea	红茶	hóng tsá
chrysanthemum tea	菊花茶	jéw hwa tsá
green tea	绿茶	lew tsá
jasmine tea	花茶	hwa tsá
oolong tea	乌龙茶	woo lúng tsá

fresh drinking yoghurt	酸奶	swǔn nài
(orange) juice	（橙）汁	(chérng) ji
lychee juice	荔枝	lēe ji
soft drink	汽水	chēe fày
sour plum drink	酸梅汤	shwǎn máy tung

I'll buy you a drink.
我请客。 ng chìng kay

What would you like?
吃啥？ chěe sā

Cheers!
干！ gun

I'm feeling drunk.
我有点儿喝高咧。 ng yò dyèn·er hér gao lye

西安话 – eating out

a ... of beer	一 … 啤酒	yee ... pée jyò
glass	杯	bay
large bottle	大瓶	dā píng
small bottle	小瓶	shyào píng
a shot of (whisky)	一杯(威士忌)	yée bay (wāy shèe jèe)
a bottle/glass of ... wine	一瓶/杯 … 葡萄酒	yěe píng/bay ... póo tao jyò
red	红	hóng
white	白	báy

street eats

deep-fried persimmon pastry	黄桂柿子饼	hwúng gwāy sī zi bìng
dumpling stuffed with hot gravy	贾三灌汤包	jyà sun·er gwūn túng bao
Qíshān pancake	岐山锅盔	chée sun gwor kway
Qíshān spiced noodles	岐山哨子面	chée sun sāo zi myēn
rice and jujube cake	甑糕	jīng gao
roasted mutton cubes on spit	烤羊肉串	kào yúng ro chwùn·er
Shaanxi sandwich	肉夹馍	rō jya mōr
shredded pancake with beef	牛羊肉泡馍	nyó yúng ro pāo mōr
steamed cold noodles	凉皮	lyúng pée

special diets & allergies

Do you have vegetarian food?
有没有素食食品? yò mer yò sōo shí

Could you prepare a meal without ...?
能不能做一个不放 … 的菜? nérng boo nérng zō yee ge bǒo fūng ... dee tsāi

I'm allergic to ...	我对 … 过敏。	ng dwāy ... gwōr mìn
dairy produce	奶制品	nài jī pìn
eggs	鸡蛋	jěe dūn
meat	肉	rō
nuts	果仁	gwòr rérn·er
seafood	海鲜	hài shyen

emergencies & health

Help!	救命！	jyō mīng
Go away!	走开！	zò kai
Fire!	着火咧！	chwór hwòr lye
Watch out!	操心！	tsáo shin

Where's the nearest ...?	最近的 … 在哪儿?	zwāy jīn dee ... zāi nà
dentist	牙医	yá yee
doctor	医生	yēe serng
hospital	医院	yěe ywūn
pharmacist	药房	yěwe fúng

Could you please help?
能帮个忙不？ — nérng bŭng ger múng boo

Can I use your phone?
能借你电话用一下不? — nérng jyē nèe dyēn hwā yōng yee ha boo

Where's the police station?
派出所在哪里? — pāi choo swòr zāi nà

Where are the toilets?
厕所在哪儿? — tsăy swòr zāi nà

I'm lost.
我迷路咧。 — ng mée lōo lye

english–xi'an dictionary

...ictionary, words are marked as n (noun), a (adjective), v (verb), sg (singular), pl (plural), inf (informal) and ...lite) where necessary.

A

accident (mishap) 灾祸 zǎi hwōr
accident (traffic) 交通事故 jyǎo tong sī gōo
accommodation 食宿 shí sōo
adaptor 编剧 byěn jēw
address n 地址 dēe zì
after 之后 zǐ hō
air conditioning 空调 kòng tyáo
airplane 飞机 fáy jee
airport 机场 jēe chùng
alcohol 酒 jyò
all 所有的 swòr yò dee
allergy 过敏 gwōr mìn
ambulance 救护车 jyō hōo cher
and 和 hér
ankle 踝 hwái
antibiotics 抗生素 kūng serng sōo
arm 手臂 shò bēe
ATM 自动取款机 zīr dōng chèw kwèn jee

B

baby 婴儿 yǐng er
back (of body) 背 bāy
backpack 背包 bāy bao
bad 坏的 hwāi dee
bag 包 bao
baggage 行李 shíng lee
bank 银行 yín húng
bar 酒吧 jyò ba
bathroom 澡堂 zao tung
battery 电池 dyēn chí
beautiful 漂亮的 pyāo lyung dee
bed 床 chwúng
beer 啤酒 pée jyò
before 之前 zǐ chyén
behind 之后 zǐ hō
bicycle 自行车 zī shíng cher
big 大的 dā dee
bill 帐单 jūng dun
blanket 毛毯 máo tùn
blood group 血型 shěwe shíng
boat 船 shwún
book (make a reservation) v 预订 yēw dīng
bottle 瓶 píng
boy 男娃 nún wā
brakes (car) 煞车 sá cher
breakfast 早饭 zào fūn
broken (out of order) 坏掉的 hwāi dyāo dee
bus 车 cher
business 生意 sěrng yee
buy v 买 mài

C

camera 相机 shyūng jee
cancel 取消 chèw shyǎo
car 汽车 chēe cher
cash n 现金 shyēn jin
cash (a cheque) v 取钱 chèw chyén
cell phone 手机 shò jee
centre n 中心 jōng shin
change (money) v 零钱 líng chyén
cheap 便宜的 pyén yee dee
check (bill) 帐单 jūng dun
check-in n 登记 děrng jēe
chest (body) 胸膛 shyǒng túng
children 儿童 ér tóng
cigarette 香烟 shyūng yun
city 城市 chérng sī
clean a 干净的 gūn jīng dee
closed 关闭的 gwǔn bēe dee
cold a 冷的 lèrng dee
collect call 对方付费电话 dwāy fung fōo fāy dyēn hwā
come 来 lái
computer 电脑 dyēn nào
condom 避孕套 bēe yōon tāo
contact lenses 隐形眼镜 yìn shíng nyèn jīng
cook v 烹饪 pěrng rērn
cost n 价格 jyā gay
credit card 信用卡 shīn yōng kà
currency exchange 货币汇兑 hwōr bēe dwāy hwūn
customs (immigration) 海关 hài gwūn

D

dangerous 危险的 way shyèn dee
date (time) 日子 er zi
day 天 tyen
delay v 延迟 yún tsí

A

english–xi'an

dentist 牙医 yā yee
depart 出发 chóo fa
diaper 尿布 nyāo bōo
dinner 晚饭 wùn fūn
direct a 直接的 jī jye dee
dirty 脏的 zung dee
disabled 残废的 tsún fāy dee
discount v 打折 dà jér
doctor 医生 yěe serng
double bed 双人床 shwǔng rérn chwúng
double room 双人房 shwǔng rérn fúng
drink n 饮料 yìn lyāo
drive v 开车 kái cher
driving licence 驾照 jyā jāo
drug (illicit) 毒品 dóo pìn

E

ear 耳朵 èr dwor
east 东 dong
eat 吃 chi
economy class 经济舱 jīng jēe tsung
electricity 电 dyēn
elevator 电梯 dyēn tee
email 电子邮件 dyēn zì yó jyēn
embassy 大使馆 dā sì gwùn
emergency 紧急状况 jìn jée jwūng kwūng
English (language) 英语 yǐng yèw
evening 傍晚 būng wùn
exit n 出口 chǒo kò
expensive 贵的很 gwāy dee hèrn
eye 眼睛 nyèn jing

F

far 远的很 ywùn dee hèrn
fast 快的很 kwāi dee hèrn
father 爸 bā
film (camera) 胶卷 jyǎo jwùn
finger 指头 zǐ to
first-aid kit 急救箱 jée jyō shyung
first class 头等舱 tó dèrng tsung
fish n 鱼 yéw
food 食物 shí pìn
foot 脚 jewe
free (of charge) 免费的 myèn fāy dee
friend 朋友 pérng yo
fruit 水果 shway gwòr
full 满的 mùn dee

G

gift 礼物 lèe woo
girl 女娃 nèw wā
glass (drinking) 杯子 bāy zi
glasses 眼镜 nyèn jīng
go 去 chēe
good 好的 hào dee
guide n 导游 dào yó

H

half n 一半 yěe ber
hand 手 shò
happy 高兴的 gǎo shīng dee
he 他 tà
head n 头 tó
heart 心 shing
heavy 重的很 jōng dee hèrn
help 帮助 búng zō
here 制达 jí da
high 高的 gǎo dee
highway 高速公路 gǎo sōo gǒng lōo
hike v 徒步旅行 tóo bōo lèw shíng
holiday 假期 jyà chee
homosexual 同性恋 tóng shīng lyēn
hospital 医院 yěe ywūn
hot 热的 rěr dee
hotel 旅馆 lèw gwùn
(be) hungry 饿的很 ng dee hèrn
husband 丈夫 jūng foo

I

I 我 ng
identification (card) 身份证 shěrn fern jērng
ill 有病的 yò bīng dee
important 重要的 jōng yāo dee
injury (harm) 侮辱 wǒo ròo
injury (wound) 伤口 shǔng kò
insurance 保险 bǎo shyèn
internet 因特网 yǐn ter wùng
interpreter 翻译 fūn yee

J

jewellery 首饰 shò shi
job 工作 gǒng zwor

K

key 钥匙 yěwe si
kilogram 公斤 gǒng jin
kitchen 厨房 chóo fúng
knife 小刀 shyào dao

L

undry (place) 洗衣店 sèe yee dyēn
wyer 律师 lēw si
ft (direction) 左 zwòr
g (body) 腿 twày
sbian 女同性恋 nèw tóng shīng lyēn
ss 少 shào
tter (mail) 信 shīn
ght n 光 gwung
ke v 喜欢 shèe hwun
ck n 锁 swòr
ng 长的 chúng dee
st (items) 遗失的 yée shi dee
ve v 爱 āi
uggage 行李 shíng lèe
unch 午饭 wòo fūn

M

nail n 信 shīn
nan 男人 nún rérn
nap 地图 dēe tóo
narket 市场 sī chùng
natches 火柴 hwòr tsái
neat 肉 rō
nedicine 药 yewe
nessage 信息 shīn shēe
nilk 牛奶 nyó nài
ninute 分钟 fērn jong
nobile phone 手机 shò jee
noney 钱 chyén
nonth 月 yewe
norning 早上 zào shung
nother 妈 ma
notorcycle 摩托车 mwór twór cher
nouth 口 kò

N

name 名字 míng zi
near 近的 jīn dee
neck n 脖子 bór zi
new 新的 shīn dee
newspaper 报纸 bāo zi
night 晚上 wùn shung
no (not at all) 一点儿也不 yěe dyèn·er yè boo
no (not this) 不是 bǒo si
noisy 喧闹的 shyūn nāo dee
nonsmoking 禁止吸烟 jīn zì shēe yun
north 北 bay
nose 鼻子 bée zi
now 现在 shyēn zāi
number 数字 shōo zī

O

old (people) 老 lào
old (things) 旧 jyō
one-way ticket 单程票 dūn chérng pyāo
open a 开着的 kǎi jer dee
outside 外部的 wāi bōo dee

P

passport 护照 hōo jāo
pay v 付钱 fōo chyén
pharmacy 药房 yēwe fúng
phonecard 电话卡 dyēn hwā kà
photo 照片 jāo pyèn
police 警察 jìng tsa
postcard 明信片 míng shīn pyèn
post office 邮局 yó jóo
pregnant 怀孕的 hwái yōon dee
price n 价格 jyā ger

Q

quiet a 安静的 ūn jīng dee

R

rain n 雨 yèw
razor 刮胡刀 gwǎ hóo dao
receipt n 收据 shǒ jēw
refund n 退款 twāy kwùn
registered (mail) 记名的 jēe míng dee
rent v 出租 chóo zoo
repair v 修理 shyǒ lèe
reserve v 预订 yèw dīng
restaurant 饭店 fūn dyen
return (give back) 还 hwún
return (go back) 回来 hwáy lai
return ticket 返程票 fùn chérng pyāo
right (direction) 右 yō
road 路 lōo
room n 房间 fúng jyen

S

safe a 安全的 ūn chwún dee
sanitary napkin 卫生棉 wāy sěrng myén
seat n 座位 zwōr wāy
send 发送 fā sōng
sex (intercourse) 性行为 shīng shíng way
sex (gender) 性别 shīng byé
shampoo 洗发香波 shèe fǎ shyúng bor
share (a dorm) 分享 fērn shyùng

she 她 tà
sheet (bed) 床单 chwúng dun
shirt 衬衫 tsern sun
shoes 鞋 hái
shop n 商店 shŭng dyēn
short 短的 dwùn dee
shower n 洗澡 shèe zào
single room 单人房 dŭn rérn fúng
skin n 皮肤 pée foo
skirt n 裙子 chóon zi
sleep v 睡眠 shwāy myén
slow 慢的 mūn dee
small 小的 swāy dee
soap 肥皂 fáy zāo
some 一些 yĕe shye
soon 马上 mà shūng
south 南 nún
souvenir 纪念品 jēe nyēn pìn
stamp 邮票 yó pyāo
stand-by ticket 站台票 zūn tái pyāo
station (train) 火车站 hwòr cher zūn
stomach 胃 wāy
stop v 停止 tíng zì
stop (bus) n 站台 zūn tái
street 街 jye
student 学生 shéwe serng
sun 太阳 tāi yung
sunscreen 防晒油 fúng sāi yó
swim v 游泳 yó yòng

T

tampon 止血棉球 zì shĕwe myēn chyó
telephone n 电话 dyēn hwā
temperature (weather) 温度 wĕrn dōo
that 为个 wày ger
they 他们 ta mern
(be) thirsty 口渴的 kò kĕr dee
this 这个 jày ger
throat 喉咙 hó long
ticket 票 pyāo
time 时间 sí jyen
tired 累的 lāy dee
tissues 卫生纸 wāy sĕrng zì
today 今天 jĭn tyen
toilet 厕所 tsāy swòr
tomorrow 明天 míng tyen
tonight 今晚 jĭn wùn
tooth 牙 nyá
toothbrush 牙刷 nyá shwa
toothpaste 牙膏 nyá găo
torch (flashlight) 手电筒 shò dyēn tòng
tour n 旅行 lèw shíng
tourist office 旅行社 lèw shíng shēr
towel 毛巾 máo jin
train n 火车 hwòr cher
translate 翻译 fŭn yee
travel agency 旅行社 lèw shíng shēr
travellers cheque 旅行支票 lèw shíng zĭ pyāo
trousers 裤子 kōo zi
twin-bed room 标间 byăo jyen

U

underwear 内衣裤 nāy yĕe kōo
urgent 紧急的 jìn jée dee

V

vacancy 空缺 kōng chewe
vegetable n 蔬菜 shŏo tsai
vegetarian a 素 sōo
visa 签证 chyĕn jērng

W

walk v 步行 bōo shíng
wallet 钱包 chyén bao
wash (something) 洗 shèe
watch n 观看 gwŭn kūn
water n 水 fày
we 我们 ng mern
weekend 周末 jó mor
west 西 shee
wheelchair 轮椅 lóon yèe
when 当 … 时 dŭng … sír
where 在啊达 zāi á da
who 谁 sáy
why 为啥 wāy sā
wife 老婆 lào pwor
window 窗户 chŭng hoo
with 和 hér
without 没有 mĕr yò
woman 女人 nèw rern
write 写 shyè

Y

yes 是 sī
yesterday 昨天 zó tyen
you sg inf 你 nì
you sg pol 您 ní
you pl 你们 ni mern

Yunnan Hua

TONES	230
ABOUT YUNNAN HUA	231
PRONUNCIATION	232
LANGUAGE DIFFICULTIES	233
TIME & DATES	234
TRANSPORT & DIRECTIONS	235
ACCOMMODATION	236
BANKING & COMMUNICATIONS	237
SIGHTSEEING	238
SHOPPING	239
MEETING PEOPLE	240
MAKING CONVERSATION	241
FEELINGS & OPINIONS	243
FAREWELLS	244
EATING OUT	245
SPECIAL DIETS & ALLERGIES	248
EMERGENCIES & HEALTH	248
ENGLISH–YUNNAN HUA DICTIONARY	249

tones

Yunnan Hua is a tonal language ('tonal quality' refers to the raising and lowe of pitch on certain syllables). In this chapter Yunnan Hua is represented with f tones, as well as a fifth one, the neutral tone. Apart from the unmarked neutral tc we have used symbols above the vowels to indicate each tone, as shown in the ta below for the vowel 'a'. Bear in mind that the tones are relative to the natural vc range of the speaker, eg the high tone is pronounced at the top of one's vocal ran Note also that some tones slide up or down in pitch.

high tone ā	high rising tone á	low falling-rising tone ǎ	high fallinց tone à

about Yunnan Hua

Yúnnán may well be China's most diverse province. In the far southwest of the country it borders Vietnam, Laos, Burma and Tibet; it's noted for the variety of its topography and myriad plant species, and is the most ethnically diverse province in China, boasting communities of 25 of China's 56 recognised nationalities. These various communities speak a range of tongues from Tibeto-Burmese, Tai and Hmong-Mien language families. Despite this linguistic diversity, Yunnan Hua (yìn nùn hwà 云南话) is broadly lumped together with other southwestern dialects of Mandarin because of its similarity to Standard Mandarin. Yunnan Hua evolved this way due to the influx of Mandarin speakers from northern China in recent centuries. To the trained ear the only different elements of Yunnan Hua are a strong accent and some minor differences in pronunciation and grammatical structure. The idiom of the 'City of Eternal Spring', Kūnmíng, capital of Yúnnán province, is said to constitute a distinct dialect of Yunnan Hua, featuring some idiosyncratic pronunciations.

yunnan hua

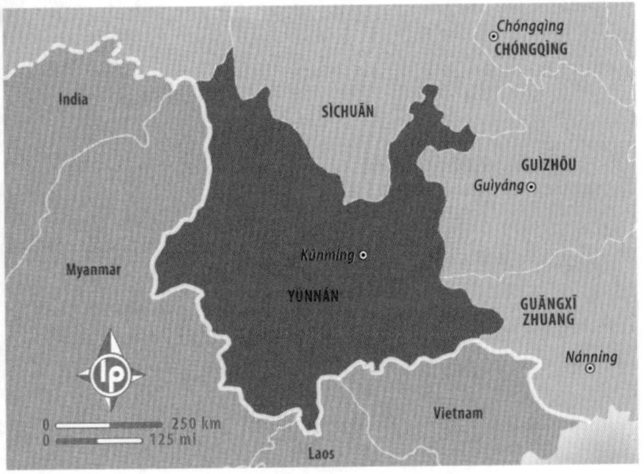

Vowels		Consonants	
Symbol	**English sound**	**Symbol**	**English sound**
a	father	b	bed
ai	aisle	ch	cheat
air	lair with strong 'r'	d	dog
ao	Mao	f	fun
ay	say	g	go
e	taken	h	hat
ea	yeah	j	jump
ee	see	k	kid
er	her	l	lot
ew	as in new, with rounded lips	m	man
i	hit	n	no
o	low	ng	ring
oo	tool	p	pet
or	more	r	run
u	cut	s	sun
In this chapter, the Yunnan Hua pronunciation is given in brown after each phrase. For pronunciation of tones, see p230.		sh	shot
		t	top
		ts	cats
		w	win
		y	yes
		z	lads

essentials		
Yes.	活呢。	hòr nē
No.	不活。	bóo hòr
Please …	请 …	chìng …
Hello.	你好。	nī hào
Goodbye.	再见咯。	zài jyèn gèr
Thank you.	谢谢你噶。	shàir shāir nì gà
Excuse me.	麻烦一哈。	mà fún yì hà
Sorry.	不好意思咯。	bòo háo yì sī gē

language difficulties

Do you speak English?
你咯会讲英文? — ní gē hwày jùng yīng wèn

Do you understand?
你咯懂呢? — ní gē dòng nē

I (don't) understand.
我认(不)得。 — wór ryèn (bōo) dèr

I (don't) speak Yunnan Hua.
我讲得(不)来云南话。 — wór júng dè (bōo) lài yìn nùn hwà

Could you please …?	你咯能 …?	ní gē nyèn …
repeat that	重新讲一遍	chòng shīng júng yì byén
speak more slowly	说慢叠	shòr mùn déa

numbers					
0	零	lìng	20	二十	ér shì
1	一	yì	30	三十	sūn shì
2	二	ér	40	四十	sì shì
3	三	sūn	50	五十	wóo shì
4	四	sì	60	陆十	lòo shì
5	五	wóo	70	七十	chì shì
6	陆	lòo	80	八十	bà shì
7	七	chì	90	九十	jyéw shì
8	八	bà	100	一百	yí bèr
9	九	jyéw	1000	一千	yí chyēn
10	十	shì	1,000,000	一百万	yí bèr wǔn

time & dates

What time is it?	这阵几点？	jyè jyèn jée dyén
It's (10) o'clock.	（十）点。	(shì) dyén
Quarter past (10).	（十）点过十五。	(shì) dyén gōr shì wōo
Half past (10).	（十）点半。	(shì) dyén bùn
Quarter to (11). (literally: Forty-five minutes past (10).)	（十）点过四十五。	(shì) dyén gōr sì shí wōo
At what time (does it start)?	哪哈（开始）？	ná hà (kāi shì)
(It starts) At 10.	十点（开始）。	shì dyén (kāi shì)
It's (18 October).	（十月十八号）。	(shì yeā shì bà hào)

yesterday	昨天	zòr tyēn
today	今天	jīn tyēn
now	这哈	jyè hà
tonight	今天晚上	jīn tyēn wún shùng
tomorrow	明天	mìng tyēn
sunrise	日出	rí chòo
sunset	日落	rí lòr
this …	这个 …	jyè gè …
morning (after breakfast)	早上	záo shùng
morning (before lunch)	上午	shúng wóo
afternoon	下午	shyàr wóo
spring	春天	chwēn tyēn
summer	夏天	shyàr tyēn
autumn	秋天	chyēw tyēn
winter	冬天	dōng tyēn

Monday	星期一	shīng chī yì
Tuesday	星期二	shīng chī ér
Wednesday	星期三	shīng chī sūn
Thursday	星期四	shīng chī sì
Friday	星期五	shīng chī wóo
Saturday	星期陆	shīng chī lòo
Sunday	星期天	shīng chī tyēn

January	一月	yì yeā
February	二月	ér yeā
March	三月	sūn yeā
April	四月	sì yeā
May	五月	wóo yeā
June	陆月	lòo yeā
July	七月	chì yeā
August	八月	bà yeā
September	九月	jéw yeā
October	十月	shì yeā
November	十一月	shì yì yeā
December	十二月	shì ér yeā

transport & directions

Is this the … to (Kūnmíng)?	这个 … 咯克 (昆明)呢?	jyè gè … gē kè (kwēn mìng) nē
boat	船	chùn
bus	公交车	gōng jyāo chē
train	火车	hór chē

Where's a/the …?	… 在哪叠?	… zài nā dèa
bank	银行	yìn hùng
place to change foreign money	换外币呢地方	hùn wài bì nē dì fūng
post office	邮局	yèw jèe

Is this the road to (the Green Lake)?

这个咯是克(翠湖)呢路? — jèr gè gē shì kè (tswày hóo) nē lòo

Can you show me where it is on the map?

麻烦帮我找一哈它在地图上呢位置。	mà fún būng wòr jyào yì hā tā zài dì tóo shùng nē wày jyì

What's the address?	地址是哪样?	dì jyī shì ná yùng
How far is it?	隔多远啊?	gè dōr yēn ā
Is it walking distance?	走过去咯远呢?	zō gòr kè gē yēn nē
How do I get there?	咋个走?	zà gè zō
Turn left/right.	往左/右拐。	wūng zòr/yèw gwài
It's straight ahead.	一直朝前。	yí jyì chào chyèn

It's …	在 …	zài …
behind …	… 呢后首	… nē hò shò
in front of …	… 呢前首	… nē chyèn shò
near …	… 呢附近	… nē fòo jìn
on the corner	… 拐角	… gwài jòr
opposite …	… 呢对面	… nē dwáy myèn
there	内叠	này dèa

accommodation

Where's a guest house?	
哪叠有宾馆?	nà dèa yèw bīn gùn
Where's a hotel?	
哪叠有酒店?	nà dèa yèw jéw dyèn
Can you recommend somewhere cheap?	
你咯能推荐一个便宜叠呢地方住?	nì gē nyèn twāy jyèn yì gè pyèn yì dèa nē dì fùng jyòo
Can you recommend somewhere good?	
你咯能推荐一个好叠呢地方住	nì gē nyèn twāy jyèn yì gè hào dèa nē dì fùng jyòo
I'd like to book a room.	
我想订哈房间。	wōr shyūng dìng hà fùng jyen
I have a reservation.	
我有预定呢。	wōr yéw yée dìng nē

Do you have a … room?	嗝有 … 房间呢?	gē yéw … fùng jyēn nē
double	套	tào
single	单人	dūn ryèn
twin	双人	shwūng ryèn

How much is it per night?
多少钱一天? — dōr shào chyèn yì tyēn

How much is it per person?
多少钱一个人? — dōr shào chyèn yì gè ryèn

I'd like to stay for (three) nights.
住上(三)天。 — jyòo shùng (sān) tyēn

Could I have my key, please?
咯能个我房间呢钥匙? — gē nyèn gē wòr fùng jyēn nē yòr chī

Can I get an extra (blanket)?
我咯能多拿一条(毛毯)? — wòr gē nyèn dōr nà yì tyǎo (mào tún)

The (air conditioning) doesn't work.
(空调)有毛病。 — (kōng tyào) yéw mào bìn

What time is checkout?
几点退房? — jí dyēn twày fùng

Could I have my …, please?	我想拿哈 我呢 …	wòr shyūng nà hà wòr nē …
deposit	押金	yà jīn
passport	护照	hòo jyào

banking & communications

Where's the local internet cafe?
附近咯有网吧? — fòo jìn gē yēw wùng bā

Where's a/an …?	… 在哪叠?	… zài ná dèa
ATM	自动取款机	zì dòng chí kùn jī
public phone	公用电话	gōng yòng dyèn hwà

I'd like to …	我想 …	wōr shyūng …
get internet access	上网	shùng wūng
use a printer	打印	dā yìn
use a scanner	扫描	sāo myào

What's your phone number?

你呢电话号码是多少?	nì nē dyèn hwà hào mā shì dōr shào

The number is ...

号码是 ···	hào mā shì ...

sightseeing

I'd like to see some local sights.

我想逛哈本地风光。	wōr shyūng gwùng hà byēn dì fōng gwūn

I'd like to go somewhere off the beaten track.

我想去人少叠呢景点。	wōr shyung kè ryèn shào dèa nē jīng dyēn

How long is the tour?

这趟旅游要花多长时间?	jyè tùng lī yèw yào hwā dōr chùng shì jyēn

I'd like to see ...

我想看哈 ···	wōr shyūng kùn hà ...

What's that?

内个是哪样?	này gè shì ná yùng

Can I take a photo?

我咯能拍呢?	wōr gē nyèn pè nē

sightseeing		
Dàlǐ three pagodas	大理三塔	dà lī sūn tà
Ěrhǎi Hú (Ear-shaped Lake)	洱海湖	eā hài hóo
Green Lake	翠湖	tswày hóo
Hǔtiào Xiá (Tiger Leaping Gorge)	虎跳峡	hōo tyào shyà
Lìjiāng	丽江	lì jyūng
Shangri-la	香格里拉	shyūng gè lée lā
Téngchōng	腾冲	tyèn chōng
Yùlóng Xuěshān (Jade Dragon Snow Mountain)	玉龙雪山	yì lòng shyeá shūn

shopping

Where's a ...?	… 在哪叠?	... zài nā dèa
camera shop	照相馆	jyào shyung gwūn
market	市场	shì chūng
souvenir shop	纪念品店	jì nyèn pīn dyèn
supermarket	超市	chāo shì

Where can I buy locally produced souvenirs?
哪叠有卖纪念品呢? ná dèa yéw mài jì nyèn pīn nē

What's this made from?
这个是拿哪样整呢? jyè gè shì nà ná yùng jyéng nē

I'd like to buy ...	我想买 …	wōr shyūng māi ...
Can I look at it?	我咯能看一哈?	wōr gē nyèn kùn yì hà
How much is it?	多少钱?	dōr shào chyèn
That's too expensive.	太贵了。	tài gwày lē

Please write down the price.
麻烦把价钱写下来的。 mà fún bà jyà chyèn shyēa shyàr lài dē

I'll give you (five kuai).
给你(五块)钱。 gē nī (wōo kwāi) chyèn

Do you accept credit cards?
你们咯收信用卡呢? nì myēn gē shō shìn yòng kà nē

less	少	shào
enough	足够	zòo gò
more	多	dōr
bigger	更大	gyèn dà
smaller	更小	gyèn shyāo

meeting people

Hello.	你好。	nī hào
Good morning.	你早。	nī zào
Good afternoon.	下午好。	shyàr wōo hào
Good evening.	晚上好。	wūn shùng hào
Goodbye.	再见噶。	zài jyèn gè
Good night.	休息啦。	shēw shì lā

Mr	大哥	dà gōr
Mrs	大姐	dà jēa
Ms/Miss	姑娘	gōo nyūng

How are you?	你咯好呢?	nī gē hāo nē
Fine. And you?	好呢。你呢?	hāo nē, nī nē
What's your name?	你叫哪样名字?	nī jyào nà yùng mìng zì
My name is ...	我叫 ···	wōr jyào ...
I'm pleased to meet you.	幸会。	shìng hwày

This is my ...	这个是我呢 ···	jyè gè shì wōr nē ...
brother	兄弟	shyōng dì
child	娃娃	wà wā
daughter	姑娘	gōo nyūng
father	爹	dēa
friend	朋友	pòng yēw
husband	男人	nùn ryèn
mother	妈妈	mā mā
partner (intimate)	对象	dwày shyung
sister	姊妹	zí mày
son	男娃娃	nùn wà wā
wife	媳妇	shèe fòo

making conversation

Do you live here?	你住的这叠咯?	nì jyòo dē jyè dèa gē
Where are you going?	克哪叠克?	kè nā dèa kè
Do you like it here?	咯喜欢这叠?	gē shī hūn jyè dèa
I love it here.	我很喜欢这叠。	wōr hyèn shī hūn jyè dèa
Have you eaten?	咯吃的啦?	gē chì dè lā
Are you here on holidays?	你咯是来这叠玩呢?	nī gē shì lài jyè dèa wùn nē

I'm here ...	我来这叠 …	wōr lài jyè dèa ...
for a holiday	玩	wùn
on business	出差	chù chāi
to study	留学	lyèw shòr

How long are you here for?
你要在这叠住到哪哈? — nī yào zài jyè dèa jyòo dào nā hà

I'm here for (four) weeks.
我住(四)周。 — wōr jyòo (sì) jyō

Can I take a photo (of you)?
我咯可以拍(你)? — wōr gē kòr yì pè (nī)

Do you speak (Yunnan Hua)?
你咯讲(云南话)? — nī gē jùng (yìn nùn hwà)

What language do you speak at home?
你在家头讲哪样话? — nī zài jyā tò jùng nā yùng hwà

What do you call this in (Yunnan Hua)?
你们用(云南话)喊这个喊哪样? — nī myēn yòng (yìn nùn hwà) hùn jyè gè hùn nā yàng

What's this called?
这个喊哪样? — jyè gè hùn nā yàng

I'd like to learn some (Yunnan Hua).
我想学一哈(云南话)咋个喊法。 — wōr shyùng shyòr yì hà (yìn nùn hwà) zà gè hūn fà

Would you like me to teach you some English?
你咯想跟的我学英语? — ní gé shyùng gēn dē wōr shyòr yīng yì

Is this a local custom?
这个咯是地方上呢风俗? — jyè gè gē shì dì fūng shùng nē fōng sòo

local talk		
Great!	板扎！	bún jyà
Hey!	麻烦！	mà fùn
It's OK.	整的成！	jyéng dè chèng
Just a minute.	等一头。	dyén yī tò
Just joking.	开玩笑。	kāi wùn shyào
Maybe.	有可能。	jéw kór nyèn
No problem.	某得事。	mó dè sì
No way!	不可能！	bòo kór nyèn
Sure, whatever.	好呢，好呢。	hào nē, bòo pà dè nē
That's enough!	可以了噶！	kór yí lē gà

Where are you from?	你从哪叠来?	ní tsòng nā déa lài
I'm from ...	我从 … 来。	wór tsòng ... lài
Australia	澳大利亚	ào dà lì yà
Canada	加拿大	jyā nà dà
England	英国	yīng gòr
New Zealand	新西兰	shīn shī lùn
the USA	美国	máy gòr
What's your occupation?	你是整哪样呢?	ní shì jyéng ná yùng nē
I'm a/an ...	我当 …	wór dūng ...
businessperson	做生意呢	zòr sēn yì nē
office worker	白领	bèr líng
tradesperson	师傅	sī fōo
How old ...?	… 几岁啦?	... jí swày lā
are you	你	ní
is your daughter	你呢姑娘	ní jyā gōo nyūng
is your son	你呢儿子	ní jyā éer zì

I'm … years old.	我 … 岁。	wór … swày
He/She is … years old.	他/她 … 岁。	tā/tā … swày
Too old!	太老啦！	tài láo lā
I'm younger than I look.	我还是小呢。	wór hài shì shyāo nē
Are you married?	你咯结的婚啦？	ní gē jèa dè hwēn lā
I live with someone.	我有伴。	wór yéw bèr
Do you have a family?	你咯成家啦？	ní gē chèn jyā là

I'm …	我 …	wór …
married	结的婚了	jèa dè hwēn lē
single	单个	dūn shēn

Do you like …?	你咯喜欢 …？	ní gē shí hūn …
I (don't) like …	我(不)喜欢 …	wór (bòo) shí hūn …
art	艺术	yí shòo
film	电影	dyèn yíng
music	听歌	yīng yòr
reading	看书	kùn shōo
sport	体育	tí yì

feelings & opinions

I'm (not) …	我(不)…	wór (bòo) …
Are you …?	你咯 …？	ní gē …
cold	冷呢	lèng nē
hot	热呢	rèr nē
hungry	饿呢	òr nē
thirsty	口渴呢	kó kòr nē
tired	累呢	lày nē

I (don't) feel …	我(不)觉得 …	wór (bòo) jòr dè …
Do you feel …?	你咯觉得 …？	ní gē jòr dè …
happy	高兴呢	gāo shìng nē
sad	不高兴	bòo gāo shìng
worried	着急	jyòr jì

What do you think of it?	你觉得咋个样？	ní jòr dè zá gè yùng

It's …	它 …	tā …
awful	差得很	chá dè hyén
beautiful	美丽呢	máy lì nē
boring	太无聊啦	tài wóo lyáo là
great	板扎	bún jyà
interesting	好玩呢	háo wùn nē
OK	还可以	hài kór yí
strange	稀奇	shī chì

farewells

Tomorrow I'm leaving.
明天我要克啦。 mìng tyēn wór yào kè lā

If you come to (Scotland) you can stay with me.
有机会么来(苏格兰)，可以来找我呢。 yéw jī hwày mē lài (sōo gè lún) kòr yī lài jyāo wór nē

Keep in touch!
常联系！ chùng lyèn shì

Here's my (address).
个你我呢(地址)。 gē ní wór nē (dì jyī)

What's your (email)?
你呢(网址)是哪样? ní nē (wúng jyī) shì ná yùng

well-wishing

Bon voyage!	一路平安！	yì lù píng ōn
Congratulations!	恭喜，恭喜！	gōng shì, gōng shì
Good luck!	祝你好运！	jyù ní hào yìn
Happy birthday!	生日快乐！	sēn rì kwài lòr
Happy New Year!	新年好！	shīn nyén hào

eating out

Where would you go for (a) ...?	…该克哪叠克?	... gāi kè ná dèa kè
banquet	办酒席	bùn jéw shì
celebration	举行庆祝会	jí shìng chìng jyóo hwày
cheap meal	吃呢稍微便宜叠呢	chì nē shāo wāy pyèn yí dèa nē
local specialities	地方小吃	dì fūng shyáo chì
yum cha	喝茶	hōr chà

Can you recommend a ...?	你咯能推荐一个 …?	ní gē nyèn twāy jyèn yì gè ...
bar	酒吧	jéw bā
cafe	咖啡馆	kā fāy gùn
dish	盘子	pùn zī
noodle house	面馆	myèn gùn
restaurant	馆子	gùn zī
snack shop	小吃店	shyáo chì dyèn
(wonton) stall	(馄饨)摊	(hwèn dyèn) tān
street vendor	街头小吃	jēa tò shyáo chì
teahouse	茶室	chà shì

I'd like (a/the) ...	我要 …	wór yào ...
table for (five)	一张(五个人呢)桌子	yì jyūng (wóo gè ryèn nē) jyòr zì
bill	账单	jyùng dūn
drink list	酒水单	jéw shwāy dūn
local speciality	一个地方特色菜	yì gè dì fūng tè sè tsài
menu	菜单	tsài dūn
(non)smoking table	(不)抽烟呢桌子	(bòo) chō yēn nē jyòr zì

Are you still serving food?
你们咯还营业呢? — ní mēn gē hài yíng yè nē

What would you recommend?
咯有喃菜可以推荐一哈? — gē yéw nùn tsài kòr yī twāy jyèn yì hà

What do you normally eat for (breakfast)?
(早点)吃喃? — (zāo dyēn) chì nùn

What's in that dish?	这道菜是用喃做呢?	**jyè dào tsài shì yòng nùn zòr nē**
What's that called?	内个喊哪样?	**này gè hùn ná yùng**
I'll have that.	整叠来嘛。	**jyèng dèa lài mà**
I'd like it with …	多放叠 …	**dōr fùng dèa …**
I'd like it without …	不要放 …	**bòo yào fùng …**
chilli	辣子	**là zī**
garlic	大蒜	**dà swùn**
MSG	味精	**wày jīng**
nuts	果仁	**gōr ryèn**
oil	油	**yèw**
I'd like …, please.	请给我 … 一哈。	**chìng gē wór … yì hà**
one slice	一块	**yí kwài**
a piece	一份	**yí fyèn**
a sandwich	一个三明治	**yí gè sūn mìng jyì**
that one	内一个	**náy yí gè**
two	两个	**lyùng gè**
This dish is …	这个菜 … 了。	**jyè gè tsài … lē**
(too) spicy	(太)辣啦	**(tái) là lā**
superb	太好啦	**tái hào lā**
That was delicious!	太好吃啦!	**tái hào chì lā**
I'm full.	吃饱的了。	**chì báo dè lē**
breakfast	早点	**zào dyèn**
lunch	中午饭	**jyōng wóo fùn**
dinner	晚饭	**wún fùn**
drink (alcoholic)	酒	**jèw**
drink (nonalcoholic)	饮料	**yīng lyào**
… water	… 水	**… shwày**
boiled	涨	**jyùng**
cold	冷开	**lèng kāi**
sparkling mineral	矿泉汽	**kùng chwùn chì**
still mineral	矿泉	**kùng chwùn**
(cup of) coffee …	(一杯)咖啡 …	**(yì bāy) kā fāy …**
(cup of) tea …	(一杯)茶 …	**(yì bāy) chà …**
with (milk)	加(牛奶)	**jyā (nèw nài)**
without (sugar)	不要加(糖)	**bòo yào jyā (tàng)**

black tea	红茶	hòng chà
chrysanthemum tea	菊花茶	jí hwā chà
green tea	绿茶	lòo chà
jasmine tea	花茶	hwā chà
oolong tea	乌龙茶	wōo lóng chà
fresh drinking yoghurt	酸奶	swūn nái
(orange) juice	(橙)汁	(chèng) jyī
lychee juice	荔枝汁	lì jyī jyì
soft drink	汽水	chèe shwày
sour plum drink	酸梅汁	swūn mày jyī
I'll buy you a drink.	我请客。	wóo chíng kèr
What would you like?	你喜欢哪样?	nì shì hūn ná yùng
Cheers!	干掉!	gūn dyào
I'm feeling drunk.	我有叠醉啦。	wóo yéw dèa zwày lá
a … of beer	一 … 啤酒	yì … pèe jèw
glass	杯	bāy
large bottle	大瓶	dà pìng
small bottle	小瓶	shyáo pìng
a shot of (whisky)	一樽(威士忌)	yì zūn (wāy sì jì)
a bottle/glass of	一瓶/杯	yì píng/bāy
… wine	… 葡萄酒	… pòo tāo jèw
red	红	hòng
white	白	bèr

street eats

cold clear bean-flour noodles	凉粉	lyùng fèn
corn on the cob	包谷	bāo gòo
dumpling (boiled)	饺子	jáo zī
dumpling (fried)	煎饺	jyēn jyào
dumpling (steamed)	包子	bāo zì
pork pie (small)	馅饼	shyèn bìng
rice cake	饵块	ér kwài
rice noodles	米线	mí shyèn
sticky rice in bamboo leaves	粽子	zòng zī
wonton soup	馄饨	hwèn dyèn

special diets & allergies

Do you have vegetarian food?
咯有素食？ gē yéw sòo shì

Could you prepare a meal without ...?
咯能做一个不放 … 呢菜？ gē nyèn zòr yì gè bòo fùng ... nē tsài

I'm allergic to ...	我 … 过敏。	wóo ... gòr mìn
dairy produce	奶制品	nái jyì pìn
eggs	鸡蛋	jī dùn
meat	肉	rò
nuts	果仁	gór ryèn
seafood	海鲜	hái shyēn

emergencies & health

Help!	救命！	jèw mìng
Go away!	让开！	rùng kāi
Fire!	着火啦！	jyòr hór lā
Watch out!	小心咯！	shyáo shīn gè

Where's the nearest ...?	最近呢 … 在哪叠？	zwày jìn nē ... zài ná dèa
dentist	牙医	yàr yī
doctor	医生	yī sēn
hospital	医院	yī yèn
pharmacist	药房	yòr fùng

Could you please help?
你咯能帮哈我呢忙？ ní gé nyèn bùng hà wór nē mùng

Can I use your phone?
我咯能借哈你呢电话用用？ wór gé nyèn jèa hà ní nē dyèn hwà yòng yōng

Where's the police station?
派出所在哪叠？ pài chòo sór zài ná dèa

Where are the toilets?
厕所在哪叠？ tsè sór zài ná dèa

I'm lost.
我迷路了说。 wór mèe lóo lē shòr

english–yunnan hua dictionary

dictionary, words are marked as n (noun), a (adjective), v (verb), sg (singular), pl (plural), inf (informal) and
polite) where necessary.

A

accident (mishap) 灾祸 zāi hòr
accident (traffic) 交通事故 jyāo tōng sì gòo
accommodation 食宿 shí sòo
adaptor 编剧 byēn jèe
address n 地址 dì jyī
after 之后 jyī hò
air conditioning 空调 kōng tyào
airplane 飞机 fāy jī
airport 机场 jī chùng
alcohol 酒 jéw
all 所有呢 sòr yèw nē
allergy 过敏 gòr mìn
ambulance 救护车 jèw hòo chē
and 和 hòr
ankle 踝 hwái
antibiotics 抗生素 kùn sēn sòo
arm 手膀子 shò būng zī
ATM 自动取款机 zì dòng chí kùn jī

B

baby 毛娃娃 mào wà wā
back (of body) 背 bāy
backpack 背包 bāy bāo
bad 坏呢 hwài nē
bag 包 bāo
baggage 行李 shíng lǐ
bank 银行 yìn hùng
bar 酒吧 jéw bā
bathroom 浴室 yée shì
battery 电池 dyén chì
beautiful 美丽呢 máy lì nē
bed 床 chùng
beer 啤酒 pée jéw
before 之前 jyī chyén
behind 后首 hò shò
bicycle 单车 dūn chē
big 大呢 dà nē
bill 帐单 jyùng dūn
blanket 毛毯 máo tún
blood group 血型 shyeá shìng
boat 船 chún
book (make a reservation) v 预订 yèe dìng
bottle 瓶 píng
boy 男娃娃 nùn wà wā
brakes (car) 煞车 sà chē
breakfast 早点 zāo dyèn
broken (out of order) 坏掉呢 hwài dyáo nē
bus 公交车 gōng jyāo chē
business 生意 sēn yì
buy v 购买 gò māi

C

camera 相机 shyùng jī
cancel 取消 chée shyāo
car 汽车 chì chē
cash n 现金 shyèn jīn
cash (a cheque) v 兑现 dwày shyèn
cell phone 手机 shò jī
centre n 中心 jyōng shīn
change (money) v 零钱 lìng chyèn
cheap 便宜呢 pyèn yì nē
check (bill) 帐单 jyùng dūn
check-in n 登记 dēn jì
chest (body) 胸膛 shyōng tùng
children 儿童 wà wā
cigarette 香烟 shyūng yēn
city 城市 chèng shì
clean a 干净呢 gūn jìng nē
closed 关闭呢 gwūn bì nē
cold a 冷呢 lèng nē
collect call 对方付费电话
dwày fūn fòo fày dyèn hwà
come 来 lài
computer 电脑 dyèn náo
condom 避孕套 bì yìn tào
contact lenses 隐形眼镜 yín shìng yēn jìng
cook v 烹饪 pēng ryèn
cost n 花费 hwā fày
credit card 信用卡 shìn yòng kā
currency exchange 货币汇兑 hòr bì hwày dwày
customs (immigration) 海关 hái gwūn

D

dangerous 危险呢 wāy shyēn nē
date (time) 日期 rì chēe
day 天 tyēn

delay v 延迟 yén chí
dentist 牙医 yàr yī
depart 出发 chòo fā
diaper 尿布 nyào bòo
dinner 晚饭 wún fùn
direct a 直接呢 jyì jèa nē
dirty 脏呢 zūng nē
disabled 残废呢 tsún fày nē
discount v 打折 dá jyè
doctor 医生 yī sēn
double bed 双人床 shwūng ryèn chùng
double room 套房 tào fúng
drink n 饮料 yīn lyào
drive v 开车 kāi chē
driving licence 驾照 jyà jyào
drug (illicit) 毒品 dòo pīn

E

ear 耳朵 āir dōr
east 东 dōng
eat 吃 chì
economy class 经济舱 jīng jì tsūng
electricity 电 dyèn
elevator 电梯 dyèn tī
email 电子邮件 dyèn zī yéw jyèn
embassy 大使馆 dà shī gwūn
emergency 紧急状况 jīn jì jyùng kwùng
English (language) 英语 yīng yì
evening 傍晚 bùn wún
exit n 出口 chòo kō
expensive 贵呢 gwày nē
eye 眼睛 yēn jīng

F

far 远呢 yēn nē
fast 快呢 kwài nē
father 爹 dēa
film (camera) 影片 dyèn yíng
finger 手指头 shō jyì tō
first-aid kit 急救箱 jí jèw shyūng
first class 头等舱 tò dèng tsūng
fish n 鱼 yèe
food 食物 shì wòo
foot 脚 jòr
free (of charge) 免费呢 myēn fày nē
friend 朋友 pòng yēw
fruit 水果 shwāy gòr
full 饱呢 bào nē

G

gift 礼物 lī wòo
girl 姑娘 shyào gōo nyūng
glass (drinking) 杯子 bāy zì
glasses 眼镜 yēn jìng
go 去 kè
good 好呢 hào nē
guide n 导游 dāo yèw

H

half n 一半 yì bùn
hand 手 shò
happy 高兴呢 gāo shìng nē
he 他 tā
head n 头 tò
heart 心 shīn
heavy 重呢 jyòng nē
help 帮助 būng jyòo
here 这叠 jyè déa
high 高呢 gāo nē
highway 高速公路 gāo sòo gōng lòo
hike v 徒步旅行 tòo bòo lí shìng
holiday 假期 jyà chī
homosexual 同性恋 tòng shìng lyèn
hospital 医院 yī yèn
hot 热呢 rèr nē
hotel 酒店 jéw dyèn
(be) hungry 饿呢 òr nē
husband 老公 lào gōng

I

I 我 wòr
identification (card) 身份证 shēn fèn jyèng
ill 生病呢 sēn bìng nē
important 重要呢 jyòng yào nē
injury (harm) 侮辱 wōo ròo
injury (wound) 伤口 shūng kò
insurance 保险 bào shyèn
internet 因特网 yīn tè wùng
interpreter 翻译 fūn yèe

J

jewellery 珠宝 jyōo bào
job 工作 gōng zòr

K

key 钥匙 yòr chī
kilogram 公斤 gōng jīn

kitchen 厨房 chòo fùng
knife 小刀 shyào dāo

L

laundry (place) 洗衣店 shī yī dyèn
lawyer 律师 lì sī
left (direction) 左 zòr
leg (body) 腿 twày
lesbian 女同性恋 nī tòng shìng lyèn
less 少 shào
letter (mail) 信 shìn
light n 光 gwūng
like v 喜欢 shí hūn
lock n 锁 sòr
long 长呢 chùng nē
lost 失去呢 shì chì nē
love v 爱 ài
luggage 行李 shìng lī
lunch 中午饭 jyōng wóo fùn

M

mail n 信 shìn
man 男人 nùn ryèn
map 地图 dì tòo
market 市场 shì chūng
matches 火柴 hōr chài
meat 肉 rò
medicine 药 yòr
message 信息 shìn shī
milk 牛奶 nèw nài
minute 分钟 fēn jyōng
mobile phone 手机 shò jī
money 钱 chyèn
month 月 yeā
morning 早上 záo shùng
mother 妈妈 mā mā
motorcycle 摩托车 mòr tòr chē
mouth 嘴巴 zwày bā

N

name 名字 mìng zì
near 附近 fòo jìn
neck n 脖子 bòr zī
new 新呢 shīn nē
newspaper 报纸 bào jyī
night 夜晚 yeà wūn
no (not at all) 一叠也不 yī dèa yē bòo
no (not this) 不活 bóo hòr
noisy 喧闹呢 shyēn nào nē
nonsmoking 禁止吸烟 jìn jyī shì yēn
north 北 bèr
nose 鼻子 bì zī
now 这哈 jyè hà
number 数字 shòo zì

O

old (people) 老 lào
old (things) 旧 jèw
one-way ticket 单程票 dūn chyèn pyào
open a 开呢 kāi nē
outside 外面呢 wài myèn nē

P

passport 护照 hòo jyào
pay v 付钱 fòo chyèn
pharmacy 药房 yòr fùng
phonecard 电话卡 dyèn hwà kā
photo 照片 jyào pyèn
police 警察 jīn chà
postcard 明信片 mìng shìn pyèn
post office 邮局 yèw jèe
pregnant 怀孕呢 hwài yìn nē
price n 价格 jyà gè

Q

quiet a 安静呢 ōn jìng nē

R

rain n 雨 yèe
razor 剃刀 tì dāo
receipt n 收据 shō jì
refund n 退款 twày kūn
registered (mail) 已挂号呢 yī gwà hào nē
rent v 出租 chòo zōo
repair v 修理 shyēw lì
reserve v 预订 yée dìng
restaurant 馆子 gùn zī
return (give back) 还 hài
return (go back) 回来 hwày lài
return ticket 返程票 fūn chèng pyào
right (direction) 右 yèw
road 路 lòo
room n 房间 fùng jyēn

S

safe a 安全呢 ōn chyèn nē
sanitary napkin 卫生棉 wày sēn myèn
seat n 座位 zòr wày
send 发送 fà sòng
sex (intercourse) 性 shìng

sex (gender) 性别 shìng beàr
shampoo 洗发精 shī fā jīng
share (a dorm) 分享 fēn shyùng
she 她 tā
sheet (bed) 床单 chùng dūn
shirt T恤 tī sheà
shoes 啡子 hài zī
shop n 商店 shūng dyèn
short 短呢 dwùn nē
shower n 淋浴 lìn yée
single room 单人房 dūn ryèn fùng
skin n 皮肤 pèe fōo
skirt n 裙子 chìn zī
sleep v 睡 shwày
slow 慢呢 mùn nē
small 小呢 shyào nē
soap 肥皂 fày zào
some 一些 yì sheā
soon 马上 mā shùng
south 南 nùn
souvenir 纪念品 jì nyèn pīn
stamp 邮票 yèw pyào
stand-by ticket 站台票 jyùn tài pyào
station (train) 火车站 hór chē jyùn
stomach 胃 wày
stop v 停止 tìn jyī
stop (bus) n 站台 jyùn tài
street 街 gāi
student 学生 shòr sēn
sun 太阳 tài yùng
sunscreen 防晒油 fùng shài yèw
swim v 游泳 yèw yōng

T

tampon 止血棉球 jyī sheà myēn chèw
telephone n 电话 dyèn hwà
temperature (weather) 温度 wēn dòo
that 那个 này gè
they 他们 tā mēn
(be) thirsty 口渴呢 kó kòr nē
this 这个 jyè gè
throat 喉咙 hó lòng
ticket 票 pyào
time 时间 shì jyēn
tired 累呢 lày nē
tissues 卫生纸 wày sēn jyī
today 今天 jīn tyēn
toilet 厕所 tsè sór
tomorrow 明天 mìng tyēn
tonight 今晚 jīn wùn
tooth 牙齿 yàr chī
toothbrush 牙刷 yàr shwà
toothpaste 牙膏 yàr gāo
torch (flashlight) 手电筒 shō dyèn tōng
tour n 旅游 lī yèw
tourist office 旅行社 lī shìng shè
towel 毛巾 mào jīn
train n 火车 hór chē
translate 翻译 fūn yèe
travel agency 旅行社 lī shìng shè
travellers cheque 旅行支票 lī shìng jyī pyào
trousers 裤子 kòo zī
twin-bed room 双人间 shwūng ryèn jyēn

U

underwear 内衣裤 này yēe kòo
urgent 紧急呢 jīn jì nē

V

vacancy 空缺 kòng chyeà
vegetable n 蔬菜 sōo tsài
vegetarian 素食呢 sòo shì nē
visa 签证 chyēn jyèng

W

walk v 步行 bòo shìng
wallet 钱包 chyèn bāo
wash (something) 洗 shì
watch n 观看 gwūn kùn
water n 水 shwày
we 我们 wòr mēn
weekend 周末 jyō mòr
west 西 shī
wheelchair 轮椅 lwèn ēe
when 哪哈 nā hà
where 在哪叠 zài nā dèa
who 哪个 nā gè
why 为哪样 wày nā yùng
wife 媳妇 shèe fòo
window 窗户 chūng hōo
with 和 hòr
without 没得 māy dè
woman 女人 nī ryèn
write 写 shyèa

Y

yes 是 shì
yesterday 昨天 zòr tyēn
you sg inf 你 nì
you sg pol 您 nīn
you pl 你们 nì mēn

Zhuang

TONES	254
ABOUT ZHUANG	255
PRONUNCIATION	256
LANGUAGE DIFFICULTIES	257
TIME & DATES	258
TRANSPORT & DIRECTIONS	259
ACCOMMODATION	260
BANKING & COMMUNICATIONS	261
SIGHTSEEING	262
SHOPPING	262
MEETING PEOPLE	263
MAKING CONVERSATION	264
FEELINGS & OPINIONS	267
FAREWELLS	268
EATING OUT	268
SPECIAL DIETS & ALLERGIES	272
EMERGENCIES & HEALTH	272
ENGLISH–ZHUANG DICTIONARY	273

tones

Zhuang is a tonal language ('tonal quality' refers to the raising and lowering of pitch on certain syllables). Tones in Zhuang fall on vowels. The same combination of sounds pronounced with different tones can have a very different meaning.

Zhuang has nine tones. In our pronunciation guide they've been simplified to six tones, indicated with accents on the letters, as shown in the tables below for the vowel 'a'. We've represented the following tones with one symbol: high flat, high even and high even short (eg ā); high rising and high rising long (eg á); mid flat and mid flat short (eg a). The last value for all three tones applies when the syllable ends in k, p or t.

Higher tones involve tightening the vocal cords to get a higher sounding pitch, while lower tones are made by relaxing the vocal cords to get a lower pitch. Bear in mind that the tones are relative to the natural vocal range of the speaker, eg the high tone is pronounced at the top of one's vocal range. Note also that some tones slide up or down in pitch.

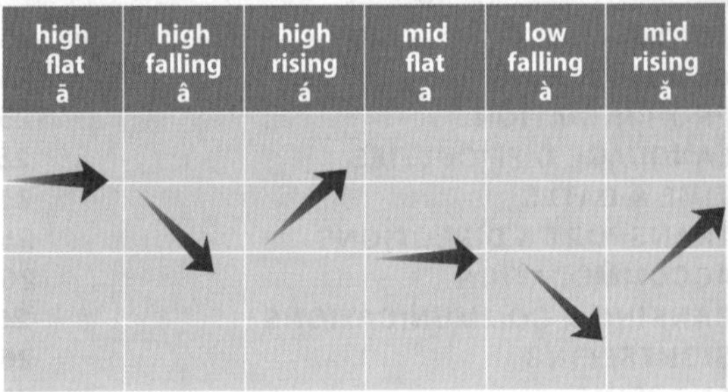

high flat ā	high falling â	high rising á	mid flat a	low falling à	mid rising ǎ

about Zhuang

Zhuang (vaa·shueng) is a Tai-Kadai language related to Thai and Lao. It's spoken primarily in the Guǎngxī Autonomous Region of southern China, but also in nearby areas of Guìzhou, Guǎngdōng, Húnán and Yúnnán. The Zhuang are China's largest minority group, with a population of around 18 million. Zhuang is tonal and largely monosyllabic. For many centuries, Zhuang has been written with a script borrowed from Chinese (the so-called *fangkuaizi*, 'square characters'), but since the 1950s the government has promoted a system of romanisation called Zhuangwen. Zhuangwen can be seen on road signs, official documents and in newspapers, and educated people may be able to read and write it. Often, however, people continue to use the Chinese script to write Zhuang. In this chapter, we have provided a more user-friendly transliteration system rather than Zhuangwen. There are two main dialects of Zhuang: northern and southern. The northern dialect represented here is based on that of Wǔmíng, a county directly to the north of Nánníng. Travellers going to other areas in Guǎngxī may find that the vocabulary varies somewhat, but armed with this phrasebook and a spirit of goodwill and adventure, you'll get along surprisingly well.

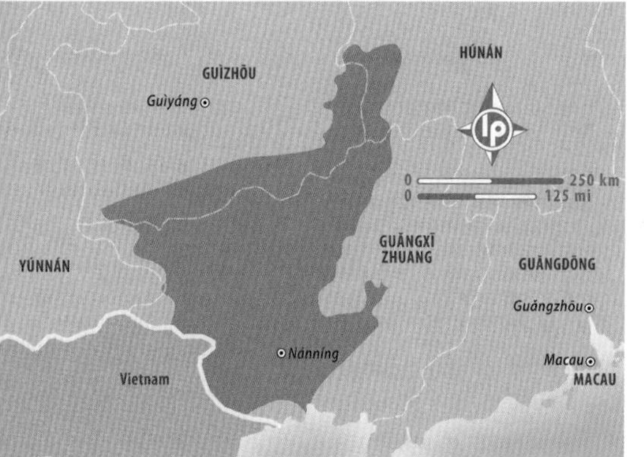

pronunciation

Vowels		Consonants	
Symbol	**English sound**	**Symbol**	**English sound**
a	run	b	like English b, but unvoiced
aa	father	d	like English d, but unvoiced
e	bet	f	fat
ee	like e, but longer	g	like English g, but unvoiced
ew	as the 'oo' in 'soon', with the lips spread widely	h	hat
i	hit	k	as in 'luck', but with no puff of air following
ii	machine	l	lot
o	vote	m	man
oo	like o, but longer	mb	a strongly voiced b
u	put	n	not
uu	like u, but longer	nd	a strongly voiced d
In this chapter, the Zhuang pronunciation is given in blue after each phrase.		ng	ring (both at the start and at the end of words)
In Zhuang, vowels can appear in combinations of two (diphthongs) or three (triphthongs). At the beginning of a word some consonants can also appear in combination, eg by, gv, gy, my, ngv, ny. All sounds in these combinations are simply pronounced in series.		p	as in 'nap', but with no puff of air following
		r	roach (guttural)
		sh	ship
		t	as in 'hat', but with no puff of air following
Syllables within a word are separated by a dot, eg: dŏo·shii.		th	thing
		v	vote
For pronunciation of tones, see p254.		y	yes

essentials

Yes./No.	dewk/mbōu dewk
Hello.	mèwng ndĕi
Goodbye. (said by person leaving)	gŏu băi góon lo
Goodbye. (said by person staying)	ndĕi byāai
Please …	shīng …
Thank you.	dŏo·shii
Excuse me. (to get past)	shīng vée ndăang di
Excuse me. (asking for assistance)	gŏu thīeng hēeu mèwng …
Sorry.	dói·mbōu·hēwn

language difficulties

Do you speak (English)?
mèwng rôo gāang (vaa·ying·yīi) mbōu

Do you understand?
mèwng rôo·yīu mbōu shàng

I (don't) understand.
gŏu (mbōu·shàng) rôo·yīu

I (don't) speak Mandarin.
gŏu (mbōu) rôo gāang būu·dung·vāa

Could you please repeat that?
shīng mèwng sháai gāang bài hee

Could you please speak more slowly?
shīng mèwng gāang meen dii

numbers

0	lìng	20	ngei·ship
1	īt/ndĕu	30	thăam·ship
2	ngei/thŏong	40	théi·ship
3	thăam	50	hāa·ship
4	théi	60	rōk·ship
5	hāa/ngûu	70	shāt·ship
6	rōk/lok	80	béet·ship
7	shāt	90	gōu·ship
8	béet/báat	100	īt·báak
9	gōu	1000	īt·shīen
10	ship	1,000,000	īt·báak·faan

time & dates

What time is it?
thèi·nêi gēi·dīem shŭng
It's (10) o'clock.
(ship) dīem lo
Quarter past (10).
(ship) dīem ship·hāa făn lo
Half past (10).
(ship) dīem búen shŭng lo
Quarter to (11). (literally: Forty-five minutes past (10).)
(ship) dīem théi·ship·hāa făn lo
At what time (does it start)?
dāa thèi·làew (hăai·shīi)
(It starts) At 10.
ship dīem shŭng (hăai·shīi)
It's (18 October).
ngòn·nêi (ship nyiet ship·béet haau)

this ...	... nêi
morning (after breakfast)	gyăang·hāt
morning (before lunch)	băan·ngòn
afternoon	băan·rìng·gváa
yesterday	ngòn·lèw·en
today	ngòn·nêi
now	thèi·nêi
tonight	ham·nêi
tomorrow	ngòn·shook
sunrise	băan·hāt
sunset	gyăang·ham
spring	thèi·shĭn
summer	thèi·haa
autumn	thèi·shŏu
winter	thèi·dŏng

Monday	thing·gìi·īt
Tuesday	thing·gìi·ngei
Wednesday	thing·gìi·tháam
Thursday	thing·gìi·théi
Friday	thing·gìi·hāa
Saturday	thing·gìi·rōk
Sunday	ngòn·thing·gìi

January	īt·nyiet
February	ngei·nyiet
March	thǎam·nyiet
April	théi·nyiet
May	ngûu·nyiet
June	lok·nyiet
July	shāt·nyiet
August	béet·nyiet
September	gōu·nyiet
October	ship·nyiet
November	ship·īt·nyiet
December	ship·ngei·nyiet

transport & directions

Is this the … to (Wǔmíng)?	… nêi bǎi (vūu·mìng) ma
boat	ǎn·rùu
bus	gung·gǔng gǐi·shee
train	ǎn·hōo·shee

Where's a/the …?	… yóu gìi·làew
bank	ngàn·hàang
place to change foreign money	diek vuen shìen gúek·rook
post office	yòu·děen·gìi

Is this the way to (Nánníng)?
dìu rǒn nêi dewk bǎi (nàam·nìng) mbōu
What village is this?
mbāan·nêi mbāan màa
Can you show me where it is on the map?
shīng mèwng ǎu mbǎew dei·dòo nêi rǎa ǎn dei·fǖeng nêi óok·dāu

What's the address?
diek·yóu yóu gìi·làew

How far is it?
mìi gēi·lǎai gyǎi

Can I get there on foot?
byāai rǒn gváa·bǎi ndāi mbōu

How do I get there?
bàn·làew byāai

Turn towards the left/right.
yieng baai·sêwi/baai·gvàa vǎan·gváa·bǎi

It's straight ahead.
īt·shik byāai·bǎi shoo baai·nāa

It's ...	yóu ...
behind ...	baai·lǎng ...
in front of ...	baai·nāa ...
near ...	théi·hèen ...
on the corner	báak·rǒn
opposite ...	dóoi·mien ...
there	gìi·hân

accommodation

Where's a guest house/hotel?
gìi·làew mìi bin·gvāan/līi·gvāan

Can you recommend somewhere cheap/good?
mèwng hāew gǒu gāew ǎn diek shien/nděi·yóu, ndāi mbōu

I'd like to stay at a locally run hotel.
gǒu thīeng yóu ǎn héek·díem dǎang·diek ging·yìng nei dòo

I'd like to book a room, please.
gǒu thīeng ding fùeng

I have a reservation.
gǒu théen shīi yāew·ding gváa

Do you have a ... room?	mìi fùeng ... rô nděwi
double (suite)	dáau
single	dǎan vùn
twin	thǒong vùn

How much is it per night/person?
ngòn·nděu/bôu·nděu gēi·lǎai shìen

I'd like to stay for (three) nights.
dāa·thúen dòo (thǎam) ngòn

Could I have my key, please?
fáak·yāk·thèi ǎn fùeng hāew gǒu, ndāi mbōu

Can I get an extra (blanket)?
sháai hāew gǒu (fǎan·dāam) nděu, ndāi mbōu

The (air conditioning) doesn't work.
(gung·dìu) vaai lo

What time is checkout?
thèi·làew dóoi fùeng

Could I have my ..., please?	shīng mèwng dóoi ... hāew gǒu
deposit	shìen·áat
passport	hǔu·shǎau

banking & communications

Where's the local internet cafe?
gìi·nêi mìi vāang·baa lewi

Where's a/an ...?	... yóu gìi·làew
ATM	thěw·dūng lîng·shìen·gii
public phone	gung·yung děen·vǎa

I'd like to ...	gǒu thīeng ...
get internet access	hēwn vāang
use a printer/scanner	yung dāa·yǐn·gii/thāau·myàau·gii

What's your phone number?
děen·vǎa mèwng dewk gēi·lǎai

The number is ...
haau·mâa dewk ...

sightseeing

I'd like to see some local sights.
gǒu thīeng bǎi yāew gīi gīng·thāk bōon·diek
I'd like to see ...
gǒu thīeng bǎi yāew ...
What's that?
gìi·hân dewk gīi·màa
Can I take a photo?
gǒu īng thíeng ndāi lewi
I'd like to go somewhere off the beaten track.
gǒu thīeng bǎi yāew gīi līi·yòu·dēen dōk·gûng dii
How long is the tour?
dāau·yòu ǎu gēi·lǎai thèi·gǎan

sightseeing	
Guìlín	gvěi·lìn
Huà Shān cliff paintings	vee·bâang·dáat byǎa·ràai
International Song Festival	shíet·fěwen tháam nyiet tháam
local chieftain's residence in Xīnchéng	yin·shìng háak·dōo yàa·mòon
museum	bǒo·vùu·gvāan
Yiling Cave in Wǔmíng	vūu·mìng yii·līng·ngàan
Zhuang village	mbāan shueng

shopping

Where's a ...?	... yóu gìi·làew
camera shop	shǎau·thǐeng·gvāan
market	shìeng·hǎew
souvenir shop	gīi·něen·gvāan
supermarket	shaau·gìi thǐi·shàang

Where can I buy locally produced goods/souvenirs?
gīi dô·gáai géi·niem dǎang·diek hân yóu gìi·làew shâew ndāi
What's this made from?
ǎn dô·gáai nêi yung gīi·màa shàai·lǐu shâau ha

I'd like to buy …
gǒu thīeng shâew …
Can I look at it?
gǒu yāew·yāew ndāi lewi
How much is it?
gēi·lǎai ngàn
Please write down the price.
shīng ràai gīi gyáa·shìen ròng·dāu hāew gǒu
That's too expensive.
dáai bèeng lo
I'll give you (five kuai).
hāew mèwng (hāa màn) ngàn
Do you accept credit cards?
yung thǐn·yǔng·gāa gyǎau shìen ndāi lewi
There's a mistake in the bill.
mbǎew dǎan nêi mìi věwn·dìi

less	dáai nôoi
enough	gáu
more	dáai lǎai
bigger	hǔng dii
smaller	íi dii

meeting people

Hello. (said to one person)	mèwng
Hello. (said to more than one person)	thǒu nděi
Welcome.	hoon·yìng
Goodbye. (said by person leaving)	gǒu bǎi góon lo
Goodbye. (said by person staying)	nděi byāai
Good night.	māa nìn lo
How are you?	mèwng nděi ma
Fine. And you?	nděi, mèwng ne
What's your name?	mìng·shoo mèwng heu·guu màa
My name is …	gǒu heu·guu …
I'm pleased to meet you.	sháu mèwng rǎn·nāa, áang râai·shâai

> **a manner of speaking**
>
> When approaching people to ask assistance, it's polite to address them with one of the following terms, which differ according to the gender and age of the person you're speaking to.
>
> | | |
> |---|---|
> | **female older than your parents** | mee·bāa |
> | **female (adult) younger than your parents** | mee·thīm |
> | **male older than your parents** | boo·lùng |
> | **male (adult) younger than your parents** | boo·ăau |

This is my ...	bôu·vùn nêi dewk ... gŏu
brother (older/younger)	dak·gŏo/dak·nûeng
child	lewk
daughter	daa·lewk
father	dâa·boo
friend	bàng·yôu
husband	gvăan
mother	dâa·mee
partner (intimate)	dak·yôu/daa·yôu m/f
sister (older/younger)	daa·shēe/daa·nûeng
son	dak·lewk
wife	yaa

making conversation

Do you live here?
mèwng yóu gìi·làew dòo
Where are you going?
mèwng băi gìi·làew
Do you like it here?
diek·nêi dewk·gyài lewi
I love it here.
diek·nêi dewk·gyài râai·shâai
Have you eaten?
mèwng gĕwn hâu shàng
Are you here on holidays?
mèwng dàng gìi·nêi lĩi·yòu ma

I'm here ...	gǒu dàng gìi·nêi ...
for a holiday	līi·yòu
on business	óok·shǎai
to study	lòu·haak

How long are you here for?
mèwng yóu gìi·nêi yóu gēi·nàan

I'm here for (four) weeks.
gǒu yóu gìi·nêi yóu (théi) ǎn thing·gìi

Can I take a photo (of you)?
gǒu īng thíeng (mèwng) ndāi lewi

Do you speak (Zhuang)?
mèwng rôo gāang (vaa·shueng) lewi

What language do you speak at home?
mèwng yóu ndǎew ràan gāang vaa gīi·màa

What do you call this in (Zhuang)?
gáai·nêi gāang (vaa·shueng) heeu·guu màa

What's this called?
gáai·nêi heeu·guu màa

I'd like to learn some (Zhuang).
gǒu thīeng haak dii (vaa·shueng) yāew

Would you like me to teach you some English?
gǒu thǒon mèwng/thǒu vaa·ying·yīi nděi mbōu sg/pl

Is this a local custom?
yieng·nêi guu dewk fǔng·thuk dǎang·diek ma

local talk

Great!	shǎn nděi
Hey!	vei
It's OK.	līi ndāi ba
Just a minute.	shāa dii
Just joking.	mèwng sháu gǒu gāang·rǐu
Maybe.	lǎau dewk yieng·nêi
No problem.	mbōu mìi màa
No way!	mbōu ndāi lo
Oh, spare me!	mbōu guu lo
Sure, whatever.	ndāi, ndāi
That's enough!	gáu lo, gáu lo

Where are you from?	mèwng dāa gìi·làew dāu
I'm from …	gǒu dewk vùn …
Australia	aáu·dǎa·lîi·yáa
Canada	gyaa·nàa·dǎa
England	ying·gòo
New Zealand	thin·thii·làan
the USA	mēi·gòo
What's your occupation?	mèwng guu gīi·màa hǒong
I'm a/an …	gǒu dewk …
businessperson	vùn thěeng·éi
office worker	vùn·baan·gǒng
tradesperson	vùn shaang
How old …?	… mìi gēi·lǎai bǐi lo
are you	mèwng
is your daughter	daa·lewk mèwng
is your son	dak·lewk mèwng

I'm … years old.
gǒu mìi … bǐi

He/She is … years old.
děe mìi … bǐi

Too old!
dáai lâau lo

I'm younger than I look.
gǒu hâau·thěeng gváa gīi yieng gǒu

Are you married? (asking a man)
mèwng ǎu la

Are you married? (asking a woman)
mèwng háa la

I'm …	gǒu …
married (said by a man)	ǎu yaa lo
married (said by a woman)	háa vùn lo
single	bôu·dok
I live with someone.	gǒu sháu yôu gǒu dòng·yóu
Do you have a family of your own?	mèwng bàn·gyǎa shàng

Do you like ...?	mèwng gyài ... ma
I (don't) like ...	gŏu (mbōu) gyài ...
art	yĭi·thùu
film	băi yāew dĕen·yīng
music	díng yin·yòo
reading	dok thăew
sport	dīi·yù

feelings & opinions

I'm (not) ...	gŏu (mbōu) ...
Are you ...?	mèwng ... ma
cold	nīt
hot	héwng
hungry	dûng íek
thirsty	hòo·háew
tired	bak

I (don't) feel ...	gŏu (mbōu) rôo·nyin ...
Do you feel ...?	mèwng rôo·nyin ... ma
happy	áang
sad	mbōu áang
worried	vŭeng

What do you think of it?	mèwng rôo·nyin ndĕi mbōu ndĕi

It's ...	dĕe ...
awful	yáak râai·shâai
beautiful	gyău·ndĕi
boring	shăn mbéw
great	gik ndĕi
interesting	yîn râai·shâai
OK	lĭi ndĕi
strange	gìi·gváai/gèi·hei

farewells

Tomorrow I'm leaving.
ngòn·shook gǒu yāk bǎi lo
If you come to (Scotland), you can stay with me.
daang·nàu mèwng dāu (thuu·gew·làan) hoon·yìng mèwng dāu sháu dǒu dòo yóu
Keep in touch!
shìeng·thèi ràai thín
It's been great meeting you.
sháu mèwng rôo·nāa shǎn váai·vuet
Here's my (address).
gīi·nêi dewk (diek·yóu) gǒu
What's your (email)?
(děen·thēw thǐn·thieng) mèwng bàn·làew ràai

well-wishing

Bon voyage!	nděi byāai
Congratulations!	gǒng·hěi
Good luck!	hoo mèwng thèi·héi nděi
Happy birthday!	ngòn·thěeng váai·vuet
Happy (Chinese) New Year!	bīi·móo váai·vuet

eating out

Where would you go for (a) ...?	... shéi nděi dàng gìi·làew bǎi
banquet	baan dàai·lāu
celebration	baan hoi hoo
cheap meal	gīi hâu byāk bìen·ngèi
local specialities	hâu byāk bōon·dei
yum cha	gěwn shàa

Can you recommend a ...? | mèwng gāang ... shéi nděi yóu gìi·làew

bar	bóu·lāu
cafe	gaa·fei·gvāan
dish	byāk
noodle house	bóu mien·fān
restaurant	bóu·hâu
snack shop	dǎan thīi·thīk
(wonton) stall	dǎan (vùn·dan)
street vendor	dǎan hèen·gǎai
teahouse	shàa·gūen

I'd like (a/the) ... | gǒu ǎu ...

table for (five)	ǎn dàai (hāa vùn)
bill	shǎang·daan
drink list	dǎan·lāu
local speciality	shūng byāk mìi dak·dīem bōon·dei hân
menu	shǎai·daan
(non)smoking table	ǎn dàai (mbōu) hāew shīt ĭen

Are you still serving food?
thǒu thèi·nêi līi hǎai·dǒu ma

What would you recommend?
mìi gīi·màa byāk shéi nděi

What's in that dish?
shūng byāk nêi yung gīi·màa dong·yieng mǎa long

I'll have that.
ǎu shūng nêi

I'd like it with ... | lǎai shúeng dii ...
I'd like it without ... | shīng gāi shúeng ...

chilli	lewk·maan
garlic	hǒo
MSG	věi·shing
nuts	máak·fâi
oil	yòu

What do you normally eat for breakfast?
hāt·nàng gěwn màa

What's that called?
shūng·nêi heeu·guu màa

I'd like ..., please.	shīng hāew gǒu ...
one slice	gáai nděu
a piece	fan nděu
a sandwich	ăn thaan·mìng·shíi nděu
that one	ăn·hân
two	thǒong ăn

This dish is ...	shūng byāk nêi ... lo
(too) spicy	(dáai) maan
superb	nděi gěwn râai·shâai

I love this dish.
shūng byāk nêi shăn hǒom
I love the local cuisine.
byāk bōon·dei shăn nděi·gěwn
That was delicious!
shăn nděi·gěwn
I'm full.
gěwn ím lo

breakfast	ngàai
lunch	rìng
dinner	shàu
drink (alcoholic)	lāu
drink (nonalcoholic)	yīn·lǐu

... water	... râm
boiled	gōn
cold	gyōt
sparkling mineral	gvăang·shèen·thūi dăai gǐi·băau
still mineral	gvăang·shèen·thūi

(cup of) coffee ...	(shēen) gaa·fei nděu ...
(cup of) tea ...	(shēen) shàa nděu ...
with (milk)	dēwk (nìu·nāai)
without (sugar)	mbōu dēwk (dàang)

black tea	hòng·shàa
chrysanthemum tea	shàa văa·gūt
green tea	shàa hěeu
jasmine tea	văa·shàa
oolong tea	vuu·lùng shàa

fresh drinking yoghurt	thoom nìu·nāai
(orange) juice	râm (máak·dōng)
lychee juice	râm lei·cĕi
soft drink	gĭi·thūi

a … of beer	… bìi·shīu ndĕu
glass	shēen
large bottle	bìng hŭng
small bottle	bìng íi

a shot of (whisky)	shŭng (vĕi·thĕw·gĭi) ndĕu

a bottle of … wine	bìng bùu·dàau·shīu … ndĕu
a glass of … wine	bòoi bùu·dàau·shīu … ndĕu
red	hòng
white	hăau

What are you drinking?	gĕwn màa
I'll buy you a drink.	gŏu shīng héek
What would you like?	gĕwn gīi·màa lāu
Cheers!	gĕwn lāu
This is hitting the spot.	dáai ndĕi gĕwn lo
I think I've had one too many.	gŏu lăau gĕwn dáai lăai lo
I'm feeling drunk.	gŏu mìi dii fii

street eats

corn on the cob	lûn hâu·yàang
dumpling (boiled)	shèi
dumpling (fried)	shèi shĭen
dumpling (steamed)	băau
flat bread with sesame seeds	thaau·bīng
rice noodles	fān
sticky rice in bamboo leaves	fâng
wonton soup	vùn·dan

special diets & allergies

Do you have vegetarian food?
mìi byāk shǎai nděwi
Could you prepare a meal without ...?
guu byāk mbōu shúeng ... ndāi mbōu

I'm allergic to ...	gǒu dóoi ... gǒo·mīn
dairy produce	nāai·bīn
eggs	gyái·gái
meat	noo
nuts	ngvei·máak
seafood	gīi dô·gěwn ndǎew hāai

emergencies & health

Help!	góu ming
Go away!	váai byāai bǎi
Fire!	dàew fèi lo
Watch out!	thīu·thǐm

Could you please help?
mèwng bǎang gǒu ndāi mbōu
Can I use your phone?
gǒu shíi ǎn děen·vǎa·gǐi mèwng ndāi mbōu
I'm lost.
gǒu byāai lǒng lo
Where are the toilets?
shèe·thōo yóu gìi·làew
Where's the police station?
bǎai·shùu·thōo yóu gìi·làew

Where's the nearest ...?	... shéi gyāew yóu gìi·làew
dentist	yàa·yii
doctor	shaang·yěw
hospital	yii·yěn
pharmacist	yòo·fàang

english–zhuang dictionary

dictionary, words are marked as n (noun), a (adjective), v (verb), sg (singular) and pl (plural) where necessary.

A

accident (mishap) thai·mēwt
accident (traffic) óok·thai
accommodation diek·gěwn·yóu
adaptor shàa·dòu shōon·shêe·gīi
address n diek·yóu
after dōk·lǎng
air conditioning gung·đìu
airplane fei·gii
airport fei·gii·shàang
alcohol lāu
all dâng
allergy gǒ·mīn·shěwng
ambulance giu·hūu·shee
and sháu
ankle dǎa·bǎu
antibiotics gǎang·gīn·thǔu
arm gěen
ATM thěw·dūng līng·shìen·gii

B

baby lewk·ndīng
back (of body) baai·lǎng
backpack dai·thǎew
bad yáak
bag dai
baggage hìng·lī
bank ngàn·hàang
bar bóu·lāu
bathroom théwi·fèwng·geen
battery děen·shìi
beautiful gyǎu·ndēi
bed shòong
beer bìi·shīu
before (time) góon
behind baai·lǎng
bicycle daan·shee
big hūng
bill shǎang·daan
blanket dǎam
blood group lewt·hìng
boat ǎn·rù
book (make a reservation) v ding
bottle bìng
boy lewk·thǎai
brakes (car) kaap·shīi
breakfast ngàai
broken (out of order) vaai lo
bus gung·gūng gīi·shee
business thěeng·éi
buy v shǎew

C

camera shǎau·thīeng·gii
cancel mbōu ǎu
car gīi·shee
cash n shìen·ngàn
cash (a cheque) v dóoi·yien (shii·byǎau)
cell phone thōu·gii
centre n shúng·gyǎang
change (money) v vuen (shìen)
cheap bìen·ngèi
check (bill) shǎang·daan
check-in n dewng·gīi
chest (body) nāa·āk
children lewk·nyèe
cigarette ìen
city ndǎew·thìng
clean a thǎew
closed gvěen dǒu lo
cold (food/water) a shāp
cold (weather) a nīt
collect call děen·vǎa dóoi·fūeng hāew·shìen
come dǎu
computer děen·nǎau
condom bìi·yìn·dǎu
contact lenses ngâan·gíng yīn·hìng
cook v thǎew
cost n bōon·shìen
credit card thīn·yūng·gāa
currency exchange diek vuen shìen
customs (immigration) hǎai·gvaan

dangerous yūng·yīem
date (time) that·shēi
day ngòn
delay v ngu

dentist yàa·yii
depart lìi
diaper vāa·nyou
dinner shàu
direct a shik·thoo
dirty úu
disabled féi
discount v dāa shīng·thóo
doctor shaang·yěw
double bed shòong thǒong·vùn
double room fūeng thǒong·vùn
drink n yīn·līu
drive v hǎai (shīi)
drivers licence gyǎa·thīi shìi·shǎau
drug (illicit) dùu·bīn

E

ear rèw
east dǒng
eat gěwn
economy class ging·shii shaang
electricity děen·gīi
elevator děen·dii
email děen·thēw yòu·gēen
embassy dǎa·thīi·gvāan
emergency thai gān·gīp
English (language) vaa ying·yii
evening gyǎang·ham
exit n shùu·gōu
expensive bèeng
eye dǎa

F

far gyǎi
fast váai
father dâa·boo
film (camera) gyaau·gēen
finger lewk·fèwng
first-aid kit gìi·gīu yòo·thieng
first class shaang dàu·dāng
fish n byǎa
food gīi·gěwn
foot dīn
free (of charge) mēen·fāi
friend bàng·yôu
fruit máak
full (container) rīm
full (stomach) ím

G

gift lâi
girl lewk·mbēwk
glass (drinking) shēen
glasses yàang·gíng
go bǎi
good nděi
guide n bôu·dáai·rǒn

H

half n búen
hand fèwng
happy áang
he děe
head n gyāu
heart thīm
heavy nāk
help v bǎang
here gìi·nêi
high thǎang
highway gung·lǔu
hike v byāai loo
holiday gyǎa·gèi
homosexual dùng·thīng·lěen·shēe
hospital yii·yěn
hot (temperature/weather) ndáat
hotel līi·gvāan
(be) hungry dūng·íek
husband gvǎan

I

I gǒu
identification (card) thin·fēwn·shěwng
ill bing lo
important yóu·gān
injury (harm) thīeng·haai
injury (wound) báak·thīeng
insurance bāau·yēen
internet hǔu·lèen·vāang
interpreter faan·yìi·yèen

J

jewellery shǎew·bāau
job hǒong

K

key yāk·thèi
kilogram gǒng·gǎn

kitchen ràan·dāa·shāew
knife shāa

L

laundry (place) thīi·yii·díem
lawyer līi·thew
left (direction) thêwi
leg (body) gǎa
lesbian nīi·thīng dùng·thīng·lěen·shēe
less nôoi
letter (mail) thín
light n děn·dewng
like v gyài
lock n thūu
long rài
lost lǒng·rǒn
love v gyài
luggage hìng·līi
lunch rìng

M

mail n yòu·gěen
man vùn
map dei·dòo
market shìeng·hǎew
matches haab·fèi
meat noo
medicine yěw
message shìen·vaa
milk nìu·nāai
minute fǎn
mobile phone thōu·gii
money shìen
month nděwen
morning gyǎang·hāt
mother dāa·mee
motorcycle moo·dòo·shee
mouth báak

N

name mìng·shoo
near gyǎew
neck n hòo
new móo
newspaper báau·shēi
night gyǎang·ham
no mbōu
noisy shàau
nonsmoking mbōu shīt īen
north bāk
nose ndǎng
now thèi·nêi
number haau

O

old (people) lâau
old (things) gée
one-way ticket bíu daan·shèwng
open a hǎai·dēwk
outside baai·roog

P

passport hǔu·shǎau
pay v gyǎau shìen
pharmacy yòo·fāang
phonecard děen·vǎa·gāa
photo mbǎew·thíeng
police gīng·shàa
postcard mìng·thǐn·bēen
post office yòu·děen·gìi
pregnant mìi ndǎang
price n gyáa·shìen

Q

quiet a yàm

R

rain n fěwn
razor faak·dái
receipt n thǒu·dìu
refund n bòoi
registered mail yòu·gěen gváa·haau
rent v shǒo ràan
repair v shooi
reserve v bǎau·lòu
restaurant bóu·hâu
return (give back) hòoi
return (go back) bǎi·mǎa
return ticket bíu bǎi·dáau
right (direction) baai gváa
road rǒn
room n fūeng

S

safe a ǎan·shìen
sanitary napkin thǎai dàew·thak
seat n diek·nang
send thóng

sex (intercourse) dô·ēe
sex (gender) dak rô daa
shampoo thīi·fàa·shīi
share (a dorm) dòng·yóu
she dĕe
sheet (bed) dāam
shirt buu
shoes hàai
shop n bóu
short dám
shower n lìn·yù·thìi
single room fùeng vùn·ndēu
skin n năng
skirt n gùn
sleep v nìn
slow meen
small îi
soap gēen
some mbāng
soon shou
south nàam
souvenir dô·gáai géi·niem
stamp yòu·biu
stand-by ticket bĕi·yung·bíu
station (train) shee·shăan
stomach dûng
stop v dìng
stop (bus) n gung·gūng gīi·shee shăan
street găai
student haak·thĕeng
sun dăng·ngòn
sunscreen fàang·thăai·yòu
swim v yòu·râm

T

tampon mèen·thăai
telephone n dĕen·văa
temperature (weather) gīi·vewn
that hân
they gyóng·dĕe
(be) thirsty hòo·háew
this nêi
throat hòo
ticket bíu
time thèi·găan
tired bak
tissues shēi·găn
today ngòn·nêi
toilet shèe·thōo
tomorrow ngòn·shook
tonight ham·nêi
tooth hēeu
toothbrush gáai·sháat·hēeu
toothpaste yàa·gaau
torch (flashlight) thōu·dĕn·dùng
tour n līi·hìng
tourist office līi·hìng băan·gung·thìi
towel thūu·bía
train n hōo·shee
translate faan·yìi
travel agency līi·hìng·thĕe
travellers cheque līi·hìng shii·byăau
trousers váa
twin-bed room fùeng thŏong shòong

U

underwear buu·ndăew
urgent găn·gīp

V

vacancy fùeng hóng
vegetable n byăk
vegetarian a bôu gĕwn shăai
visa shīem·shíng

W

walk v byăai
wallet shìen·băau
wash (something) thak
watch n thōu·byăau
water n râm
we (including 'you') ràu
we (not including 'you') dōu
weekend shōu·mòo
west thăi
wheelchair ēi·lōk
when thèi·làew
where gìi·làew
who bôu·làew
why vii·màa
wife yaa
window báak·dáang
with sháu
without mbōu mìi
woman mee·mbēwk
write ràai

Y

yes dewk
yesterday ngòn·lèwen
you sg mèwng
you pl thōu

Mongolian

ALPHABET 278
ABOUT MONGOLIAN 279
PRONUNCIATION 280
LANGUAGE DIFFICULTIES 281
TIME & DATES 282
TRANSPORT & DIRECTIONS 283
ACCOMMODATION 285
BANKING & COMMUNICATIONS 286
SIGHTSEEING 286
SHOPPING 288
MEETING PEOPLE 289
MAKING CONVERSATION 290
FEELINGS & OPINIONS 294
FAREWELLS 295
EATING OUT 296
SPECIAL DIETS & ALLERGIES 300
IN THE GRASSLANDS 301
EMERGENCIES & HEALTH 303
ENGLISH–MONGOLIAN DICTIONARY 305

alphabet

Initial	Medial	Final	Romanisation
			a, aa
			u
			i, ee
			o, ŭ
			ŭ, oo
			n
			ng
			b, v, w
			p
			h, kh
			h, kh
			g
			g
			l
			m
			s, sh
			sh
			t, d
			ch
			j

Initial	Medial	Final	Romanisati
			y
			r
			w, v, e

Extended letters (for Chinese and other foreign words) are listed below.

Initial	Medial	Final	Romanisati
			f
			k
			lh
			ts
			z
			h
			zh
			zh
			chö

Mongolian is written vertically, ie from to to bottom (and read from left to right), ir a cursive alphabetic script consisting of 2 basic letters with the addition of several extra characters used mainly to write worc borrowed from other languages.

Not all sounds listed in this table are foun in the phrases within this chapter. See th pronunciation guide, p280.

Where two options are given in the table, you might see either symbol used.

MONGOLIAN

about Mongolian

Mongolian (*mong*·gol hul) is a Mongolic language, thought to be related to Turkish, Japanese and Korean. It's written using a cursive script in vertical lines read from left to right (also see p282) – one of few languages to be written this way. According to legend, the script was instituted by order of Genghis Khan in 1204. Today, there are estimated to be around 10 million Mongols worldwide, the majority living in the Inner Mongolia Autonomous Region of China. The standard language for Mongols in China is based on the Chahar dialect (used in this chapter), an official language alongside Mandarin Chinese. Mongolian restaurants and stores can be found throughout Inner Mongolia, and if the Mongolian writing on the signs is larger than the Chinese, you can be sure those inside speak Mongolian. Of course, a trip to Inner Mongolia should include a visit to its famous grasslands. Travellers here will often be met by locals and presented with a ceremonial scarf, called a *khadag* (*had*·dug), along with verbal blessings. Foreigners speaking Mongolian cause great delight – even more so if you say *tan*·nē yir·*rool tog*·tukh bol·*too*·gē, meaning 'May your blessings come to pass!'

mongolian

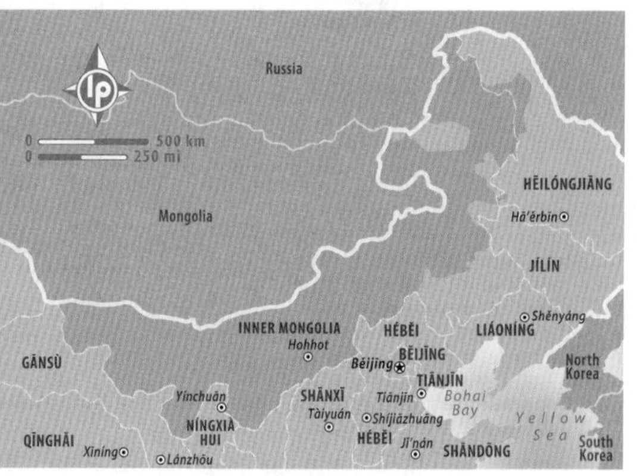

pronunciation

Vowels		Consonants	
Symbol	**English sound**	**Symbol**	**English sound**
a	fat	b	bit
aa	father	ch	chin
ai	aisle	d	dog
ao	Mao	f	fun
ay	day	g	go
e	bet	h	hot
ē	there	j	jump
ee	see	k	kid
i	pig	kh	as the 'ch' in Scottish 'loch'
o	hot	l	lip
ô	alone	m	map
ö	'e' pronounced with rounded lips	n	no
oi	oil	ng	sing
öö	slightly longer ö	p	pet
oo	tool	r	run (very strong and trilled)
u	cut	s	sip
ŭ	good	sh	shoe
		t	top
		ts	cats
		v	very
		w	win
		y	you
		z	lads

In this chapter, the Mongolian pronunciation is given in green after each phrase. The 'r' in Mongolian is a hard, trilled sound. Note that s should always be pronounced as in 'sip' regardless of the sounds around it.

Syllables are separated by a dot and the stressed syllable is marked by italics.

For example: *ar*·bun

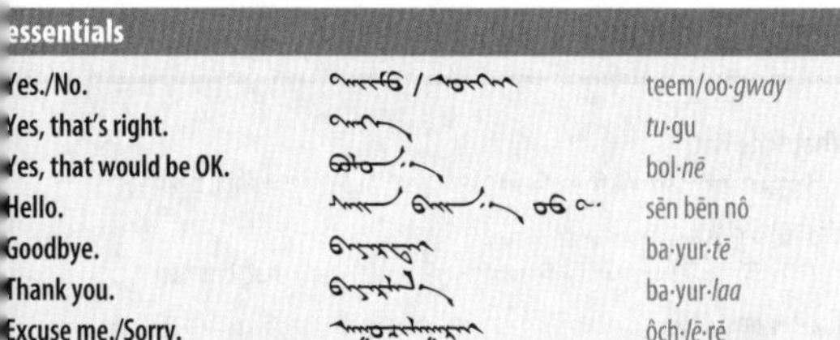

essentials	
Yes./No.	teem/oo·*gway*
Yes, that's right.	*tu*·gu
Yes, that would be OK.	bol·*nē*
Hello.	sēn bēn nô
Goodbye.	ba·yur·*tē*
Thank you.	ba·yur·*laa*
Excuse me./Sorry.	ôch·*lē*·rē

language difficulties

Do you speak English?
ta *ang*·gul hul *mu*·tun nô

Do you understand?
ta *oil*·goj jô

I (don't) understand.
bee *oil*·og·sun·(gway)

Could you please repeat that?
dēkh·*aad* nig ŭd·*daa*
hilj *bol*·un nô

Could you please speak more slowly?
aa·jim shig hilj *bol*·un nô

numbers				
0	tig		20	hur
1	nig		30	gŭch
2	*hoi*·yur		40	dŭch
3	gŭ·*roo*		50	teb
4	dŭ·*roo*		60	jir
5	tav		70	dal
6	jŭr·*gaa*		80	nai
7	dol·*lô*		90	yir
8	nēm		100	jô
9	yis		1000	myang
10	*a*·ra·oo		1,000,000	jôn tŭm

time & dates

What time is it?
hut·tee chag bolj bēkh vē

It's (10) o'clock.
(*ar*·bun) chag bolj bēn

Quarter past (10).
(*ar*·bun) chag *ar*·ban *ta*·vun *min*·nut

Half past (10).
(*ar*·bun) chag *ha*·gas

Forty-five minutes past (10).
(*ar*·bun) chag *dŭ*·chin *ta*·vun *min*·nut

At what time (does it start)?
hut·tee chagt (*ukh*·lukh vē)

(It starts) At 10.
ar·bun chag·*aas* (ukh·lun·*nē*)

It's (18 October).
oo·*noo*·dur (ar·bun sar·in ar·bun nē·mun)

the day before yesterday	ŭr·*jee*·dur
yesterday	*oo*·chig·dur
today	oo·*noo*·dur
tomorrow	mar·*gaash*
the day after tomorrow	nŭg·*oo*·dur

just a twist to the right

Mongolian script is written vertically and read from left to right. So if you want to have a go at reading the script in this chapter, or when asking a local to read it for you, simply turn the book 90 degrees clockwise. Our coloured pronunciation guides, however, should simply be read the same way you read English.

Monday	ga·rug·*een nig*·un
Tuesday	ga·rug·*een* hoir
Wednesday	ga·rug·*een gŭr*·bun
Thursday	ga·rug·*een dŭr*·bun
Friday	ga·rug·*een ta*·vun
Saturday	ga·rug·*een* jur·*gaa*
Sunday	ga·rug·*een ŭd*·dur

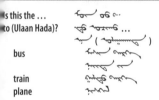

transport & directions

Is this the ... to (Ulaan Hada)?	un (ŭ·*laan*·ad) *och*·ikh ... mŭn ô
bus	*neet*·in *ma*·shin *tur*·rug
train	galt *tur*·rug
plane	*nis*·gul

Where's a/the ...?	... haa bēkh vē
bank	benk
convenience store	khit dul·*goor*
currency exchange	jôs *so*·likh *gaj*·jur
pharmacy	um·*meen* dul·*goor*
post office	*shô*·dang tob·*chô*
restaurant	*hô*·lan gur

Is this the road to (the Inner Mongolia Museum)?

un bol (*oo*·woor *mong*·gol·in moo·*zēi*)·d *ya*·vukh jam mŭn nô

Can you show me where it is on the map?
oon·*ee gaj*·rin *jir*·rug döör *nad*·ad jaaj *üg*·gün nô

Where is it located?
haa *bē*·dug vē

How far is it?
hut·tee hol vē

How do I get there?
bee yaaj tund *och*·chikh vē

Turn towards the left.
joonsh·ön

Turn towards the right.
ba·*rônsh*·ön

It's straight ahead.
shôt *ya*·vun

Can I get there on foot?
bee *yav*·gun *o*·chij *bol*·un nô

behind	*ar*·dun
in front of	*oom*·nun
near	oi·rul·*chô*
on the corner	*ŭn*·chŭgt bēn
opposite	*us*·rug *tal*·dun
there	tund

accommodation

Where's a guest house?

joch·*deen bô*·tul
haa bēkh vē

Can you recommend somewhere cheap/good?

nad·ud nig *hyemd*·hun/sēn shig
gaj·jur tan·il·*chôlj*
ŭg·gun nô

I'd like to book a room, please.

bee nig ŭr·*röö*
jakh·*aal*·dakh san·*naa*·tē

I have a reservation.

bee nig ŭr·*röö* jakh·*aald*·jai

Do you have a … room?	tand … ŭr·*röö* bēn nô
double (suite)	*hoi*·yur *hoo*·nē
single	ganch *hoo*·nē
twin	*hoi*·yur or·*tē*

How much is it per night/person?

nig *ho*·nug/hoon
hut·tee jôs vē

I'd like to stay for (three) nights.

bee (*gŭ*·roo) *hon*·nokh san·*naa*·tē

Could I have my key, please?

tŭl·*khoor*·öön *ŭgch*
bol·un nô

Can I get an extra (blanket)?

öör nig (tans) ŭgch *bol*·un nô

The (air conditioning) doesn't work.

(*kong*·tee·aa·oo) uv·dur·*jē*

What time is checkout?

mar·*gaash hut*·tee chagt
yav·vakh vē

Could I have my …, please?	*min*·nee … *bô*·chaj ŭgch *bol*·un nô
deposit	bar·ree·*chaan*·nē mŭngk
passport	*pas*·port

banking & communications

Where's a/an …?	… haa bēkh vē
ATM	tee kwan jee
public phone	*neet*·in *ô*·tas
internet cafe	net baar

How much is it per hour?
nig chag *hut*·tee jôs vē

What's your phone number?
tan·*nē ŭ*·tus·un *no*·mur *hut*·tee vē

The number is …
min·nee *no*·mur bol …

sightseeing

What time does it open/close?
hut·tun chagt *nö*·dug/*haa*·dug vē

What's the admission charge?
pee·*aa*·oo *hut*·tee jôs vē

Is there a discount for student/children?
sŭ·ragch·*een*/hookh·*deen* pee·*aa*·oo bēn nô

I'd like a …	bee … av·*yaa*
catalogue	jô·*gaa*·chul·een *div*·tir
guide	jam·*chee*·lugch
map	*gaj*·reen *jŭ*·rug

'd like to see …

… *ŭ*·jikh san·*naa*·tē

Vhat's that?

tir yoo bē

'an I take a photo?

bee *soo*·dur avch
bol·un nô

'an I take photos here?

und *soo*·dur avch
bol·un nô

Vhen's the next tour?

hut·tee chag·*aas* da·*raa*·cheen
jô·*gaa*·chikh ölj *bol*·ukh vē

How long is the tour?

hut·tee *hŭg*·chaa vē

sightseeing

Arjai Grotto (Utag Banner)	*ar*·jai *a*·goi
Bái Tǎ (White Pagoda)	cha·*gaan sŭv*·rag
Dà Zhào Monastery	yikh jô som
Dali Lake	dal nôr
Daqingqou Nature Reserve (Tōngliáo)	*chŭng*·khul·een gao
Five Pagoda Temple	*ta*·vun *sŭv*·ragt som
Genghis Khan's Mausoleum in Ordos	*ching*·gis·seen *ong*·gun
Tomb of Zhaojun	jao jee·yun·*nē ong*·gun
Yuan Dynasty Upper Capital (Shàngdū/Xanadu)	*yoo*·an *ŭl*·seen dööd *nees*·lul

shopping

Where's a ...?	... haa *bē*·dug vē
camera shop	*soo*·dur *ta*·takh *ga*·jar
market	jakh dul·*goor*
souvenir shop	*mong*·gol·een onch *ga*·rul·teen dul·*goor*

Where can I buy locally produced goods/souvenirs?

haan·aas *tan*·nē und·*kheen* onch *gar*·ult avch *dee*·lukh vē

What's this made from?
un·*nee yoo*·gaar *hee*·sun vē

I'd like to buy ...
bee ... *a*·vukh san·*naa*·tē

Can I look at it?
bee *ŭ*·jij *bol*·un nô

Can I have it sent overseas?
gad·*aad ŭl*·sud ya·*vôlj* *bol*·un nô

How much is it?
hut·tee jôs vē

Please write down the price.
ŭ·*nee*·geen *bi*·chij ŭgch *bol*·un nô

That's too expensive.
mash ŭn·*tē*

I'll give you (five kuai).
tand (*ta*·vun *tŭg*·rug) ŭg·gee·*yöö*

shopping

Can you lower the price?
hyamd·run nô

Is that enough?
jôs *hŭ*·run nô

It's faulty.
uv·dur·*jē*

I'd like a refund.
mŭngk·*öön bo*·chaj avch *bol*·un nô

I'd like ..., please.	... ŭg·*gē*·rē
a bag	*sô*·lee·ao ôt
a receipt	*ba*·rimt

meeting people

Hello.	sēn bēn nô
Hi.	sēn nô
Goodbye.	ba·yur·*tē*
Good night.	sēn am·*raa*·rē
Mr/Mrs	av·*gē*
Ms/Miss	av·*khē*
How are you?	sēn bēn nô
Fine. And you?	sēn sēn sēn nô
What's your name?	tan·*nē al*·dur
My name is ...	min·*nee* nur ...
I'm pleased to meet you.	sē·khun ta·nilch·*laa*

This is my …	un bol min·*nee* …
brother (older)	akh
brother (younger)	doo
child	*hoo*·khud
daughter	*hoo*·khun
father	aav
friend	nēj
husband	*nŭ*·khur
mother	ööj
partner (intimate)	*gu*·reen hoon
sister (older)	ugch
sister (younger)	*hoo*·khun doo
son	hoo
wife	*ukh*·nur

making conversation

Do you live here?
und sôj bēn nô

Where are you going?
haa *ya*·vukh vē

Do you like it here?
und sôkh *dŭr*·tē yô

I love it here.
mash *dŭr*·tē

Have you eaten?
id·sun nô

Are you here on holidays?
und *am*·rilt ŭng·gö·*rö*·khör *yir*·sun nô

local talk

Great!	*yaa*·sun sēn bē
Hey!	hoo·*yee*
It's OK.	ha·*maa*·gway
Just a minute.	bag hŭl·*lēj* bē
Just joking.	*sho*·gulj bēn
Maybe.	bol·ul·*chô*·tē
No problem.	ha·*maa*·gway
No way!	*bolkh*·gway
Sure, whatever.	*bol*·un *bol*·un
That's enough!	*bol*·chi·khun

I'm here …	bee … und yir·*jē*
on business	*mē*·mē *hee*·khöör
for a holiday	*am*·rilt ŭng·gö·*rö*·khöör
for a meeting	hŭ·rul hee·*khöör*
to study	sŭ·rŭlch·*khaar*
for travel	jô·gaach·*khaar*
to work	a·jil·*khaar*
to visit family	sa·dun·*aan* ŭj·*khöör*

How long are you here for?

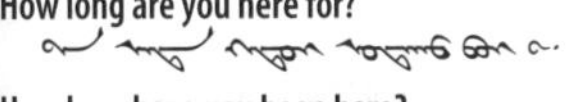

ta und *hut*·tee *ŭ*·dukh vē

How long have you been here?

ta und yi·*rööd hut*·tee *ŭ*·daj bēkh vē

I'm here for (four) weeks.

bee und (*dŭr*·bun *ga*·rag) sôkh san·*naa*·tē

Can I take a photo of you?

tan·*nee soo*·durlj *bol*·un nô

Are you Mongolian?

ta *mong*·gol hoon nô

Do you speak Mongolian?

ta *mong*·gol hul *chat*·tun nô

What's this called?

un yoo bē

How do you say … in Mongolian?

… *gu*·sun ŭ·*gee mong*·gol·ôr yaaj *hu*·lukh vē

I'd like to learn some (Mongolian).

bee (*mong*·gol hul) sŭrkh san·*naa*·tē

Would you like me to teach you some English?

ta nad·*aar ang*·gul hul jaal·gan·*nô*

Sorry, I didn't mean to do anything wrong.

ôch·*lē*·rē bee al·*vaar* bish

I didn't do it on purpose.

bee al·*vaar* bish

Is this a local custom?

un *tan*·nē end·*kheen jang*·shil mŭn·*nô*

Where are you from?

ta *haa*·naas *yir*·see

Where is your home county?

tan·*nē nŭ*·tug chin

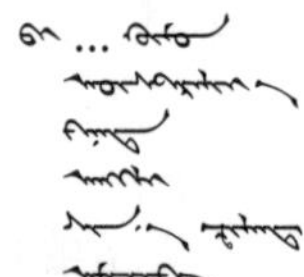

I'm from …	bee … hoon
Australia	av·straa·*lee*·yaa
Canada	*ka*·na·da
England	*ang*·gul
New Zealand	shin *zee*·land
the USA	am·e·rik

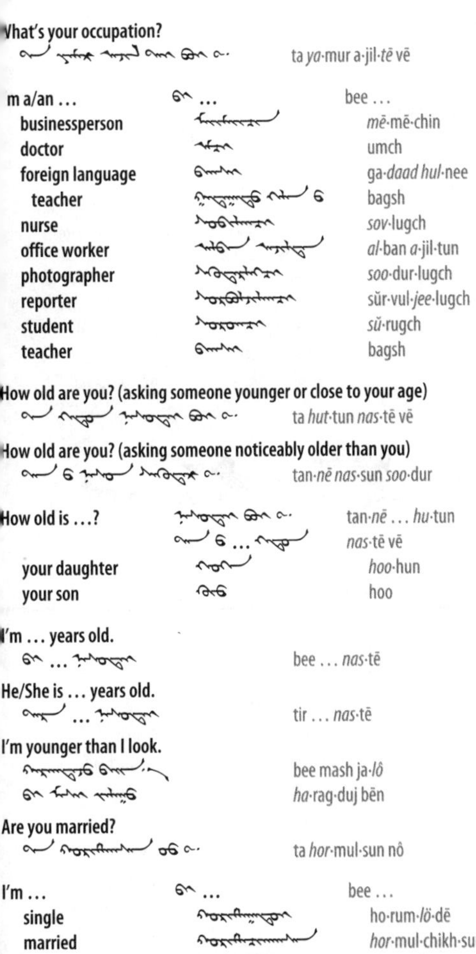

What's your occupation?
ta *ya*·mur a·jil·*tē* vē

I'm a/an … — bee …

businessperson	*mē*·mē·chin
doctor	umch
foreign language teacher	ga·*daad hul*·nee bagsh
nurse	*sov*·lugch
office worker	*al*·ban *a*·jil·tun
photographer	*soo*·dur·lugch
reporter	sŭr·vul·*jee*·lugch
student	*sŭ*·rugch
teacher	bagsh

How old are you? (asking someone younger or close to your age)
ta *hut*·tun *nas*·tē vē

How old are you? (asking someone noticeably older than you)
tan·*nē nas*·sun *soo*·dur

How old is …? — tan·*nē* … *hu*·tun *nas*·tē vē

your daughter	*hoo*·hun
your son	hoo

I'm … years old.
bee … *nas*·tē

He/She is … years old.
tir … *nas*·tē

I'm younger than I look.
bee mash ja·*lô* *ha*·rag·duj bēn

Are you married?
ta *hor*·mul·sun nô

I'm … — bee …

single	ho·rum·*lö*·dē
married	*hor*·mul·chikh·sun

I live with someone.

[illegible] — bee nig *hoon*·tē hamt sôj bēn

Do you have a family of your own?

[illegible] — ta *hookhd*·tē yô

Do you like ...?	[illegible]	ta ... *dŭr*·tē yô
I like ...	[illegible]	bee ... *dŭr*·tē
I don't like ...	[illegible]	bee ... dür *oo*·gway
art	[illegible]	*jŭ*·rugt
film	[illegible]	*kee*·nô *ŭ*·jikh
music	[illegible]	*hŭg*·jimt
reading	[illegible]	nom *ŭn*·shikh
sport	[illegible]	tem·*reen* hŭ·dul·*göönd*

feelings & opinions

I feel ...	[illegible]	bee ... bēn
I don't feel ...	[illegible]	bee ... *oo*·gway
Are you ...?	[illegible]	ta ... bēn nô
cold	[illegible]	daarch
drunk	[illegible]	*sog*·tuj bēn
happy	[illegible]	*ba*·yurlj bēn
hot	[illegible]	ha·*lô*·chij
hungry	[illegible]	ŭlsch
sad	[illegible]	jobj bēn
thirsty	[illegible]	ŭn·*daasch*
tired	[illegible]	*ya*·durj

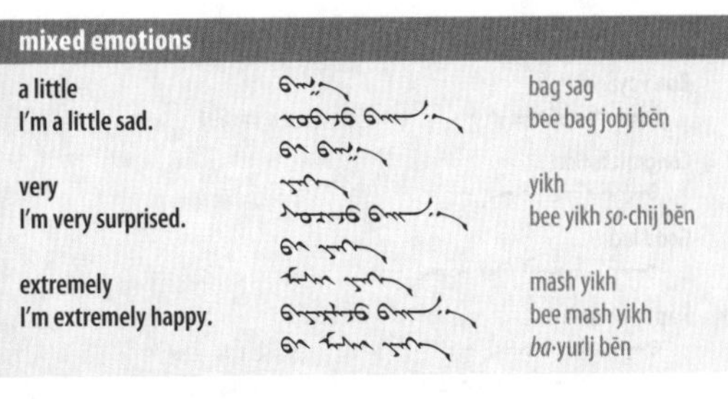

mixed emotions

a little	bag sag
I'm a little sad.	bee bag jobj bēn
very	yikh
I'm very surprised.	bee yikh *so*·chij bēn
extremely	mash yikh
I'm extremely happy.	bee mash yikh *ba*·yurlj bēn

What do you think of it?
oon·nē to·*khē* yoo *bo*·duj bēn nô

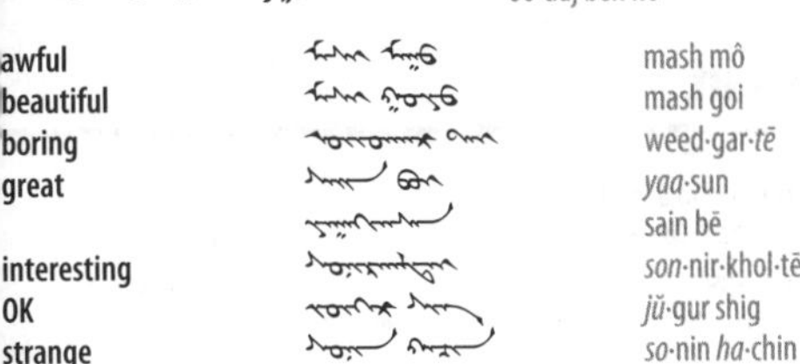

awful	mash mô
beautiful	mash goi
boring	weed·gar·*tē*
great	*yaa*·sun
	sain bē
interesting	*son*·nir·khol·tē
OK	*jŭ*·gur shig
strange	*so*·nin *ha*·chin

farewells

Tomorrow I'm leaving.
bee mar·*gaash ya*·vun

If you come to my country you can stay with me.
ta *min*·nee *ŭls*·ad *och*·bul *nad*·tē hamt sôj *bol*·un

Keep in touch!
ha·ril·chij bē·ga·*rē*

Here's my (address).
un bol *min*·nee (gir·*reen ha*·yig)

What's your (email)?
tan·*nē* (*ee*·mēl) chin

well-wishing

Bon voyage!
sēn ya·va·*rē*

Congratulations!
ba·yur hŭr·*gee*

Good luck!
aaj *jar*·gal hoo·*see*

Happy birthday!
tŭr·sun *ŭd*·reen
ba·yur hŭr·*gee*

Happy New Year!
sēn shin·ul·*voo*

eating out

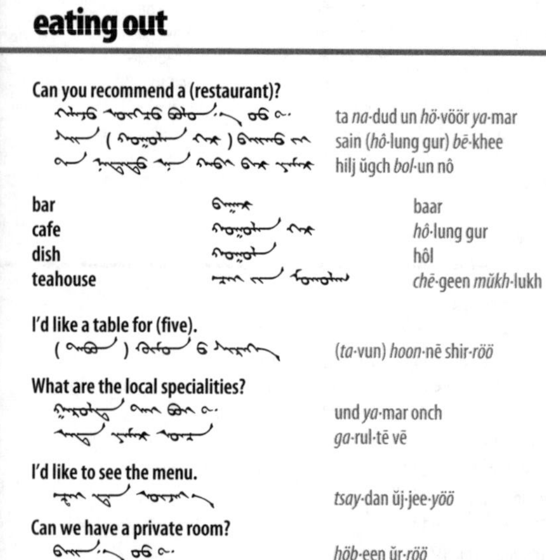

Can you recommend a (restaurant)?
ta *na*·dud un *hö*·vöör *ya*·mar
sain (*hô*·lung gur) *bē*·khee
hilj ŭgch *bol*·un nô

bar	baar
cafe	*hô*·lung gur
dish	hôl
teahouse	*chē*·geen *mŭkh*·lukh

I'd like a table for (five).
(*ta*·vun) *hoon*·nē shir·*röö*

What are the local specialities?
und *ya*·mar onch
ga·rul·tē vē

I'd like to see the menu.
tsay·dan ŭj·jee·*yöö*

Can we have a private room?
höb·een ŭr·*röö*
bēn nô

Can we have the bill?
dang·*saan* bod·dee·*yöö*

Are you still serving food?
o·*dô* bas hôl bēn nô

What would you recommend?
und *ya*·mar *sē*·khun hôl bēkh vē

What do you normally eat for (breakfast)?
ta yŭr·*döön ya*·mar (ŭg·*löö*·geen hôl) *it*·dug vē

What's that called?
tur yoo vē

What's in that dish?
yoo·gur *hee*·dug vē

I'll have that.
tur·*ee* a·*vee*

I'd like it with …	… *gee*·gin i·*loo* *hee*·chikh
I'd like it without …	*bit*·gee … hee
chilli	*laa*·jao
garlic	*sa*·rim·sug
MSG	wee jing
nuts	*ho*·shig
oil	tos

I'd like …	bee … a·*vee*
a piece	nig *hu*·sug
one bottle	nig longk
one box/carton	nig *hēr*·chug
one *jing* (500gm)	nig jing
that one	tu·*ree*
two	*hoi*·ree

This dish is … — un hôl …
- (too) spicy — (mash) ha·*lôn*
- superb — mash *amt*·tē

I love this dish. — bee un hôl·*lee i*·dukh *dŭr*·tē

I love the local cuisine. — bee un *gaj*·reen *hôl*·lund *dŭr*·tē

That was delicious! — mash *amt*·tē

I'm full. — bee *chat*·tul id·*löö*

breakfast	ŭg·*löö*·geen hôl
lunch	ŭd·*een* hôl
dinner	ö·*röö*·geen hôl
drink (alcoholic)	*a*·rikh
drink (nonalcoholic)	un·*daan*

… water — … ŭs
- boiled — *bo*·chil·sun
- cold — *hwee*·tun
- still mineral — *chu*·vur

not your cup of tea?

Mongols are generally tea, rather than coffee, drinkers. Be warned, though, that Mongolian food and drink customs are quite different to those in other parts of China. For instance, 'milk tea' sounds innocent enough, but many people are surprised to find lumps of flour and meat, as well as animal fats, butter, millet and salt added to a Mongolian cuppa. And don't expect a cup and saucer – locals usually drink their tea from a bowl.

(cup of) coffee — kôf
(cup of) tea — chē

black tea — har chē
fresh drinking yoghurt — ē·rug
kumiss (fermented mare's milk) — *chu*·gu
milk tea — *soo*·tē·chē

… of beer — … peev
- a glass — nig cho·*mo*
- a large bottle — tom *longk*·tē
- a small bottle — bag *longk*·tē

red/white wine — ŭl·*aan*/cha·*gaan* *ŭj*·meen *a*·rikh
a shot of (rice wine) — nig *hŭn*·dug (har *a*·rikh)

What are you drinking?
ta yoo ôkh vē

I'll buy you a drink.
tand un·*daan* avch ŭg·*yöö*

What would you like?
ta yoond *dŭr*·tē vē

Cheers!
tog·toi·*yo*

This is hitting the spot.
yaa·sun sēn bē

I'm feeling drunk!
bee *sog*·tuj bēn

I'm totally drunk!
(lit: I've become a domestic animal)
bee mal bol·chikh·*lô*

street eats

boiled dumplings	bēnsh
boiled meat	*chan*·sun makh
butter (to add to milk tea)	shar tos
dried beef strips	borch
fried bread	*hēr*·sun bôb
fried-meat pancake	*shal*·bing
fried millet	*hôr*·sun bo·*daa*
fried millet with sweet cream	*jöö*·khē·tē bo·*daa*
huruud (a type of curd)	hŭr·*ood*
noodles	*mee*·en·ti·yor
öröm (hardened skin of milk)	oo·*room*
steamed dumplings	bôs

special diets & allergies

I'm a vegetarian.	bee *saa*·yô
I can't eat pork.	bee *ga*·khēn makh *it*·dug·gway
Where can I find halal food?	haa *ho*·tŭng *ŭn*·dus·tun·nē hôl bēkh vē
I only want to eat vegetables.	bee no·*gô* id·ee·*yöö* gij *bo*·doj bēn

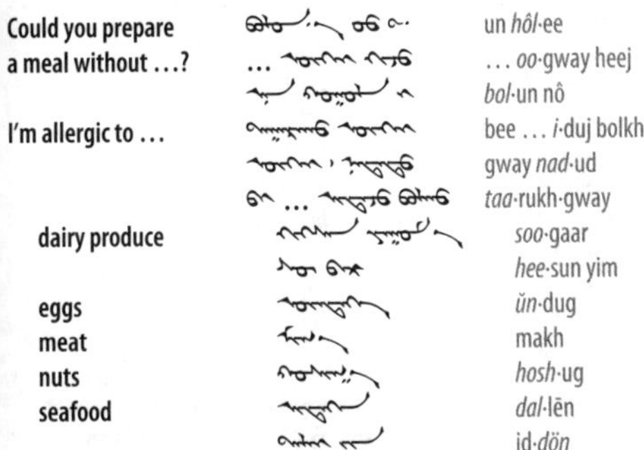

Could you prepare a meal without …?	un *hôl*·ee … *oo*·gway heej *bol*·un nô
I'm allergic to …	bee … *i*·duj bolkh gway *nad*·ud *taa*·rukh·gway
dairy produce	*soo*·gaar *hee*·sun yim
eggs	*ŭn*·dug
meat	makh
nuts	*hosh*·ug
seafood	*dal*·lēn id·*dön*

in the grasslands

I'd like to visit a Mongolian family on the steppe.
bee hu·*döö*·geen *mong*·gol ēlt *o*·chij ŭ·jikh san·*naa*·tē

I'd like to see some traditional Mongolian life.
bee ŭ·lam·jee·lalt *mong*·gol *am*·dur·lee ŭ·jikh san·*naa*·tē

I'd like to find a company that arranges tours of the grasslands.
bee tal *nŭt*·geen jŭ·*gaa*·chil·een *kom*·pan *ur*·ikh san·*naa*·tē

Can you help me?
ta na·*mēg* tŭs·ul·*nô*

How much is it per person?
nig hoon *hut*·tee jôs vē

I'd like to see a traditional Mongolian yurt.
bee *mong*·gol gur ŭ·jikh san·*naa*·tē

Where can I hire a horse?

haa·naas mur
tŭr·*öös*·ulj
bol·ukh vē

How much is it per hour?

nig chag
hut·tee jôs vē

Can I have a guide?

jamch olj ŭgch
bol·un nô

I'd like to ...	bee ... san·*naa*·tē
do some archery	nŭm sŭm *har*·vukh
ride a buggy	*tu*·rug *ba*·rikh
do some wrestling	bŭkh *ba*·ril·dukh

horse	mur
horse riding	mur *ô*·nakh
reins	jol·*lô*
saddle	um·*ööl*
steppe/grasslands	tal *nŭ*·tug
stirrup	dŭ·*röö*

Stop!

jogs·*sôch*

My saddle is hurting me.

un um·*ööl* na·*mēg*
ŭbt·göj bēn

Can I change horses?

bee mur·*öön* sol·*lee*·yô
bol·un nô

Can we stop here?

und jogs·ô·*yöö*
bol·un nô

just a twist to the right

Mongolian script is written vertically and read from left to right. So if you want to have a go at reading the script in this chapter, or when asking a local to read it for you, simply turn the book 90 degrees clockwise. Our coloured pronunciation guides, however, should simply be read the same way you read English.

Can we go back now?
bid o·*dô* *he*·rij
bol·un nô

Let's go back now.
bid o·*dô* he·ree·*yaa*

Can you help me get off this horse?
nad·dee bôl·gaa·*gaach*

emergencies & health

Help!
em av·*raa*

Could you help me, please?
ta *nad*·dee *khav*·sŭrch
bol·un nô

I've been injured.
bee shar·khug·tich·ukh·*laa*

My friend has been injured.
min·*nee* nēj shar·khug·tich·ukh·*laa*

There's been an accident.
un·dul gar·chikh·*laa*

Where's the nearest phone?
ham·geen öör *ô*·tas
haa bēkh vē

We need to get to a doctor.
bid *umch*·ud
hŭr·dun *och*·ikh *hu*·rug·tē

Where's the nearest …?	*ham*·geen öör … haa bēkh vē
dentist	*shood*·nē umch
doctor	umch
hospital	*um*·nul·geen
	hor·*rô*
pharmacist	*um*·een dul·*goor*

I'm ill.

bee ŭvd·chikh·*löö*

My friend is ill.

min·*nee* nēj ŭvd·chikh·*löö*

emergencies & health

english–mongolian dictionary

In this dictionary, words are marked as n (noun), a (adjective), v (verb), sg (singular), pl (plural), inf (informal) and pol (polite) where necessary.

A

accident (mishap) *üs*·sul *un*·dul
accommodation bēr
adaptor *bee*·yen yaa chee
after da·*raa*
air conditioning *kong*·tee·aa·oo
airplane *nis*·gul
airport *nis*·gul·een *bô*·tul
alcohol *a*·rikh
all bükh
ambulance *tür*·gun av·ral·*teen ma*·shin
and ba
ankle shaa
arm gar

B

baby *nyel*·ukh *khoo*·khud
back (of body) nü·*rô*
backpack bogch
bad mô
bag ôt
baggage *bô*·tul
bank benk
bar baar
bathroom ü·*gaal*·gin gur
battery *dee*·en chö
beautiful goi
bed or
beer peev
before *ü*·mŭn
behind höön
bicycle dü·*gway*
big tom
bill dangs
blanket *khoon*·jil
blood group *chŭ*·sun *too*·rool
boat jab
book (make a reservation) v jakh·*aa*·lukh
bottle longk
boy hoo
breakfast üg·*löö*·geen hôl
broken (out of order) uv·dur·*hē*
bus *neet*·in *ma*·shin *tur*·rug
buy v *a*·vakh

C

camera *soo*·dur·lukh *ma*·shin
car *ma*·shin *tur*·rug
cash n *bul*·lun mongk
cell phone gar *ô*·tas
centre n tŭv
change (money) v jôs *so*·likh
cheap hyemd
check (bill) n dangs
chest (body) chööj
children *hoo*·hud
cigarette *ta*·mukh
city hot
clean a *chu*·vur
closed ood haa·*jē*
cold a *hwee*·tun
come *yi*·rukh
computer kom·*pyoo*·tur
condom bee *yoo*·wun tao
cook v hôl heekh
cost n ün
credit card it·gum·*jeen* kaart
currency exchange jôs *so*·likh *ga*·jur
customs (immigration) *bôm*·teen gēl

D

dangerous *a*·yul·tē
date (time) *ü*·dur
day *ü*·dur
delay v *hoch*·rukh
dentist *shood*·nē umch
depart *ya*·vakh
dinner ö·*röö*·geen hôl
direct a shôt
dirty *bŭ*·jir

disabled *jim*·dug
discount v hyemt·*rô*·lukh
doctor umch
double bed *hoi*·yur *hoo*·nē or
double room *hoi*·yur *hoo*·nē ür·*röö*
drink n *un*·daan
drink v ôkh
drive v jo·*lô*·dukh
driving licence jo·*lô*·cheen *tum*·dug
drug (illicit) hôrt um

E

ear chikh
east joon
eat *id*·dukh
electricity *cha*·khil·gun
elevator *cha*·khil·gun shat
email *ee*·mël
embassy *ul*·chin sē·deen *ya*·mun
emergency *ba*·chim *hu*·rug
English (language) *ang*·gul hul
evening ö·*röö*
exit n ood
expensive *ün*·tē
eye nüd

F

far hol
fast *hur*·dun
father aav
finger hür·*rô*
first-aid kit *ba*·chim av·ral·*teen* hĕr·chug
first class tur·*roon jir*·geen
fish n *jag*·gas
food hôl
foot hül
free (of charge) *jü*·göör
friend nēj
fruit *ji*·mus
full *doo*·rung

G

gift *bul*·lug
girl *o*·khin
glass (drinking) cho·*mô*
glasses *nüd*·un shil
go *ya*·vakh
good sēn
guide n jamch

H

half n *ha*·gus
hand gar
happy *ba*·yurlj bēn
he tir
head n tol·*gē*
heart jürkh
heavy hünd
help *tŭs*·lamj
here und
high *ün*·dür
hike v *yav*·gun *ya*·vakh
holiday *am*·rult
homosexual i·jil *hwees*·tun·nē *am*·rug·lui
horse mur
hospital *um*·nul·geen hor·*rô*
hot ha·*lôn*
hotel *joch*·deen *bô*·tul
(be) hungry *ül*·sukh
husband ur *nŭ*·khur

I

I bee
identification (card) *bay*·yeen gurch
ill *ub*·chin·tē
injury n *sha*·rakh
insurance *bay*·yeen *daat*·gul
internet sŭl·*jöö*
interpreter *hul*·murch

J

jewellery *ur*·dun·is
job *a*·jil

K

key tül·*khoor*
kilogram kee·*lô*·gram

tchen to·*gôn* gur
ife *khut*·ag

-

undry (place) *hub*·chus ô·*gaakh* *ga*·jur
wyer hölch
ft (direction) joon
g (body) hül
ss chöön
tter (mail) *jakh*·dul
ght n *gu*·rul
ke v *dür*·tē
ck n *ün*·us
ng ürt
st (items) *göö*·sun
ve v *hēr*·tē
ggage *bô*·tul
nch *üd*·een hôl

M

mail n *shô*·dang
man hoon
map *gaj*·rin *jü*·ug
market jakh dul·*goor*
matches *chwee*·dung
meat makh
medicine um
message *jakh*·aa
milk soo
minute *min*·nut
mobile phone gar *ô*·tas
money jôs
month sar
morning üg·*löö*
mother ööj
motorcycle *mo*·tur
mouth em

N

name nur
near öör
neck n hüj·*joo*
new shin
newspaper *so*·nin
night sün
no (not at all) oo·*gway*
no (not this) bish
noisy shô·*gaan*·tē

north hööt
nose *ha*·mur
now o·*dô*
number *no*·mēr

O

old (people) *nas*·tē
old (things) *hô*·chin
open a *nölt*·tē
outside *ga*·dun

P

passport *pas*·port
pay v jôs *üg*·gukh
pharmacy *um*·meen dul·*goor*
photo *soo*·dur
police chag·*daa*
post office *shô*·dang tob·*chô*
pregnant *jir*·um·sun
price n ün

Q

quiet a *tē*·vung

R

rain n bor·*ôn*
razor *sakh*·leen *hü*·tug
receipt n *pee*·ao
rent v khoo·*loos*·lukh
repair v *jas*·sukh
restaurant *hô*·lung gur
return (give back) *üg*·gukh
return (go back) *bo*·chuj *ya*·vakh
return ticket yavj *ha*·rikh bil·*lēt*
right (direction) ba·*rôn*
road jam
room n ür·*röö*

S

safe a a·mur *tüb*·shin
seat n *sô*·dul
send ya·*vô*·lukh
sex (act) *hor*·chul
sex (gender) *chan*·reen *yil*·gul
shampoo *gu*·jig üg·*aakh* *shing*·gun

she tir
sheet (bed) *khoon*·jil
shirt chamch
shoes *shaa*·khē
shop n dul·*goor*
short *bo*·gun
single room ganch *hoo*·nē ŭr·*röö*
skin n ars
skirt n *bang*·jil
sleep v *ŭn*·tukh
slow ŭd·*daan*
small *ji*·jig
soap *saa*·vung
some *jar*·rim
soon ô·dul·gway
south *ŭm*·un
souvenir *dürs*·khul·een ud
stamp *yô*·oo *pee*·ao
station (train) *galt tur*·gun ŭr·*töö*
stomach *gu*·dus
stop v *jog*·sukh
stop (bus) n jog·*sôl*
street *gô*·dumj
student ô·*yoo*·tun
sun nar
sunscreen fang *shaa*·yee *shoo*·wong
swim v *om*·bukh

T

telephone n ô·tas
temperature (weather) dŭ·*laa*·nē hum·*jöö*
that tir
they tund
(be) thirsty un·*daa*·sukh
this un
throat *hô*·lē
ticket *pee*·ao
time chag
tired *ya*·darch bēn
tissues chaas
today oo·*noo*·dur
toilet *jor*·long
tomorrow mar·*gaash*
tonight ŭ·*noo* or·*röö*
tooth shŭd
toothbrush *shŭ*·dun umch
toothpaste yaa gao
torch (flashlight) *dee*·am·bur
tour n *ay*·lul
towel *al*·choor
train n galt *tur*·rug
translate orch·ô·lukh
trousers ŭ·mud
twin-bed room *hoi*·yur or·*tē* ŭr·*röö*

U

underwear *do*·tur ŭ·mud
urgent *yaa*·rul·tē

V

vegetable n nog·*gô*
vegetarian a *saa*·yô
visa veez

W

walk v *yab*·gun *ya*·vakh
wallet *jôs*·un bogch
wash (something) v ŭ·*gaakh*
watch n gar chag
water n ŭs
we bid
weekend *gar*·geen soolch
west ba·*rôn*
when hu·*jöö*
where haa
who hun
why *yaa*·gaad
wife *ukh*·nur
window chongk
with … … tē
without oo·*gway*
woman *um*·ug·tē
write *bi*·chikh

Y

yes teem
yesterday *oo*·chig·dur
you sg inf chee
you sg pol ta
you pl ta nar
yurt gur

Tibetan

ALPHABET 310
ABOUT TIBETAN 311
PRONUNCIATION 312
LANGUAGE DIFFICULTIES 313
TIME & DATES 314
TRANSPORT & DIRECTIONS 315
ACCOMMODATION 317
BANKING & COMMUNICATIONS 318
SIGHTSEEING 319
SHOPPING 320
MEETING PEOPLE 321
MAKING CONVERSATION 322
FEELINGS & OPINIONS 325
FAREWELLS 326
EATING OUT 327
SPECIAL DIETS & ALLERGIES 329
EMERGENCIES & HEALTH 329
ENGLISH–TIBETAN DICTIONARY 331

alphabet

Tibetan script consists of 30 basic characters and four symbols for vowels, which can be added to these characters.

Each of the consonants in the writing system includes an 'a'. This is because consonants in Tibetan are represented as syllabic units and all have an inherent 'a' sound in their basic form. Consonants are arranged according to where the sound comes from in your mouth (from the throat to the lips).

Symbols are added above or below the consonant to indicate different vowel sounds – we've used the first consonant, ཀ (ka), as an example. Note that the Tibetan symbol for each vowel can be pronounced in different ways because the pronunciation is affected by the letters around it.

Vowels (consonant 'ka' used as example)			
ཀི་ ki	ཀུ་ ku	ཀེ་ ke	ཀོ་ ko

Consonants			
ཀ་ ka	ཁ་ kha	ག་ ga	ང་ nga
ཅ་ ca	ཆ་ cha	ཇ་ ja	ཉ་ nya
ཏ་ ta	ཐ་ tha	ད་ da	ན་ na
པ་ pa	ཕ་ pha	བ་ ba	མ་ ma
ཙ་ tsa	ཚ་ tsha	ཛ་ dza	
ཝ་ wa	ཞ་ zha	ཟ་ za	
འ་ 'a	ཡ་ ya	ར་ ra	ལ་ la
ཤ་ sha	ས་ sa		
ཧ་ ha	ཨ་ a		

about Tibetan

The language of His Holiness the Dalai Lama, Tibetan (bod·skad བོད་སྐད), belongs to the Tibeto-Burman group of the Sino-Tibetan language family, with Burmese its closest relative. It's spoken by more than six million people, mainly in Tibet but also in neighbouring Nepal, Bhutan, India and Pakistan. Tibetan has many dialects, but the Lhasa dialect (used in this chapter) is the most influential and considered the standard. Written Tibetan was devised in the 7th century by a scholar sent to India by the Tibetan King Songtsen Gampo to enable the translation of Buddhist literature into Tibetan. The new script was based on the Devanagari characters used to write many Indian languages. Since its introduction, the writing system of Tibetan has barely changed, but the spoken language has evolved considerably. As a result, written and spoken Tibetan are quite different. The importance of Mandarin Chinese is also a reality in Tibet – in urban areas almost all Tibetans speak Mandarin. Nevertheless, making an effort to get a few Tibetan phrases together will be greatly appreciated by the Tibetans you encounter on your travels.

tibetan

pronunciation

Vowels		Consonants	
Symbol	**English sound**	**Symbol**	**English sound**
a	run	b	bed
â	ago	c	cheat
aw	law	d	dog
ay	say	dz	adds
e	bet	g	go
ee	see	h	hat
i	hit	j	jar
o	so	k	kit
ö	her	l	lot
oo	zoo	m	man
u	glue	n	not
ü	flute (with a raised tongue)	ng	ring
		ny	canyon
		p	pet
		r	run (pronounced deep in the throat)
		s	sun
		sh	shot
		t	top
		ts	hats
		w	win
		y	yes
		z	zero
		zh	pleasure

In this chapter, the Tibetan pronunciation is given in pink after each phrase.

Some consonants in Tibetan can be aspirated (pronounced with a puff of air after the sound). Aspirated sounds are represented with an h following the consonant: ch, kh, ph, th and tsh. An n, m or ng following a vowel indicates a nasalised sound (pronounced with air escaping through the nose).

Tibetan also has tones but, unlike in some Asian languages, they aren't crucial to meaning and haven't been indicated in this chapter.

Syllables are separated by a dot. For example: ཐུགས་རྗེ་ཆེ། tu·jay·chay

essentials

Hello.	བཀྲ་ཤིས་བདེ་ལེགས།	ta·shi de·lek
Goodbye. (by person staying)	ག་ལེར་ཕེབས།	ka·lee pay
Goodbye. (by person leaving)	ག་ལེར་བཞུགས།	ka·lee shu
Please.	ཐུགས་རྗེ་གཟིགས།	tu·jay·sig
Thank you.	ཐུགས་རྗེ་ཆེ།	tu·jay·chay
Sorry./Excuse me.	དགོངས་དག	gong·da

language difficulties

Do you speak English?
ཁྱེད་རང་དབྱིན་ཇི་སྐད་ཤེས་ཀྱི་ཡོད་པས། kay·râng in·ji·kay shing·gi yö·bay

Do you understand?
ཧ་གོ་སོང་ངས། ha ko song·ngay

I understand.
ཧ་གོ་སོང་། ha ko·song

I don't understand.
ཧ་གོ་མ་སོང་། ha ko ma·song

Could you speak more slowly, please?
ཡང་སྐྱུར་ག་ལེར་ག་ལེར་གསུང་གནང་དང་། yâng·kya ka·lee ka·lee soong nâng da

Could you repeat that, please?
དེ་ཡང་སྐྱུར་གསུང་གནང་དང་། te yâng·kya soong nâng·da

numbers

0	༠	lay·koh	20	༢༠	nyi·shu
1	༡	chig	30	༣༠	soom·chu
2	༢	nyi	40	༤༠	shib·chu
3	༣	soom	50	༥༠	ngâb·chu
4	༤	shi	60	༦༠	doog·chu
5	༥	nga	70	༧༠	dün·chu
6	༦	doog	80	༨༠	gyay·chu
7	༧	dün	90	༩༠	goob·chu
8	༨	gye	100	༡༠༠	gya
9	༩	gu	1000	༡༠༠༠	chig·tong
10	༡༠	chu	1,000,000	༡༠༠༠༠༠༠	sa·ya·chig

time & dates

What time is it? ད་ལྟ་ཆུ་ཚོད་ག་ཚོད་རེད།	tân·da chu·tsö kâ·tsay·ray
It's (two) o'clock. ཆུ་ཚོད་ (གཉིས་) པ་རེད།	chu·tsö (nyi)·pa ray
It's quarter past (six). ཆུ་ཚོད་ (དྲུག་) དང་སྐར་མ་ བཅོ་ལྔ་རེད།	chu·tsö (doog)·dâng ka·ma chö·nga ray
It's half past (two). ཆུ་ཚོད་ (གཉིས་) དང་ཕྱེད་ཀ་རེད།	chu·tsö (nyi)·dâng chay·ka ray
It's quarter to (three). (གསུམ་) པ་ཟིན་པ་སྐར་མ་ བཅོ་ལྔ་	(soom)·pa sin·ba ka·ma cho·nga
The Western calendar date is (28 June). དེ་རིང་ཕྱི་ཟླ་ (དྲུག་པའི་ཚེས་ ཉི་ཤུ་རྩ་བརྒྱད་) རེད།	te·ring chin·da (doog·bay tsay nyi·shu tsâb·gye) ray

now	ད་ལྟ་	tân·da
today	དེ་རིང་	te·ring
tonight	དོ་གོང་མཚན་	dho·gong·tshen
this morning	དེ་རིང་ཞོགས་སྐད་	te·ring shoh·gay
this afternoon	དེ་རིང་ཕྱི་དྲོ་	te·ring chi·toh
yesterday	ཁ་ས་	kay·sa
tomorrow	སང་ཉིན་	sa·nyin
sunrise	ཉི་མ་ཤར་དུས་	nyin·ma shar·dü
sunset	ཉི་མ་ནུབ་དུས་	nyin·ma noob·dü

spring	དཔྱིད་ཀ	chi·ka
summer	དབྱར་ཁ	yar·ga
autumn	སྟོན་ཀ	tön·ga
winter	དགུན་ཁ	gün·ga

Monday	གཟའ་ཟླ་བ	sa da·wa
Tuesday	གཟའ་མིག་དམར	sa mig·ma
Wednesday	གཟའ་ལྷག་པ	sa lhâg·bâ
Thursday	གཟའ་ཕུར་བུ	sa phu·bu
Friday	གཟའ་པ་སངས	sa pa·sâng
Saturday	གཟའ་སྤེན་པ	sa pem·pa
Sunday	གཟའ་ཉི་མ	sa nyi·mâ

Tibet uses both the traditional lunar calendar, in which each month has 30 days, and the Gregorian calendar, as used in the West. There are 12 months in each, and they are simply referred to as the '1st month', the '2nd month' etc. However, the Lunar New Year is about six weeks after the Western New Year.

1st month (Tibetan lunar)	ཟླ་བ་དང་པོ	da·wa dâng·po
2nd month	ཟླ་བ་གཉིས་པ	da·wa nyi·pa
3rd month	ཟླ་བ་གསུམ་པ	da·wa soom·pa
4th month	ཟླ་བ་བཞི་པ	da·wa shi·pa
5th month	ཟླ་བ་ལྔ་པ	da·wa nga·pa
6th month	ཟླ་བ་དྲུག་པ	da·wa doog·pa
7th month	ཟླ་བ་བདུན་པ	da·wa dün·pa
8th month	ཟླ་བ་བརྒྱད་པ	da·wa gye·pa
9th month	ཟླ་བ་དགུ་པ	da·wa gu·pa
10th month	ཟླ་བ་བཅུ་པ	da·wa chu·pa
11th month	ཟླ་བ་བཅུ་གཅིག་པ	da·wa chu·chig·pa
12th month	ཟླ་བ་བཅུ་གཉིས་པ	da·wa chu·nyi·pa

transport & directions

Where is this ... going?	... འདི་ག་པར་འགྲོ་གི་རེད།	... ka·bah doh·gi ray
boat	གྲུ་གཟིངས	dru·zing
bus	སྤྱི་སྤྱོད་རླངས་འཁོར	chi·chö lâng·kho·di
plane	གནམ་གྲུ	nâm·du

What time's the	སྤྱི་སྤྱོད་རླངས་འཁོར	chi·chö lâng·kho
... bus?	... ཆུ་ཚོད་ག་ཚོད་ལ་	... chu·tsö kâ·tsay·la
	འགྲོ་གྱི་རེད།	doh·gi ray
first	དང་པོ་དེ་	tâng·po·te
last	མཐའ་མ་དེ་	tha·ma·te
next	རྗེས་མ་དེ་	je·ma·te

I'd like to hire a ...	ང་ ... གཡར་འདོད་ཡོད།	nga ...·chig yar dhö·yö
car	མོ་ཊ་	mo·ta
donkey	བོང་གུ་	boong·gu
landcruiser	ལེནྜ་ཀྲུ་རུ་ས་	len cu·ru·sa

How much is it daily/weekly?
ཉིན་/བདུན་ཕྲག་རེ་རེར་ nyin/dun·tâg ray·ray
གོང་ག་ཚོད་རེད། gong kâ·tsay ray

Where's the ...?	... ག་བར་ཡོད་རེད།	... ka·bah yö·ray
bank	དངུལ་ཁང་	ngü·khâng
post office	སྦྲག་ཁང་	da·khâng
tourist information	ཡུལ་སྐོར་སྤྲོ་འཆམ་གྱི་	yu·kor to·châm
office	ལས་ཁུངས་	lay·khoong

Does this road lead to ...?
ལམ་ཀ་འདི་ ... lâm·ga·di ...
འགྲོ་ཡག་རེད་པས། doh·ya re·bay

Can you show me (on the map)?
(ས་བཀྲ་འདི་ནང་) སྟོན་གནང་དང་། (sâp·ta di·nâng) tön nâng·da

What's the address?
ཁ་བྱང་ག་རེ་རེད། ka·châng kâ·ray ray

Is it far?
ཐག་རིང་པོ་རེད་པས། ta ring·po re·bay

How do I get to ...?
... ལ་གང་འདྲས་འགྲོ་དགོས་རེད། ...·la kân·teh·si doh·gö ray

Turn left/right.
གཡོན་ལ་/གཡས་ལ་སྐྱོགས་གནང་། yön·la/yeh·la kyog·nâng

Go straight ahead.
ཁ་ཐུག་འགྲོ། ka·toog·do

ehind …	… རྒྱབ་ལ་	… gyâb·lâ
n front of …	… མདུན་ལ་	… dün·lâ
ear (to) …	… འཁྲིས་ལ་	… tee·lâ
pposite …	… ཕར་ཕྱོགས་ལ་	… pha·chog·lâ
here	ཕ་གིར་	pha·kay

accommodation

I'm looking for a …	… གཅིག་མིག་བལྟ་གྱི་ཡོད།	…·chig mig ta·gi·yö
campsite	གུར་བརྒྱབ་ནས་ སྡོད་སའི་ས་ཆ་	gur gyâb·nay dö·say sa·cha
guest house	མགྲོན་ཁང་	drön·khâng
hotel	འགྲུལ་ཁང	drü·khâng

Where's the … hotel?	འགྲུལ་ཁང་ … ག་བར་ཡོད་རེད།	drü·khâng … ka·bah yö·ray
best	ཡག་ཤོས་	yâg·shö
cheapest	ཁེ་ཤོས་	ke·shö

I'd like to book a room, please.

ཁང་མིག་ཅིག་གླ་དགོས་ཡོད། — khâng·mi·chig la gö·yö

Do you have a room with two beds?

ཉལ་ཁྲི་གཉིས་བྲེད་པའི་ཁང་མིག་ཡོད་པས། — nye·ti·nyi chay·pay khâng·mi yö·bay

Do you have a room with a double bed?

མི་གཉིས་གཤོང་སའི་ཉལ་ཁྲི་
བྲེད་པའི་ཁང་མིག་ཡོད་པས། — mi·nyi shong·say nye·ti
chay·pay khâng·mi yö·bay

How much for …?	…ལ་གོང་ག་ཚད་རེད།	…·la gong kâ·tsay ray
one night	མཚན་གཅིག་	tsen chig
a week	བདུན་ཕྲག་གཅིག་	dun·tâ chig
two people	མི་གཉིས་	mi·nyi

For (three) nights. མཚན་(གསུམ་) རིང་ tsen (soom) ring

Could we have (a/an) …? ང་ཚོར་ … དགོས། ngân·tsoh … gö

- (extra) blanket ཉལ་ཆས་(་(ཐོལ་པ་)) nye·chay (tö·bâ)
- mosquito net ཉལ་གུར་ nye·gur
- our key ང་ཚོའི་ལྡེའུ་མིག་ ngân·tsö di·mig

The (heater) doesn't work.
(ཚ་གློག་) འདི་སྐྱོན་ ཤོར་ཤག་
(tsa·log) di kyön shor·sha

Is there somewhere to wash clothes?
དུག་ལོག་འཁྲུ་ས་ཡོད་རེད་པས།
du·log trü·sa yö re·bay

Can we use the kitchen?
ཐབ་ཚང་བེད་སྤྱོད་བྱེད་ན་ འགྲིག་གི་རེད་པས།
tâb·tsâng bay·chö chay·na di·gi re·bay

Do you have a safe where I can leave my valuables?
རིན་ཐང་ཅན་ཅ་ལག་བ ཅོལ་ས་ཡོད་པས།
rin·tâng·chen cha·lâg chö·sa yö·bay

What time do we have to check out?
ང་ཚོ་ཆུ་ཚོད་ག་ཚོད་ ཐོན་དགོས་རེད།
ngân·tso chu·tsö ka·tsay tön·gö·ray

banking & communications

I'm looking for a/the … … ག་བར་ཡོད་མེད་བ ལྟ་གི་ཡོད། … ka·bah yö·may ta·gi yö

- bank དངུལ་ཁང་ ngü·khâng
- public telephone མི་དམངས་ཁ་པར་ mi·mâng kha·pah

I want to exchange some money.
ང་ཕྱི་རྒྱལ་དངུལ་བརྗེ་དགོས་ཡོད།
nga chi·gay ngü jay·gö·yö

What's the exchange rate?
དངུལ་བརྗེའི་གོང་ཚད་ག་རེ་རེད།
ngü·je·gong·tsay kâ·ray ray

Is there a local internet cafe?
ས་གནས་དེར་ཨིན་ཊ་ནེཊ་བེད་སྤྱོད་གཏོང་ས་ཡོད་ པའི་ཇ་ཁང་ཡོད་རེད་པས།
sa·nay·day in·ta·net bay·chö tong·sa yö·pay cha·khâng

'd like to get internet access.

ང་ཨིན་ཊ་ནེཊ་བེད་སྤྱོད་བྱེད་དགོས་ཡོད། — nga in·ta·net bay·chö chay·go yö

ow much is it for an hour?

ཆུ་ཚོད་གཅིག་གླ་ཆ་ག་ཚད་རེད། — chu·tsö·chig la·ja kâ·tsay ray

want to make a long-distance call to (Australia).

ང་ (ཨོ་ཊ་ལི་ཡ་) ལ་ཁ་པར་ག
ཏང་དགོས་ཡོད། — nga (o·ta·li·ya)·la kha·pah
tâng·go yö

want to make a collect call.

ཁ་པར་གཏོང་གླ་ཕ་ཕྱོགས་ནས་རྩིས་རྒྱག
ཆོག་པའི་ཁ་པར་གཅིག་གཏང་དགོས་ཡོད། — kha·pah tong·la phâ·chog·nay tsi·gya
chog·pay kha·pah·chi tâng go·yö

The number is …

ཁ་པར་ཨང་གྲངས་ … རེད། — kha·pah ahng·dâng … ray

sightseeing

I'd like to see …

… མིག་བལྟ་འདོད་ཡོད། — … mig ta·dö yö

What's that place?

ས་ཆ་ཕ་གི་ག་རེ་རེད། — sa·cha pha·gi kâ·ray ray

Is it OK if I take a photo?

པར་རྒྱབ་ན་འགྲིག་གི་རེད་པས། — par gyâb·na di·gi re·bay

How long is the tour?

བལྟ་སྐོར་རྒྱུན་རིང་ལོས་འགྲོ་ཡག་ཡོད་རེད། — ta·kor gyün ring·lö do·ya yö·ray

What time does it open/close?

ཆུ་ཚོད་ག་ཚད་ལ་སྒོ་ཕྱེ་/
སྒོ་བརྒྱབ་གི་རེད། — chu·tsö kâ·tsay·la go chay·gi/
gyâb·gi ray

Is there an admission charge?

འཛུལ་གླ་སྤྲོད་དགོས་རེད་པས། — zü·la tay·go re·bay

sightseeing

monastery	དགོན་པ་	gom·pa
mosque	ཁ་ཆེའི་ལྷ་ཁང་	ka·chay lha·khâng
mountain	རི་	ri
museum	འགྲེམས་སྟོན་ཁང་	dem·tön khâng
old city	གྲོང་ཁྱེར་རྙིང་པ་	dron·kay nying·ba
palace	ཕོ་བྲང་	pho·dâng
park	གླིང་ག་	ling·ga
statues	འདྲ་སྐུ་	dâ·ku
temple	ལྷ་ཁང་	lha·khâng
waterfall	འབབ་ཆུ་	bâb·chu

How much is a guide?

གནས་བཤད་རྒྱག་མཁན་
གླ་ཆ་ག་ཚོད་རེད། — nay·shay gya·khen la·cha kâ·tsay ray

Where can I get a local map?

ས་གནས་ཀྱི་ས་བཀྲ་ག་ནས་རག་གི་རེད། — sa·nay·ki sâp·ta kâ·nay ra·gi·ray

shopping

Where's the nearest ...?	... ཉེ་ཤོས་ག་བར་ ཡོད་རེད།	... nyay·shö ka·bah yö·ray
camera shop	པར་ཚོང་ཁང་	par tsong·khâng
market	ཁྲོམ་	trom
souvenir shop	དྲན་རྟེན་ཅ་ལག་ ཚོང་ཁང་	dren·ten cha·lâg tsong·khâng

Do you have any ...?

ཁྱེད་རང་ལ་ ... བཙོང་ཡག་ཡོད་པས། — kay·râng·la ... tsong·ya yö·bay

Can you show me that?

ཕ་གི་ངར་མིག་སྟོན་དང་། — pha·gi ngah mik tön·dâ

Where can I buy locally produced souvenirs?

ས་གནས་རང་ནས་འཐོན་པའི་
དྲན་རྟེན་ཅ་ལག་
ཉོ་ས་ག་བར་ཡོད་རེད། — sa·nay râng·nay tön·pay den·ten cha·lâg nyo·sa ga·bah yö·ray

Is this made from …?	འདིའི་རྒྱུ་ཆ་ … རེད་པས།	diy gyub·ja … re·bay
leopard bone	གཟིག་གི་རུས་གོག་	sig·ki rü·koh
leopard skin	གཟིག་པགས་	sig·pâg
onyx	གཟི་	si
tiger bone	སྟག་གི་རུས་གོག་	tâg·gi rü·koh
tiger skin	སྟག་པགས་	tâg·pâg
turquoise	གཡུ་	yu

How much is it?
གོང་ག་ཚོད་རེད། — gong kâ·tsay ray

Can you write down the price?
གོང་ཤོག་བུ་ཐོག་བྲིས་གནང་དང་། — gong shu·gu·tog dih nâng·da

It's too expensive.
གོང་ཆེ་དྲགས་ཤག — gong chay·ta·sha

I'll give you …
ངས་ … སྤྲད་དགོས། — ngay … tay go

Do you accept credit cards?
བུ་ལོན་ཤོག་བྱང་ཐོག་
རིན་པ་སྤྲད་ན་འགྲིག་གི་རེད་པས། — bu·lön shog·jâng·tog
rim·pa tay·na di·gi re·bay

There's a mistake in the bill.
དངུལ་རྩིས་ནང་ནོར་འཁྲུལ་ཤོར་ཤག — ngü·tsi·nâng non·tü shor·sha

less	ཉུང་ང་	nyoong·nga
enough	འགྲིགས་པ་	dig·pa
more	མང་བ་	mâng·wa

meeting people

Hello.	བཀྲ་ཤིས་བདེ་ལེགས།	ta·shi de·lek
Goodbye. (said by person staying/ leaving)	ག་ལེར་ཕེབས།/ ག་ལེར་བཞུགས།	ka·lee pay/ ka·lee shu
Good night.	གཟིམ་འཇམ་གནང་དགོས།	sim·ja nâng·go

How are you?
ཁྱེད་རང་སྐུ་གཟུགས་བདེ་པོ་ཡིན་པས། kay·râng ku·su de·po yin·bay

Fine. And you?
བདེ་པོ་ཡིན། ཁྱེད་རང་ཡང་ de·bo·yin kay·râng·yâng
སྐུ་གཟུགས་བདེ་པོ་ཡིན་པས། ku·su de·po yin·bay

What's your name?
ཁྱེད་རང་གི་མཚན་ལ་ག་རེ་རེད། kay·râng·gi tsen·lâ kâ·ray·ray

My name is …
ངའི་མིང་ལ་ … རེད། ngay·ming·la … ray

Pleased to meet you.
ཁྱེད་རང་མཇལ་པ་དགའ་པོ་བྱུང་། kay·râng jel·pa gâh·po choong

This is my …	ཁོང་ངའི་…རེད།	khong ngay·… ray
brother	སྤུན་སྐྱ་བུ	pün·kya bu
daughter	བུ་མོ	bu·mo
father	པ་ཕ	pa·pha
friend	གྲོགས་པོ/གྲོགས་མོ	tok·po/tok·mo **m/f**
husband	ཁྱོ་ག	kyo·ka
mother	ཨ་མ	ah·ma
sister	སྤུན་སྐྱ་བུ་མོ	pün·kya bu·mo
son	བུ	bu
wife	སྐྱེས་དམན	kye·man

making conversation

Do you live here?
ཁྱེད་རང་འདིར་བཞུགས་ཀྱི་ཡོད་པས། kay·râng·day shu·gi yö·bay

Where are you going?
ཁྱེད་རང་ག་བར་ཕེབས་གས། kay·râng ka·bah pay·kay

Do you like it here?
ཁྱེད་རང་འདིར་སྐྱིད་པོ་འདུག་གས། kay·râng·day kyi·po du·gay

I love it here.
ངོ་འདིར་སྐྱིད་པོ་འདུག nga day kyi·po du

I'm here …	ང་འདིར་ … ཡིན།	nga day … yin
on business	ཚོང་ལས་ཆེད་	tsong·lay·chay
on holiday	གུང་གསེང་ཆེད་	goong·seng·chay
to study	སློབ་སྦྱོང་བྱེད་ཆེད་	lob·jong je·chay

How long are you here for?

ཁྱེད་རང་འདིར་ཡུན་རིང་ལོས་
བསྡད་ཀྱི་ཡིན།

kay·râng·day yün ring·lö
day·ki·yin

I'm here for … weeks/days.

ང་འདིར་བདུན་ཕྲག་/
ཉིན་མ་ … བསྡད་ཀྱི་ཡིན།

nga day dün·ta/
nyin·ma … day·ki·yin

Can I take a photo (of you)?

(ཁྱེད་རང་) པར་ཅིག་རྒྱག་ན་
འགྲིག་གི་རེད་པས།

(kay·râng) par·chig gyâb·na
di·giy ray·bay

I'd like to learn some of your local dialects.

ང་ཡུལ་མིའི་སྐད་སྦྱང་འདོད་ཡོད།

nga yü·miy·kay jâng·dö·yö

Would you like me to teach you some English?

ངས་ཁྱེད་རང་ལ་དབྱིན་ཇི་སྐད་
བསླབ་དགོས་པས།

ngay kay·râng·la in·ji·kay
lâb gö·bay

What's this called?

འདི་ལ་ག་རེ་ཟ།

di·la kâ·ray sa

How do you do this in your country?

ཁྱེད་རང་གི་ལུང་པའི་ལུགས་སྲོལ་
ལ་འདི་གང་

kay·râng·gi loong·pay
loog·sö·la

Is this a local or national custom?

འདི་ཡུལ་མིའི་ལུགས་སྲོལ་ཡིན་ནམ།
རྒྱལ་ཁབ་སྤྱི་ཡོངས་ཀྱི་
ལུགས་སྲོལ་ཡིན་ནམ།

di yü·miy loog·söl yin·na
gya·kâb chi·yong·gi
loog·söl yin·na

I'm sorry, it's not the custom in my country.

དགོངས་དག་ དེ་འདྲ་
ཚོའི་ལུང་པའི་ལུགས་
སྲོལ་ལ་ཡོད་མ་རེད།

gong·ta te·da
ngân·tsö loong·pay
loog·sö·la yö·ma·ray

Thank you for your hospitality.

སྣེ་ལེན་ཡག་པོ་གནང་དབར་
ཐུགས་རྗེ་ཆེ།

nay·len yak·po nâng·wa
tu·jay·chay

local talk

Just a minute.	ཏོག་ཙམ་སྒུག་ཨ།	teh·si gu·ah
I see.	ཨ་ལེ་	ah·leh
It's OK.	འགྲིག་གི་རེད།	di·gi ray
Sure.	ཡིན་དང་ཡིན།	yin·da·yin

Where are you from?
ཁྱེད་རང་ལུང་པ་ག་ནས་ཡིན། kay·râng loong·pa ka·nay yin

I'm from ...	ང་ ... ནས་ཡིན།	nga ... ·nay yin
Australia	ཨོ་སི་ཀྲ་ལི་ཡ་	o·ta·li·ya
Canada	ཁེ་ན་ཌ་	ka·na·da
England	དབྱིན་ཇི་ལུང་པ་	in·ji loong·pa
New Zealand	ནེའུ་ཛི་ལེནཌ་	nu·zee·land
the USA	ཡུ་ཨེས་ཨེ་/ཨ་མི་རི་ཀ་	yu·es·ay/ah·mi·ri·ka

What do you do (for a living)?
ཁྱེད་རང་ (འཚོ་ཐབས་ཆེད་) ལས་ཀ་ ག་རེ་བྱེད་ཀྱི་ཡོད། kay·râng (tso·tâb·che) lay·kâ kâ·ray chay·ki·yö

I'm a/an ...	ང་ ... ཡིན།	nga ... yin
businessperson	ཚོང་པ་	tsong·pa
office worker	ལས་ཁུངས་ལས་ཀ་ བྱེད་མཁན་	lay·koong lay·ka chay·khen
teacher	དགེ་རྒན་	gay·gan

How old are you?
ཁྱེད་རག་ལོ་ག་ཚོད་ཡིན། kay·râng lo kâ·tsay yin

I'm ... years old.
ང་ལོ་ ... ཡིན། nga lo ... yin

How old is your ...?	... ལོ་ག་ཚོད་རེད།	... lo kâ·tsay ray
daughter	ཁྱེད་རང་གི་བུ་མོ་	kay·râng·gi bu·mo
son	ཁྱེད་རང་གི་བུ་	kay·râng·gi bu

Are you married?

ཁྱེད་རང་ཆང་ས་བརྒྱོན་ཚར་པས། kay·râng châng·sa kyön tsa·bay

We live together, but we're not married.

ང་གཉིས་མཉམ་དུ་སྡོད་ཀྱི་ཡོད་དེ་ འཆང་ས་བརྒྱབ་མེད། nga·nyi nyâm·tu dö·ki yö·te châng·sa gyâb·may

I'm …	ང་ …	nga …
single	མི་ཧྲང་ཡིན།	mi·hreng yin
married	འཆང་ས་བརྒྱབ་ཚར།	châng·sa gyâb·tsah

Do you like …?

ཁྱེད་རང་ … ལ་དགའ་པོ་ཡོད་པས། kay·râng …·la ka·bo yö·bay

I don't like …

ང་ …ལ་དགའ་པོ་མེད། nga …·la ka·bo may

I like reading.

ང་དེབ་ཀློག་ཡག་ལ་དགའ་པོ་ཡོད། nga teb lo·ya·la ka·bo yö

I like music.

ང་རོལ་ཆ་གཏོང་ཡག་དགའ་པོ་ཡོད། nga rö·ja tong·ya ka·bo yö

I like playing sport.

ང་རྩེད་མོ་རྩེ་ཡག་དགའ་པོ་ཡོད། nga tsay·mo tsi·ya ka·bo yö

feelings & opinions

I'm …	ང་ …གི་འདུག	nga …·gi du
Are you …?	ཁྱེད་རང་ … གི་འདུག་གས།	kay·râng …·gi du·gay
cold	ཁྱག་	khya
hot	ཚ་བ་འཚིག་	tsa·wa tsi
hungry	གྲོད་ཁོག་ལྟོགས་	drö·kog tog
sad	སེམས་སྐྱོ་	sem kyo
thirsty	ཁ་སྐོམ་	ka kom
tired	དཀའ་ལས་ཁ་	kâ·lay ka
worried	སེམས་འཁྲལ་ལང་	sem·tel lâng

I'm happy.

ང་སྐྱིད་པོ་འདུག nga kyi·po du

I'm well.

ང་བདེ་པོ་ཡིན། nga de·po yin

I'm in a hurry.

ང་བྲེལ་བ་ཡོད། — nga te·wa yö

What do you think about …?

ཁྱེད་རང་ … ཐོག་ལ་བསམ་ཚུལ་ ག་རེད་ཡོད། — kay·râng … tog·la sâm·tsü kâ·ray·yö

I thought it was …	ངའི་བསམ་པར་ དེ་ …ཅིག་རེད་ཤག	ngay sâm·pâh te …·chi ray·sha
boring	ཉོ་ཏོ་	nyob·to
great	དཔེ་ཡག་པོ་	pay yâg·po
horrible	དཔེ་སྡུག་ཆག་	pay doog·châg
OK	འགྲིག་ཙམ་	dig·tsâm
too expensive	འགྲོ་སོང་ཆེན་པོ་	doh·song chen·po

farewells

Tomorrow is my last day here.

སང་ཉིན་ང་འདིར་སྡོད་ཡག་ཉིན་མ་ མཐའ་མ་དེ་ཡིན། — sa·nyin nga day dö·ya nyin ta·ma·te yin

If you come to (Scotland) you must come and visit us.

ཁྱེད་རང་གལ་སྲིད་ (སོ་ཀོ་ཊ་ལེན་) ལ་ཕེབས་ན་ང་ ཚོའི་སར་རེས་པ་དུ་ཕེབས་གནང་། — kay·râng gay·si (so·kot·land)·la pheb·na nga·tsö·sah ngay·pa·du

What's your address?

ཁྱེད་རང་གི་ཁ་བྱང་ག་རེ་རེད། — kay·râng·gi ka·châng kâ·ray ray

What's your (email address)?

ཁྱེད་རང་གི་ (ཨི་མེལ་ ཁ་བྱང་) ག་རེ་རེད། — kay·râng·gi (ee·mel ka·châng) kâ·ray ray

Here's my (address).

ངའི་ (ཁ་བྱང་) འདི་རེད། — ngay (ka·châng) di·ray

Keep in touch!

མུ་མཐུད་ནས་འབྲེལ་བ་གནང་ཨ།། — mu·tü·nay day·wa nâng·ah

well-wishing

Congratulations!
བཀྲ་ཤིས་བདེ་ལེགས་ — ta·shi de·lek

Happy birthday!
སྐྱེས་སྐར་ཉིན་བཀྲ་ཤིས་བདེ་ལེགས། — kye·kah·nyin ta·shi de·lek

Happy New Year!
ལོ་གསར་བཀྲ་ཤིས་བདེ་ལེགས། — lo·sar ta·shi de·lek

eating out

I'm looking for a restaurant.
ཟ་ཁང་ག་པར་ཡོད་མེད་བལྟ་གི་ཡོད། — sa·khâng ka·bah yö·may ta·gi yö

A table for …, please.
མི་ …ལ་ཅོག་ཙེ་གཅིག་གནང་རོགས། — mi …·la chog·tse·chig nang·ro

Can I see the menu, please?
ངར་ཁ་ལག་གི་ཐོ་སྟོན་གནང་དང་། — ngah kha·la·gi·tho tön nang·da

What do you recommend?
ཁྱེད་རང་ཁྱེད་ན་ག་རེ་ཡག་གི་རེད། — kay·râng chay·na kâ·ray yâ·gi·ray

What's the local speciality?
ས་གནས་ཀྱི་བཟའ་ཆས་དམིགས་བསལ་
ག་རེ་ག་རེ་བཙོང་ཡག་ཡོད་རེད། — sa·nay·ki sa·chay mig·say kâ·ray kâ·ray tsong·ya yö·ray

I'll have …
ང་ … དགོས། — nga … gö

I'll have what they're having.
ཁོང་ཚོས་མཆོད་ཡག་དེ་ན་བཞིན་ང་ལ་དགོས། — khong·tsö chö·ya·te na·shin nga·la gö

What's in that dish?
ཁ་ལག་ཕ་གིའི་ནང་ག་རེ་ཡོད་རེད། — kha·la pha·gi·nâng kâ·ray yö·ray

I love this dish.
ང་ཁ་ལག་འདི་ལ་དགའ་པོ་ཡོད། — nga kha·la di·la ka·bo yö

We love the local cuisine.
ང་ཚོས་གནས་ཀྱི་ཁ་ལག་ལ་དགའ་པོ་ཡོད། — ngân·tso sa·nay·ki kha·la·la ka·bo yö

street eats

fried meat dumplings	མོག་མོག་བརྔོས་པ་	mo·mo ngö·pa
fried rice	འབྲས་བརྔོས་པ་	day ngö·pa
noodle soup	རྒྱ་ཐུག	gya·thuk
pork spare ribs	རྩིབ་ཤ་	tsib·sha
rice soup	འབྲས་ཐུག	day·thuk
roasted pancake (bread)	ཨ་མདོ་བག་ལེབ་	ahm·dho bâk·lay
soup with meat, vegetables and noodles	ཐེན་ཐུག	ten·thuk
steamed meat dumplings	མོག་མོག་	mo·mo
vegetable dumplings	ཚལ་མོག་མོག་	tsay mo·mo

The meal was delicious!
ཁ་ལག་ཞིམ་པོ་ཞེ་དྲགས་བྱུང་། — kha·la shim·bu shay·ta choong

Please bring the (bill).
(ཁ་ལག་གི་འཛིན་) ཅིག་གནང་དང་། — (kha·la·gi zihn)·chig nâng·da

breakfast	ཞོགས་སྐད་ཁ་ལག	shog·kay kha·la
lunch	ཉིན་གུང་ཁ་ལག	nyin·goong kha·la
dinner	དགོང་དག་ཁ་ལག་	gong·da kha·la
a bottle of ...	... ཤེལ་དམ་གཅིག་	... shay·tâm·chig
(boiled) water	ཆུ་ (འཁོལ་མ་)	chu (khö·ma)
(mineral) water	(བུལ་ཏོག་) ཆུ་	(bu·tog)·chu
(orange) juice	(ཚ་ལུ་མའི་) ཁུ་བ་	(tsâ·lu·may) khu·wa
soda	ཆུ་མངར་མོ་	chu nga·mo
coffee (without milk)	ཇ་ཀོ་ཕི་ (འོ་མ་མེད་པ་)	cha ka·bi (oh·ma may·pa)
black tea	ཇ་ཇ་ཐང་	cha·tâng
tea	ཇ	cha
tea with sugar	ཇ་མངར་མོ་	cha nga·mo

I'll buy you a drink.
འཐུང་ཡག་ཅིག་ངས་ཉོ་གོ — toong·ya·chig ngay nyo·go

What would you like?
ཁྱེད་རང་ག་རེ་དགོས། — kay·râng kâ·ray gö

You can get the next one.
རྗེས་མ་དེ་མངག་ཆོག་གི་རེད། — je·ma·te ngâg cho·gi ray

beer (home-brew)	ཆང་	châng
beer (bottled)	བི་ཡར་	bee·yar
Chinese brandy	རྒྱ་མིའི་ཨ་རག་	gya·mee ah·râk
liquor	ཨ་རག་	ah·râk
wine	རྒུན་འབྲུམ་ཆང་རག་	gün·doom châng·râk

special diets & allergies

I'm vegetarian.
ང་ཤ་མི་ཟ་མཁན་ཡིན། — nga sha mi·sa·ken yin

Not too spicy, please.
སྨན་སྣ་ཞེ་དྲགས་
མ་རྒྱག་རོགས་གནང་། — men·na shay·ta ma·gyâ·ro·nâng

I'm allergic to ...	ངར་ ... ཕོག་གི་ཡོད།	ngah ... pho·gi·yö
eggs	སྒོ་ང་	go·nga
dairy products	དཀར་ཆུ་	kar·chu
fish	ཉ་ཤ་	nya·sha
meat	ཤ་	sha
peanuts	བ་དམ་	ba·tâm

emergencies & health

Help!	རོགས་གནང་དང་།	rog nâng·da
Stop!	ཁ་བཀག་དང་།	kha kâg·dâng
Go away!	ཕར་རྒྱུགས།	phâh gyook
Thief!	རྐུ་མ་འདུག	ku·ma du
Fire!	མེ་འབར་གྱིས།	may bâh·gee
Watch out!	གཟབ་གཟབ་གནང་།	sâb sâb nâng

Call …!	… སྐད་གཏོང་དང་།	… kay tong·da
a doctor	ཨེམ་ཆི་	ahm·chi
an ambulance	ནད་པ་དབོར་མཁན་མོ་ཊ་	nay·pa or·khen mo·ta
the police	སྐོར་སྲུང་བ་	kor·soong·wa

Please help me.
ང་ལ་རོགས་གནང་དང་། — ngah ro nâng·dâ

Could I please use the telephone?
ཁ་པར་བེད་སྤྱོད་བྱེད་ན་འ གྲིགས་ཀྱི་རེད་པས། — kha·pah bay·chö chay·na di·gi re·bay

I'm lost.
ང་ལམ་ཀ་བརླགས་ཤག — nga lâm·ga la·sha

Where are the toilets?
གསང་སྤྱོད་ག་པར་ཡོད་རེད། — sâng·chö ka·bah yö·ray

Where's the police station?
སྐོར་སྲུང་བའི་ལས་ཁུངས་ ག་པར་ཡོད་རེད། — kor·soong·way le·koong ka·bah yö·ray

english–tibetan dictionary

n this dictionary, words are marked as n (noun), a (adjective), v (verb), m (masculine), f (feminine), sg (singular) and pl (plural) where necessary.

A

accident (collision) གདོང་ཐུག་བརྒྱབ་པ dhong·tu gyâb·pa
accommodation སྡོད་གནས dhö·nay
adaptor གློག་ཤུགས་གཅོག་ཡག log·shoog cho·ya
address ཁ་བྱང ka·châng
after རྗེས་ལ je·la
air-conditioned གྲང་གློག dâng·log
airplane གནམ་གྲུ nâm·du
airport གནམ་ཐང nâm·tâng
all ཚང་མ tshâng·ma
allergy ཕོགས་ནད phog·nay
ambulance ནད་པ་དོར་མཁན་མོ་ཊ nay·pa or·khen mo·ta
and དང dâng
ankle རྐང་ཚིག kâng·tsig
antibiotics ནད་འབུ་འགོག་སྨན་ཨེན་ཏི་བྷ་ཡེ་ཨོ་ཊིཀ
nay·bu gok·men an·ti·ba·ye·ot·ik
arm ལག་པ lâg·pa

B

baby ཕྲུ་གུ pu·gu
back (of body) རྒྱབ gyâb
backpack རྒྱབ་ཕེད gya·phay
bad སྡུག་ཆགས dhuk·cha
bag འབེག་ལ bag·la
baggage claim རྟོག་ཐྲས་ལེན་ས tog·tay len·sa
bank དངུལ་ཁང ngü·khâng
bar ཆང་ཁང châng·khâng
bathroom ཁྲུས་ཁང trü·khâng
battery སྦེ་ཏི་རི bay·ti·ri
beautiful སྙིང་རྗེ་པོ nying je·po
bed ཉལ་ཁྲི nye·ti
beer (bottled) བྷི་ཡར་/ཕི་ཆུ bee·yar
beer (home-brew) ཆང châng
before སྔོན་ལ ngön·la
behind རྒྱབ་ལ gyâb·la
bicycle རྐང་སྒ་རིལ kâng·ga·ri
big ཆེན་པོ chen·po
bill (account) དངུལ་རྩིས ngü·tsi
blanket ཉལ་ཆས nye·chay
blood group ཁྲག་རིགས tâg·rig
boat གྲུ་གཟིངས dru·zing
book (make a reservation) སྔོན་མངགས་བྱེད་པ
ngön·ngâg chay·pa
bottle ཤེལ་དམ shay·tâm
boy བུ bu
breakfast ཞོག་སྐད་ཁ་ལག shog·kay kha·la
broken ཆག་པ châg·pa
bus སྤྱི་སྤྱོད་རླངས་འཁོར chi·chö lâng·kho
business ཚོང tsong
buy v ཉོ་བ nyo·wa

C

camera པར་ཆས par·chay
cancel ཕྱིར་འཐེན་བྱེད་པ chi·ten chay·pa
car མོ་ཊ mo·ta
cell phone ལག་པར་འཁྱེར་ཡག་ཁ་པར lâg·pa kye·ya kha·pa
centre (city) གྲོང་ཁྱེར་དཀྱིལ drong·kay·kyil
change v བརྗེ་བ je·wa
cheap ཁེ་པོ kay·po
chest (body) བྲང་ཁོག bâng·go
child/children ཕྲུ་གུ pu·gu
cigarettes ཐ་མག tha·ma
city གྲོང་ཁྱེར dong·kay
clean གཙང་མ tsâng·ma
closed སྒོ་བརྒྱབ་པ go gyâb·pa
cold a གྲང་མོ dâng·mo
come ཡོང་བ yong·wa
computer ཀམ་པུ་ཊར câm·pu·tah
condoms ལྡིག་ཤུབས lig·shoob
cook v ཁ་ལག་བཟོ་བ kha·la so·wa
cost n གོང gong
credit card བུ་ལོན་ཤོག་བྱང bu·lön shog·jâng
customs (at border) གོམས་སྲོལ gom·söl

D

dangerous ཉེན་ཀ nyan·ga
date (time) ཚེས་པ tshe·pa
day ཉིན nyin·ma
delay འགྱང་བ gyâng·wa
dentist སོ་ཨེམ་ཆི so ahm·chi
depart ཕྱིར་ཐོན་པ chi thön·pa
diaper ཕྲུ་གུའི་ཆུ་གདན pu·gü chu·den
dinner དགོང་དག་ཁ་ལག gong·da kha·la
direct ཁ་ཐུག ka·thoog
dirty བཙོག་པ་ཅན tsog·ba·chen
disabled དབང་པོ་སྐྱོན་ཅན wâng·po kyön·chen

discount གོང་བཅག་པ gong châg·pa
doctor ཨེམ་ཆི ahm·chi
double bed མི་གཉིས་ག་ཤོང་སའི་ཉལ་ཁྲི
mi·nyi shong·say nye·ti
double room མི་གཉིས་སྡོད་སའི་ཁང་མིག
mi·nyi dö·say khâng·mi
drink n འཐུང་ཡག toong·ya
drive v མོ་ཊ་གཏོང་བ mo·ta tong·wa
driving licence མོ་ཊ་གཏོང་ཡག་ལག་ཁྱེར mo·ta tong·ya lâg·kay
drug བཟི་སྨན si·men

E

ear ཨམ་ཅོག ahm·chog
east ཤར shâr
eat ཟ་བ sa·wa
electricity གློག log
email ཨི་མེལ ee·mel
embassy གཞུང་ཚབ shoong·tsab
emergency ཛ་དྲག za·dâg
English (language) དབྱིན་ཇི in·ji
evening དགོང་དག gong·da
exit ཐོན་ས dön·sa
expensive གོང་ཆེན་པོ gong chen·po
eye མིག mig

F

far ཐག་རིང་པོ ta ring·po
fast མགྱོགས་པོ gyok·po
father པ་ཕ pa·pha
film (camera) ཕིང་ཤོག phing·sho
finger མཛུབ་གུ zu·gu
first-aid kit ཁ་ཐུག་བེད་སྤྱོད་བྱེད་ཡག་སྨན་བཅོས་ཡོ་བྱད
ka·toog bay·chö chay·ya·men·chö yo·chay
fish (alive) ཉ nya
fish (as food) ཉ་ཤ nya·sha
food ཁ་ལག kha·la
foot རྐང་པ kâng·pa
free (of charge) རིན་མེད་པ rin may·pa
friend གྲོགས་པོ/གྲོགས་མོ tok·po/tok·mo m/f
fruit ཤིང་ཏོག shing·tog
full ཁེངས་པ kheng·pa

G

gift ལག་རྟགས lâg·tâg
girl བུ་མོ bu·mo
glass གེ་ལ་སི ge·la·si
go འགྲོ་བ doh·wa
good ཡག་པོ yâg·po
guide (person) ལམ་སྟོན་པ lâm·tön·pa

H

half ཕྱེད་ཀ chay·ka
hand ལག་པ lâg·pa
happy སྐྱིད་པོ kyi·po
have ཡོད་པ yö·pa
he ཁོ kho
head མགོ go
heart སྙིང nying
heavy ལྗིད་ཁོག ji·kog
help v རོགས་གནང་བ rog nâng·wa
here འདིར day
high མཐོ་པོ tho·po
hike v རྐང་འགྲོས་རྒྱག་པ kâng·drö gyâk·pa
holiday (vacation) གུང་གསེང goong·seng
homosexual ཕོ་ཕོ་ལ་ཆགས་པ་བྱེད་པ
phö pho·la châg·pa chay·pa
hospital སྨན་ཁང men·khâng
hot ཚ་པོ tsha·po
hotel འགྲུལ་ཁང drü·khâng
hungry གྲོད་ཁོག་ལྟོགས་པ drö·kog tog·pa
husband ཁྱོ་ག kyo·ka

I

I ང nga
identification (card) ངོ་སྤྲོད་ལག་ཁྱེར ngo·trö lâg·kay
ill ན་བ na·wa
important གལ་ཆེན་པོ kay·chen·po
injury རྨས་སྐྱོན may·kyön
insurance ཨིན་ཤུ་རན་འགན་རྒྱ in·shu·ren gan·gya
internet ཨིན་ཊ་ནེཊ in·ta·net

J

jewellery རྒྱན་ཆ gyen·jâ
job ལས་ཀ lay·ka

K

key ལྡེ་མིག di·mig
kilogram ཀི་ལོ་ག་རམ ki·lo·ga·râm
kitchen ཐབ་ཚང thâb·tsang
knife གྲི ti

L

laundry དུག་ལོག་འཁྲུད་ཁང tu·log trü·khâng
lawyer ཁྲིམས་རྩོད་པ tim·tsö·pa
left (direction) གཡོན yön
leg (body) རྐང་པ kâng·pa

sbian མོས་མོ་ལ་ཆགས་པ་བྱེད་མཁན
mö mo·la châg·pa chay·khen
ss ཉུང་བ nyoong·wa
tter ཡི་གེ yi·ge
ght (sun/lamp) འོད wö
ke དགའ་པོ་བྱེད ga·po chay
ck སྒོ་ལྕགས gon·châg
ng རིང་པོ ring·po
ove v དགའ་པོ་བྱེད ga·po chay
iggage དོག་ཁྲེས tog·tay
inch ཉིན་གུང་ཁ་ལག nyin·goong kha·la

M

nail སྦྲག dâg
nan ཕོ pho
nap ས་བཀྲ sâp·ta
narket འཁྲོམ trom
natches ཙག་ཏྲ tsâg·ta
neat ཤ sha
nedicine སྨན men
nessage ཁ་ལན kha·len
nilk འོ་མ oh·ma
minute སྐར་མ་གཅིག ka·ma·chig
mobile phone ལག་པར་འཁྱེར་ཡག་ཁ་པར lâg·pa kye·ya kha·pa
noney དངུལ ngü
nonth ཟླ་བ da·wa
morning སྔ་དྲོ nga·toh
mother ཨ་མ ah·ma
motorcycle སྦག་སྦག bâhg·bâhg
mouth ཁ kha

N

name མིང ming
near འཁྲིས་ལ tih·la
new གསར་པ sar·ba
newspaper ཚགས་པར tsâg·ba
night དགོང་དག gong·da
no མིན/ མེད/མ་རེད/མིན་འདུག min/may/ma·ray/min·du
noisy སྐད་ཅོར kay·choh
north བྱང châng
nose སྣ་ཁུག na·khoog
now ད་ལྟ tân·da

O

old རྙིང་པ nying·pa
one-way ticket ཡར་ལམ་གཅིག་པོ་འགྲོ་ཡག་ཏི་ཀ་ས
ya·lâm chig·po do·ya ti·ka·sî
open a ཁ་ཕྱེ kha·chay
outside ཕྱིར་ལོགས chi·log

P

passport པ་སེ་པོད pa·se·pot
pay v རིན་སྤྲོད་པ rin trö·pa
pharmacy སྨན་ཚོང་ཁང men tsong·khâng
phonecard ཁ་པར་གཏོང་ཡག་ལག་ཁྱེར kha·pah tong·ya lâg·kye
photo པར par
police སྐོར་སྲུང་བ kor·soong·wa
postcard སྦྲག་ཤོག dâg·shog
post office སྦྲག་ཁང da·khâng
pregnant ཕྲུ་གུ་སྐྱེ་ཡག་ཡོད་པ pu·gu kye·ya yö·pa
price n གོང gong

Q

quiet a ཁ་ཁུ་སིམ་པོ kha·khu sim·bu

R

rain འཆར་པ chah·pa
razor སྐྲ་གྲི ta·di
receipt བྱུང་འཛིན choong·zin
refund n ཕྱིར་ལོག chi·log
registered mail དེབ་སྐྱེལ་སྦྲག teb·kyel·dâg
rent v གཡར་བ yâr·wa
repair v བཟོ་བཅོས་རྒྱག་པ so·chö gyâk·pa
reservation སྔོན་མངགས ngön·ngâg
reserve v སྔོན་མངགས་བྱེད་པ ngön·ngâg chay·pa
restaurant ཟ་ཁང sa·khâng
return v ཕྱིར་ལོག་པ chih log·pa
return ticket ཡར་ལམ་མར་ལམ་འགྲོ་ཡག་ཏི་ཀ་སི
ya·lâm ma·lâm do·ya ti·ka·si
right (direction) གཡས yeh
road (main) ལམ་ཆེན lâm·chen
room ཁང་མིག khâng·mi

S

safe a ཉེན་ཁ་མེད་པ nyen·ga may·pa
sanitary napkins གཙང་སྦྲའི་ཤོག་བུ tsâng·day shu·gu
seat རྐུབ་ཀྱག koob·kya
send གཏོང་བ tong·wa
sex ཕོ་མོ་རྟགས pho·mo tâg
shampoo སྐྲ་འཁྲུད་ཤམ་པུ ta·trü·ya shâm·bu
share (a dorm) ཕྱི་ཁང་ནང་མཉམ་དུ་སྡོད་པ
chi·khâng·nâng nyâm·tu dhö·pa
she མོ mo
sheet (bed) ཅག་དར cha·tah
shirt སྟོད་ཐུང tö·toong
shoes ལྷམ་ཀོག lhâm·ko
shop n ཚོང་ཁང tsong·khâng

short (height) དམའ་པོ mâ·po
short (length) ཐུང་ཐུང་ toong·toong
shower གཟུགས་ཁྲུད་ཐོར་ཆུ་ soog·po tru·ya tor·cho
single room ཁང་མིག་གཅིག khâng·mi·chig
skin པགས་པ pâg·pa
skirt སྨད་གཡོག may·yog
sleep v གཉིད་ཉལ་བ nyi nyay·wa
slowly ག་ལེ་ག་ལེ་ ka·lee ka·lee
small ཆུང་ཆུང་ choong·choong
soap ཡི་ཙི་ yi·tsi
some ཁ་ཤས ka·shay
soon མགྱོགས་པོ gyok·po
south ལྷོ lho
souvenir shop དྲན་རྟེན་ཅ་ལག་ཚོང་ཁང་
dren·ten cha·lâg tsong·khâng
stamp སྦྲག་རྟགས dâg·tâg
station འབབ་ཚུགས bâb·tsoog
stomach གྲོད་ཁོག drö·kog
stop v བཀག་པ kâg·pa
stop (bus) n བཀག་ས kâg·sa
street ལམ་ཁ lâm·ga
student སློབ་ཕྲུག lob·toog
sun ཉི་མ nyi·ma
sunscreen ཉི་བཀྲག་འགོག nyib·ta gok
swim v ཆུ་རྐྱལ་རྒྱག་པ chu·kye gyâk·pa

T

tampons མ་ཁ་འགོག་བྱེད་སྲིན་བལ ma·kha gok·chay sin·bay
teeth སོ་ so
telephone n ཁ་པར་ kha·pah
temperature (weather) གནམ་གཤིས nâm·shi
that ཕ་གི་ pha·gi
they ཁོང་ཚོ khong·tso
thirsty ཁ་སྐོམ་པོར་ kha kom·po
this འདི་ di
throat མིད་པ mik·pa
ticket ཏི་ཀ་སི་ ti·ka·si
time དུས་ཚོད་ dü·tsö
tired ཐང་ཆད་པ tâng chay·pa
tissues གཙང་སྦྲ་ཤོག་བུ tsâng·ta shu·gu
today དེ་རིང་ te·ring
toilet གསང་སྤྱོད་ sâng·chö
tomorrow སང་ཉིན་ sa·nyin
tonight དོ་དགོང་ toh·gong
toothbrush སོ་ཁྲུས་ so·trü
toothpaste སོ་སྨན་ so·men
torch (flashlight) གློག་བཞུ་ log·shu
tour བལྟ་སྐོར་ ta·kor
tourist information office ཡུལ་སྐོར་སྟོ་འཆམ་པའི་ལས་ཁུངས་
yu·kor to·châm·pay lay·khoong
train རི་ལི་ ri·li
translate v ཕབ་སྒྱུར་བྱེད་པ phâb·gyur chay·pa
travel agency འགྲིམ་འགྲུལ་ལས་ཁུངས dim·drü lay·koong
travellers cheques འགྲུལ་བཞུད་དངུལ་འཛིན་ drü·shü ngü·zin
trousers གོས་ཐུང་ gö·toong
twin beds ཉལ་ཁྲི་ཆ་གཅིག nye·ti cha·chig

U

underwear ནང་གོན་ཧ་པན་ nâng·gyön ha·pan
urgent གལ་ཆེན་པོ kay chen·po

V

vacant སྟོང་པ tong·pa
vegetable སྔོ་ཚལ ngo·tsay
vegetarian ཤ་མི་ཟ་མཁན་ sha mi·sa·khen
visa ཝི་ཛ་ vi·za

W

walk v གོམ་པ་རྒྱག་པ gom·pa gyâk·pa
wash (something) v ཁྲུས་རྒྱག་པ trü gyâk·pa
watch n ཆུ་ཚོད་ chu·tsö
water n ཆུ་ chu
we ང་ཚོ་ ngân·tso
weekend གཟའ་སྤེན་པ་དང་ཉི་མ sa pen·pa dâng nyin·ma
west ནུབ noob
wheelchair འཁོར་ལོ་རྐུབ་ཀྱག kho·lö koob·gya
when ག་དུས ka·dü
where ག་པར་ ka·bah
who སུ su
why ག་རེ་བྱས་ནས kâ·ray chay·nay
wife སྐྱེ་དམན་ kye·man
window སྒེའུ་ཁུང་ gay·koong
with མཉམ་དུ་ nyâm·tu
without མེད་པ/མིན་པ may·pa/min·pa
woman སྐྱེ་དམན་ kye·man
write འབྲི་བ ti·wa

Y

yes ཡིན/རེད་/ཡོད་/འདུག yin/ray/yö/du
yesterday ཁ་སང་ kay·sa
you sg/pl ཁྱེད་རང་/ཁྱེད་རང་ཚོ kay·râng/kay·râng·tso

Uighur

ALPHABET 336
ABOUT UIGHUR 337
PRONUNCIATION 338
LANGUAGE DIFFICULTIES 339
TIME & DATES 340
TRANSPORT & DIRECTIONS 342
ACCOMMODATION 343
BANKING & COMMUNICATIONS 344
SIGHTSEEING 344
SHOPPING 345
MEETING PEOPLE 346
MAKING CONVERSATION 347
FEELINGS & OPINIONS 350
FAREWELLS 351
EATING OUT 352
SPECIAL DIETS & ALLERGIES 355
EMERGENCIES & HEALTH 356
ENGLISH–UIGHUR DICTIONARY 357

uighur alphabet				
word-final	**word-medial**	**word-initial**	**alone**	**sound**
ـا		ئا	ئا	aa
ـە	ـئھـ	ئھ	ئە	a
ـب	ـبـ	بـ	ب	b
ـپ	ـپـ	پـ	پ	p
ـت	ـتـ	تـ	ت	t
ـج	ـجـ	جـ	ج	j
ـچ	ـچـ	چـ	چ	ch
ـخ	ـخـ	خـ	خ	h
ـد		د	د	d
ـر		ر	ر	r
ـز		ز	ز	z
ـژ		ژ	ژ	z
ـس	ـسـ	سـ	س	s
ـش	ـشـ	شـ	ش	sh
ـغ	ـغـ	غـ	غ	r
ـف	ـفـ	فـ	ف	f
ـق	ـقـ	قـ	ق	k
ـك	ـكـ	كـ	ك	k
ـگ	ـگـ	گـ	گ	g
ـڭ	ـڭـ	ڭـ	ڭ	ng
ـل	ـلـ	لـ	ل	l
ـم	ـمـ	مـ	م	m
ـن	ـنـ	نـ	ن	n
ـھ	ـھـ	ھـ	ھ	ee
ـو		ئو	ئو	o
ـۇ		ئۇ	ئۇ	u
ـۆ		ئۆ	ئۆ	v
ـۈ		ئۈ	ئۈ	ü
ـۋ		ۋ	ۋ	v
ـې		ئې	ئې	e
ـى		ئىـ	ئى	i
ـي	ـيـ	يـ	ي	y

about Uighur

The old language of the Central Asian steppe, Uighur (ooy·*roor*·cha ئۇيغۇرچە) is spoken by more than 10 million people in the oases, bazaars and mosques of China's Xīnjiāng Uighur Autonomous Region. True to its history as a language of the Silk Road, Uighur has absorbed elements of Arabic and Persian and can be heard in pockets of neighbouring Kazakhstan, Kyrgyzstan, Mongolia, Uzbekistan and Russia. Buddhist texts from the 9th century were written in old Uighur script (read from bottom to top) and for much of the following 1000 years Uighur scribes dutifully recorded the history of Central Asia using a modified Arabic script. Since the 1970s some Uighur speakers have used the Roman alphabet, but the modified Arabic script (written from right to left) still predominates in China. Uighur is a Turkic language closely related to Uzbek and similar to modern Turkish. As the guardians of a venerable language, the Muslim Uighurs also enjoy a reputation for longevity, with over 25% of all centenarians in China being Uighur. It's not unusual for Uighur people to invite foreigners into their homes – with a few of the phrases in this chapter you're sure to impress your hosts.

uighur

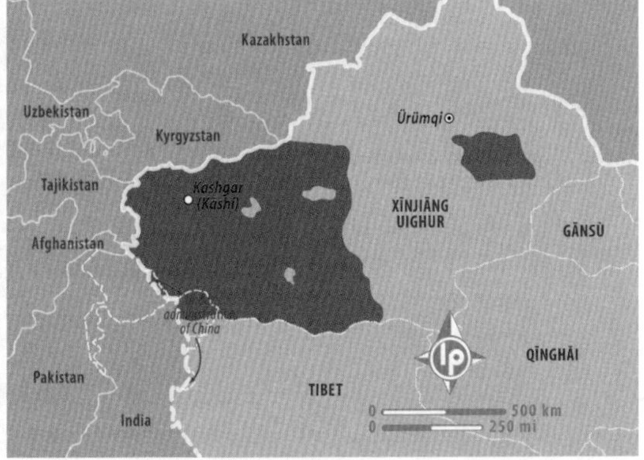

pronunciation

Vowels		Consonants	
Symbol	**English sound**	**Symbol**	**English sound**
a	hat	b	bed
aa	father	ch	cheat
e	bet	d	dog
ee	as the 'ee' in 'sleep', but produced from the throat	f	fat
i	hit	g	go
o	go	h	hat (pronounced with a puff of air)
ö	as the 'e' in 'her', pronounced with rounded lips	j	joke
oo	tool	k	king
u	put	l	live
ü	i pronounced with rounded lips	m	man
		n	not
		ng	sing
		p	pet
		r	room (produced from the throat)
		s	sun
		sh	shut
		t	top
		v	very
		y	yes
		z	zoo

In this chapter, Uighur pronunciation is given in purple after each phrase.

Syllables are separated by a dot, and stressed syllables are indicated with italics.

For example:
كەچۈرۈڭ ka·chü·*rueng*

essentials

Yes./No.	ھەئە./ياق.	ee·a·*a*/yaak
Please …	مەرھەممەت …	ma·ree·am·*mat* …
Hello.	ياخشىمۇسىز.	yaah·shi·mu·*siz*
Goodbye.	خەير-خوش.	hayr·*hosh*
Thank you.	رەھمەت سىزگە.	rah·*mat* siz·ga
Excuse me. (to get past)	كەچۈرۈڭ ئۆتۈۋالاي.	ka·chü·*rüng* ö·tü·vaa·*laay*
Excuse me. (to get assistance)	كەچۈرۈڭ گە قانداق بارىدۇ؟	ka·chü·*rüng* ga kaan·*daak* baar·i·du
Sorry.	كەچۈرۈڭ.	ka·chü·*rüng*

language difficulties

Do you speak English?

سىز ئىنگلىزچە بىلەمسىز؟ siz ing·gi·lis·*ka* bi·*lam*·siz

Do you understand?

سىزچۈشەندىڭىزمۇ؟ siz chü·*shan*·di·ngiz·moo

I understand/don't understand.

مەن چۈشەندىم/چۈشەنمىدىم. man chü·*shan*·dim/chu·*shan*·mi·dim

I speak/don't speak Mandarin.

مەن ئورتاق تىلدا سۆزلىيەلەيمەن/ سۆزلىيەلمەيمەن. man or·*taak* til·*daa* söz·li·*ya*·lay·man/ söz·li·*yal*·may·man

Do you speak (Uighur)?

سىز (ئۇيغۇرچە) سۆزلىيەلەمسىز؟ siz (ooy·*roor*·cha) söz·li·ya·lam·*siz*

What do you call this in (Uighur)?

بۇنى (ئۇيغۇر تىلىدا) نىمە دەپ ئاتايسىلەر؟ bu·*ni* (ooy·*roor* ti·*li*·daa) ni·*ma* dap aa·taay·*si*·lar

Can we try to speak in (Uighur)?

مەن (ئۇيغۇرچە) سۆزلەپ سىناپ باقسام بولامدۇ؟ man (ooy·roor·*cha*) söz·*lap* si·*naap* baak·saam *bo*·laam·*doo*

Could you please …?	خاپابولماي … قىلىپ بېرەلەمسىز؟	haa·*paa* bol·*maay* … *ki*·lip bi·ra·lam·*siz*
repeat that	يەنەبىر دەڭە	ya·*na* bir da·*nga*
speak more slowly	ئاستىراق سۆزلەڭ	aas·*ti*·raak söz·*lang*

numbers

0	نۆل	nöl	20	يىگىرمە	yi·*gir*·ma
1	بىر	bir	30	ئوتتۇز	ot·*tuz*
2	ئىككى	ik·ki	40	قىرىق	ki·*rik*
3	ئۈچ	üch	50	ئەللىك	al·*lik*
4	تۆت	töt	60	ئاتمىش	at·*mish*
5	بەش	bash	70	يەتمىش	yat·*mish*
6	ئالتە	aal·*ta*	80	سەكسەن	sak·*san*
7	يەتتە	yat·*ta*	90	توقسان	tok·*saan*
8	سەككىز	sak·*kiz*	100	بىر يۈز	bir *yüz*
9	توققۇز	tok·*kuz*	1,000	بىر مىڭ	bir mng
10	ئون	on	1,000,000	بىر مىلىيون	bir mil·*yoon*

time & dates

What time is it?

هازىر سائەت قانچە بولدى؟ — ee·aa·*zir* saa·*at* kan·*cha* bol·*di*

It's (10) o'clock.

سائەت (ئون) بولدى. — saa·*at* (on) bol·*di*

Quarter past (10).

(ئون)دىن بىرچارەك ئۆتتى. — (on) din bir chaa·*rak* öt·*ti*

Half past (10).

(ئون) يېرىم بولدى. — (on) ye·*rim* bol·*di*

Quarter to (11).

(ئونبىر)غا بىر چارەك قالدى. — (oon·bir) raa bir kaa·*rak* üt·*ti*

At what time (does it start)?

سائەت قانچىدە (باشلايدۇ)؟ — saa·*at* kaan·ki·*da* (baash·*laay*·doo)

(It starts) At 10.

سائەت ئوندا(باشلايدۇ). — saa·*at* oon·*daa* (baash·laay·*doo*)

It's (18 October).

(ئونىنچى ئاينىڭ ئونسەككىزىنچى كۈنى) بولدى. — (o·nin·*chi* aay·*ning* on·sak·*ki*·zin·chi kü·*ni*) bol·*di*

now	هازىر	ee·aa·*zir*
today	بۈگۈن	bü·*gün*
tonight	بۈگۈن ئاخشام	bü·*gün* aah·*shaam*

this …	بۈگۈن …	bü·*gün* …
afternoon	چۈشتىن كېيىن	chüsh·*tin* ke·*yin*
morning (after breakfast)	ئەتتىگەن	a·ti·*gan*
morning (before lunch)	چۈشتىن بۇرۇن	chüsh·*tin* bu·*run*
yesterday	تۈنۈگۈن	tü·nü·*gün*
tomorrow	ئەتە	a·*ta*
sunrise	كۈن چىقىش	kün chi·*kish*
sunset	كۈن ئولتۇرۇش	kün ol·tu·*roosh*
spring	باهار	baa·*ee*·*aar*
summer	ياز	yaaz
autumn	كۈز	küz
winter	قىش	kish

Monday	دۈشەنبە	dü·shan·*ba*
Tuesday	سەيشەنبە	say·shan·*ba*
Wednesday	چارشەنبە	chaar·shan·*ba*
Thursday	پەيشەنبە	pay·shan·*ba*
Friday	جۈمە	jü·*ma*
Saturday	شەنبە	shan·*ba*
Sunday	يەكشەنبە	yak·shan·*ba*
January	يانۋار	yaan·*vaar*
February	فېۋرال	fi·vi·*raal*
March	مارت	maart
April	ئاپرېل	aap·*ril*
May	ماي	maay
June	ئىيۇن	i·*yoon*
July	ئىيۇل	i·*yool*
August	ئاۋغۇست	aav·*roost*
September	سېنتەبىر	sin·ta·*bir*
October	ئۆكتەبىر	ök·ta·*bir*
November	نويابىر	no·yaa·*bir*
December	دېكابىر	de·kaa·*bir*

transport & directions

Is this the ... to (Kashgar)?	بۇ ... (قەشقەر)گە بارامدۇ؟	bu ... (kash·*kar*)·ga baa·raam·*du*
boat	كېمە	ki·*ma*
bus	ئاپتوبۇس	aap·too·*boos*
train	پويىز	po·*yiz*
Where's a/the ...?	... نەدە؟	... na·*da*
bank	بانكا	baan·*kaa*
place to change foreign money	چەتئەل پۇلى ئالماشتۇرىدىغان ئورۇن	chat·*al* poo·*li* aal·maash·too·ri·*di*·raan o·*roon*
post office	پوچتاخانا	*posh*·taa·haa·naa

Is this the road to (Kashgar)?

بۇ (قەشقەر)گە بارىدىغان يولمۇ؟	bo (kash·*kar*)·ga baa·ri·di·*haan* yol·*mo*

Can you show me where it is on the map?

ماڭا بۇ يەرنىڭ خەرىتىدىكى ئورنىنى كۆرسىتىپ بېرەمسىز؟	maa·*ngaa* bu *yar*·ning ha·ri·*ti*·di·*ki* or·ni·*ni* kör·si·*tip* bi·ram·*siz*

What's the address?

ئادرېسى قەيەر؟	aa·di·*ri*·si ka·*yar*

How far is it?

قانچىلىك يىراق؟	kaan·chi·*lik* yi·*raak*

Can I get there on foot?

ئۇيەرگە پىيادە بارغىلى بولامدۇ؟	u yar·ga pi·*yaa*·da bar·*ri*·li boo·*laam*·du

How do I get there?	قانداق ماڭىدۇ؟	kaan·*daak* maa·*ngi*·du
Turn right/left.	ئوڭغا/سولغا قايرىلىپ.	ong·*raa*/sol·*raa* kaay·ri·*lip*
It's straight ahead.	ئۇدۇل ئالدىغا مېڭىپ.	u·*dul* aal·*di*·raa me·*ngip*
It's ...	... نىڭ	... ning
behind ...	... ئارقىدا	... aar·*ki*·daa
in front of ...	... ئالدىدا	... aal·*di*·daa
near ...	... ئەتراپىدا	... at·raa·*pi*·daa
on the corner	نىڭ بۇلۇڭىدا	ning bu·lu·*ngi*·daa
opposite ...	... نىڭ قارشى تەرىپىدە	... ning kaar·*shi* ta·ri·*pi*·da
there	ئۇيەر	u·*yar*

accommodation

Where's a guest house/hotel?
قەيەردە مهمانخانا بار؟ ka·yar·*da* mee·maan·*haa*·naa baar

Can you recommend somewhere cheap/good?
ياخشىراق/ئەرزانراق yaah·*shi*·raak/*ar*·zaan·raak
ياتىدىغان يەردىن بىرنى yaa·ti·*di*·raan yar·din bir·*ni*
تەۋسىيە قىلىڭە؟ tav·si·*ya* ki·li·*nga*

I'd like to stay at a locally run hotel.
مىنىڭ يەرلىك مهمانخانىدا mi·*ning* yar·*lik* mee·maan·haa·ni·*daa*
تۇرغۇم بار. toor·*room* baar

I'd like to book a room, please.
مەن ياتاق زاكاس قىلماقچى ئىدىم. man yaa·*taak* zaa·*kaas* kil·maak·*chi* i·*dim*

I have a reservation.
مەن ئالدىن تىزىملىتىپ قويغان. man aal·*din* ti·zim·*li*·*tip* koy·*raan*

Do you have a … room?	… ياتاق بارمۇ؟	… yaa·*taak* baar·*mu*
double (suite)	بىر يۈرۈش	*bir* yü·*rüsh*
single	يالغۇز كىشلىك	yaal·*rooz* kish·*lik*
twin	قوش كىشلىك	kosh kish·*lik*

How much is it per night/person?
ھەربىر كۈنلىكى/ئادەمگە ee·*ar* bir kün·li·*ki*/aa·*dam*·*gee*
نەچچە پۇل؟ nach·*cha* pool

I'd like to stay for (three) nights.
مەن (ئۈچ) كۈن ياتماقچى ئىدىم. man (üch) kün *yaat*·maak·chi i·*dim*

Could I have my key, please?
ياتاقنىڭ ئاچقۇچىنى بىرەمسىز؟ yaa·taak·*ning* aach·*ku*·chi·ni *bi*·ram·siz

Can I get an extra (blanket)?
مەن بىرتال (ئەديال) ئارتۇق man bir taal (a·*di*·yaal) *aar*·took
ئالسام بولامدۇ؟ aal·*saam* boo·laam·*doo*

The (air conditioning) doesn't work.
(ھاۋا تەڭشىگۈچنىڭ) (ee·aa·*vaa* tang·shi·güch·*ning*)
چاتىقى بار كەن. *chaa*·ti·ki baar·*kan*

What time is checkout?
سائەت قانچىدە ياتاق قايتۇرىدۇ؟ saa·*at* kaan·*chi*·da yaa·*taak* kaay·too·ri·*du*

Could I have my ..., please?	مەن ئۆزەمنىڭكى ... نى ئېلىۋالسام بولامدۇ؟	man ö·züm·ning·*ki* ... ni e·*li*·vaal·saam bo·laam·*doo*
deposit	زاكالەت پۇلى	zaa·*kaa*·lat pu·*li*
passport	پاسپورت	paas·*port*

banking & communications

Where's a/an ...?	... نەدە؟	... na·*da*
ATM	ئاپتوماتىك پۇل ئېلىش ماشىنىسى	aap·to·maa·*tik* pool e·*lish* maa·*shi*·ni·si
public phone	ئاممىۋى تېلېفون	aam·*mi*·vi te·li·*foon*
What's your phone number?	تېلېفون نومۇرىڭىز قانچە؟	te·li·*foon* nu·mu·ri·*ngiz* kaan·*cha*
The number is ...	نومۇرى بولسا ...	nu·mu·*ri* *bol*·saa ...
Where's the local internet cafe?	يېقىن ئەتراپتا تورخانا بارمۇ؟	yi·*kin* at·raap·*taa* tor·haa·*naa* baar·*mu*
I'd like to ...	مەن ... قىلاي دېگەن	man ... *ki*·laay *di*·gan
get internet access	تورغا چىقىش	tor·*raa* *chi*·kish
use a printer/scanner	پرىنتېر/سكەنېر	pi·rin·*tir*/si·*ka*·nir

sightseeing

I'd like to see some local sights.	مەن يەرلىك مەنزىرىنى كۆرەي دېگەن.	man yar·*lik* man·zir·*ni* *kü*·ray *de*·gan
I'd like to see ...	مەن ... كۆرەي دېگەن.	man ... *kü*·ray *de*·gan
What's that?	ئۇ نىمە؟	u *ni*·ma
Can I take a photo?	سۈرەتكە تارتىۋالسام بولامدۇ؟	sü·*rat*·ka taar·*ti*·vaal·saam bo·laam·*doo*
I'd like to go somewhere off the beaten track.	مىنىڭ بۇ يەرنىڭ يەرلىك مەنزىرىسىنى كۆرگۈم بار.	mi·*ning* bu yar·*ning* yar·*lik* man·zir·*si*·ni *kör*·güm baar

How long is the tour?

بۇ يەرنى قانچىلىك ۋاقىتتا ساياھەت قىلىپ بولغىلى بولىدۇ؟	bu yar·*ni* kaan·chi·*lik* vaa·*kit*·taa saa·*yaa*·ee·at ki·*lip* bol·*ri*·li bo·*li*·doo

sightseeing		
Etgal Mosque	ھېيتكار جەمە مەسچىتى	eeyt·*kaar* ja·*ma* mas·*chi*·ti
Heaven Pool	بوغدا كۆلى	boor·*daa* kü·*li*
Kanasi Lake	قاناس كۆلى	kaa·*naas* kü·*li*
Lake Sayram	سايرام كۆلى	say·*raam* kü·*li*
Mahmud's Tomb	مەخموت قەشقەرەى قەبرىسى	mah·*moot* kash·*ki*·ri kab·*ri*·si
Thousand-Buddha Cave	مىڭ ئۆي	ming öy
Xiangfei Tomb	ئىپپارخان قەبرىسى	i·paar·*haan* kab·*ri*·si

shopping

Where's a …?	… نەدە؟	… na·*da*
camera shop	سۈرەتخانا	sü·*rat*·haa·naa
market	بازار	baa·*zaar*
souvenir shop	خاتىرە بۇيۇملىرى ماگزىنى	haa·*ti*·ra bo·yoom·*li*·ri maag·zi·ni
supermarket	تۈلۈك ماللار ماگزىنى	tür·*lük* maal·*laar* maag·*zi*·ni

I'd like to buy …	
مېنىڭ … نى سېتىۋالغۇم بار.	mi·*ning* … ni se·*ti*·vaal·room baar
Can I look at it?	
كۆرۈپ باقسام بولامدۇ؟	kö·*rüp* baak·*saam* bo·laam·*doo*
How much is it?	
قانچە پۇل؟	kaan·*cha* pool
Please write down the price.	
باھاسىنى خاتىرلەپ قويۇڭ.	baa·*ee*·aa·si·ni haa·*tir*·lap *ko*·yong
That's too expensive.	
بەك قىممەتكەن.	bak *kim*·mat·kan
I'll give you (five yuan).	
سىزگە (بەش يۇەن) بېرەي.	siz·*ga* (bash *yu*·an) *bi*·ray

Do you accept credit cards?

بۇيەردە ئىناۋەتلىك كارتوچكا ئىشلىتىشكە بولامدۇ؟ — bu yar·*da* i·*naa*·vat·*lik* kaar·tuch·*kaa* ish·li·tish·*ka* boo·laam·*doo*

There's a mistake in the bill.

ھېساۋات تالۇنىدا مەسىلە بار ئىكەن. — eey·saa·vaat taa·*lu*·ni·*daa* *ma*·si·*la* baar i·*kan*

Where can I buy locally produced goods/souvenirs?

نەدىن يەرلىك مەھسۇلاتلىرىنى سېتىۋالغىلى بولىدۇ؟ — na·*din* yar·*lik* ma·ee·*soo*·laat·laar·*ni* se·*ti*·vaal·*ri*·li boo·li·*doo*

What's this made from?

بۇ نەدە ياسالغان؟ — bu na·*da* yaa·saal·*raan*

less	ئاز	aaz
enough	يېتەرلىك	yi·tar·*lik*
more	كۆپ	köp
bigger	چوڭراق	chong·*raak*
smaller	كىچىكرەك	ki·*chik*·rak

meeting people

Hello.	ئەسسالامۇ ئەلەيكۇم./ ياخشىمۇسىز.	as·saa·laa·*mu* a·lay·*kom*/ yaah·shi·mu·*siz*
Good morning.	خەيرلىك سەھەر.	hayr·*lik* sa·*ee*·ar
Good afternoon.	چۈشتىن كېيىنلىكىڭىز خەيرلىك بولسۇن.	*chüsh*·tin ke·*yin*·li·ki·ngiz *hayr*·lik *bol*·soon
Good evening.	كەچلىكىڭىز خەيرلىك بولسۇن.	kach·*li*·ki·ngiz *hayr*·lik *bol*·soon
Goodbye.	خەير-خوش.	hayr·*hosh*
Good night.	خەيرلىك كەچ.	hayr·*lik* kach

Mr	ئەپەندىم	a·*pan*·dim
Mrs	خانىم	haa·*nim*
Ms/Miss	خېنىم	he·*nim*

How are you?	قانداق ئەھۋالىڭىز؟	kaan·*daak* a·ee·vaa·*li*·ngiz
Fine, and you?	ياخشى، سىزچۇ؟	yaah·*shi* siz·*chu*
What's your name?	سىزنىڭ ئىسمىڭىز نېمە؟	siz·*ning* is·mi·*ngiz* ni·*ma*
My name is ...	مېنىڭ ئىسمىم ...	mi·*ning* is·*mim* ...
Pleased to meet you.	دىدار غەنىمەت.	di·*daar* ra·ni·*mat*

This is my…	بۇ مېنىڭ …	bu me·*ning* …
brother (older)	ئۇكا	u·*kaam*
brother (younger)	ئىنىم	i·*nim*
child	بالام	baa·*laam*
daughter	قىزىم	ki·*zim*
father	دادىم/ئاتام	daa·*daam*/aa·*taam*
friend	دوستۇم	dos·*toom*
husband	ئەر	ar
mother	ئاپام/ئانام	aa·*paam*/aa·*naam*
partner (intimate)	لايىقىم	laa·*yi*·kim
sister (older)	ئاچام	aa·*cham*
sister (younger)	سىڭلىم	sing·*lim*
son	ئوغلۇم	or·*lum*
wife	ئايالىم	aa·yaa·*lim*

making conversation

Do you live here?	سىز بۇ يەردە تۇرامسىز؟	siz bu yar·*da* too·raam·*siz*
Where are you going?	نەگە بارىسىز؟	na·*ga* baa·*ri*·siz
Do you like it here?	بۇ يەرنى ياقتۇردىڭىزمۇ؟	bu yar·*ni* yaak·toor·di·ngiz·*mu*
I love it here.	بۇ يەرنى بەك ياقتۇردۇم.	bu yar·*ni* bak yaak·toor·*doom*
Have you eaten?	تاماق يېدىڭىزمۇ؟	taa·*maak* yi·di·ngiz·*mu*
Are you here on holidays?	بۇ يەرگە ساياھەت قىلغىلى كەلگەنمۇ؟	bu yar·*ga* saa·yaa·*ee*·at kil·ri·*li* kal·gan·*mu*
I'm here …	مەن بۇ يەرگە … كەلگەن.	man bu yar·*ga* … kal·*gan*
for a holiday	ساياھەت قىلىش	saa·*yaa*·ee·at ki·*lish*
on business	كوماندۇرۇپكىغا چىقىش	ko·maan·*do*·roop·*ki*·raa chi·*kish*
to study	ئوقۇش	o·*koosh*

How long are you here for?

سىز بۇيەردە قانچىلىك تۇرىسىز؟ — siz·*bu* yar·*da* kaan·chi·*lik* too·*ri*·siz

I'm here for (four) weeks.

مەن (تۆت) ھەپتە تۇرىمەن. — man (töt) ee·ap·*ta* too·*ri*·man

Can I take a photo (of you)?

مەن (سىزنى) سۈرەتكە تارتىۋالسام بولامدۇ؟ — man (siz·*ni*) sü·rat·*ka* taar·*ti*·vaal·saam boo·laam·*doo*

making conversation – UIGHUR

What language/dialect do you speak at home?

سىلەر يۇرتۇڭلاردا قايسى تىلدا سۆزلىشىسىلەر؟ — si·*lar* yoor·toong·laar·*daa* kaay·*si* til·daa söz·li·shi·si·*lar*

Do most of the people here speak (Uighur)?

بۇيەردە كۆپۈنچە ئادەم (ئۇيغۇرچە) سۆزلىشەمدۇ؟ — bu yar·*da* kö·pün·*cha* aa·*dam* (ooy·rur·*cha*) söz·li·sham·*doo*

I'd like to learn some (Uighur).

مېنىڭ (ئۇيغۇرتىلى)نى ئۈگەنگىم بار. — mi·*ning* (ooy·*roor* ti·*li*)·ni ü·gan·*gim* baar

Would you like me to teach you some English?

ماڭا ئازراق ئىنگلىچە ئۈگۈتۈپ قويۇشنى خالامسىز؟ — maa·*ngaa* aaz·*raak* ing·gi·lis·*cha* ü·gü·*tüp* ko·yoosh·*ni* haa·laam·*siz*

What's this called?

بۇنى نىمە دەيدۇ؟ — bu·*ni* ni·*ma* day·*doo*

local talk

Great!	قالتىس!	kaal·*tis*
Hey!	قانداق ئەھۋال.	kaan·*daak* aee·*vaal*
It's OK.	خېلى ياخشى.	he·*li* yaah·*shi*
Just a minute.	بىردەم ساقلاپ تۇرۇڭ.	bir·*dam* saak·*laap* too·*roong*
Just joking.	چاقچاق قىلىپ قويدۇم.	chaak·*chaak* ki·*lip* koy·*doom*
Maybe.	بەلكىم.	bal·*kim*
No problem.	ھېچقىسى يوق.	*eech*·ki·si yook
No way!	مۇمكىن ئەمەس.	moom·*kin* a·*mas*
Sure, whatever.	بولىدۇ،ماقۇل.	bo·li·doo maa·*kol*
That's enough!	بولدى،يېتەرلىك!	bol·*di* yi·tar·*lik*

Where are you from? سىز نەدىن كەلدىڭىز؟ — siz na·*din* kal·di·*ngiz*

I'm from ...	مەن ... دىن كەلدىم.	man ... din kal·*dim*
Australia	ئاۋىستىرالىيە	aa·vis·*ti*·raa·*li*·ya
Canada	كانادا	kaa·*naa*·daa
England	ئەنگلىيە	an·gi·*li*·ya
New Zealand	يېڭى زىنلاندىيە	ye·*ngi* zin·laan·di·*ya*
the USA	ئامرىكا	aa·mri·*kaa*

What's your occupation?

سىز نىمە ئىش بىلەن شۇغۇللىنىسىز؟ — siz ni·*ma* ish bi·*lan* shoo·roon·li·*ni*·siz

I'm a/an ...	مېنىڭ كەسپىم ...	mi·*ning* kas·*pim* ...
businessperson	سودىگەر	soo·*di*·gar
office worker	ئىشخانا خىزمەت خادىمى	ish·*haa*·naa hiz·*mat* haa·di·*mi*
tradesperson	ئىشچى	ish·*chi*
How old ...?	... قانچە ياشقا كىردىڭىز؟	... kaan·*cha* yaash·*kaa* kir·*di*·ngiz
are you	سىز/سەن	siz/san pol/inf
is your daughter	قىزىڭىز	ki·*zi*·ngiz
is your son	ئوغلىڭىز	or·*li*·ngiz
I'm ... years old.	مەن ... ياشقا كىردىم.	man ... yaash·*kaa* kir·*dim*
He/She is ... years old.	ئۇ ... ياشقا كىردى.	oo ... yaash·*kaa* kir·*di*
Too old!	بەك قېرى ئىكەن!	bak ke·*ri* i·*kan*
I'm younger than I look.	مەن كىچىك كۆرۈنىمەن.	man ki·*chik* kü·ru·ni·*man*
Are you married?	سىز توي قىلدىڭىز مۇ؟	siz toy kil·di·ngiz·*mu*
Do you have a family of your own?	سىز ياتلىق بولدىڭىزمۇ؟	siz yaat·*lik* bol·di·ngiz·*mu*
I live with someone.	مېنىڭ جۈپتىم بار.	mi·*ning* jüp·*tim* baar
I'm ...	مەن ...	man ...
single	بويتاق	boy·*taak*
married	توي قىلدىم	toy kil·*dim*
Do you like ...?	سىز ... نى ياخشى كۆرەمسىز؟	siz ... ni yaah·*shi* kü·*ram*·siz
I like/don't like ...	مەن ... نى ياخشى كۆرىمەن/كۆرمەيمەن.	man ... ni yaah·*shi* kü·*ri*·man/kör·may·*man*
art	سەنئەت	san·*at*
film	كىنو كۆرۈش	ki·*no* kü·*rüsh*
music	مۇزىكا ئاڭلاش	mu·zi·*kaa* aang·*laash*
reading	كىتاپ كۆرۈش	ki·*taap* kö·*rüsh*
sport	تەنتەربىيە	tan·tar·*bi*·ya

feelings & opinions

Are you ...?	سىز ... بولدىڭىزمۇ؟	siz ... bol·di·ngiz·*mu*
cold	سوغوق	so·*rook*
hot	ئىسسىق	is·*sik*
hungry	ئاچ	aach
thirsty	ئۇسساش	oos·*saash*
tired	ھېرىش	ee·*rish*

I feel ...	مەن ... ھېس قىلدىم.	man ... ees kil·*dim*
I don't feel ...	مەن ... ھېس قىلمىدىم.	man ... ees kil·mi·*dim*
Do you feel ...?	سىز ... بولىۋاتامسىز؟	siz ... bo·li·vaa·*taam*·siz
happy	خۇشال بولۇش	hoo·*shaal* bo·*loosh*
sad	خاپا بولۇش	haa·*paa* bo·*loosh*
worried	ئەنسىرەش	an·si·*rash*

What do you think of it?	سىزنىڭچە قانداقراق؟	siz·ning·*cha* kaan·daak·*raak*

It's ...	ئۇ ...	u ...
awful	بەك ناچار	bak naa·*chaar*
beautiful	بەك گۈزەل	bak gü·*zal*
boring	بەك زېرىكىشلىك	bak ze·*ri*·kish·*lik*
great	بەك ياخشى	bak yaah·*shi*
interesting	بەك مەنىلىك	bak ma·ni·*lik*
OK	بوپ قالىدۇ	bop kaa·li·*doo*
strange	غەلىتە	ra·*li*·ta

mixed emotions

a little	ئازراق	aaz·*raak*
very	بەك	bak
extremely	ئىنتايىن	in·*taa*·yin

I'm a little sad.
مەن ئازراق خاپا بولۇپ قالدىم. — man aaz·*raak* haa·*paa* bo·*loop* kaal·*dim*

I'm very surprised.
مەن بەك ھەيران قالدىم. — man bak ee·ay·*raan* kaal·*dim*

I'm extremely happy.
مەن ناھايىتى خۇشال. — man naa·ee·aa·*ti* hoo·*shaal*

I didn't mean to do anything wrong.

مىنىڭ خاتا ئىش قىلغۇم يوق.	mi·*ning* haa·*taa* ish kil·*room* yok

Is this a local custom?

بۇ يەرلىك ئۆرۈپ-ئادەت مۇ؟	bu yar·*lik* ö·*rüp* aa·dat·*mu*

farewells

Tomorrow I'm leaving.

مەن ئەتە ماڭىمەن.	man a·*ta* maa·ngi·*man*

If you come to (Scotland) you can stay with me.

پۇرسەت بولۇپ قالسا (شوتلاندىيە)گە بارسىڭىز مىنى ئىزدەڭ.	poor·*sat* bo·*loop* kaal·*saa* (shot·laan·*di*·ya) ga baar·*si*·ngiz me·*ni* iz·*dang*

Keep in touch!

ئالاقىلىشىپ تۇرايلى.	aa·laa·ki·li·*ship* tu·raay·*li*

It's been great meeting you.

سىز بىلەن تونۇشقانلىقىمدىن ئىنتايىن خۇشال.	siz bi·*lan* to·*nush*·kan·*li*·kim·*din* in·*taa*·yin hoo·shaal·*man*

Here's my address.

ئادىرسىمنى سىزگەيېزىپ دەپ بىرەي.	aa·dir·sim·*ni* siz·*ga* dap bi·*ray*

What's your email?

سىزنىڭ تور ئادىرسىڭىز چۇ؟	siz ning tor aa·dir·*si*·ngiz chu

well-wishing

Bon voyage!	سەپىرىڭىزگە ئاقيول بولسۇن!	sa·pi·ri·ngiz·*ga* aak·*yol* bol·*soon*
Congratulations!	مۇبارەك بولسۇن!	mu·*baa*·rak bool·*soon*
Good luck!	سىزگە ئامەت تىلەيمەن!	sya·*ga* aa·*mat* ti·lay·*man*
Happy birthday!	تۇغۇلغان كۈنىڭىزگە مۇبارەك بولسۇن!	too·rool·*raan* kü·ni·ngiz·*ga* moo·baa·*rak* bol·*soon*
Happy New Year!	يېڭى يىلىڭىزغا مۇبارەك بولسۇن!	*ye*·ngi yi·li·ngiz·*raa* moo·*baa*·rak bol·*soon*

eating out

Where would you go for (a) ...?	... ئۇچۇن نەگە بېرىش كېرەك؟	... u·*chun* na·*ga* be·*rish* ki·*rak*
banquet	مۇراسىم ئۆتكۈزۈش	mu·raa·*sim* öt·kü·*züsh*
celebration	تەبرىكلەش پائالىيىتى ئۆتكۈزۈش	tab·*rik*·lash paa·aa·li·yi·*ti* öt·kü·*züsh*
cheap meal	ئەرزانراق يېمەكلىكلەرنى يېيىش	ar·zaan·*rak* yi·mak·lik·lar·*ni* yi·*yish*
local specialities	يەرلىك يېمەكلىكلەر	yar·*lik* yi·mak·lik·*lar*
yum cha	چاي ئىچىش	chaay i·*chish*
Can you recommend a ...?	ماڭا بىرەر ... راق تىن بىرنى تەۋسىيە قىلامسىز؟	maa·*ngaa* bi·*rar*... raak tin bir·*ni* tav·si·*ya* ki·laam·*siz*
bar	قاۋاقخانا	kaa·vaak·haa·*naa*
cafe	قەھۋەخانا	ka·ee·va·haa·*naa*
noodle house	ئۈگرەخانا	üg·ra·haa·*naa*
dish	تەخسە	tah·*sa*
restaurant	ئاشخانا	aash·ha·*naa*
snack shop	ئۇششاق يېمەكلىكلەر ماگزىنى	oosh·*shaak* yi·mak·*lik*·lar maag·*zi*·ni
(wonton) stall	چۆچۈرەخانا	chö·kü·ra·haa·*naa*
street vendor	كوچىدىكى ئۇششاق يېمەكلىكلەر	ko·chi·di·*ki* oosh·*shaak* yi·mak·lik·*lar*
teahouse	چايخانا	chaay·haa·*naa*
I'd like a/the ...	مەن ... قىلاي دىگەن.	man ... ki·*laay* di·*gan*
table for (five)	(بەش) كىشىلىك ئۈستەل	(bash) kish·*lik* üs·*tal*
bill	ھېساۋات تالونى	hi·*saa*·vaat taa·loo·*ni*
drink list	ئىچىملىك تىزىملىكى	i·chim·*lik* ti·zim·*li*·ki
local speciality	يەرلىك ئالاھىدە قورۇما	yar·*lik* aa·laa·eey·*da* ko·ru·*maa*
menu	قورۇما تىزىملىكى	ko·ru·*maa* ti·zim·*li*·ki
(non)smoking table	تاماكا چېكىش (مەنئى قىلىنغان) ئۈستەل	taa·maa·*ka* chi·*kish* (*man*·i ki·lin·*raan*) üs·*tal*

Are you still serving food?

سىلەر يەنە سودا قىلامسىلەر؟ — si·*lar* ya·*na* so·*daa* ki·laam·*si*·lar

What would you recommend?

قانداق قورومنى تەۋسىيە قىلىسىز؟ — kaan·*daak* ko·rum·*ni* tav·si·*ya* ki·*li*·siz

What do you normally eat for breakfast?

ئەتتىگەنلىك تاماقتا — at·ti·gan·*lik* taa·maak·*taa*
ئادەتتە نىمە يەيدۇ؟ — aa·dat·*ta* *ni*·ma yay·*doo*

What's that called?

ئۇنى نىمە دەيدۇ؟ — oo·ni ni·*ma* day·*doo*

What's in that dish?

بۇ قورۇمىنىڭ خۇرۇچلىرى نىمە؟ — bu ko·ro·mi·*ning* hu·ruch·*li*·ri ni·*ma*

I'll have that.

ماڭا بىر كىشلىك بىرىڭ. — maa·*ngaa* bir kish·*lik* be·*ring*

I'd like it with …	… نى كۆپرەك سېلىڭ.	… ni köp·*rak* se·*ling*
I'd like it without …	… بۇنى ئارلاشتۇرماي.	… bu·*ni* aar·laash·toor·*maay*
chilli	قىزىل مۇچ	ki·*zil* mooch
garlic	سامساق	saam·*saak*
MSG	ئىسپىرت	is·*pirt*
nuts	مېغىز	me·*riz*
oil	ماي	maay

I'd like …, please.	ماڭا … نى.	maa·*ngaa* … ni
one slice	بىر پارچە	bir paar·*cha*
a piece	بىر كىشلىك	bir kish·*lik*
that one	ئاشۇ شۇ	aa·*shoo* shoo
two	ئىككى	ik·*ki*

This dish is …	بۇ … نىڭ قورىمىسى.	bu … ning ko·ru·*mi*·si
(too) spicy	(بەك) ئاچچىق	(bak) aach·*chik*
superb	بەك ياخشى	bak yaah·*shi*

I love this dish.

بۇ قورۇما شۇنداق مىزىلىك بوپتۇ. — bu ko·ru·*maa* shoon·*daak* mi·*zi*·lik bop·*too*

I love the local cuisine.

بۇ يەرنىڭ قورۇملىرى شۇنداق — bu yar·*ning* ko·ru·mi·li·*ri* shoon·*daak*
ئوخشاپتۇ. — oh·shaap·*too*

That was delicious!

شۇنداق يىيىشلىك بوپتۇ. — shoon·*daak* yi·*yish*·lik bop·*too*

I'm full.

مەن تويدۇم. — man toy·*doom*

breakfast	ئەتتىگەنلىك تاماق	a·ti·gan·*lik* taa·*maak*
lunch	چۈشلۈك تاماق	chüsh·*lük* taa·*maak*
dinner	كەچلىك تاماق	kach·*lik* taa·*maak*
drink (alcoholic)	هاراق	ee·aa·*raak*
drink (nonalcoholic)	ئىچىملىكلەر	i·chim·*lik*·lar
… water	سۇ …	… soo
boiled	قايناق	kaay·*naak*
cold	سۇۋۇتۇلغان	soo·voo·tool·*raan*
sparkling mineral	مىنېرالنى	min·ral·*ni*
still mineral	بۇلاق	bu·*laak*
(cup of) coffee …	(بىر ئىستاكان) قەھۋە …	(bir is·taa·*kaan*) kaee·*va* …
(cup of) tea …	(بىر پىيالا) چاي …	(bir pi·yaa·*la*) chaay …
with milk	سۈت قوشقان	süt kosh·*kaan*
without sugar	شېكەر قوشمىغان	shi·*kar* kosh·*mi*·raan
fresh drinking yoghurt	قېتىق	ke·*tik*
(orange) juice	ئەپلىسىن (سۈيى)	ap·*li*·sin (sü·*yi*)
soft drink	گازسۈيى	gaaz sü·*yi*
black tea	قىزىل چاي	ki·*zil* chaay
chrysanthemum tea	جۇخاگۇل چېيى	jo·ee·aa·*gül* che·*yi*
green tea	كۆك چاي	kök chaay
jasmine tea	گۇل چېيى	gül che·*yi*
oolong tea	ۋۇلۇڭ چېيى	vu·*long* che·*yi*
a … of beer	بىر … پىۋا	bir … pi·*va*
glass	رۇمكا	rum·*kaa*
large bottle	چوڭ بوتۇلكا	chong bo·tool·*kaa*
small bottle	كىچىك بوتۇلكا	ki·*chik* bo·tool·*kaa*
a shot of (whisky)	بىر رومكا (ۋىسكى)	bir rum·*kaa* (vis·*ki*)
a bottle/glass of	بىر بوتۇلكا/رۇمكا	bir bo·tool·*kaa*/rum·*kaa*
… wine	… ئۈزۈم هارىقى.	… ü·*züm* ee·aa·*ri*·ki
What are you drinking?	نىمە ئىچكىڭىز بار؟	ni·*ma* ich·*ki*·ngiz baar
I'll buy you one.	مەن مېھمان قىلىمەن.	man mee·*maan* ki·*li*·man

Vhat would you like?

نـمـمـنـى خالايسىز؟	ne·mi·*ni* haa·*laay*·siz

heers!

خوشـهـا!	ho·*sha* ee

his is hitting the spot.

تەمى تازا ياختى!	ta·*mi* taa·*zaa* yaah·*ti*

think I've had one too many.

كۆپ ئىچىپ قويغاندەك قىلىمەن.	köp i·*chip* koy·raan·*dak* ki·*li*·man

'm feeling drunk.

مەن ئازراق مەس بولۇپ قالدىم.	man aaz·*raak* mas bo·*loop* kaal·*dim*

street eats		
cold clear bean-flour noodles	لەڭپۇڭ	lang·*poong*
corn on the cob	كۆكباش قوناق	kök·*baash* ku·*naak*
dumpling (boiled)	بەشرە	ban·*shi*·ra
egg pancake	پوشكال	posh·*kaal*
fried stuffed (meat) bun	سامسا	saam·*saa*
hand pilaf	پولو	po·*lo*
pork pie (large)	گۆشنان	gösh naan
pork pie (small)	قىيمىلىق پىرەنىك	key·*mi*·lik pi·ra·*nik*
pulled noodles	ئۆي لەغمىنى	öy lar·*mi*·ni
shish kebab	كاۋاپ	kaa·*vaap*
stuffed naan bread	نان	naan
wonton soup	چۆچۈرە	chö·chü·*ra*

special diets & allergies

Do you have vegetarian food?

كۆكتاتلىق يېمەكلىكلەر بارمۇ؟	kök·taat·*lik* yi·mak·lik·*lar* baar·*mu*

Could you prepare a meal without ...?

... نى ئارلاشتۇرماي بىر قورۇما قورىسا بوپتىكەن؟	... ni aar·laash·toor·*maay* bir ko·ru·*maa* ko·*ri*·sa bop·*ti*·kan

I'm allergic to ...	ماڭا ... رېئاكسىيە قىلىدۇ.	maa·*ngaa* ... ri·*aak*·si·ya ki·li·*doo*
dairy produce	سۈتلۈك مەھسۇلاتلار	süt·*lük* mah·*soo*·laat·laa
eggs	تۇخۇم	tu·*hoom*
meat	گۆش	gösh
nuts	مېغىز	me·*riz*
seafood	دېڭىز مەھسۇلاتلىرى	de·*ngiz* mah·*soo*·laat·li·r

emergencies & health

Help!	قۇتقۇزۇڭلار!	kut·ku·zung·*laar*
Go away!	يوقال!	yo·*kaal*
Fire!	ئوت كەتتى!	ot kat·*ti*
Watch out!	ئېھتىيات قىلىڭ!	ee·ti·*yaat* ki·*ling*

Could you please help?
ماڭا ياردەم قىلالامسىز؟ maa·*ngaa* yaar·*dam* ki·*laa*·laam·siz

Can I use your phone?
تېلېفونىڭىزنى ئىشلىتىپ تۇرسام بولامدۇ؟ te·*li*·fu·ni·ngiz·*ni* ish·li·*tip* toor·*sam* bo·laam·*doo*

I'm lost.
مەن ئېزىپ قالدىم. man e·*zip* kaal·*dim*

Where are the toilets?
تازلىق ئۆيى قەيەردە؟ taz·*lik* ü·*yi* ka·yar·*da*

Where's the police station?
ساقچىخانا قەيەردە؟ sak·chi·haa·*naa* ka·yar·*da*

Where's the nearest ...?	ئەڭ يېقىن ... قەيەردە؟	ang ye·*kin*... ka·yar·*da*
dentist	چىش دوختۇرى	chish doh·too·*ri*
doctor	دوختۇر	doh·*toor*
hospital	دوختۇرخانا	doh·toor·*haa*·naa
pharmacist	دورىخانا	do·ri·haa·*naa*

english–uighur dictionary

dictionary, words are marked as n (noun), a (adjective), v (verb), sg (singular), pl (plural), inf (informal) l (polite) where necessary.

A

accident (mishap) كۆتۈلمىگەن بەختسىزلىك kü·*tül*·mi·gan ba·*hit*·siz·lik
accommodation قونالغۇ koo·*naal*·ru
adaptor ماسلاشقۇچى maas·*laash*·koo·chi
address n لىكسىيە سۆزلەش lik·*si*·ya süz·*lash*
after دىن كىيىن din *ki*·yin
air conditioning ھاۋا تەڭشىگۈچ ee·aa·*vaa* tang·shi·*güch*
airplane ئايروپىلان aay·roo·pi·*laan*
airport ئايدورۇم aay·*doo*·room
alcohol ئىسپىرت is·*pirt*
all ھەممىسى ee·am·*mi*·si
allergy زىيان قىلىش zi·*yaan ki*·lish
ambulance جىددى قوتقۇزۇش ماشىنىسى jid·*di* koot·*koo*·zoosh maa·*shi*·ni·si
and بىلەن bi·*lan*
ankle ھوشۇق hoo·*shouk*
antibiotics ئانتى بىئوكتىپ aan·*ti* bi·*ok*·tip
arm بىلەك bi·*lak*
ATM ئاپتوماتىك پۇل ئىلىش ماشىنىسى aap·to·maa·*tik* pool e·*lish* maa·*shi*·ni·si

B

baby بوۋاق bo·*vak*
back (of body) دۈمبە düm·*ba*
backpack يۈك-تاق yük taak
bad ئەسكى as·*ki*
bag سومكا som·*kaa*
baggage سەپەر لازىمەتلىكلىرى sa·*par* laa·zi·mat·lik·*li*·ri
bank بانكا baan·*kaa*
bar قاۋاقخانا *kaa*·vaak·haa·*naa*
bathroom مونچا moon·*chaa*
battery باتارىيە baa·*taa*·ri·ya
beautiful چىرايلىق *chi*·raay·lik
bed كارۋات *kaar*·vaat
beer پىۋا pi·*va*
before بورۇن boo·*roon*
behind كەينىدە *kay*·ni·da
bicycle ۋەلسىپىت val·si·*pit*
big چوڭ chong
bill تالون taa·*loon*
blanket ئەديال ad·*yaal*
blood group قان تىپى kaan ti·*pi*
boat كىمە ki·*ma*
bottle بوتۇلكا bo·tool·*kaa*
boy ئوغۇل بالا o·*rool* baa·*laa*
brakes (car) تورمۇز toor·*mooz*
breakfast ئەتتىگەنلىك تاماق at·*ti*·gan·lik taa·*maak*
broken (out of order) تەرتىپسىز tar·tip·*siz*
bus ئاپتوبۇس aap·too·*boos*
business سودا ساھەسى so·*daa* saa·ha·*si*
buy v سىتىۋىلىش *se*·ti·ve·lish

C

camera ئاپارات aa·paa·*raat*
cancel ئەمەلدىن قالدۇرۇش a·mal·*din* kaal·doo·*roosh*
car كىچىك ماشىنا ki·*chik* maa·*shi*·naa
cash n نەق پۇل nak *pool*
cash (a cheque) v پۇل چىكى pool chi·*ki*
cell phone يان تىلىفون *yaan* te·li·*foon*
centre n مەركەز mar·*kaz*
change (money) v پۇل ئلماشتۇرۇش pool aal·maash·too·*roosh*
cheap ئەرزان ar·*zaan*
check (bill) تالون taa·*loon*
check-in n يوقلىمىغا ئۆتۈش yok·loo·mi·*raa* ö·*tüsh*
chest (body) مەيدە may·*da*
children باللار baa·li·*laar*
cigarette تاماكا taa·maa·*kaa*
city شەھەر sha·*har*
clean a پاكىز paa·*kiz*
closed تاقاق taa·*kaak*
cold a سوغۇق so·*rook*
come كىلىش ki·*lish*
computer كومپيۇتىر kom·poo·yo·*tir*
contact lenses مىكرو ئەينەك *mik*·ro ay·*nak*
cook v تاماق ئىتىش taa·*maak* i·*tish*
cost n چىقىم chi·*kim*
credit card ئىناۋەتلىك كارتوچكىسى i·naa·*vat*·lik kaar·*toch*·ki·si
currency exchange پۇل ئالماشتۇرۇش pool aal·*maash*·too·*roosh*
customs (immigration) چەتئەللىك كۆچمەنلەر chat·al·*lik köch*·man·lar

A

english–uighur

D

dangerous خەتەرلىك ha·*tar*·lik
date (time) چېسلا chis·*laa*
day كۈن kün
delay v كېچىكتۈرۈش ki·chik·tü·*rüsh*
dentist چىش دوختۇرى chish doh·*too*·ri
depart ئايرىلىش aay·ri·*lish*
diaper زاكا zaa·*kaa*
dinner كەچلىك تاماق kach·*lik* taa·*maak*
direct a بىۋاستە bi·vaas·*ta*
dirty مەينەت may·*nat*
disabled مېيىپ mi·*yip*
discount v ئېتىبار بېرىش i·ti·*baar* bi·*rish*
doctor دوختۇر doh·*toor*
double room قوش كىشلىك ياتاق
kosh kish·*lik* yaa·*taak*
drink n ئىچىملىك i·chim·*lik*
drive v ھەيدەش hay·*dash*
driving licence شوپۇرلۇق پراۋىسى
sho·poor·look praa·*vi*·si
drug (illicit) زەھەرلىك چېكىملىك
za·har·*lik* chi·*kim*·lik

E

ear قۇلاق koo·*laak*
east شەرق shark
eat يېيىش yi·*yish*
economy class ئادەتتىكى ئورۇن aa·*dat*·ti·*ki* o·*roon*
electricity توك tok
elevator لىفت li·*fit*
email ئېلخەت il·*hat*
embassy دۆلەت كونسۇلخانىسى dö·*lat* kon·sul·haa·ni·*si*
emergency جىددى ئەھۋال jid·*di* ah·*vaal*
English (language) ئىنگلىز تىلى ing·*gi*·liz *ti*·li
evening كەچ kach
exit n چىقىش ئېغىزى chi·*kish* e·*ri*·zi
expensive قىممەت kim·*mat*
eye كۆز köz

F

far يىراق yi·*raak*
fast تېز tiz
father دادا/ئاتا daa·*daa*/aa·*taa*
film (camera) نېگاتىپ ni·gaa·*tip*
finger بارماق baar·*maak*
first-aid kit جىددى قۇتقۇزۇش ساندۇقى
jid·*di* koot·*koo*·zoosh saan·*doo*·ki
first class بىرىنچى دەرىجىلىك bi·rin·*chi* da·ri·ji·*lik*
fish n بېلىق be·*lik*
food يېمەكلىك yi·mak·*lik*
foot پۇت poot
free (of charge) ھەقسىز ee·ak·*siz*
friend دوست dost
fruit مېۋە mi·*va*
full تويۇش to·*yoosh*

G

gift سوۋغات soo·*raat*
girl قىز بالا kiz baa·*laa*
glass (drinking) ئىستاكان is·taa·*kaan*
glasses كۆز ئەينەك köz ay·*nak*
go بېرىش be·*rish*
good ياخشى yaak·*shi*
guide n ساياھەت يېتەكچىسى saa·yaa·*hat* yi·tak·chi·

H

half n يېرىم ye·*rim*
hand قول kol
happy خۇشال بولۇش hoo·*shaal* bo·*loosh*
he ئۇ oo
head n باش baash
heart يۈرەك yü·rak
heavy ئېغىر e·*rir*
help ياردەم yaar·*dam*
here بۇيەر boo·*yar*
high ئېگىز i·*giz*
highway تېز سۈرئەتلىك تاشيول tiz sü·*rat*·lik taash·*yol*
hike v پىيادە مېڭىش pi·*yaa*·da me·*ngish*
holiday تەتىل ta·*til*
hospital دوختۇرخانا doh·toor·*haa*·naa
hot ئىسسىق is·*sik*
hotel مېھمانخانا mee·maan·*haa*·naa
(be) hungry قورسىقى ئېچىش kor·si·*ki* e·*chish*
husband ئېرى e·*ri*

I

I مەن man
identification (card) كىملىك kim·*lik*
ill كېسەل ki·*sal*
important مۇھىم moo·*eeim*
injury (wound) يارا yaa·*raa*
insurance ئىستىراخۇۋانىيە is·ti·raa·hoo·*aa*·ni·*ya*
internet تور tor
interpreter چۈشەندۈرۈش chü·*shan*·dü·rüsh

J

jewellery ئۈنچە-مەرۋايىت ün·*cha* mar·*vaa*·yit
job خىزمەت hiz·*mat*

K

ey ئاچقۇچ aach·*kooch*
itchen ئاشخانا aash·*haa*·naa
nife پىچاق pi·*chaak*

L

aundry (place) كىرخانا kir·*haa*·naa
awyer ئادۇكات aa·doo·*kaat*
eft (direction) سول sol
eg (body) پاچاق paa·*chaak*
ess ئازراق aaz·*raak*
etter (mail) تور خەت-چەكلىرى tor hat·*chak*·li·ri
ight n چىراغ chi·*raar*
ike v ئامراق aam·*raak*
ock n قۇلۇپ koo·*loop*
long ئۇزۇن oo·*zoon*
lost ئېزىپ قېلىش e·*zip ke*·lish
love v ياخشى كۆرۈش yaah·*shi* kö·*rüsh*
luggage يۈك-تاق yük *taak*
lunch چۈشلۈك تاماق chüsh·*lük* taa·*maak*

M

mail n خەت hat
man ئەر ar
map خەرىتە ha·ri·*ta*
market بازار baa·*zaar*
matches سەرەڭگە sa·*rang*·ga
meat گۆش gösh
medicine دورا *do*·raa
message ئۇچۇر oo·*choor*
milk سۈت süt
minute مىنۇت mi·*noot*
mobile phone يان تېلېفون *yaan* te·li·*foon*
money پۇل pool
month ئاي aay
morning ئەتىگەن at·*ti*·gan
mother ئانا/ئاپا aa·*naa*/aa·*paa*
motorcycle موتوسىكلىت mo·to·si·ki·*lit*
mouth ئېغىز e·*riz*

N

name ئىسىم i·*sim*
near يېقىن ئەتراپ ye·*kin* at·*raap*
neck n بويان bo·*yaan*
new يېڭى ye·*ngi*
newspaper گېزىت ge·*zit*
night ئاخشام aah·*shaam*
no (not at all) ھېچقىسى يوق eech·*ki*·si yok
noisy ۋاراڭ-چۇرۇڭ vaa·*raang* choo·*roong*
north شىمال shi·*maal*
nose بۇرۇن boo·*roon*
now ھازىر ee·aa·*zir*
number نۇمۇر noo·*moor*

O

old (people) ياشانغانلار yaa·*shaan*·raan·*laar*
old (things) كونا نەرسىلەر ko·*naa* nar·si·*lar*
one-way ticket بىر يوللۇق بېلەت bir yol·*look* bi·*lat*
open a ئوچۇق o·*chook*
outside سىرت sirt

P

passport پاسپورت paas·*port*
pay v تۆلەش tö·*lash*
pharmacy دورىخانا do·ri·ee·aa·*naa*
phonecard تېلېفون كارتىسى te·li·*foon* kaar·*ti*·si
photo سۈرەت sü·*rat*
police ساقچى saak·*chi*
postcard ئاتكىرتكا aat·*kirt*·kaa
post office پوچتىخانا *posh*·taa·haa·naa
pregnant ھامىلدار ee·aa·mil·*daar*
price n باھا baa·*ee*·aa

Q

quiet a جىمجىت jim·*jit*

R

rain n يامغۇر yaam·*roor*
razor ئۇستۇر oos·*toor*
receipt n تالون taa·*loon*
refund n قايتۇرۇش kaay·too·*roosh*
registered (mail) رويخەتكە ئېلىش roy·*hat*·ka e·*lish*
rent v ئارىيەتكە ئېلىش aa·ri·yat·*ka* e·*lish*
repair v رېمونت قىلىش ri·*mot* ki·*lish*
reserve v زاكاس قىلىش zaa·*kaas* ki·*lish*
restaurant تاماقخانا taa·maak·haa·*naa*
return (go back) قايتىپ كېتىش kaay·*tip* ki·*tish*
return ticket قايتىپ كېلىش بېلىتى kaay·*tip* ki·*lish* be·li·*ti*
right (direction) ئوڭ ong
road يول yol
room n ئۆي öy

S

safe a بىخەتەر bi·ha·*tar*
sanitary napkin تازلىق قەغىزى taa·zi·*lik* ka·*ri*·zi

seat n ئورۇن o·*roon*
send يوللاش yol·*laash*
sex (gender) جىنسى jin·*si*
shampoo چاچ سوپۇنى chaach soo·poo·*ni*
share (a dorm) تەڭ ئىشلىتىش tang ish·li·*tish*
she ئۇ oo
sheet (bed) كىرلىك kir·*lik*
shirt كۆينەك köy·*nak*
shoes ئاياغ aa·*yaar*
shop n ماگزىن maag·*zin*
short قىسقا kis·*kaa*
shower n يۇيۇنۇش yoo·yoo·*noosh*
single room بىر كىشلىك ياتاق bir kish·*lik* yaa·*taak*
skin n تېرە ti·*ra*
skirt n يوپكا *yop*·kaa
sleep v ئۇخلاش *ooh*·laash
slow ئاستا *aas*·taa
small كىچىك ki·*chik*
soap شورپا *shor*·paa
some بەزەن ba·*zan*
son ئوغۇل o·*rool*
south جەنۇپ ja·*noop*
souvenir خاتىرە بويۇمى haa·*ti*·ra bo·yoo·*mi*
stamp پوچتا ماركىسى poch·*ta* maar·*ki*·si
station (train) بېكەت bi·*kat*
stomach ئاشقازان aash·kaa·*zaan*
stop v توختاش toh·*taash*
stop (bus) n ئاپتوبۇس بېكىتى aap·*too*·boos bi·ki·*ti*
street كوچا ko·*chaa*
student ئوقۇغۇچى o·koo·*roo*·chi
sun قۇياش koo·*yaash*
sunscreen قۇياش نۇرىدىن ساقلىنىدىغان koo·*yaash* noo·ri·*din* saak·li·ni·di·*raan*
swim v سۇ ئۈزۈش soo ü·*züsh*

T

tampon قان توختۇش پاختىسى kaan toh·*ti*·tish *paah*·ti·si
telephone n تېلېفون te·li·*foon*
temperature (weather) تېمپېراتورا tim·*poo*·raa·too·raa
that ئۇ oo
they ئۇلار oo·*laar*
(be) thirsty ئۇسساش oos·*saash*
this بۇ boo
throat بوغۇز bo·*rooz*
ticket بېلەت bi·*lat*
time ۋاقىت vaa·*kit*
tired ھېرىش ee·*rish*
tissues تالا taa·*laa*
today بۈگۈن bü·*gün*
toilet ئوبۇرنى o·*boor*·ni
tomorrow ئەتە a·*ta*
tonight بۈگۈن ئاخشام bü·*gün* aah·*shaam*
tooth چىش chish
toothbrush چىش پاستىسى chish *paas*·ti·si
toothpaste چىش مەلھىمى chish *mal*·hi·mi
torch (flashlight) مەشئەل mash·*al*
tour n ساياھەت saa·yaa·*ee*·at
tourist office ساياھەت ئىدارىسى saa·yaa·*ee*·at i·*daa*·ri·s
towel لۆڭگە löng·*ga*
train n پويىز po·*yiz*
translate تەرجىمە قىلىش tar·*ji*·ma ki·*lish*
travel agency ساتاھەت شىركىتى saa·yaa·*ee*·at shir·ki·*ti*
travellers cheque ساياھەت چېكى saa·yaa·*ee*·at che·*ki*
trousers ئىشتان ish·*taan*

U

underwear ئىچ كىيىم ich ki·*yim*
urgent جددى jid·*di*

V

vacancy بىكار خىزمەت ئورنى bi·*kaar* *hiz*·mat *or*·ni
vegetable n كۆكتات *kök*·taat
vegetarian a گۆشسىز تاماق يېگۈچىلەر gösh·*siz* taa·*maak* yi·*gü*·chi·lar
visa يۆتكەش رەسمىيىتى yöt·*kash* ras·*mi*·yi·ti

W

walk v مېڭىش me·*ngish*
wallet ھەميان *ee*·am·yaan
wash (something) يۇيۇش yoo·*yoosh*
watch n سائەت saa·*at*
water n سۇ soo
we بىز biz
weekend ھەپتە ئاخىرى hap·*ta* aa·*hi*·ri
west غەرب *ra*·rip
wheelchair چاقلىق ئورۇندۇق *chaak*·lik o·roon·*dook*
when قاچان kaa·*chaan*
where قەيەر ka·*yar*
who كىم kim
why نىمە ئۈچۈن ni·*ma* ü·*chün*
wife ئايالى aa·*yaa*·li
window دەرىزە da·*ri*·za
with بىلەن bi·*lan*
without يوق yok
woman ئايال كىشى aa·*yaal* ki·shi
write يېزىش ye·*zish*

Y

yes ھەئە ee·a·*a*
yesterday تۈنۈگۈن tü·nü·*gün*
you sg inf/pol سەن/سىز san/siz
you pl سىلەر si·*lar*

Culture

The glory of China is the sheer diversity of its culture – from a rich **history** and regional **cuisines** to colourful **festivals**, China has it all. Here we present you with a cultural snapshot of the country and give you the tools to travel in an exciting and respectful way.

history timeline

Take a wander through the rich history of China …

c 4000 BC	Early settlements established in modern-day Shaanxi and Hénán.
c 3000 BC	Emperor Fúxī ushers in the period of the legendary 'Three Emperors and Five Sovereigns'.
c 2200–1700 BC	Dynastic rule commences with the Xia.
1700–1100 BC	The Shang dynasty comes to power. Bronzeware production is perfected, and the consistent use of Chinese characters is documented.
1100–221 BC	The Western and Eastern Zhou dynasties rule.
600 BC	Laotzu, the founder of Taoism, is reputedly born.
551 BC	Confucius is born.
300 BC	Petroglyphs indicate the spread of Buddhism in Tibet at this time.
221 BC	The short-lived Qin dynasty is established.
221–206 BC	The Qin kingdom conquers the surrounding states to create the first unified China.
214 BC	Emperor Qin indentures thousands of labourers to link existing city walls into one Great Wall.
206 BC	The Han dynasty takes over.
c 100 BC	Chinese traders and explorers follow the Silk Road all the way to Rome.
c 50 BC	One of the first documented accounts of tea-drinking in China.
AD 220–581	An 'age of disunion', seeing a succession of rival kingdoms and a strong division between north and south China.
581–618	The Sui dynasty rules.
c 600	The Grand Canal, the world's longest artificial canal, is constructed.
608	The first mission is sent from the Tibetan court to the Chinese emperor.

618–907	The Tang dynasty holds sway.
635	The first Christian missionaries are believed to have arrived.
c 640	Pilgrim Xuan Zhuang sets out for India, returning 16 years later with countless Buddhist holy texts.
625–705	Wu Zetian is the first and only woman to become emperor.
960–1279	The Song dynasty is in power.
c 1000	The major inventions of the premodern world – paper, printing, gunpowder and the compass – are all commonly used in China.
1215	Genghis Khan conquers Běijīng.
1279–1368	Kublai Khan's vast Mongol empire includes all of China.
1286	The Grand Canal is extended to Běijīng, assuming its current form.
1368–1644	Chinese ethnic rule is restored with the Ming dynasty.
1385–1464	The life of Tangtong Gyelpo, Tibet's 'Renaissance man' – leader, medic, inventor of Tibetan opera and builder of 108 bridges in Tibet.
1406	Ming Emperor Yongle begins the construction of the Forbidden City.
1557	The Portuguese establish a permanent trade base in Macau.
1590s	The classic tale *Journey To The West* is published – made known to many by its incarnation as 1970s TV series *Monkey Magic*.
c 1640	The *qípáo* (cheongsam) becomes a fashionable frock for women.
1644–1911	Conquerors from Manchuria establish the Qing dynasty.
1720s	Emperor Kangxi declares Tibet a protectorate of China. Two Chinese representatives, known as Ambans, are installed at Lhasa, along with a garrison of Chinese troops.
1839	British traders at Guǎngzhōu hand over 20,000 chests of opium to Chinese officials, the pretext for the First Opium War.
1842	Hong Kong is ceded to the British in perpetuity.
1856–64	The Taiping uprising establishes army rule in parts of eastern China with Nánjīng as its capital, ultimately failing following civil war.

1894–95	First Sino-Japanese war.
1908	Two-year-old Puyi ascends the throne as China's last emperor.
1911–12	Revolution brings dynastic rule to an end with Sun Yatsen's republican government and abdication of the emperor.
1921–22	Lu Xun's *The Story of Ah Q,* the first work to be written entirely in Mandarin 'vernacular', is published in serial form.
1923–27	The remains of the Peking Man, between 500,000 and 230,000 years old, are unearthed at Zhōukǒudiàn, near Běijīng.
1927	Chiang Kaishek's Kuomintang rounds up and kills thousands of communists in Shànghǎi and Guǎngzhōu.
1934	The infamous Long March of communists from Jiāngxī province begins, travelling 6400km northwest.
1935	Mao Zedong is recognised as head of the Chinese Communist Party in a meeting at Zūnyì.
1937–45	Japanese invasion and occupation of China.
1946	Communists and the Kuomintang fail to form a coalition government, and plunge China back into civil war.
1949	The People's Republic of China (PRC) is established.
1950	China supports North Korea in the Korean War.
1957	A brief period of liberalisation under the 'Hundred Flowers Movement', but criticisms of the regime lead Mao to imprison or exile thousands.
1958	The Taiwan Straits crisis.
1958–62	The Great Leap Forward ultimately causes mass starvation.
1959	Widespread revolt in Tibet is suppressed. Amid mounting violence the 14th Dalai Lama flees to exile in India.
1965	The establishment of the Tibetan Autonomous Region.
1966	The birth of the Red Guards and the Cultural Revolution. Mao's 'Little Red Book' of quotations is published.

1971	The US national table tennis team becomes the first American delegation to set foot in China in 49 years; Nixon soon follows.
1973	Deng Xiaoping returns to power as Deputy Premier.
1976	Mao Zedong dies aged 83.
1979	Diplomatic relations are established with the US.
1980	The one-child policy is enforced. Mao's 'Gang of Four' is put on trial.
1987	*The Last Emperor* collects an Oscar for best picture.
1989	Hundreds of civilian demonstrators are killed by Chinese troops in the streets around Tiananmen Square. The 14th Dalai Lama, Tenzin Gyatso, wins the Nobel Peace Prize.
1997	Deng Xiaoping dies. Britain returns Hong Kong to the PRC.
1999	Falun Gong protest silently in Běijīng, prompting a crackdown. Macau is handed over from Portugal to the PRC.
2001	The Shanghai Cooperation Organisation is formed between China, Russia, Kazakhstan, Kyrgyzstan, Tajikistan and Uzbekistan. China also joins the World Trade Organization.
2003	Hu Jintao becomes president. SARS hits Hong Kong and mainland China. China sends its first astronaut into space. The Golden Shield Project is put in place to control internet usage.
2007	Prime Minister Wen Jiabao addresses Japan's parliament. Jiang Rong wins the first Man Asia Literary Prize for his novel *Wolf Totem*.
2008	Tens of thousands are killed in the Sìchuān province earthquake. Běijīng hosts the 2008 Summer Olympic Games – topping the medal tally with 51 gold – amid pro-Tibet demonstrations.
2009	The global financial crisis sees a 10-year low in China's economic growth. A study finds China has 32 million more boys than girls.
2013	China's lunar lander Chang'e 3 touches down on the moon

the chinese & food

The Chinese live to eat – not just to eat, but to eat well, to eat indulgently and to eat flavoursome, interesting, well-cooked food at every meal.

Chinese cuisine can be divided into four main schools, summed up in the Mandarin saying *dōng suān, xī là, nán tián, běi xián* (meaning 'the east is sour, the west is spicy, the south is sweet and the north is salty'). Cantonese (southern) cuisine *(Yuècài)* is the nation's most varied and elaborate; we can also thank it for *yǐncha* (yum cha). Shànghǎi's *Zhècài* (eastern) cuisine is generally richer, sweeter and oilier, relying on preserved vegetables, pickles and salted meats. *Lǔcai* (northern) food from Shāndōng uses wheat pancakes, spring onions and fermented bean paste, while *Chuāncài* (western or Sìchuān) style is renowned for red chillies and peppercorns firing up pork, poultry, legumes and soybeans. Finally, *Huáiyáng cài* (east coast cuisine) is relatively vegetarian-friendly and is home to meat simmered in dark soy sauce, sugar and spices. And there are many other influences, like Macau's Portuguese touches, Hong Kong's gift at importing the best and Tibet's *momos* (steamed dumplings) and *chang* (fermented barley beer).

eat by number

A Chinese saying talks of seven basic daily necessities: fuel, rice, oil, salt, soy sauce, vinegar and tea. Another 'seven' is the seven tastes incorporated in dishes: sweet, salty, sour, bitter, hot, *guō qì* (wok essence) and *xiān wèi* (a kind of savoury, moreish element sometimes created with MSG). Then there are five elements that must be attended to in cooking: colour, aroma, flavour, shape and texture. In addition, food is considered medicine for the *qì* (life energy). Accordingly, a meal must balance *yīn* (cool and moist) and *yáng* (warm and solid), the five elements (wood, earth, fire, water, metal) and the four states (moist, warm, cool, dry).

staples

If it walks, crawls, slithers, swims or flies, someone in China will probably eat it. In Guǎngdōng you can sample possum, elsewhere pangolin (anteater), steamed scorpions, cicadas, land and water beetles, snakes (the bile and blood is meant to help impotence) and turtle. The term for meat is *ròu*, which will generally mean 'pork' unless otherwise stated, and lard is laced in breads and sweets alike. From the water, sample *sānwén yú* (salmon) from Hēilóngjiāng, *niān yú* (catfish) in Sìchuān, and live *xiāzi* (prawns) at Xiàmén. The best ocean fare comes from Qīngdǎo, where every self-respecting restaurant has live shellfish and fish on the front step. Eat all *hǎixiān* (seafood) hot from cooking, even the medicinally 'cold' *pángxiè* (crab), best steamed with ginger and spring onions and eaten with yellow rice wine.

Vegetables and fruit are diverse and readily available, but vegetarians will face *niúròu tāng* (beef stock) and *háoyóu* (oyster sauce) in nearly everything – don't be suckered by the term *shūcai* (vegetable dish), which is not usually vegetarian but rather features a particular vegetable. Meantime, try out the chillies of Húnán, the soft flavour of cabbage and the yammy taste of taro. In addition to *qīngcài* (green leafy vegetables), the Chinese make use of delicate, crisp turnips in salads, and fennel tops in dumplings across the north. Don't miss out on Yúnnán's coal-cooked sweet potato. Other delicacies are Běijīng's *biǎn táo* (flat peaches), the *záo* (jujube, also called Chinese date) and *lóngyǎn* ('dragon eyes', also called longan).

Although grains other than *fàn* (rice) play their part in Chinese cuisine – wheat, millet, sorghum, corn – rice is so important that *fàn* is a symbol for all meals. It is prepared as flour, noodles, porridge and more, and even the aroma from rice cooking is revered. Black rice is glutinous and used in sweets, jasmine rice dominates towards the southeast border, and red rice is used for alcohol and vinegar. In the northwest, noodles are more likely to be made from wheat, while in Inner Mongolia and Tibet millet is probably used. *Jiǎozi* (dumplings) are a must-eat, from Běijīng's pork-filled, fried or steamed wheat dough, to Guǎngdōng's yum cha. In the north, eat the big, soft dumpling called *mántou*. Breads include the famous *dà mianbāo* ('big' bread) of Hā'ěrbīn, as well as Shànghǎi's *yóutiáo* (deep-fried bread). And finally there's the versatile *huángdòu* (soy bean), which the Chinese have been fermenting, smoking, maturing and eating for over 3000 years – best known in *dòufu* (tofu) and *dòujiāng* (soy milk drink).

fishy business

An ingredient, its form and the manner of eating it may hold symbolic meaning in China. For example, serving a whole fish means prosperity, as it has a logical beginning and end. Yet you'd never turn it over once you've eaten the top side, as this is reminiscent of a boat capsizing at sea and therefore means death.

mystery ingredients

So what are China's secret herbs and spices? *Dàsuàn* (garlic) in Shāndōng and *chùng* (spring onion) in Guǎngdōng are easy to identify, while *bājiǎo* (star anise) is used continent-wide in marinades and braised dishes. Look out for *huājiāo* (Sìchuān pepper, a prickly ash bud that sends your tongue numb), as well as the ubiquitous *suī* (coriander), *zhī ma* (sesame seeds) and *wǔxiāngfěn* (five spices mix, using cassia bark, star anise, fennel seeds, black pepper and cloves).

Soy sauce, *jiàngyóu,* comes in dark and thick or light varieties, and is used for dips as well as in cooking. Toasty-flavoured *zhī ma yóu* (sesame oil) is a finishing touch, while in Sìchuān *zhīmá jiàng* (sesame paste) and *lajiāo jiàng* (chilli sauce) are ever-present. Fújiàn's Pacific oysters provide *háoyóu* (oyster sauce), and other flourishes come from *hóngcù* (red rice vinegar) and syrupy black Chinkiang vinegar.

A wealth of dried ingredients is available, with over 30 kinds of mushrooms, not to mention *gǒu qǐ zǐ* (wolfberries), *chóng cǎo* (caterpillar consumed from the inside by a rabid fungus) and dried *hǎishēn* (sea cucumber). *Xiāng gū (shiitake* mushroom) is the most common fungus, but also try *mù ěr* (wood-ear fungus) and *hóu tóu gū* (monkey-head mushrooms). Nuts and legumes abound, the more unusual ones being *xìng rén* (bitter apricot kernels) and *bái guǒ* (ginkgo nuts). Meat is also dried and the *ròu sōng* (dried beef) of Hángzhōu has a texture like fairy floss.

And then there's the outright exotic, such as bamboo worms, deer penis and wild cat. Other local treats are *sōng huā dàn* (preserved or 'thousand-year' eggs) and *yàn wō* (bird's nest – made from the saliva of swiftlets).

drinks

No true Chinese will miss out on their tea. There are at least 320 strains of the tea plant *Camellia sinensis*, processed according to six broad categories. In Xī'ān they prefer the heady, gutsy nature of *wūlongcha* (oolong) or *hóngchá* (black) teas, while the people around Hángzhōu on the eastern seaboard prefer *lǜchà* (green) tea. In Yúnnán they prefer Pu'erh tea *(pǔ-ěr chá)*, a fermented black tea. While most teas in China are drunk without milk or sugar, in Inner Mongolia they prefer to add cream or butter to their 'milk tea' *(soo tē chē)*, while Tibetans fancy it with rancid yak butter and salt *(bö cha)*. Also check out *tuóchá* (brick teas – made from tea that has been compressed into a brick shape) and *huāchá* (scented teas).

For other nonalcoholic options, try *lizhī zhi* (lychee juice), *suānméi tāng* (sour plum drink) or *xìngrén niúnǎi* (almond milk) in the south. In the north, you'll find *suānnǎi* (yoghurt) as a breakfast item. You could also sample the near-nonalcoholic lemon beer and pineapple beer, or *kāfēi* (coffee), popular with the up-and-coming younger generation.

Alcohol definitions in China are a little slippery: *bái pútáo jiǔ* (white wine) actually means near-toxic firewater, containing 40% to 60% alcohol – try Yúnnán's Long Chuan rice liqueur and Chinese flowering quince wine. Other renowned wines include red rose liqueur, and *Shàoxīng jiǔ* (yellow rice wine), with a 2400-year history in the city of Shàoxīng. Beer *(pijiǔ),* is China's universal alternative to tea. Always ask for your beer *lěng* (cold). In Macau test the evocatively named Lágrima de Cristo (Tears of Christ), a Portuguese white port.

table manners

The word *rènào* (bustling) encapsulates the atmosphere of restaurants across China, where people value enthusiastic participation in conversation as well as the meal. Meals come not in individual servings but in *dàpán* (communal plates) – do get your hepatitis A shots but don't miss out on the fun. At the table, wait until your host picks up their chopsticks before you begin eating. When choosing your food, go for the dish closest to you or ask people to pass your choice – never reach over the table. Don't tap the side of your bowl with your chopsticks (the sign of beggars), nor stick the chopsticks upright in your rice as that resembles funerary incense. Finally, it's polite to offer to pay the bill, even if you're clearly the guest. Bluffing or not, say: *Shì ní qǐngde kè, wǒ buguò shì mǎidān de* (You were tonight's host, but I'll pay the bill). And should you need a night off the dreaded white spirits, a good escape is to turn your glass upside down and explain that your doctor won't let you drink.

street food

Be prepared: any Chinese with a gas bottle and a wok can become a *jiētóu xiǎochī* (street vendor). Eat only freshly made *xiǎochī* (snacks) and only where appreciative crowds are gathered, and you needn't miss out on local delicacies such as *zòngzi* (sticky rice in bamboo leaves), *húntun* (wonton soup) or *jiānbǐng* (egg and spring onion pancake). Ubiquitous *shuǐjiǎo* (meat- or vegetable-stuffed dumplings) are a treat – locals mix *làjiāo* (chilli), *cù* (vinegar) and *jiàngyóu* (soy sauce) according to taste in a little bowl, then dip. Postparty in Hong Kong, grab some *dím sàm* (dim sum) to soak up the beer – try *hàa gáau* (steamed shrimp dumplings) or *chéung fán* (steamed rice-flour rolls with shrimp, beef or pork). Some Chinese street-fare shows a Persian influence, like *shashlick* and kebab. While in Běijīng try *chòu dòufu* (astonishingly stinky tofu fermented in cabbage juice), in Shànghǎi go for the half-moon *xiǎolóng* dumplings, and in Macau don't miss the distinctive pastries on Rua da Felicidade. Hong Kong tempts with *ngàu zaap* (cow's organs), *yèw dáan* (fish balls), *cháau fùng léut* (roasted chestnuts) and *jèw chèung fán* (rice noodles). Tibetan markets offer the challenge of *chura kâmpo* (dried yak cheese), white balls eaten like a boiled sweet.

festivals

festivals in china

A-Ma Festival (A-Ma Temple, Inner Harbour, Macau) *The birth of the Taoist goddess of fisherfolk A-Ma is celebrated on the 23rd day of the third lunar month (March/April). One legend has it that a junk sailing across the South China Sea was embroiled in a storm, the passengers facing certain death. Behold, a beautiful young woman on the boat stood and ordered the sea be calm, saving all on board. A temple was built in her honour in 1488 – at the location of their safe return to land – and A-Ma is worshipped along the coast under the names Mazu, Tin Hau and Niangniang. On the festival day, seafarers and their families throng the Ming dynasty temple, leaving offerings, burning incense and praying for safe journeys. Enjoy the Chinese opera performances and take in the gorgeous poetry inscribed on the surrounding cliff walls.*

Cheung Chau Bun Festival (Cheung Chau, Hong Kong) *On the island of Cheung Chau the Buddha's birthday public holiday is marked by the construction of rocket-shaped towers, standing up to 20m high, covered with sacred bread rolls. At midnight on the eighth day of the fourth lunar month (April/May), competitors scramble up the towers, grabbing a bun for good luck – the higher the bun, the better the fortune. For 26 years the festivities were kept to ground level after a tower collapsed in 1978, but the bamboo structures have been replaced by metal and climbers now use safety ropes. Swirling around the towers is the greater festival, with processions featuring floats, stilt walkers and people dressed as characters from legend and opera. Most interesting are the 'floating children', carried through the streets atop long poles. Make the most of the vegetarian feast and check out the colourful fishing boats in the harbour.*

Chinese New Year (Shànghǎi) *There's something special about being in one of China's major cities for Lunar New Year (January/February), the 'real thing' after seeing it in your local Chinatown. Also known as Chūn Jié (Spring Festival), it's the high point of the Chinese year, and for the most part this is a family festival. Throughout the country, the weeks building up to the festival are an explosion of colour, with chūnlián (spring couplets) pasted on door posts, door gods brightening up alleys and streets, and shops glistening with red and gold decorations. Work colleagues and relatives present each other with hóng bāo (red envelopes) of money and the streets ring with cries of Gōngxi fācái! (Congratulations! May you make money!). Shànghǎi-side, check out the explosion of fireworks at midnight both to welcome in the New Year and ward off bad spirits, plus the special services held at Longhua and Jing'an Temples. Stay hungry for the eight- or nine-course banquet coming your way!*

Dragon Boat Festival (Mi Lo River, Húnán) *During the Dragon Boat Festival (fifth day of the fifth lunar month, May/June), the Mi Lo fills with colourful crafts decked out to imitate dragons, from fearsome snout to scaly tail. The China-wide festival commemorates Qu Yuan, a revered poet-statesman who drowned himself in 278 BC to protest the Qin state's invasion. Onlookers tried to keep fish and evil spirits from Qu Yuan's body by splashing their oars and beating drums. Today festival spectators snack on zòngzi (sticky rice in bamboo leaves) in memory of the rice scattered as an offering to the poet's ghost. Arrive waterside early to see the dragon-head prows blessed with incense and gongs. The race is won when a rower straddles his craft's dragon head and grabs the flag. The festival is also a tribute to the god of water, and homes fill with invocations of physical and spiritual well-*

being. The herbs calamus and moxa are hung from front doors and pictures of Chung Kuei, the demon slayer, are pinned up. Adults also enjoy hsiung huang (a type of rice wine) and the party continues after dark with firecrackers and dragon dances.

International Ice & Snow Festival (Zhaolin Park & Sun Island Park, Hā'ěrbīn) *China's northern Hēilóngjiāng province may be cursed with one of the coldest climates in Asia, but its capital Hā'ěrbīn has made the best of a bad thing with its International Ice and Snow Festival. Held in the depths of winter (5 January to 5 February), the festival revolves around over 1300 fanciful and elaborate ice sculptures built by teams from about 20 countries, including recreations of famous buildings and structures (such as a scaled-down Forbidden City, or a Great Wall of China that doubles as an ice slide). The bulk of the sculptures can be found in central Zhaolin Park and Sun Island Park, while the hardiest of festival-goers can join Hā'ěrbīn's winter swimmers for a dip in the frozen Songhua River. Attractions include ice lanterns, skiing, ice skating, outdoor swimming, hunting, dog-sled rides and art performances – not to mention whooshing down ice slides and the ice-axe free-for-all that marks the festival's end.*

Mid-Autumn Festival (West Lake, Hángzhōu) *Also known as the Moon Festival or the Moon Cake Festival, this festival on the full moon of the eighth lunar month (September/October) is a holiday for lovers, families and the homesick. Loved ones meet under the lunar symbol of unity to barbecue, eat pomelos (draping the rinds on their heads), do fire-dragon dances, and hang lanterns from towers. Incense is burnt for the lunar goddess Chang'e, who lives on the moon with a jade rabbit. The yuè bǐng (moon cakes) themselves are made of a thin dough shell containing fillings such as jelly, dates and nuts or red bean paste – during an uprising against the Mongols in the 14th century, revolutionary plans were secretly passed around in the cakes. A popular spot to moonbathe is Hángzhōu's West Lake, with its three candlelit towers.*

Nánníng International Folk Song Art Festival (Nánníng, Guǎngxī) *The Nánníng International Folk Song Art Festival has become a spectacular affair, held each Novemb since 1999. Entertainment comes in the form of local and foreign folksingers showing off their modern and classical numbers, dancing galas and dramatic lighting displays. It's come a long way from its roots as a ge'wei (song gathering) for the Zhuang minority whose omnipresent musical culture led to the province of Guǎngxī earning the name 'Ocean of Folk Songs'. The Zhuang sing their way through daily life, while working the fields, collecting firewood, attending funerals and, of course, courting. At a ge'wei, youn people sing an impromptu antiphonal song cycle (a one-to-one song competition) tellin of their love; women hand the successful swain xiuqiu, a ball made of 12 silk stripes like flower petals.*

Qīng Míng Jié (across China) *A celebration held around 5 April (or 4 April in leap years Tomb-Sweeping Day, also called Clear and Bright Festival, sees families returning to the ancestors' graves. The dead are honoured by cleaning weeds from gravestones, touching up inscriptions, offering chrysanthemums and favourite foods, and burning paper goods and zhiqian ('Bank of Hell' money) so the ancestor will be wealthy in the afterlife. The particularly devout hang a willow branch in the doorway to their homes, preventing the dead from entering if they roam free of the cemetery. For most it's a spring celebration rather than a day of mourning, with families feasting on the offerings and flying kites. Traditionally, trees are planted to welcome the warmer weather, and tea leaves picked before this date are prized for their subtle aromas (and priced accordingly).*

Qurban Festival (Xīnjiāng Uighur AR) *Also known as Eid al-Adha, this major Islamic festival sees the faithful remember the story of Ibrahim, who offered his son as a sacrifice in order to show his obedience to Allah. Allah saved the boy and a lamb was sacrificed in his place, and today an important part of Qurban is the sacrifice of a goat or cow to commemorate this occasion. During the three-day festival, Muslims across China dress in their finest and head to the mosque for prayer and thanksgiving. It's not all prayer and sacrifice, though – this is also a time for entertaining family and friends, gift-giving and partaking in traditional festival foods, including sanzi, a deep-fried noodle-shaped dough. The festival begins on the tenth day of the final month of the Islamic calendar (falling in September until 2017, then August). This is a particularly interesting time for visitors to be in the Xīnjiāng Uighur region.*

Saga Dawa Festival (Lhasa & Mt Kailash, Tibet) *Buddha Sakyamuni's conception, enlightenment and entry into nirvana is marked on the 15th day of Tibet's fourth lunar month (May/June). It falls during the year's holiest month, when the karmic effect of all wholesome or unwholesome actions is multiplied by 100,000 – another good reason for most of Lhasa's population to walk the Lingkhor circuit. Prayer wheels are turned on the streets, Tibetan operas recount history and legend, and boats are paddled in the Dragon King Pool at the foot of the Potala Palace. Alternatively, you can trek to holy Mt Kailash to see the 25m Tarboche prayer-pole being raised in accordance with a Lama's instructions. Lung ta (prayer flags; literally 'wind horses') are hung to the tune of sacred horn-and-cymbal music, the faithful circle the pole, and if it's positioned correctly all bodes well for Tibet.*

Sister's Meal Festival (Shīdòng, Guìzhōu) *Love is in the air during this courtship ritual in eastern Guìzhōu when young Miao (or Hmong) people find partners through the medium of sticky rice. To a soundtrack of music from the lúshēng (a reed instrument), and amid dancing, paper-dragon fights and buffalo fighting, young women dress in exquisite embroidery and kilograms of silver jewellery shaped into neck rings, loin chains, and multiple headdresses. The suitors arrive, serenading the women and presenting a parcel of dyed rice to the ladies who have taken their fancy. In return, the damsels hand back rice parcels containing unspoken messages – two chopsticks indicate acceptance, one means 'no thank you', a leaf is a request for some satin before giving a decision, while a chilli is the most definite of rebukes. The celebration, held on the 15th day of the third lunar month (March/April), marks the time when married women return home and see their parents.*

Wéifáng International Kite Festival (Wéifáng, Shāndōng) *Tradition has it that the world's first kite – an eagle made out of wood – was held aloft from Mount Lu (in Wéifáng) more than 2000 years ago by philosopher Mozi. Thanks to his discovery, Wéifáng is now home to both the International Kite Festival (launched, pun intended, in 1984) and the Wéifáng World Kite Museum. Come April, international teams and thousands of enthusiasts arrive to display and compete over three days. Visitors will be awestruck by enormous structures being hauled aloft by jeeps, or dragon kites over 800m long. The creativity and presentation of the kites, which are often based on traditional folk designs, is the focus of the festival. Performances include an opening parade of participants, an impressive fireworks display to close and regional songs and dances. Be sure to take in the kite museum, whose peacock-blue roof is designed to resemble a dragon-head centipede kite.*

INDEX

A	Mandarin	Cantonese	Chaozhou	Dongbei Hua	Hakka	Hunanese	Shanghainese	Sichuan	Xi'an	Yunnan Hua	Zhuang	Mongolian	Tibetan	Uighur
accommodation	19	44	68	92	116	140	164	188	212	236	260	285	317	343
addresses	17, 18	43,51	67, 76	92, 100	115, 123	140, 147	164, 171	188, 195	212, 219	236, 244	260, 268	295	316, 326	342, 351
addressing people	24	50	72	96	119	143	168	191	216	240	268	289	–	346
admission (sightseeing)	21	47	–	–	–	–	–	–	–	–	264	286	319	–
age	–	–	74	98	122	146	170	194	218	242, 243	266	293	324	349
alcoholic drinks	27	53	79	103	126	151	174	198, 199	223	247	271	299	329	354,
allergies	27, 30	54, 56	80	104	127	152	175	199	223	248	272	300	329	355
alphabet	–	–	–	–	–	–	–	–	–	–	–	278	310	336
ambulances	28	54	–	–	–	–	–	–	–	–	–	–	330	–
amounts	23	49	71	95	119	143	167	191	215	239	263	297	321	346
apologising	13	39	65	89	113	137	161	185	209	233	257	281, 292	313	339, 351
art & architecture	362-5													
B														
baggage	16, 29	42, 55	–	–	–	–	–	–	–	–	–	–	–	–
banking	18, 20	43, 45	67, 69	92, 93	115, 117	139, 141	163, 165	187, 189	211, 213	235, 237	259, 261	283	316, 318	342, 344
bars	26	52	76	101	124	148	172	196	220	245	269	296	–	352
bargaining	23	49	71	95	118	143	167	191	215	239	263	289	321	345
basic phrases	13	39	65	89	113	137	161	185	209	233	257	281	313	339

	Mandarin	Cantonese	Chaozhou	Dongbei Hua	Hakka	Hunanese	Shanghainese	Sichuan	Xi'an	Yunnan Hua	Zhuang	Mongolian	Tibetan	Uighur
bill (restaurant)	26	52	77	101	124	148	172	196	220	245	269	297	328	352
bill (shopping)	23	49	71	95	119	143	167	–	–	–	263	–	321	346
boats	16	42	67	91	115	139	163	187	211	235	259	–	315	342
booking (accommodation)	19	44	68	93	116	140	164	188	212	236	260	285	317	343
booking (tickets)	15	41	–	–	–	–	–	–	–	–	–	–	–	–
border crossings	15	40	–	–	–	–	–	–	–	–	–	–	–	–
bus	16, 17	42	67	91	115	139	163	187	211	235	259	283	315, 316	342
C														
cameras	22, 24	48, 50	70	95	118	142	166	190	215	239	262	288	320	345
car	17	43	–	–	–	–	–	–	–	–	–	–	316	–
changing money	18, 20	43, 45	67	92	115	139	163	187	211	235	259	283	318	342
checking out	19	45	69	93	117	141	164	189	213	237	261	285	318	343
civilities	13	39	65	89	113	137	161	185	209	233	257	281	313	339
communications	20	45	69	93	117	141	165	189	213	237	261	286	318	344
complaints (shopping)	23	49	71	95	119	143	167	–	–	–	263	289	321	346
consonants	12	38	64	88	112	136	160	184	208	232	256	280	312	338
contact details	25	51	76	100	123	147	171	195	219	244	268	295	326	351
cost (accommodation)	19	45	68	93	116	141	164	188	213	237	261	285	317	343
cost (general)	23	49	71	95	118	143	167	191	215	239	263	288	321	345
cost (internet)	20	46	–	–	–	–	–	–	–	–	–	286	319	–
cost (phone)	21	46	–	–	–	–	–	–	–	–	–	286	319	–

	Mandarin	Cantonese	Chaozhou	Dongbei Hua	Hakka	Hunanese	Shanghainese	Sichuan	Xi'an	Yunnan Hua	Zhuang	Mongolian	Tibetan	Uighur
cost (sightseeing)	21	47	–	–	–	–	–	–	–	–	–	286	319	–
cost (taxi)	17	43	–	–	–	–	–	–	–	–	–	–	–	–
countries	25	51	74	98	121	146	170	193	218	242	266	292	324	348
credit cards	23, 29	49, 55	71	95	119	143	167	191	215	239	263	–	321	346
cuisine	366-9													
culture	362-73													
customs (local)	–	52	73	97	121	145	169	193	217	241	265	292, 301	323	351
D														
dates	14	40	66	90	114	138	162	186	210	234	258	282	314	340
days of the week	14	40	66	91	114	138	163	186	211	235	259	283	315	340
dentist	29	55	80	104	128	152	176	200	224	248	272	304	–	356
dictionary	31	57	81	105	129	153	177	201	225	249	273	305	331	357
directions	18	43	67	91	115	139	163	187	212	236	260	283	315	342
doctor	28, 29	54, 55	80	104	128	152	176	200	224	248	272	303, 304	330	356
drinks	26, 27	53	78, 79	102, 103	126	150, 151	174	198, 199	222, 223	246, 247	270, 271	298, 299	328, 329	354
drinks (China)	368													
E														
eating out	26	52	76	100	124	148	172	196	220	245	268	296	327	352
email	20, 25	46, 51	69, 76	94, 100	117, 123	141, 147	165, 171	189, 195	213, 219	237, 244	261, 268	286, 295	319, 326	344, 351
embassies	28	55	–	–	–	–	–	–	–	–	–	–	–	–
emergencies	28	54	80	104	127	152	175	200	224	248	272	303	329	356
English, use of	13, 29	39, 52, 56	65, 73	89, 97	113, 121	137, 145	161, 169	185, 193	209, 217	233, 241	257, 265	281, 292	313, 323	339, 348
entertainment	370-3													

F	Mandarin	Cantonese	Chaozhou	Dongbei Hua	Hakka	Hunanese	Shanghainese	Sichuan	Xi'an	Yunnan Hua	Zhuang	Mongolian	Tibetan	Uighur
family	25	51	72	96	120	144	168	192	216	240	264	290	322	347
farewells	24	50	71, 75	96, 100	119, 123	143, 147	167, 171	191, 195	215, 219	240, 244	263, 268	289, 295	321, 326	346, 351
feelings	–	–	75	99	122	147	171	194	219	243	267	294	325	350
festivals	370-3													
food & drink	26	52	76	101	124	148	172	196	220	245	268	296	327	352
food (China)	366-9													
G														
goodbyes	24	50	71, 75	96, 100	119, 123	143, 147	167, 171	191, 195	215, 219	240, 244	263, 268	289, 295	321, 326	346, 351
greetings	24	50	71	96	119	143	167	191	215	240	263	289	321	346
guides	21	47	–	–	–	–	–	–	–	–	–	286, 302	320	–
H														
health	29	55	80	104	128	152	176	200	224	248	272	303	329	356
hire (car)	17	43	–	–	–	–	–	–	–	–	–	–	316	–
history	362-5													
hospitals	29	55	80	104	128	152	176	200	224	248	272	304	–	356
hotels	15, 19	41, 44	68	92	116	140	164	188	212	236	260	285	317	343
I														
illnesses	30	56	–	–	–	–	–	–	–	–	–	304	–	–
interests	25	52	74	99	122	146	170	194	218	243	267	294	325	349
internet	20	46	69	93, 94	117	141	165	189	213	237	261	286	318, 319	344
introductions	24	50	72	96	119	144	168	191	216	240	263	289	322	346
J														
jobs	25	51	74	98	122	146	170	193	218	242	266	293	324	348, 349

L	Mandarin	Cantonese	Chaozhou	Dongbei Hua	Hakka	Hunanese	Shanghainese	Sichuan	Xi'an	Yunnan Hua	Zhuang	Mongolian	Tibetan	Uighur
language difficulties	13	39	65	89	113	137	161	185	209	233	257	281	313	339
language history	11	37	63	87	111	135	159	183	207	231	255	279	311	337
language map	11	37	63	87	111	135	159	183	207	231	255	279	311	337
language speakers	11	37	63	87	111	135	159	183	207	231	255	279	311	337
literature	362-5													
local food	26	53	76, 77, 79	100, 101, 103	124, 127	148, 151	172, 175	196, 199	220, 223	245, 247	268, 269, 271	296, 298, 300	327, 328	352, 353, 355
lost	16, 29	42, 55	80	104	128	152	176	200	224	248	272	–	330	356
luggage	16, 29	42, 55	–	–	–	–	–	–	–	–	–	–	–	–
M														
mail	21	47	–	–	–	–	–	–	–	–	–	–	–	–
making conversation	24	50	72	96	120	144	168	192	216	241	264	290	322	347
map (language)	6-7													
maps	18, 21	43, 47	67	92	115	139	163	187	212	236	259	284, 286	316, 320	342
markets	22	48	70	95	118	142	166	190	215	239	262	288	320	345
marriage	–	–	74	99	122	146	170	194	218	243	266	293	325	349
meals	26	53	78	102	125	150	173	197	222	246	270	298	328	354
medicine	29	56	–	–	–	–	–	–	–	–	–	–	–	–
meeting people	24	50	71	96	119	143	167	191	215	240	263	289	321	346
menus	26	52	77	101	124	148	172	196	220	245	269	296	327	352
money	18, 20, 23, 29	43, 45, 49, 55	67	92	115	139	163	187	211	235	259	283	318	342
months			67	91	115	139	163	187	211	235	259	–	315	341

	Mandarin	Cantonese	Chaozhou	Dongbei Hua	Hakka	Hunanese	Shanghainese	Sichuan	Xi'an	Yunnan Hua	Zhuang	Mongolian	Tibetan	Uighur
N														
nationalities	25	51	74	98	121	146	170	193	218	242	266	292	324	348
nonalcoholic drinks	26	53	78	102	126	150	174	198	222	246, 247	270, 271	298	328	354
numbers	13	39	65	90	113	137	162	185	209	233	257	281	313	340
O														
occupations	25	51	74	98	122	146	170	193	218	242	266	293	324	348, 349
opinions	–	–	75	99	122	147	171	194	219	243	267	294	325	350
ordering (restaurant)	26	52	77	101	124, 125	148, 149	172, 173	196, 197	220, 221	246	269, 270	296	327	352
ordering (taxi)	17	42	–	–	–	–	–	–	–	–	–	–	–	–
P														
pharmacies	29	55	80	104	128	152	176	200	224	248	272	283, 304	–	356
phone	20, 21, 28	45, 46, 55	69, 80	93, 94, 104	117, 128	141, 142, 152	165, 176	189, 200	213, 214, 224	237, 238, 248	261, 272	286, 303	318, 319, 330	344, 356
photography	24	50	–	–	–	–	–	–	–	–	–	–	–	–
photos, taking	22	47	70, 73	94, 97	117, 120	142, 145	166, 169	190, 192	214, 217	238, 241	262, 265	287, 291	319, 323	344, 347
plane	16	42	–	–	–	–	–	–	–	–	–	283	315	–
police	29	54, 55	80	104	128	152	176	200	224	248	272	–	330	356
post office	18, 21	43, 47	67	92	115	139	163	187	211	235	259	283	316	342
pronunciation	12	38	64	88	112	136	160	184	208	232	256	280	312	338
Q														
quantities	23	49	71	95	119	143	167	191	215	239	263	297	321	346
R														
receipts	23	49	–	–	–	–	–	–	–	–	–	289	–	–
refunds	23	49	–	–	–	–	–	–	–	–	–	289	–	–

	Mandarin	Cantonese	Chaozhou	Dongbei Hua	Hakka	Hunanese	Shanghainese	Sichuan	Xi'an	Yunnan Hua	Zhuang	Mongolian	Tibetan	Uighur
religion							362-5							
repairs	23	49	–	–	–	–	–	–	–	–	–	–	–	–
reservations (accommodation)	19	44	68	93	116	140	164	188	212	236	260	285	317	343
reservations (tickets)	15	41	–	–	–	–	–	–	–	–	–	–	–	–
restaurants	26	52	76	101	124	148	172	196	220	245	269	283, 296	327	352
rooms (hotel)	19	44	68	93	116	140	164	188	212	236	260	285	317	343
S														
script (alphabet)	–	–	–	–	–	–	–	–	–	–	–	278, 282	310	336
seasons	–	–	66	91	114	138	162	186	210	234	258	–	315	341
seating	16, 17, 26	41, 42, 52	77	101	124	148	172	196	220	245	269	296	327	352
shopping	22	48	70	95	118	142	166	190	215	239	262	288	320	345
sightseeing	21	47	70	94	117	142	166	190	214	238	262	286	319	344
souvenirs	22	48	70, 71	95	118	142	166, 167	190	215	239	262	288	320	345, 346
special diets	27	54	79	104	127	151	175	199	223	248	272	300	329	355
street food							369							
T														
taxis	17	42	–	–	–	–	–	–	–	–	–	–	–	–
telephone	20, 21, 28	45, 46, 55	69, 80	93, 94, 104	117, 128	141, 142, 152	165, 176	189, 200	213, 214, 224	237, 238, 248	261, 272	286, 303	318, 319, 330	344, 356
telling the time	14	40	66	90	114	138	161, 162	186	210	234	258	282	314	340
theft	16, 29	42, 55	–	–	–	–	–	–	–	–	–	–	329	–
tickets	15	41	–	–	–	–	–	–	–	–	–	–	–	–

	Mandarin	Cantonese	Chaozhou	Dongbei Hua	Hakka	Hunanese	Shanghainese	Sichuan	Xi'an	Yunnan Hua	Zhuang	Mongolian	Tibetan	Uighur
timeline	362-5													
titles (addressing people)	24	50	72	96	119	143	168	191	216	240	264	289	–	346
toilets	28	55	80	104	128	152	176	200	224	248	272	–	330	356
tones (pronunciation)	10	36	62	86	110	134	158	182	206	230	254	–	–	–
tours	22	47	70	94	118	142	166	190	214	238	262	287, 301	319	345
trains	16	42	67	91	115	139	163	187	211	235	259	283	–	342
transport	16	42	67	91	115	139	163	187	211	235	259	283	315	342
travellers cheques	20, 23, 29	45, 49, 55	–	–	–	–	–	–	–	–	–	–	–	–
V														
valuables	20, 29	45, 55	–	–	–	–	–	–	–	–	–	–	318	–
vegetarian food	27	54	79	104	127	151	175	199	223	248	272	300	329	355
vowels	12	38	64	88	112	136	160	184	208	232	256	280	312	338
W														
water (drinkable)	27	53	78	102	126	150	174	197	222	246	270	298	328	354
well-wishing	–	–	76	100	123	148	172	195	220	244	268	296	327	351
women's health	29	56	–	–	–	–	–	–	–	–	–	–	–	–
work	25	51	74	98	122	146	170	193	218	242	266	293	324	348, 349

NOTES

NOTES

Read it, hear it, speak it!

The right phrasebook for every trip

FAST TALK
- Perfect for a short trip
- All your essential needs covered

PHRASEBOOK & DICTIONARY
- The original
- Comprehensive
- Easy to use

LANGUAGE & CULTURE SERIES
- Spoken English around the world
- Fun, quirky and easy-to-use

Plus digital products to suit every traveller

BOOK & CD
- Read, listen and talk like a local
- Practise your pronunciation before you go

FAST TALK APP
- Practise hundreds of phrases on the go
- Save key phrases for easy use
- Works offline

EBOOKS
- Full phrasebook plus 400 audio files available on your reader
- Fun and interactive

lonelyplanet.com/shop

lonelyplanet.com/apps-and-ebooks